Mexico's Cold War

Mexico's Cold War examines the history of the Cold War in Mexico and Mexico in the Cold War. Renata Keller draws on declassified Mexican and US intelligence sources and Cuban diplomatic records to challenge earlier interpretations that depicted Mexico as a peaceful haven and a weak neighbor forced to submit to US pressure. Mexico did in fact suffer from the political and social turbulence that characterized the Cold War era in general, and by maintaining relations with Cuba it played a unique, and heretofore overlooked, role in the hemispheric Cold War. The Cuban Revolution was an especially destabilizing force in Mexico because Fidel Castro's dedication to many of the same nationalist and populist causes that the Mexican revolutionaries had originally pursued in the early twentieth century called attention to the fact that the government had abandoned those promises. A dynamic combination of domestic and international pressures thus initiated Mexico's Cold War and shaped its distinct evolution and outcomes.

Renata Keller is an Assistant Professor of International Relations in the Frederick S. Pardee School of Global Studies at Boston University.

Cambridge Studies in US Foreign Relations

Edited by

Paul Thomas Chamberlin, *University of Kentucky*
Lien-Hang T. Nguyen, *University of Kentucky*

This series showcases cutting-edge scholarship in US foreign relations that employs dynamic new methodological approaches and archives from the colonial era to the present. The series will be guided by the ethos of transnationalism, focusing on the history of American foreign relations in a global context rather than privileging the United States as the dominant actor on the world stage.

Mexico's Cold War

*Cuba, the United States, and the Legacy
of the Mexican Revolution*

RENATA KELLER

Boston University

CAMBRIDGE
UNIVERSITY PRESS

32 Avenue of the Americas, New York NY 10013-2473, USA

Cambridge University Press is part of the University of Cambridge.

It furthers the University's mission by disseminating knowledge in the pursuit of education, learning and research at the highest international levels of excellence.

www.cambridge.org
Information on this title: www.cambridge.org/9781107079588

First published 2015

A catalogue record for this publication is available from the British Library

Library of Congress Cataloguing in Publication data
Keller, Renata, 1981–
Mexico's Cold War : Cuba, the United States, and the legacy of the
Mexican Revolution / Renata Keller.
pages   cm. – (Cambridge studies in US foreign relations)
Includes bibliographical references and index.
ISBN 978-1-107-07958-8 (hardback)
1. Mexico – Foreign relations – 1946–1970.   2. Mexico – Foreign relations –
1970–1988.   3. Cold War.   4. Mexico – Foreign relations – United States.
5. United States – Foreign relations – Mexico.   6. Mexico – Foreign relations –
Cuba.   7. Cuba – Foreign relations – Mexico.   I. Title.
F1228.K45   2015
327.72073–dc23   2015009550

ISBN 978-1-107-07958-8 Hardback

I dedicate this book to my parents.

Contents

Figures

Tables

Acknowledgments

I am deeply grateful to all of the people and institutions that helped make this book possible.

I was fortunate enough to receive a world-class education in Arizona's public school system. The teachers I had at Lineweaver, Pistor, and University High, especially Mark Olbin, Dana Elmer, and Steve Reff, remain among the most gifted and dedicated educators I have ever met. The Flinn Foundation generously covered not only the entire cost of my college education at Arizona State University, but also my first academic trips to Latin America. My mentors at ASU – Lynn Stoner, Janet Burke, and Ted Humphrey – provided excellent advice as I wrote my first piece of substantial scholarship for my honors thesis. I am also grateful for the friendships I made during all those years. Thanks especially to Emily Areinoff, Lauren Cleff, Brian Decker, Maura Dell, Jennifer Finney, John Hamman, Brandon Kelley, Monica Morales Diaz, Joe Nguyen, Michelle Noelck, North Noelck, Alberto Ranjel, Joyanne Rolph, Jessica Ziegler, and the entire Chile crew for all the adventures and sugar-fueled study sessions.

I thank my lucky stars on a daily basis that I decided to go to the University of Texas for graduate school. My advisor, Jonathan Brown, met my initial ideas about a Mexico-Cuba project with equal parts enthusiasm and good humor, and he has continued to provide both at every step along the way. The other members of my doctoral committee – Ann Twinam, Virginia Garrard-Burnett, Mark Lawrence, and Peter Trubowitz – also supported and challenged me, and helped me make the transition from student to scholar. The classes that I took with Seth Garfield, Frank Guridy, Susan Deans-Smith, H. W. Brands, and Jacinto

Rodríguez Munguía shaped the ways I think about the history of Mexico and inter-American relations. Jeremi Suri, Jorge Cañizares-Esguerra, and Lina del Castillo became friends and mentors in my later years at the University of Texas. The History Department, Mexican Center, and College of Liberal Arts at the University of Texas all provided funding for my dissertation, as did the Social Science Research Council and the Philanthropic Educational Organization. Most of all, I treasure the friendships that I made during my time in Texas. Cheasty Anderson (who comes first even though it slightly violates my tidy alphabetical ordering), Amber Abbas, Chris Albi, José Barragán, Juandrea Bates, Ben Breen, Mikki Brock, Paul Conrad, Jesse Cromwell, Felipe Cruz, Chris Dietrich, Stephen Dove, Sam Frazier, Michelle Getchell, Andrew Gillette, Larry Gutman, John Harney, Chris Heaney, Bonar Hernández, Rachel Herrmann, Jennifer Hoyt, Brian McNeil, Aragorn Storm Miller, Rachel Ozanne, Marc Palen, Jeff Parker, Andrew Paxman, Heather Peterson, Claudia Rueda, Kyle Shelton, Susan Somers, Sarah Steinbock-Pratt, and Susan Zakaib – thank you for the conversations, the Subalterns games, the Tweed parties, the research tips, and everything else.

I did most of the research for this book in Mexico, and I owe a great deal to the archivists and librarians who made that work possible and the friends who kept me sane. The staffs of the Archivo General, the Biblioteca Lerdo de Tejada, the Hemeroteca Nacional, and the Secretaría de Relaciones Exteriores were all professional, friendly, and quick to help. During my time in Mexico, I benefited greatly from conversations with Ana Covarrubias, Gastón Martínez Rivera, Daniela Spenser, Soledad Loaeza, and Alonso Aguilar Monteverde. Claudia Carreta and Pablo Mijangos, two fellow Longhorns, helped me find doctors and tacos when I needed them most. Research can be a lonely endeavor, but my roommates, Catherine Vézina and Mini-Miri, and my friends Steve Allen, Jennifer Boles, Ted Cohen, Shane Dillingham, Stuart Easterling, Alberto Hernández Sánchez, and Michael Lettieri provided entertainment as well as emotional and intellectual support. Special thanks to Catherine and the staff of the Biblioteca Lerdo de Tejada for helping me get permission to use the images from *Política*.

Getting access to Cuban archives required some patience, and I probably would not have even tried a second trip back to Havana if not for a timely tip from Aaron Moulton that the Foreign Ministry archives had finally opened. Belkis Quesada of the Instituto de Historia de Cuba went out of her way to process my visa quickly, and working with Eduardo Válido at the Archivo del Ministerio de Relaciones Exteriores was a delight. Ben Narvaez and William Morgan offered advice and connections for my first trip to Cuba, and Meg Vail and Maikel Fariñas Borrego helped assuage the frustration of that experience.

Archival work in the United States may be somewhat less "glamorous" than Havana or Mexico City, but no less rewarding. I am grateful to the staffs of the Nettie Lee Benson and Lyndon B. Johnson Libraries in Austin for patiently guiding my early forays into this project. The staffs of the John F. Kennedy Library in Boston, the National Archives in College Park, and the National Security Archive at George Washington University all provided crucial assistance. A long-lost friend from elementary school, Leslie McCall Dervan, let me stay with her in Boston when my housing plans fell through at the last minute.

Since leaving Texas, I have been lucky enough to find a new home at Boston University. My colleagues took a chance when they hired a graduate student who hadn't even finished her dissertation, and I will always be grateful for their leap of faith. My mentors, Erik Goldstein and Susan Eckstein, have provided excellent advice and support. Scott Palmer, Bill Keylor, Bill Grimes, Vivien Schmidt, Kevin Gallagher, Jeff Rubin, Steven Kinzer, Andy Bacevich, Joe Wippl, and Ann Helwege all gave me a warm welcome and have continued to aid my professional growth, even though some of them are no longer at Boston University. My fellow junior faculty members are a fantastic, fun group. Manjari Chatterjee Miller, Cornel Ban, Jeremy Menchik, Kaija Schilde, Ivan Arreguín-Toft, Noora Lori, Michael Woldemariam, Min Ye, and all the Tertulia regulars – thanks for your friendship and collegiality. I am also grateful to the leadership and staff of the Pardee School of Global Studies, especially Dean Adil Najam, Christian Estrella, Victoria Puyat, and Noorjehan Khan, and to my research assistants Lindsay Hamsik and Mariana Echaniz.

I was able to take a year away from teaching to transform my dissertation into this book thanks to generous funding from Boston University and the Kluge Center at the U.S. Library of Congress. At the Library of Congress, special thanks must go to the staffs of the Kluge Center and the Hispanic, Historical Newspapers, Prints and Photographs, and Manuscript Divisions. Mary Lou Reker, Carolyn Brown, Travis Hensley, Jason Steinhauer, Barbara Tenenbaum, Tracy North, and Thomas Mann went out of their way to make my time in Washington, DC, as productive as possible, and William Austin Baker was an outstanding research assistant. I also thank Michele Navakas for leading the happy hour effort, the Finney family for following me from Boston to DC, and Chris Darnton and his wife Jessica for their friendship and hospitality.

I have received much aid and encouragement from other people and institutions along the way. Boston University's Center for the Humanities covered the costs of the expensive photographs that I wanted to include in the book. Clark Whitehorn at the University of New Mexico Press gave me permission to include some of the material from my contribution to an earlier edited volume. Conversations with Jaime Pensado, Sergio Aguayo, Amy Kiddle, Tanalís Padilla, Louise Walker, Ben Smith, Paul Gillingham, Alex Aviña, Peter Kornbluh, Andy Kirkendall, Stephen Rabe, Monica Rankin, Dina Berger, Thomas Field, Thomas Tunstall Allcock, Rob Alegre, and Tom Long helped me think through my arguments. Ignacio Chávez de la Lama sent me countless articles about student politics in Mexico, and Jonathan Brown, Sergio Aguayo, Jacinto Rodríguez Munguía, and Aaron Moulton selflessly shared scanned documents with me. Tanya Harmer, Gilbert Joseph, Jeffrey Taffet, Piero Gleijeses, Max Paul Friedman, Eric Zolov, Hal Brands, Jonathan Hunt, and Fernando Calderón read all or part of this research in one form or another and were extremely generous with their feedback. The four anonymous reviewers who read my manuscript gave me just the kind of constructive criticism that I needed – and wanted – to hear. Working with Cambridge University Press has been a delight, thanks to the hard work of my editor Deborah Gershenowitz, her assistant Dana Bricken, copy editor Christine Dunn, and series editors Hang Nguyen and Paul Chamberlin.

My family has never wavered in their support and love. My sister Rachel has always been ready to assuage my hypochondria, even when she has better things to do like saving lives. My brother Kevin not only read and edited this whole book, but also did most of the painstaking work of indexing. My new in-laws Karol, Bill, Tyson, and Tanya have welcomed me into their family. It is impossible to acknowledge all the ways that my parents have helped me over the years. They have encouraged me, challenged me, and supported me both emotionally and financially. I will never be able to pay them back, but I hope that someday I will be able to live up to their example.

And finally, Cameron Strang not only made this book better, he made my life better. Thank you for making me happy.

Abbreviations

AGN	Archivo General de la Nación/General Archive of the Nation
ALM	Adolfo López Mateos
CCI	Central Campesina Independiente/Independent Campesino Center
CIA	Central Intelligence Agency
CNC	Confederación Nacional Campesina/National Campesino Confederation
CNED	Central Nacional de Estudiantes Democráticos/National Center of Democratic Students
CNOP	Confederación Nacional de Organizaciones Populares/National Confederation of Popular Organizations
CREST	CIA Records Search Tool
CTM	Confederación de Trabajadores Mexicanos/Confederation of Mexican Workers
DFS	Dirección Federal de Seguridad/Department of Federal Security
DGI	Dirección General de Inteligencia/General Intelligence Department
FAR	Fuerzas Armadas Revolucionarias/Revolutionary Armed Forces
FBI	Federal Bureau of Intelligence
FECSM	Federación de Estudiantes Campesinos Socialistas de México/Federation of Socialist Campesino Students of Mexico
FEMOSPP	Fiscalía Especial para Movimientos Sociales y Políticos del Pasado/Special Prosecutor for Social and Political Movements of the Past

FEP	Frente Electoral del Pueblo/People's Electoral Front
FER	Frente de Estudiantes Revoluccionarios/Student Revolutionary Front
FRAP	Fuerzas Revolucionarias Armadas del Pueblo/People's Armed Revolutionary Front
FRUS	Foreign Relations of the United States
GDO	Gustavo Díaz Ordaz
IPN	Instituto Politécnico Nacional/National Polytechnic Institute
IPS	Dirección General de Investigaciones Políticas y Sociales/Department of Political and Social Investigations
JFK	John F. Kennedy Presidential Library
LBJ	Lyndon Baines Johnson Presidential Library
MAR	Movimiento de Acción Revolucionaria/Revolutionary Action Movement
MINREX	Ministerio de Relaciones Exteriores/Ministry of Foreign Relations
MLN	Movimiento de Liberación Nacional/National Liberation Movement
MRM	Movimiento Revolucionario del Magisterio/Revolutionary Teachers' Movement
MURO	Movimiento Universitario de Renovadora Orientación/University Movement of Renovating Orientation
NARA	US National Archives and Records Administration
OAS	Organization of American States
OSPAAAL	Organización de Solidaridad de los Pueblos de África, Asia, y América Latina/Solidarity Organization of the Peoples of Africa, Asia, and Latin America
PAN	Partido de Acción Nacional/Party of National Action
PCM	Partido Comunista Mexicano/Mexican Communist Party
PIPSA	Productora e Importadora de Papel, S.A/Producer and Importer of Paper
POCM	Partido Obrero-Campesino Mexicano/Mexican Worker-Peasant Party
POR	Partido Obrero Revolucionario/Revolutionary Workers' Party
PPS	Partido Popular Socialista/Popular Socialist Party
PRI	Partido Revolucionario Institucional/Institutional Revolutionary Party
SRE	Secretaría de Relaciones Exteriores/Foreign Ministry Archive

TECOS	Tarea Educativa y Cultural hacia el Orden y el Síntesis/ Educational and Cultural Work toward Order and Synthesis
UGOCM	Unión General de Obreros y Campesinos Mexicanos/ General Union of Mexican Workers and Campesinos
UNAM	Universidad Nacional Autónoma de México/National Autonomous University of Mexico
VPLC	Versión Pública de Lázaro Cárdenas/Public Version of Lázaro Cárdenas

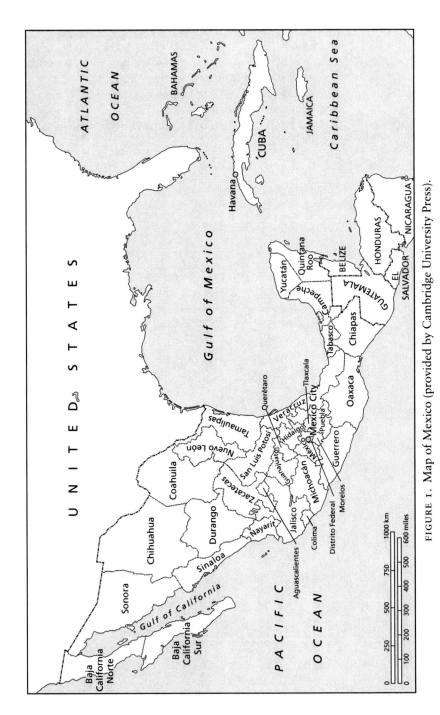

FIGURE I. Map of Mexico (provided by Cambridge University Press).

Introduction

On April 18, 1961, as U.S.-trained forces attacked Cuba in the Bay of Pigs invasion, Lázaro Cárdenas rushed to Mexico City's airport and boarded a private jet to Havana to fight alongside Fidel Castro. The flight never left the runway; Mexico's president, Adolfo López Mateos, had ordered the military to ground the plane and remove Cárdenas from the premises.[1]

But Cárdenas would not be stopped from defending Cuba. He made his way from the airport to the Zócalo – Mexico City's main plaza – where from the improvised podium of the roof of a car he denounced the invasion. Cuba needed the moral support of Mexico, Cárdenas said, and if all the people of Latin America united to help the island, there would be nothing the United States could do.[2] The presence of the ex-president was captivating; a crush of eighty thousand protesters sat silently on the ground in the plaza, overwhelming the police force tasked with keeping the area clear.[3]

Cárdenas's condemnation of the Bay of Pigs invasion also reached beyond the Zócalo. He sent a scathing message to a wide range of

[1] Luís Suárez, *Cárdenas: Retrato inédito, testimonios de Amalia Solorzano de Cárdenas y nuevos documentos* (Mexico City: Editorial Grijalbo, 1987), 214–16. See also Alfonso Corona del Rosal, *Mis Memorias Políticas* (Mexico City: Grijalbo, 1995), 131.

[2] "Cárdenas defendió a Fidel Castro anoche, en un mítin en el Zócalo," *Excélsior*, April 19, 1961.

[3] Manuel Rangel Escamilla, "[Cárdenas and students protest Bay of Pigs]," April 18, 1961, Dirección Federal de Seguridad [hereafter DFS], Versión Pública de Lázaro Cárdenas [hereafter VPLC], Leg. 2, Hoja 168, Archivo General de la Nación, Mexico City [hereafter AGN]; "Mitin Estudiantil," April 18, 1961, Dirección General de Investigaciones Políticas y Sociales [hereafter IPS] Caja 1980 B, AGN; "El país, con Cuba," *Política*, May 1, 1961.

international institutions and leaders, including the United Nations, the presidents of numerous countries, and prominent U.S. journalist Walter Lippmann, in which he called the invasion "a great crime whereby a small country is wounded by the powerful resources of imperialism."[4] He also made inflammatory statements to Cuban reporters, swearing, "[I]f the government continues to deny me permission [to go to Cuba], I will go instead to the Mexican interior to organize support for the Cuban Revolution."[5]

President López Mateos was well aware of Cárdenas's actions. Intelligence agents collected copies of Cárdenas's declarations and newspaper clippings about the protest in the Zócalo. They maintained a round-the-clock watch outside Cárdenas's house and submitted extensive reports about his activities.[6] The president also knew of students' desires to follow Cárdenas's example: according to intelligence agents, an organization called the Student Front in Defense of the Cuban Revolution had recruited more than a thousand members to form a brigade to send to the island.[7] López Mateos continued to deny permission to all those who wanted to go to Cuba, citing Mexico's traditional policy of nonintervention and threatening to revoke the citizenship of anyone who "lent his or her services" to a foreign government without permission from Congress.[8]

Displeased with Cárdenas's very public response to the Bay of Pigs invasion, López Mateos summoned the ex-president to a private meeting. There, he confronted Cárdenas about his attempt to fly to Cuba. "Mexico is passing through a difficult situation right now; the revenue from tourism has dropped. The campaign abroad is very intense and it appears to me that we are borrowing other people's troubles," López Mateos explained. When Cárdenas refused to agree about the importance of cultivating good relations with the United States, López Mateos took a more threatening tack. "They say that the communists are enclosing you in a dangerous web," he warned Cárdenas.[9]

[4] Lázaro Cárdenas, "[Cárdenas's telegram to the United Nations about the Bay of Pigs Invasion]," April 17, 1961, DFS, VPLC, Leg. 2, Hoja 165, AGN.
[5] "Luchará Cárdenas en Cuba o en México," *Revolución*, April 20, 1961.
[6] Ruben Fernández Millan, "[Vigilance outside of Cárdenas's house during Bay of Pigs]," April 17, 1961, DFS, VPLC, Leg. 2, Hoja 166, AGN.
[7] Manuel Rangel Escamilla, "[Student protests against Bay of Pigs invasion]," April 19, 1961, DFS, VPLC, Leg. 2, Hoja 172, AGN.
[8] "Ningún mexicano podrá ir a pelear," *Excélsior*, April 19, 1961.
[9] Cárdenas, *Obras: Apuntes 1957/1966*, Vol. 3 (Mexico City: Universidad Nacional Autónoma de México, 1986), 212–16.

Yet, despite all these concerns about communists, the United States, and borrowing other people's troubles, President López Mateos spent much of his time in office defending the Cuban Revolution. During a tour of South America in January 1960, he informed Venezuelan journalists that his country had been the first to recognize the new Cuban regime and compared Castro's agrarian reforms to those undertaken by the Mexican government after the Revolution of 1910.[10] He told Brazilian reporters that Mexicans' revolutionary experience gave them a unique understanding of the events in Cuba.[11] "Mexico," López Mateos explained, "has formulated an entire theory about agrarian reform and land distribution founded on the principles of justice, [and] cannot but look favorably upon a country with similar problems [that] resolves them in agreement with the needs of its own people."[12] López Mateos again demonstrated solidarity with the Cuban Revolution five months later when he welcomed Cuban President Osvaldo Dorticós Torrado in an official state visit. López Mateos greeted Dorticós at the airport in front of a crowd of thousands who cheered and waved celebratory banners. In a speech that contained numerous comparisons between the Mexican Revolution and the more recent Cuban one, López Mateos said, "We, who have travelled similar paths, understand and value the transformative effort that Cuba is undertaking."[13] By connecting the two countries' experiences, he validated Castro's actions and reasserted his own government's revolutionary credentials.

Mexico's defense of Cuba changed but did not cease as Castro increasingly allied his government with the communist bloc in 1960 and 1961. No longer praising the Cuban Revolution and comparing it to Mexico's own experience, President López Mateos and his representatives in the Organization of American States (OAS) instead began focusing on Cuba's juridical rights to self-determination and nonintervention.[14] In

---

[10] Mexico was actually among a group of countries that all recognized Castro's new government on January 5, 1959. The other countries were Venezuela, Ecuador, Bolivia, and Honduras. "Venezuela, Ecuador, Bolivia y Honduras reconocen a Urrutia," *Excélsior*, January 6, 1959.

[11] *Presencia internacional de Adolfo López Mateos*, Vol. 1 (Mexico City, 1963). López Mateos neglected to mention that Venezuela, Ecuador, Bolivia, and Honduras recognized Castro's government on the same day as Mexico.

[12] Ibid., 225.

[13] *Los presidentes de México: Discursos políticos 1910–1988*, Vol. 4 (Mexico City: El Colegio de México, 1988), 82.

[14] On Mexican foreign policy and the doctrines of self-determination and nonintervention, see Olga Pellicer de Brody and Esteban L. Mancilla, *Historia de la Revolución Mexicana 1952–1960: El entendimiento con los Estados Unidos y la gestación del desarrollo estabilizador*, Vol. 23 (Mexico City: El Colegio de México, 1978); Guillermo Garcés

January 1962, the Mexican foreign minister cited those principles when he abstained from voting on OAS resolutions that expelled Cuba from the organization. In July 1964, when the OAS resolved that all member nations that still maintained diplomatic relations with Cuba should sever them, Mexico alone refused to comply. For the rest of the decade, it was the only Latin American country to maintain diplomatic relations and air contact with Cuba.[15] In serving as a bridge between Cuba and the rest of the hemisphere, the Mexican government aided Castro and risked reprisals from the United States.

López Mateos's decision to support Cuba came at a high price. The country served as a central hub of the Cold War in Latin America, a thoroughfare for people, money, weapons, and information traveling between Cuba and the rest of the Americas. Yet, Mexico's leaders steadfastly maintained their relations with Cuba, because, despite what López Mateos told Cárdenas in their private conversation, Mexico was not borrowing someone else's problems. It was confronting its own. Castro and his fellow Cuban revolutionaries had unwittingly exposed a contradiction

---

Contreras, *México: Cincuenta Años de política internacional* (Mexico City: Partido Revolucionario Institucional and Instituto de Capacitación Política, 1982); Leticia Bobadilla González, *México y la OEA: Los debates diplomáticos, 1959–1964* (Mexico City: Secretaria de Relaciones Exteriores, 2006), 12; Arnulf Becker Lorca, *Mestizo International Law: A Global Intellectual History, 1842–1933* (Cambridge: Cambridge University Press, 2014). These principles are commonly associated with Mexico's Estrada Doctrine, established in 1930 by Minister of Foreign Relations Genaro Estrada. This doctrine stated that Mexico would not use the practice of withholding recognition from new governments because passing judgment on other governments' legitimacy represented a violation of their national sovereignty. Santiago Roel García, ed., *Genaro Estrada: Diplomático y escritor* (Mexico City: Secretaría de Relaciones Exteriores, 1978).

[15] Chile, Bolivia, and Uruguay also voted against all or part of the OAS resolution to isolate Cuba, but unlike Mexico, complied with the will of the majority and subsequently cut ties with the island. When Salvador Allende became president of Chile in 1970, he reestablished his country's relations with Cuba. Castro was isolated in the Caribbean community as well; e.g., the Jamaican government did not establish diplomatic relations with Castro's government until 1972. Canada, which did not become a member of the OAS until 1990, maintained relations with Cuba throughout the 1960s. However, trade and other forms of contact between Cuba and Canada were negligible. See Tanya Harmer, *Allende's Chile and the Inter-American Cold War* (Chapel Hill: University of North Carolina Press, 2011); Wendell Bell, "Independent Jamaica Enters World Politics: Foreign Policy in a New State," *Political Science Quarterly* 92 (Winter 1977–8): 683–703; John M. Kirk and Peter McKenna, *Canada-Cuban Relations: The Other Good Neighbor Policy* (Gainesville: Gainesville University Press of Florida, 1997); Asa McKercher, "'The Most Serious Problem'? Canada-U.S. Relations and Cuba, 1962," *Cold War History* 12, no. 1 (February 2012): 69–88.

coded deep in the DNA of Mexican politics: the tension between the country's revolutionary past and its conservative present.

This is a book about the Cold War in Mexico, and Mexico in the Cold War. It argues that a dynamic, shifting combination of domestic and international pressures initiated Mexico's Cold War and shaped its evolution and outcomes. The participants in Mexico's Cold War did not live and act in separate fields of foreign and domestic politics, but in both at the same time. Domestic problems took on international dimensions, and foreign events influenced the ways that Mexicans across the social spectrum interpreted domestic problems.[16] Just like the wider global confrontation, Mexico's Cold War was a multisided geopolitical and local contest. It was an undeclared state of war over questions of ideology, economics, culture, citizenship, and security.[17] Mexico may have appeared to be an island of stability in the turbulent sea of Latin American politics, a mere observer of the Cold War, but a closer look reveals that the peaceful haven was actually an active battleground where multiple groups debated, spied, schemed, and struggled for influence.[18] At stake was the shape of Mexico's future, and that of the inter-American community.

In Mexico, the Cold War began when the Cuban Revolution intensified the preexisting struggle over the legacy of the Mexican Revolution. Fidel Castro's triumph over the dictatorial Fulgencio Batista and his bold

[16] On the connections between foreign and domestic politics, see Gilbert M. Joseph, "What We Now Know and Should Know: Bringing Latin America More Meaningfully into Cold War Studies," in *In from the Cold: Latin America's New Encounter with the Cold War*, ed. Gilbert M. Joseph and Daniela Spenser (Durham, NC: Duke University Press, 2008), 3–46, see p. 4; Fredrik Logevall, "Politics and Foreign Relations," *The Journal of American History* 95, no. 4 (March 2009): 1074–8; Campbell Craig and Fredrik Logevall, *America's Cold War: The Politics of Insecurity* (Cambridge, MA: Belknap Press of Harvard University Press, 2009).

[17] For similar definitions of the Cold War that decenter the confrontation between the United States and the Soviet Union, see Greg Grandin, *The Last Colonial Massacre: Latin America in the Cold War* (Chicago: University of Chicago Press, 2004); Odd Arne Westad, *The Global Cold War* (Cambridge: Cambridge University Press, 2007); Greg Grandin and Gilbert Joseph, eds., *A Century of Revolution: Insurgent and Counterinsurgent Violence during Latin America's Long Cold War* (Durham, NC: Duke University Press, 2010).

[18] The most prominent hemispheric and global histories of the Cold War either overlook Mexico entirely, or mention it only in passing. See Odd Arne Westad, *The Global Cold War*; Melvyn P. Leffler and Odd Arne Westad, eds., *The Cambridge History of the Cold War*, 3 vols. (Cambridge: Cambridge University Press, 2010); Hal Brands, *Latin America's Cold War* (Cambridge, MA: Harvard University Press, 2010); Stephen G. Rabe, *The Killing Zone: The United States Wages Cold War in Latin America* (New York: Oxford University Press, 2012).

challenge to U.S. imperialism resonated among the Mexican population, serving as an inspiration to some and a warning to others. *Fidelismo* was an especially destabilizing force in Mexico because Castro's dedication to many of the same nationalist and populist causes that the Mexican revolutionaries had originally pursued called attention to the fact that the government had since abandoned those promises. Workers, *campesinos*, journalists, students, and even former presidents like Lázaro Cárdenas seized upon the Cuban example and demanded that their own government return to its revolutionary roots.[19]

Members of the Mexican public were thus central actors in Mexico's Cold War. Through their actions and organizations, Mexicans across the social and political spectrum put forward their own interpretations of domestic and international events. They held conferences, built alliances, marched in the streets, and even took up weapons. Information about the grassroots dynamics of Mexico's Cold War comes from the newspapers, magazines, cartoons, posters, and pamphlets that they created. These sources provide nonstate perspectives and vivid detail about the events on the ground in cities and towns across Mexico. They show how the battle over the legacy of the Mexican Revolution shaped not only Mexico's domestic politics, but also its relations with Cuba and the United States.

This internal struggle over the legacy of the Mexican Revolution determined Mexico's role in the hemispheric Cold War. López Mateos's fear of a domestic backlash and desperation to maintain his government's revolutionary legitimacy compelled him to defend Castro. His decision established a precedent that would endure throughout Mexico's Cold War: contradictory overt and covert foreign policies. Publicly, López Mateos declared that the United States was Mexico's "greatest problem" and predicted that the Cuban Revolution would be "one step more toward the greatness of America."[20] At the same time, he quietly decreased trade with the island, instituted travel restrictions, and facilitated U.S. efforts to spy on the Cubans. Mexico's secret cooperation with anti-Castro efforts suggests that sentiments of revolutionary or Third World solidarity did

---

[19] Though frequently treated as a synonym of "peasant," the term *campesino* refers to a specific rural social identity, describing a group "united by a shared set of political and economic interests as well as by a collective history of oppression." Christopher R. Boyer, *Becoming Campesinos: Politics, Identity, and Agrarian Struggle in Postrevolutionary Michoacán, 1920–1935* (Stanford, CA: Stanford University Press, 2003), 3. Those who considered themselves *campesinos* included small landowners, wage laborers, sharecroppers, and other agrarian workers.

[20] *Presencia internacional de Adolfo López Mateos*, 225; *Los presidentes de México: Discursos políticos 1910–1988*, 82–4.

not play as great of a role in Mexican foreign policy as some historians have suggested.[21] U.S. and Mexican intelligence agents perceived Castro as a threat, and their records demonstrate that they cooperated extensively in their efforts to monitor and obstruct Cuban activities.

In fact, perception played a crucial role in all aspects of Mexico's Cold War. Mexicans' perceptions of their own revolutionary legacy shaped their responses to the Cuban Revolution. While some saw the Cuban Revolution as a reminder of the promises that the Mexican Revolution had yet to fulfill, many others perceived it as a warning of what a new revolution in Mexico could become. At the same time, the Mexican government's perception of threats influenced the way it responded to domestic and international events. Mexican officials focused on the communist role in the Cuban Revolution, and would increasingly perceive activism among Mexican workers, *campesinos*, and students as evidence of an international communist conspiracy.

These perceptions, as well as the ideas, fears, and ambitions that drove Mexico's Cold War, are now visible in the recently opened records of Mexico's intelligence organizations. In 2002, the government declassified hundreds of thousands of pages of reports written by the agents of the Department of Federal Security and the Department of Political and Social Investigations. These organizations served as the eyes and ears of presidents Adolfo López Mateos (1958–64), Gustavo Díaz Ordaz (1964–70), and Luis Echeverría (1970–6). Some of their information was accurate; much of it was not. Yet even though the intelligence reports were often biased, exaggerated, and false, they were still the best information that Mexico's presidents had available.[22] As historical sources, therefore, the records of the intelligence organizations can sometimes tell us what was actually happening, but more often – and more importantly – they tell us what Mexico's leaders *thought* was happening. When read carefully, they reveal how intelligence agents shaped both Mexican presidents' perceptions of threat and the strategies that they used to defend themselves.[23]

[21] Christopher M. White, *Creating a Third World: Mexico, Cuba, and the United States During the Castro Era* (Albuquerque: University of New Mexico Press, 2007).

[22] On the significance of the intelligence archive for historians, see the special dossier edited by Tanalís Padilla and Louise E. Walker in "Spy Reports: Content, Methodology, and Historiography in Mexico's Secret Police Archive," *Journal of Iberian and Latin American Research* 19, no. 1 (July 2013): 1–111. Recently, in 2015, Mexico's National Archive began reclassifying most of the files of the Department of Federal Security. The current status of access to researchers remains unclear and in flux.

[23] Scholars have long argued that internal factors played a crucial role in shaping Mexico's policy toward Cuba, but they lacked the sources to prove it. See Olga Pellicer de Brody, *México y la Revolución Cubana* (Mexico City: El Colegio de México, 1972); Mario Ojeda, *Alcances y límites de la política exterior de México* (Mexico City: El Colegio

The declassified intelligence records also prove that conservative groups and government officials were responsible for instigating and perpetrating the vast majority of the violence that occurred during Mexico's Cold War. Mexico's revolutionary legacy and the Cuban Revolution did inspire people across the political spectrum to take action, but government security forces and civilians on the right wing of the spectrum were the first groups to resort to violent tactics and the ones who embraced the use of force most consistently and effectively. In Mexico, as in the rest of Latin America, the Cold War was not an equal fight.[24]

While internal struggles were fundamental to Mexico's Cold War, foreign actors also played important roles. Not surprisingly, the countries that participated the most in Mexico's Cold War and felt the greatest effects were the ones that represented the two opposing ideological poles of the hemispheric Cold War: Cuba and the United States. These countries' physical proximity to Mexico, as well as their long histories of interactions with Mexico, also influenced the trilateral relationship. Mexico presented unique challenges and opportunities for both of its neighbors, and the governments of all three countries persistently pushed and tested each other in their efforts to maximize the benefits of Mexico's exceptional position.

Fidel Castro followed Adolfo López Mateos's lead, and crafted contradictory overt and covert foreign policies toward Mexico. Publicly, he praised the Mexican government's "democratic and constitutional tradition" and pledged to maintain "inviolable norms of respect" for Mexico's sovereignty.[25] In secret internal communications, however, Castro and other Cuban officials expressed much lower opinions of Mexico's

---

de México, 1976); Ana Covarrubias-Velasco, "Mexican-Cuban Relations, 1959–1988" (PhD diss., Oxford, 1994). Kate Doyle of the National Security Archive was the first historian to use the intelligence records to reexamine Mexico's policy toward Cuba. See Kate Doyle, "Double Dealing: Mexico's Foreign Policy toward Cuba," *The National Security Archive Electronic Briefing Book*, March 2, 2003, http://www.gwu.edu/~nsarchiv/NSAEBB/NSAEBB83/index.htm#sidebar.

[24] For opposing views in the debate over apportioning blame for Cold War violence in Latin America, see Brands, *Latin America's Cold War*, and Rabe, *The Killing Zone*. For an application of the "Two Devils Thesis" to the Mexican context, see Jorge Castañeda, *Utopia Unarmed: The Latin American Left after the Cold War* (New York: Vintage Books, 1994).

[25] Fidel Castro Ruz, "Ninguna autoridad moral ni jurídica tiene la OEA para tomar medidas contra Cuba: Discurso del primer ministro y primer secretario del Partido Unido de la Revolución Socialista Cubana, Fidel Castro, el 26 de Julio de 1964," *Política*, August 1, 1964; "México mantuvo la posición más firme en su oposición a este acuerdo cínico," *Revolución*, July 27, 1964.

government. Thanks to the recent declassification in 2013 of some of Cuba's diplomatic records, we can now gain new insight into Cuban perceptions of Mexico and its leaders. These records reveal that Cuban officials did not really admire Mexico's government; rather, they frequently criticized it and saw the Mexican example as one to avoid. What was more, the Cuban government used its embassy and consulates in Mexico to spread propaganda and possibly even to support revolutionary activities in Mexico and elsewhere. In examining Cuba's foreign policy toward Mexico, this book contributes a new perspective to a body of literature that has almost exclusively focused on Cuba's relations with its allies or its enemies.[26] Just as Mexico was both friend and foe to Cuba, Cuban foreign policy toward Mexico was ambivalent, variable, and contradictory.

The United States, meanwhile, adjusted its hemispheric Cold War strategy to meet Mexican needs. U.S. leaders initially wanted to isolate Cuba completely and tried to compel Mexico to join the campaign against Castro, but they relented when their Mexican counterparts convinced them that the symbolism of ties with Cuba played a crucial stabilizing role. Eventually, the United States not only accepted but also even embraced Mexico's decision to maintain relations with Cuba. U.S. leaders realized that even though Mexico's independent foreign policy aided Castro, it also benefited Mexico and the United States.

The U.S. role in Mexico's Cold War was thus more accommodating than decisive. Though histories of the Cold War in Latin America have criticized U.S. interventionism and anticommunism for good reason, in focusing so much on the United States they have tended to overlook the ways that Latin Americans sometimes took the lead in the Cold War and shaped U.S. policy.[27] Just as the literature on inter-American relations has tended to exaggerate U.S. power, it has also overstated the centrality of the United States to Latin American foreign policy formulation.[28] While it would be

---

[26] On Cuban foreign policy, see Jorge I. Domínguez, *To Make a World Safe for Revolution: Cuba's Foreign Policy* (Cambridge, MA: Harvard University Press, 1989); Piero Gleijeses, *Conflicting Missions: Havana, Washington, and Africa, 1959–1976* (Chapel Hill: University of North Carolina Press, 2002); Piero Gleijeses, *The Cuban Drumbeat: Castro's Worldview: Cuban Foreign Policy in a Hostile World* (London: Seagull Books, 2009).

[27] On the tendency to overlook Latin American agency, see Max Paul Friedman, "Retiring the Puppets, Bringing Latin America Back In: Recent Scholarship on United States-Latin American Relations," *Diplomatic History* 27, no. 5 (November 2003): 621–36; Brands, *Latin America's Cold War*.

[28] On U.S. centrism in histories of inter-American relations, see Jürgen Buchenau, *In the Shadow of the Giant: The Making of Mexico's Central America Policy, 1876–1930* (Tuscaloosa: University of Alabama Press, 1996), x. Prominent exceptions include

ahistorical to ignore the U.S. role completely, this book argues that the United States was not the primary determinant of Mexico's Cold War or Mexico's relations with Cuba. By looking beyond the United States, we can begin to see the ways that other domestic and foreign actors influenced the processes and outcomes of inter-American relations.

Studying Mexico's Cold War experience also provides insight into more widespread dynamics of international relations and domestic politics. Understanding how and why the Mexican government pursued such Janus-faced foreign and domestic policies to ensure stability during the Cold War can serve to identify the types of entangled pressures that have created similar inconsistencies in other places and times.[29] Uncovering the roles that nonstate actors played in shaping Mexico's foreign relations helps broaden the scope of social movement research to examine the impact of domestic activism on international relations.[30] And finally, analyzing the ways that perceptions influenced Mexican politics on the international, national, and local levels can provide insight onto processes of policy construction and contestation in other nations and situations.[31]

This book combines a wide variety of sources and perspectives from Mexico, Cuba, and the United States to analyze the intersecting domestic and international struggles that constituted Mexico's Cold War. It examines multiple facets of national politics and international relations, including social mobilization, diplomacy, espionage, and cultural

---

Daniela Spenser, *Espejos de la guerra fría: México, América Central y el Caribe* (Mexico City: Secretaría de Relaciones Exteriores, 2004); Harmer, *Allende's Chile and the Inter-American Cold War*; Christopher Darnton, *Rivalry and Alliance Politics in Cold War Latin America* (Baltimore: Johns Hopkins University Press, 2014).

[29] For the classic formulation of Janus-faced policies and two-level foreign/domestic "games," see Robert D. Putnam, "Diplomacy and Domestic Politics: The Logic of Two-Level Games," *International Organization* 42, no. 3 (July 1988): 427–60. Other prominent work on the subject includes Peter B. Evans, Harold Karan Jacobson, and Robert D. Putnam, eds., *Double-Edged Diplomacy: International Bargaining and Domestic Politics* (Berkeley: University of California Press, 1993); Peter Trubowitz, *Politics and Strategy: Partisan Ambition and American Statecraft* (Princeton, NJ: Princeton University Press, 2011).

[30] This line of investigation builds on Mary Dudziak's pathbreaking work on how a social movement with domestic goals affected foreign policy in the U.S context. See Mary Dudziak, *Cold War Civil Rights: Race and the Image of American Democracy* (Princeton, NJ: Princeton University Press, 2000).

[31] On the importance of perception, see Robert Jervis, *Perception and Misperception in International Politics* (Princeton, NJ: Princeton University Press, 1976); Klaus Knorr, "Threat Perception," in *Historical Dimensions of National Security Problems*, ed. Klaus Knorr (Lawrence: University Press of Kansas, 1976), 78–119.

contestation. Its geographic scope extends beyond the traditional corridors of power in Washington and Mexico City, reaching from the northern state of Chihuahua to the Yucatán Peninsula in the south, from the Mexican embassy in New York to the one in Havana.

Mexico's Cold War proceeds chronologically. Because it is impossible to understand Mexico's Cold War outside of the context of the Mexican Revolution, the first chapter provides a brief background of that revolution and its subsequent institutionalization. It also examines the multiple ways that groups and individuals in Mexico, the United States, and Cuba supported, challenged, and took advantage of the Mexican government in the years prior to the Cuban Revolution. The first chapter ends and the second one opens with two coinciding events that heralded the beginning of Mexico's Cold War: the railroad workers' movement of 1958–9 and the Cuban Revolution. Chapter 2 explores how people across the political spectrum in Mexico responded to the Cuban Revolution, as well as the ways that the Mexican, Cuban, and U.S. governments interpreted – and exploited – those responses.

The book's middle chapters analyze how the escalating confrontation between Cuba and the United States affected Mexico's domestic politics and, at the same time, how Mexico's domestic struggles over the legacy of the Mexican Revolution shaped its international relations. Chapter 3 begins with an international peace conference in Mexico City and the Bay of Pigs invasion, and looks at why these events polarized politics in Mexico and prompted leftists and conservatives alike to build new alliances and organizations.[32] Chapter 4 examines the ways that López Mateos and other Mexican leaders resisted U.S. pressure to break relations with Cuba, and how they navigated such threats to national and hemispheric stability as the Cuban Missile Crisis in 1962 and Kennedy's assassination in 1963.

The book's closing chapters explore how and why the Mexican government found the internal aspects of the Cold War more difficult to manage than the external ones. Chapter 5 analyzes multiple instances of social activism in the second half of the 1960s, as well as the ways that intelligence agents increasingly misinterpreted that activism by claiming that Mexico was the target of an international communist conspiracy.

---

[32] By "leftist," I refer generally to those groups and individuals whose efforts stressed social equality and justice. Edward J. McCaughan, *Reinventing Revolution: The Renovation of Left Discourse in Cuba and Mexico* (Boulder, CO: Westview Press, 1997); Eric Zolov, "Expanding Our Conceptual Horizons: The Shift from an Old to a New Left in Latin America," *A Contra Corriente* 5, no. 2 (Winter 2008): 47–73.

Chapter 6 examines the process through which Mexico's Cold War evolved into a "dirty war" under presidents Díaz Ordaz and Echeverría. Looking at such developments as the student movement of 1968 and the proliferation of guerrilla groups, this chapter argues that Mexican leaders' use of repression eventually created the very thing they were trying to avoid: a new revolutionary movement.

I

The Institutionalized Revolution

Throughout the first years of the global Cold War, Mexico's self-proclaimed revolutionary government enjoyed a rare degree of stability and security. While most of the countries in Latin America reeled from dictatorship to democratic opening and back again, Mexican leaders honed a number of methods to maintain control over their country.[1] The U.S. government did its part by helping strengthen Mexico's security apparatus and tolerating Mexican revolutionary and nationalist rhetoric. Though it never actually managed to become the "perfect dictatorship" that some observers have claimed, the Mexican government did enjoy a great deal of success in its efforts to consolidate power and discourage opposition.[2] At the same time that they repressed local communist groups and suffocated the few outbreaks of domestic activism, Mexican leaders offered safe haven to foreigners, including Fidel Castro and Ernesto "Che" Guevara, who used Mexican territory to pursue their own agendas.

THE LEGACY OF THE MEXICAN REVOLUTION

The Mexican Revolution was many things: an event, a process, a promise, and, by the 1960s, a myth. The first phase consisted of a long, bloody, multisided civil war, a revolution from both above and below against Porfirio

---

[1] On postwar politics in the rest of Latin America, see Leslie Bethell and Ian Roxborough, "The Impact of the Cold War on Latin America," in *Origins of the Cold War: An International History*, ed. Melvyn P. Leffler and D. S. Painter, 2nd ed. (New York: Routledge, 2005), 299–316.

[2] Mario Vargas Llosa, "Mexico: The Perfect Dictatorship," *New Perspectives Quarterly* 8, no. 1 (1991): 23–5.

Díaz's dictatorship and the exclusionary economic system that it supported, which culminated with the victory of one faction and the Constitution of 1917.[3] This constitution was, according to historian Mary Kay Vaughan, the cultural product of the revolution, "a shared language of values, rights, identities, and expectations."[4] The shared language encompassed ideas of nationalism, secularism, populism, and democracy that guided the second phase, a halting, limited process of revolution that saw its fullest expression in the 1930s with the presidency of Lázaro Cárdenas (1934–40).

Cárdenas became one of the foremost heroes of the Mexican Revolution for millions of his countrymen and women. Under his direction, the government finally delivered upon the constitution's populist and nationalist promises, distributing land, championing workers' rights, and nationalizing the oil industry. Yet, he also contributed significantly to the process of institutionalizing the revolution and, in the later years of his presidency, national politics began to take a conservative turn.[5] Cárdenas strengthened the state by incorporating the peasantry and the working class into the government's electoral machinery, reorganizing the official "party of parties" into a party of sectors.[6] The reorganization laid the foundations for its final transformation into the corporatist Institutional Revolutionary Party (Partido Revolucionario Institucional, or PRI) in 1946.[7]

[3] On the Mexican Revolution, see Alan Knight, *The Mexican Revolution*, 2 vols. (Cambridge: Cambridge University Press, 1986); Friedrich Katz, "Violence and Terror in the Mexican and Russian Revolutions," in *A Century of Revolution*, 45–61; Gilbert M. Joseph and Jürgen Buchenau, *Mexico's Once and Future Revolution: Social Upheaval and the Challenge of Rule since the Late Nineteenth Century* (Durham, NC: Duke University Press, 2013). On the distinction between revolution from above and revolution from below, see Peter Winn, *Weavers of Revolution: The Yarur Workers and Chile's Road to Socialism* (New York: Oxford University Press, 1986).

[4] Mary K. Vaughan, *Cultural Politics in Revolution: Teachers, Peasants, and Schools in Mexico, 1930–1940* (Tucson: University of Arizona Press, 1997), 3.

[5] On Cárdenas, see Alan Knight, "Cardenismo: Juggernaut or Jalopy?," *Journal of Latin American Studies* 26, no. 1 (February 1, 1994): 73–107; John W. Sherman, *The Mexican Right: The End of Revolutionary Reform, 1929–1940* (Westport, CT: Praeger, 1997); Stephen R. Niblo, *Mexico in the 1940s: Modernity, Politics, and Corruption* (Wilmington, DE: Scholarly Resources, 1999); Alan Knight, "Lázaro Cárdenas," in *Gobernantes Mexicanos*, Vol. 2 (Mexico City: Fondo de Cultura Económica, 2008), 179–208.

[6] Pablo González Casanova, *El estado y los partidos políticos en México: Ensayos* (Mexico City: Ediciones Era, 1981).

[7] Some scholars argue that the Institutional Revolutionary Party was a completely different party from Cárdenas's Party of the Mexican Revolution (Partido Revolucionario Mexicano) and the earlier National Revolutionary Party (Partido Revolucionario Nacional). See Gastón Martínez Rivera, *La lucha por la democracia en México* (Mexico City: Grupo Editorial Cenzontle, 2009). Regardless of whether these were three different

By the time that the official party completed this transformation, the Mexican Revolution had entered yet another phase and had shifted from process and promise to myth. The country's leaders had turned their attention to industrialization and the economic boom known as the "Mexican Miracle" encouraging foreign – especially U.S. – investment, and cracking down on labor and agrarian activism.[8] The advent of World War II further encouraged political and economic cooperation with the United States at the same time that the Soviet Union's common front strategy urged Mexican communists and other leftists to accommodate the government's increasingly conservative policies for the sake of war-time unity.[9] Historian Stanley R. Ross described this conservative turn as "the Thermidor of the Mexican Revolution," while Ian Roxborough has called it a "virtual silent revolution by the middle sectors and professional political bureaucracy."[10] Lower- and middle-class groups became formally incorporated into the state through the PRI, while those in the upper classes established more subtle and direct ties to the government, using a network of pressure groups and personal connections to influence national policy.[11]

In addition to becoming less nationalist and more economically conservative, Mexico's government also failed to deliver on another

---

parties, the fact remains that the PRI was the heir to the one-party political system that originated with the formation of the National Revolutionary Party in 1929. On the relationship between the PRI and the Mexican state, see Victoria E. Rodríguez and Peter M. Ward, "Disentangling the PRI from the Government in Mexico," *Mexican Studies/ Estudios Mexicanos* 10, no. 1 (January 1, 1994): 163–86.

[8] Ian Roxborough, "Mexico," in *Latin America between the Second World War and the Cold War, 1944–1948*, ed. Leslie Bethell and Ian Roxborough (Cambridge: Cambridge University Press, 1992), 190–216; Niblo, *Mexico in the 1940s*; Stephen R. Niblo, *War, Diplomacy, and Development: The United States and Mexico, 1938–1954* (Wilmington, DE: Scholarly Resources, 1995).

[9] Friedrich Katz, "International Wars, Mexico, and U.S. Hegemony," in *Cycles of Conflict, Centuries of Change: Crisis, Reform, and Revolution in Mexico*, ed. Elisa Servín, Leticia Reina, and John Tutino (Durham, NC: Duke University Press, 2007), 184–210; Monica A. Rankin, *¡México, La Patria! Propaganda and Production during World War II* (Lincoln: University of Nebraska Press, 2009).

[10] Stanley R. Ross, *Is the Mexican Revolution Dead?* (New York: Knopf, 1966), 18; Roxborough, "Mexico," 194.

[11] Susan Eckstein, *The Poverty of Revolution: The State and the Urban Poor in Mexico* (Princeton, NJ: Princeton University Press, 1977), 208; Pablo González Casanova, *Democracy in Mexico*, trans. Danielle Salti, 2d ed. (New York: Oxford University Press, 1970), 50. On the influence of conservative entrepreneurial groups, see also Susan Kaufman Purcell, *The Mexican Profit-Sharing Decision: Politics in an Authoritarian Regime* (Berkeley: University of California Press, 1975); Soledad Loaeza, *Clases medias y política en México: La querella escolar, 1959–1963* (Mexico City: El Colegio de México, 1988).

revolutionary promise: democracy. None of the nation's postrevolutionary leaders, including Cárdenas, were particularly dedicated to democracy. Mexican presidents handpicked their successors, the electoral
system was riddled with corruption, the executive branch dominated the
legislative and judicial branches, and state- and local-level governments
relied heavily upon the federal government.[12] Strongmen, also known as
caudillos or *caciques*, continued to dominate local politics, often commit-
ting flagrant abuses of power.[13]

Despite these authoritarian characteristics, the state was not
all-powerful, nor did it rule through imposition and repression alone.
Historians Paul Gillingham and Benjamin Smith have described the
mid-century Mexican state as a *dictablanda*, "a hybrid regime that
combine[d] democratic and authoritarian elements."[14] Mexican leaders exercised power through the construction of hegemonic consensus,
engaging in a continuous dialectical process that frequently involved
force but also required the conditional loyalty of the population.[15]
Mexico's government needed popular support, or at least acquiescence.
Economic growth, distribution of resources, and political accommoda-
tion all helped generate this support, but culture played an important role
as well.[16] The Mexican government strengthened its political legitimacy
by co-opting popular cultural symbols.[17]

[12] González Casanova, *Democracy in Mexico*; Leon Vincent Padgett, *The Mexican Political
System*, 2nd ed. (Boston: Houghton Mifflin, 1976); Dale Story, *The Mexican Ruling
Party: Stability and Authority* (New York: Praeger, 1986).

[13] On caudillos, caciques, and other strongmen, see Alan Knight and W. G Pansters, eds.,
Caciquismo in Twentieth-Century Mexico (London: Institute for the Study of the
Americas, 2005); Rogelio Hernández Rodríguez, "Strongmen and State Weakness," in
Dictablanda: Politics, Work, and Culture in Mexico, 1938–1968, ed. Paul Gillingham
and Benjamin T. Smith (Durham, NC: Duke University Press, 2014), 108–25.

[14] Paul Gillingham, "Preface," in *Dictablanda*, vii–xiv, see p. vii.

[15] Jeffrey W. Rubin, "Contextualizing the Regime: What 1938–1968 Tells Us about Mexico,
Power, and Latin America's Twentieth Century," in *Dictablanda*, 379–95. See also
Vaughan, *Cultural Politics in Revolution*; Knight, "Cardenismo: Juggernaut or Jalopy?";
Alan Knight, "Mexico's Three Fin de Siècle Crises," in *Cycles of Conflict, Centuries of
Change*, 153–83; Jeffrey W. Rubin, *Decentering the Regime: Ethnicity, Radicalism, and
Democracy in Juchitán, Mexico* (Durham, NC: Duke University Press, 1997); Arthur
Schmidt, "Making It Real Compared to What? Reconceptualizing Mexican History since
1940," in *Fragments of a Golden Age: The Politics of Culture in Mexico since 1940*, ed.
Gilbert Joseph, Anne Rubenstein, and Eric Zolov (Durham, NC: Duke University Press,
2001), 23–68, 41.

[16] Gillingham, "Preface," x.

[17] Seth Fein, "Myths of Cultural Imperialism and Nationalism in Golden Age Mexican
Cinema," in *Fragments of a Golden Age*, 159–98; Julio Moreno, *Yankee Don't Go*

There was no symbol more powerful, more popular in Mexico than the Mexican Revolution. Even as the government turned its back on the goals of the 1910 Revolution, it co-opted the event's heroes and repackaged homogenized versions of them into the official history of the regime.[18] The PRI played an especially important role in propagating the myth of the institutionalized revolution through its campaigns, slogans, and grassroots organizing. This tactic of using revolutionary mythos to maintain legitimacy meant that criticism or competition from the political left could be particularly damaging, especially when it called attention to the contradictions between Mexico's mythology and its reality.[19]

REVOLUTIONARY INSTITUTIONS

As the name of the official party indicated, the Mexican government relied on purportedly revolutionary institutions to maintain political and economic stability. One of its greatest instruments of influence was the Institutional Revolutionary Party. PRI officials dated the origins of their party to Plutarco Elías Calles's National Revolutionary Party (Partido Revolucionario Nacional), founded in 1929 in order to stabilize the country and institutionalize the rule of the group of military caudillos and politicians who had triumphed in the military phase of the Mexican Revolution. Every president of Mexico was a member of the single, government-sponsored party. Candidates from the official party occupied nearly every post in the national Congress, as well as most state and municipal government offices.

The Institutional Revolutionary Party dominated electoral politics, and the president, in turn, dominated the PRI. The official party served as a tool for those already in power to retain control over the country, providing them with political legitimacy under the symbolic mantle of the Mexican Revolution, as well as the machinery for balancing competing interests, mediating mass participation, and winning elections. In a practice known as *tapadismo*, every six years incumbent presidents chose their

Home! Mexican Nationalism, American Business Culture, and the Shaping of Modern Mexico, 1920–1950 (Chapel Hill: University of North Carolina Press, 2003), 229.

[18] Ilene V. O'Malley, *The Myth of the Revolution: Hero Cults and the Institutionalization of the Mexican State, 1920–1940* (New York: Greenwood Press, 1986).

[19] González Casanova, *El estado y los partidos políticos en México*; Story, *The Mexican Ruling Party*; Alan Knight, "The Myth of the Mexican Revolution," *Past & Present* 209 (November 1, 2010): 223–73.

own successors in consultation with top party leaders.[20] Electoral fraud was rampant; members of the government, the armed forces, and the PRI managed the registration of new parties, controlled polling sites, distributed ballots, guarded the boxes, and calculated the results. Competing groups and individuals resolved their differences through closed-door wrangling and negotiations within the official government party rather than through genuine electoral contests.[21]

Though Mexico's leaders used the presence of opposition parties as evidence that their country was a democracy, the parties other than the PRI were so weak and ineffective that they were known as the "loyal opposition." Even the two most important opposition parties – the conservative National Action Party (Partido de Acción Nacional, or PAN) and the leftist Popular Socialist Party (Partido Popular Socialista, or PPS) – posed little threat to the PRI.[22] The Ministry of the Interior went so far as to cover the expenses of another opposition party, the Authentic Party of the Mexican Revolution (Partido Auténtico de la Revolución Mexicana, or PARM), in order to maintain the illusion of democracy and funnel patronage to military officials.[23] The leaders of the so-called loyal opposition would usually support the PRI's presidential candidates in return for lower-level positions and other political and financial favors.

Mexico's leaders also used revolutionary rhetoric and mythology to strengthen their political legitimacy. As historian Thomas Benjamin put

---

[20] Daniel Cosío Villegas, *El sistema político mexicano: Las posibilidades de cambio* (Mexico City: Editorial Joaquin Mortiz, 1972), 59; Rubén Narváez, *La sucesión presidencial: Teoría y práctica del tapadismo*, 2nd ed. (Mexico City: Instituto Mexicano de Sociología Política, 1981).

[21] On the Mexican electoral system and the PRI, see Story, *The Mexican Ruling Party*; Pablo González Casanova, *La democracia en México*, 2nd ed. (Mexico City: Ediciones Era, 1991); Rodríguez and Ward, "Disentangling the PRI from the Government in Mexico"; Jorge G. Castañeda, *Perpetuating Power: How Mexican Presidents Were Chosen* (New York: The New Press, 2000); Roderic Ai Camp, *Politics in Mexico: The Democratic Consolidation*, 5th ed. (Oxford: Oxford University Press, 2006); Niblo, *Mexico in the 1940s*, 110. It is important to note that local elections tended to be more genuinely competitive. See Will Pansters, *Politics and Power in Puebla: The Political History of a Mexican State, 1937–1987* (Amsterdam: Centre for Latin American Research and Documentation, 1990); Will G. Pansters, "Tropical Passion in the Desert: Gonzalo N. Santos and Local Elections in Northern San Luis Potosí, 1943–1958," in *Dictablanda*, 126–48; Paul Gillingham, "'We Don't Have Arms, But We Do Have Balls': Fraud, Violence, and Popular Agency in Elections," in *Dictablanda*, 149–72.

[22] Soledad Loaeza, "El Partido Acción Nacional: La oposición leal en México," *Foro Internacional* 14, no. 3 (55) (January 1, 1974): 352–74.

[23] Jacinto Rodríguez Munguía, *La otra guerra secreta: Los archivos prohibidos de la prensa y el poder* (Mexico City: Random House Mondadori, 2008), 225.

it, "the Mexican government learned how to exhibit, disseminate, and perform the Revolution."[24] Vehicles of the official cultural production of the Revolution ranged from books and declarations to murals, monuments, and festivities. Ilene V. O'Malley points to the example of the yearly memorials that Mexico's leaders organized on the anniversary of Emiliano Zapata's assassination, observing that "the myth uses the figure of Zapata to imbue the campesinos with a nonrevolutionary sentiment that Zapata himself did not have: dependence on and loyalty to the government."[25]

Though the Mexican government abandoned many of its revolutionary foundations including nationalism, populism, and democracy, its leaders continued to pay lip service to those ideals. Even Mexico's most conservative president, Miguel Alemán Valdés (1946–52), would sprinkle his public speeches with references to the Mexican Revolution. He concluded his 1950 State of the Union address by declaring "We are confident that our national unity will be unshakeable in the face of any problem and that we will patriotically find solutions that satisfy our collective interests, that guarantee the principles of the Revolution, our liberties, and the progress of our country."[26]

Policy makers in the United States were not fond of their Mexican counterparts' nationalist rhetoric, especially when it was directed at the United States, but they learned to accept it. As a National Intelligence Estimate from 1957 explained, "Although all Mexican political leaders feel compelled to profess adherence to the 'Mexican Revolution,' the aggressive and combative phases of the revolution ended with Cárdenas's term in 1940. Revolutionary ideals are still loudly proclaimed, but the pace of social welfare programs has been slowed."[27] In a report about a meeting with President-elect López Mateos in August 1958, U.S. Ambassador Robert C. Hill referred to the political theater of Mexican elections, describing how López Mateos's seven-month-long political campaign had led him to "act his part as the triumphant candidate of the party of the Institutional Revolution, with its strong nationalist and

---

[24] Thomas Benjamin, *La Revolución: Mexico's Great Revolution as Memory, Myth, and History* (Austin: University of Texas Press, 2000), 13.

[25] O'Malley, *The Myth of the Revolution*, 6.

[26] Dirección de Servicios de Investigación y Análisis, "Informes presidenciales: Miguel Alemán Valdés," http://www.diputados.gob.mx/sedia/sia/re/RE-ISS-09-06-10.pdf (accessed February 26, 2015).

[27] "National Intelligence Estimate," August 13, 1957 in *Foreign Relations of the United States* [hereafter FRUS] *1955–1957, Volume VI: American Republics* (Washington, DC: U.S. Government Printing Office, 1987), 752–65.

generally leftist orientation."[28] U.S. officials understood that the PRI's nationalist and revolutionary pretensions did not necessarily translate into policy and made sure that relations between the two countries remained amicable.

One of the Mexican government's most important "revolutionary institutions" was the National Campesino Confederation (Confederación Nacional Campesina, or CNC), which Cárdenas had created to institutionalize his extensive agrarian reform campaign. Article 27 of the Constitution of 1917 had given the Mexican government the right to transfer ownership of lands, waters, and other natural resources, and thus the ability to break up large landholdings and redistribute them to individuals or communities. The state-run confederation became the institution through which the government enacted Article 27 at the same time that it indirectly incorporated rural workers and farmers into the PRI and kept them within the sphere of government control. *Campesinos* took their complaints and petitions to the CNC, which acted as their principal intermediary with the government. In return for land grants and other favors, they usually voted for PRI candidates, attended political rallies, and refrained from political opposition.[29]

As with the *campesinos*, the Mexican government also restrained the urban working class through the use of institutions. Article 123 of the Constitution had promised legal and social protections including the right to form unions and strike. Cárdenas, with the help of Marxist intellectual and labor leader Vicente Lombardo Toledano and union leader Fidel Velázquez, had sought to encourage worker mobilization and put an end to factional rivalries in the 1930s by uniting most unions under the umbrella of the Confederation of Mexican Workers (Confederación de Trabajadores Mexicanos, or CTM). As the National Campesino Confederation did with rural workers, the CTM indirectly incorporated urban workers into the PRI, encouraging them to look to the government as the arbiter of disputes and the regulator of industry. Mexico's leaders selectively distributed legal, financial, and political rewards to the workers through the CTM in exchange for obedience and electoral

---

[28] Robert C. Hill, "Despatch from the Embassy in Mexico to the Department of State," in *Foreign Relations of the United States, 1958–1960, American Republics*, Vol. 5, FRUS (Washington, DC: U.S. Government Printing Office, 1991), 832.

[29] On postrevolutionary agrarian issues in Mexico, see Boyer, *Becoming Campesinos*; John J. Dwyer, *The Agrarian Dispute: The Expropriation of American-Owned Rural Land in Postrevolutionary Mexico* (Durham, NC: Duke University Press, 2008).

support.[30] In addition, the government managed to install "*charro*" bosses in many unions, corrupt individuals whose loyalties lay with their patrons rather than their fellow workers.[31]

The government incorporated the "popular sector," or middle class, through yet another PRI-affiliated institution. The National Confederation of Popular Organizations (*Confederación Nacional de Organizaciones Populares*, or CNOP) emerged in the early 1940s in part as a reaction to the creation of the CNC and CTM, as state employees, professionals, intellectuals, merchants, and small industrialists sought to balance against the bargaining power of the worker and peasant confederations. Government leaders favored the creation of the CNOP because the "catchall" nature of this sector helped them incorporate those members of the population who were not *campesinos* or unionized workers. The flexible definition of "popular sectors" meant that the CNOP was a heterogeneous organization that also included groups that would not typically be considered middle class, such as street vendors and shantytown dwellers. Thanks to close connections between the CNOP's leadership and the state bureaucracy, this sector enjoyed more power and political clout than its *campesino* and worker counterparts.[32]

In addition to using official political organizations and institutions, the Mexican government also deployed the "fourth estate" – the media. The wealthy owners of newspapers, radio, and television stations, especially top moguls Rómulo O'Farrill and Emilio Azcárraga Vidaurreta, had close ties with the government and used political connections to build their media empires. The state business Producer and Importer of Paper (Productora e Importadora de Papel S.A., or PIPSA) monopolized newsprint and manipulated the price and availability of paper. The government subsidized friendly newspapers through loans, credits, and

---

[30] Kevin J. Middlebrook, *The Paradox of Revolution: Labor, the State, and Authoritarianism in Mexico* (Baltimore: Johns Hopkins University Press, 1995).

[31] A "charro" is a folkloric Mexican cowboy. The original "charro" union leader, Jesús Díaz de León of the railway workers association, would come to union assemblies dressed like a cowboy. He seized control of the railway union with government assistance in 1948, and since his time sell-out labor leaders have been known as "charros." Enrique Krauze, *Mexico: Biography of Power* (New York: HarperCollins, 1997), 575; Michael Snodgrass, "The Golden Age of Charrismo: Workers, Braceros, and the Political Machinery of Postrevolutionary Mexico," in *Dictablanda*, 175–95.

[32] Louise E. Walker, *Waking from the Dream: Mexico's Middle Classes after 1968* (Stanford, CA: Stanford University Press, 2013); David Schers, "The Popular Sector of the Partido Revolucionario Institucional in Mexico," PhD diss., Tel Aviv University, 1972; Loaeza, *Clases medias y política en México*.

purchases of advertising space and intervened in labor disputes between newspaper owners and their employees. On special occasions, government officials plied editors with gifts of whiskey, champagne, cognac, luggage, and crystal candlesticks.[33] More standard bribes took the form of paid inserts disguised as articles, called *gacetillas*, and monthly payments known as *embutes*; some writers allegedly earned as much as ten thousand pesos a month through these illicit channels.[34] When bribes and co-optation failed, the government applied physical and economic pressure on newspaper owners and journalists. It denied newspapers access to paper, raided their offices, and even imprisoned journalists.

As a result, the major national print media generally told their readers only what the government wanted them to hear. The newspaper *El Nacional* served as the official mouthpiece of the nation's leaders. The three most important privately owned papers, *Excélsior*, *El Universal*, and *Novedades*, usually toed the party line, while *La Prensa*, a popular purveyor of yellow journalism, was the government's favorite vent for its propaganda, fears, threats, and wrath.[35] Even the magazine *¡Siempre!*, which stayed relatively independent of official control and published a wide range of views, refrained from criticizing Mexican presidents or their policies.[36]

Like the print media, Mexican audiovisual executives, producers, and reporters cooperated closely with the government. Through their broadcasts and news coverage, creators of the mass media helped their friends stay in power by discouraging domestic dissent and spreading propaganda.[37] Moviegoers watched films and newsreels that were crafted by

---

[33] Luis Echeverría, "[Gifts from Echeverría to newspaper editors]," December 22, 1967, IPS Caja 2862 B Exp 2, AGN.

[34] "Corrupción, más que libertad," *Política*, June 15, 1961. *Embute* come from the verb *embutir*, which loosely translates as "to stuff." See also Carlos Monsiváis and Julio Scherer, *Tiempo de saber: Prensa y poder en México* (Mexico City: Nuevo Siglo Aguilar, 2003). In 1961, ten thousand pesos would have been worth $125. Banco de México, www.banxico.org.mx (accessed March 13, 2015).

[35] Rodríguez Munguía, *La otra guerra secreta*, 150.

[36] Ibid., 122. On the government's control of the press, see also Monsiváis and Scherer, *Tiempo de saber*; Roderic A. Camp, *Intellectuals and the State in Twentieth Century Mexico* (Austin: University of Texas Press, 1985); Rafael Rodríguez Castañeda, *Prensa vendida: Los presidentes y los periodistas, 40 años de relaciones* (Mexico City: Grijalbo, 1993); Chappell H. Lawson, *Building the Fourth Estate: Democratization and the Rise of a Free Press in Mexico* (Berkeley: University of California Press, 2002).

[37] Claudia Fernández and Andrew Paxman, *El Tigre: Emilio Azcárraga y su imperio Televisa* (Mexico City: Grijalbo, 2000); Celeste González de Bustamante, *"Muy Buenas Noches": Mexico, Television, and the Cold War* (Lincoln: University of Nebraska Press, 2012).

members of the political establishment and promoted a culture of celebrity around the Mexican president.[38] The country's very first television broadcast was of President Miguel Alemán delivering the 1950 State of the Union address, setting a precedent for favorable coverage of government actions and accomplishments. As television grew in popularity, Mexico's leaders built a system of microwave transmitters that spanned the nation and helped reach remote areas. In return, they demanded that radio and television stations devote a certain percentage of their airtime to government programming.[39]

When negotiation, manipulation, and co-optation failed, the Mexican government used force. In 1941, President Manuel Ávila Camacho (1940–6) sought a wartime expedient to combat Axis infiltration and enacted Article 145 of the Federal Penal Code. This article defined the crime of social dissolution as "spreading ideas, programs, or forms of action of any foreign government which disturb the public order or affect the sovereignty of the Mexican State."[40] Even after World War II ended the law remained on the books, and the government widened its scope in 1950 and continued to invoke it to discipline critics and detractors. Authorities denied civil liberties to the political prisoners jailed under Article 145 for the so-called crimes of threatening the nation's economy or security through such acts as sabotage, work stoppage, and slowdowns. Under this vague law, the Mexican government created new punishable categories of people, and political opposition became a dangerous, illegal act.[41]

While the military's role in politics had decreased significantly since the Mexican Revolution and especially since the 1940s, government leaders still relied on the army to help contain domestic opposition, especially in the countryside. In the name of maintaining national security, soldiers broke strikes, dispersed demonstrations, and intimidated and even killed protesters. The military was not only heavily involved in policing activities but also institutionally intermingled with the country's many civilian police forces, which included the Federal Judicial Police (subordinate

---

[38] Seth Fein, "New Empire into Old: Making Mexican Newsreels the Cold War Way," *Diplomatic History* 28, no. 5 (November 2004): 703–48.

[39] Fátima Fernández Christlieb, *Los medios de difusión másiva en México* (Mexico City: Juan Pablos Editor, 1982), 103–5.

[40] On the crime of social dissolution, see Evelyn P. Stevens, "Legality and Extra-Legality in Mexico," *Journal of Interamerican Studies and World Affairs* 12, no. 1 (January 1, 1970): 62–75, see pp. 62–3.

[41] On the political uses of state violence, see Carole Nagengast, "Violence, Terror, and the Crisis of the State," *Annual Review of Anthropology* 23 (January 1, 1994): 109–36.

to the attorney general), the Judicial Police of the Federal District and Territories, the Police of the Federal District, and others. Additional formal and informal groups and individuals such as *pistoleros* (gunmen), *defensas rurales* (militias), *granaderos* (riot police), and student *porras* (thugs) received support from the government and used violent methods to discourage and eliminate dissent.[42]

The Mexican government also created multiple intelligence agencies to maintain domestic order. The two main intelligence organizations were the Department of Political and Social Investigations, or IPS, which originated in the early aftermath of the Mexican Revolution, and the Department of Federal Security, or DFS, which Miguel Alemán created in order to incorporate ambitious military officials into an elite security service directly under presidential control. Both groups became increasingly professionalized and politicized throughout the 1940s and 1950s. Alemán's successor, Adolfo Ruiz Cortines (1952–8), moved the Department of Federal Security to the Ministry of the Interior, where it partially eclipsed the older Department of Political and Social Investigations. Agents from the two intelligence organizations and the police forces frequently mirrored each other's work and competed for prominence.[43]

Intelligence agents performed a wide range of services for the Mexican government. Primary among their responsibilities was the collection and analysis of information. According to historian Sergio Aguayo, the Mexican president collaborated with the minister of the interior, the director of intelligence, and other government leaders to create a list of targets that included political opponents, dissidents, and foreigners.[44] Agents kept track of the individuals and groups on the list by combing the media, infiltrating opposition groups, intercepting mail and telephone calls, and bribing informants. Over the years, intelligence officials also became increasingly responsible for the "dirty work" of maintaining

---

[42] Thomas Rath, *Myths of Demilitarization in Postrevolutionary Mexico, 1920–1960* (Chapel Hill: University of North Carolina Press, 2013); Hernández Rodríguez, "Strongmen and State Weakness"; Jaime Pensado, "Political Violence and Student Culture in Mexico: The Consolidation of Porrismo during the 1950s and 1960s," PhD diss., University of Chicago, 2008.

[43] On Mexico's intelligence organizations, see Sergio Aguayo, *La Charola: Una historia de los servicios de inteligencia en México* (Mexico City: Grijalbo, 2001); Jacinto Rodríguez Munguía, *Las nóminas secretas de Gobernación* (Mexico City: LIMAC (Libertad de Información-México A.C.), 2004); Enrique Condés Lara, *Represión y rebelión en México (1959–1985)*, Vol. 1 (Mexico City: Miguel Ángel Porrúa, 2007); Aaron Navarro, *Political Intelligence and the Creation of Modern Mexico, 1938–1954* (University Park: Pennsylvania State University Press, 2010).

[44] Aguayo, *La Charola*, 110–12.

political and social control, using threats, violence, and assassination to intimidate the population.[45]

All of these methods – institutionalization, co-optation, manipulation, and repression – combined to create the appearance of a *pax PRIista* in Mexico in the early years of the Cold War. Compared to many other countries in Latin America, Mexico did enjoy a relatively high degree of stability. Yet even in this period of peace and prosperity, the nation's leaders knew that their power was never absolute, their control over the country never complete. They had to negotiate and defend their authority in multiple arenas and on local, national, and international levels.

U.S.-MEXICAN INTELLIGENCE COOPERATION

Mexico's intelligence agencies had close connections with their U.S. counterparts, who shared their concerns over national security. The Federal Bureau of Investigation, which had maintained an office in Mexico City since the beginning of World War II, helped organize the Department of Federal Security and provided training, support, and weapons.[46] In return, Mexican security police helped track down U.S. fugitives and turned them over to the FBI.[47]

The Central Intelligence Agency, operating out of the top floor of the U.S. embassy, became intricately entwined with the DFS in the 1950s and 1960s under the leadership of Chief of Station Winston Scott. In an operation code named LITEMPO, the CIA built a network of contacts and agents within the Mexican government. President López Mateos, code named LITENSOR, and his minister of the interior and successor Díaz Ordaz, or LITEMPO-2, both cooperated with the CIA's operations.[48] By the mid-1960s, as many as two hundred "indigenous agents," or Mexican citizens, were assisting the agency.[49] These included the head of the Department

[45] Navarro, *Political Intelligence and the Creation of Modern Mexico*, 185.

[46] Ibid., 183–4; Morley, *Our Man in Mexico: Winston Scott and the Hidden History of the CIA* (Lawrence: University Press of Kansas, 2008), 85.

[47] J. Edgar Hoover, *Exposé of Soviet Espionage, May 1960: For the Use of the Subcommittee to Investigate the Administration of the Internal Security Act and Other Internal Security Laws* (Washington, DC: U.S. Government Printing Office, 1960), 20.

[48] Morley, *Our Man in Mexico*, 90, 94. For further evidence that Gustavo Díaz Ordaz was "LITEMPO-2," see Willard C. Curtis, "LITEMPO Operational Report 1–3; October 1963," November 7, 1963, RG 233 Box 90 Reel 46 JFK/CIA RIF 104-10211-10102, U.S. National Archives and Records Administration II, College Park, MD [hereafter NARA]. "Willard C. Curtis" was Winston Scott's pseudonym. Morley, *Our Man in Mexico*, 289, 356.

[49] Anne Goodpasture, "Mexico City Station History," November 16, 1978, RG 263 CIA Russ Holmes Work File Box 22 RIF 104-10414-10124, NARA.

of Federal Security, Fernando Gutiérrez Barrios or LITEMPO-4, and Díaz Ordaz's minister of the interior and successor, Luis Echeverría (1970–6) or LITEMPO-8.[50]

As the Cold War progressed, the Mexico City station grew into one of the most extensive and expensive intelligence programs in the CIA. Operations included photographic surveillance, wiretapping, infiltration, and recruitment.[51] Agents under cover as students collected information about activities at the National Autonomous University of Mexico (Universidad Nacional Autónoma de México, or UNAM) and the Colegio de México.[52] The station spent at least five thousand dollars a month to disseminate anticommunist propaganda through bulletins, articles, editorials, and advertisements.[53] It spent more than four thousand dollars a year supporting a national Catholic student group.[54] One decidedly juvenile operation involved using stink bombs against enemy targets.[55]

Personal connections formed the backbone of the relationship between the CIA and the Mexican government. Winston Scott spoke fluent Spanish and developed close friendships with Mexico's presidents. The Deputy Chief of Mission in the U.S. Embassy in Mexico City recalled that Scott "was the one man who could go in to see the president whenever he wanted."[56] The CIA station chief breakfasted with López Mateos every available Sunday, and the president served as the chief witness at Scott's Mexico City wedding.[57] López Mateos and Díaz Ordaz trusted the chief of station to such an extent that they reportedly preferred to conduct the business of U.S.-Mexican relations with him, in effect circumventing the State Department.[58] According

[50] Morley, *Our Man in Mexico*, 94.
[51] Goodpasture, "Mexico City Station History."
[52] Willard C. Curtis, "LIMOTOR Progress Report January–July 1963," October 30, 1963, RG 233 Box 90 Reel 46 JFK/CIA RIF 104-10211-10070, NARA.
[53] Willard C. Curtis, "LILISP-E Progress Report for September–October 1963," November 6, 1963, RG 233 Box 90 Reel 46 JFK/CIA RIF 104-10211-10117, NARA.
[54] Willard C. Curtis, "LIEVICT Status Report for May and June 1963," October 17, 1963, RG 233 Box 72 /32 JFK/CIA RIF 104-10092-10089, NARA.
[55] Willard C. Curtis, "Operational Monthly Report–1–30 September 1963," October 18, 1963, RG 233 Box 72 /32 JFK/CIA RIF 104-10092-10083, NARA. On Mexico City as a center of Cold War espionage, see Patrick Iber, "Paraíso de espías. La ciudad de México y la Guerra Fría," *Nexos*, April 1, 2014, http://www.nexos.com.mx/?p=20004 (accessed March 13, 2015).
[56] "Interview with Henry Dearborn," May 8, 1991, The Foreign Affairs Oral History Collection of the Association for Diplomatic Studies and Training, Library of Congress, Manuscript Division, http://hdl.loc.gov/loc.mss/mfdip.2004dea03 (accessed March 13, 2015).
[57] Morley, *Our Man in Mexico*, 112, 145.
[58] Ibid., 108; Philip Agee, *Inside the Company: CIA Diary* (New York: Stonehill Publishing Company, 1975), 525. The CIA confirmed the veracity of much of Agee's information in

to an internal history of the agency's Mexico City station, the relationship "became an unofficial channel for the exchange of selected, sensitive political information which each government wanted the other to receive but not through public protocol exchanges." U.S. Ambassadors Robert Hill (1957–60) and Thomas Mann (1961–3) approved of this arrangement, but Fulton Freeman (1964–9) resented what he perceived as the CIA's encroachment on his professional territory.[59]

Friendships between CIA agents and Mexican officials existed on lower rungs of the ladder as well. Díaz Ordaz's nephew, Emiliano Bolanos Díaz, became extremely close to the coordinator of the LITEMPO program, George Munro, a former FBI agent also known as Jeremy K. Benadum. Munro had met Bolanos while working for the FBI and had built a large part of the LITEMPO network from that initial contact. The two men even served as godparents to each other's children.[60]

Cooperating with the CIA was good business for Mexican officials. Scott helped arrange wiretaps of López Mateos and Díaz Ordaz's most powerful rivals and critics, including Lázaro Cárdenas, Vicente Lombardo Toledano, and painter David Álfaro Siqueiros.[61] The CIA gave the Mexican presidents daily intelligence summaries of domestic and international developments and provided advice and equipment for a secret communications network to connect the Ministry of the Interior in Mexico City with principal cities in the rest of the country.[62] Bribery also abounded. Díaz Ordaz received four hundred dollars a month from the CIA during his presidential campaign and, if rumors were true, an automobile for his mistress.[63]

In spite of all the personal ties and close cooperation between the Mexican and U.S. intelligence organizations, professional tensions also existed. In a monthly operational report to CIA headquarters, Scott described the DFS agents as "largely poorly trained, insecure, and unreliable." According to the chief of station, Mexico's security officials were "dishonest, cruel, and abusive." U.S. distrust of the Mexican agents ran so deep that the CIA included the DFS among its targets for observation and wiretapped two of its telephone lines.[64]

a classified book review: Anonymous, "Book review of 'Inside the Company: CIA Diary' by Philip Agee," *Studies in Intelligence* 19, no. 2 (Summer 1975): 35–38.

[59] Goodpasture, "Mexico City Station History."

[60] On the friendship between Bolanos Díaz and Munro, see ibid. On Munro's identification as Benadum, see Morley, *Our Man in Mexico*, 91.

[61] Morley, *Our Man in Mexico*, 93.

[62] Agee, *Inside the Company*, 526.

[63] Goodpasture, "Mexico City Station History"; Agee, *Inside the Company*, 275.

[64] CIA, "Monthly Operational Report for Project LIENVOY," October 8, 1963, 104-10052-10083, Mary Ferrell Foundation Digital Archive.

CONTAINING DOMESTIC OPPOSITION

Mexico's intelligence organizations helped the government maintain semiauthoritarian control over the country, but Mexican leaders still faced a number of political, social, and economic challenges. In the 1940s, intellectuals and politicians began criticizing the government's claims to revolutionary legitimacy, at the same time that students, *campesinos*, and workers demanded that the government live up to the promises of the Mexican Revolution. Mexico's leaders used a variety of increasingly repressive tactics to counter and contain their various critics.

In the realm of letters, some of Mexico's most prominent intellectuals began undermining the government's claims to revolutionary legitimacy. In 1943, economist and historian Jesús Silva Herzog published an essay in the journal *Cuadernos Americanos* in which he declared that the Mexican Revolution was in full crisis and called the nation's leaders "profiteer[s] of the Revolution, concerned exclusively with personal profit."[65] Four years later, another economist and historian, Daniel Cosío Villegas, published an equally influential essay in the same journal. Cosío Villegas examined in detail each of the Mexican Revolution's original intentions – democracy, agrarian reform, workers' rights, and nationalism – and explained when and how each goal had been abandoned or perverted. "The crisis comes from the fact that the goals of the Revolution have become exhausted to such a degree that the very term 'revolution' now means nothing," Cosío Villegas contended.[66] Also in 1947, intellectual José Iturriaga published yet another essay on the subject in *Cuadernos Americanos* that diagnosed the Revolution as "gravely ill."[67] Two years later, Jesús Silva Herzog pronounced the Revolution officially dead and conducted a postmortem. "Revolutions are not immortal," he concluded.[68] *Excélsior* columnist José R. Colín provided a figurative burial, titling one of his columns "The Mexican Revolution: R.I.P."[69] These intellectual critics publicly challenged Mexican leaders' claims that they were still carrying out the work of the Mexican Revolution.

Beginning in 1943, a movement emerged within the PRI among those opposed to the military reforms and conservative politics of President

---

[65] Ross, *Is the Mexican Revolution Dead?*, 22–3.
[66] Daniel Cosío Villegas, *Ensayos y notas*, Vol. 1 (Mexico City: Editorial Hermes, 1966), 113.
[67] Ross, *Is the Mexican Revolution Dead?*, 93.
[68] Ibid., 100.
[69] Ibid., 110.

Ávila Camacho. These dissidents, many of them military leaders and followers of Lázaro Cárdenas, declared themselves the legitimate heirs of the Mexican Revolution and coalesced around the general and revolutionary veteran Miguel Henríquez Guzmán. The *henriquistas* created a new organization called the Federation of Parties of the Mexican People (Federación de Partidos del Pueblo Mexicano, or FPPM) to promote his candidacy for the elections of 1946, but were frustrated when Ávila Camacho designated his minister of the interior, Miguel Alemán, as his successor. Henríquez returned to the political battlefield in 1950 in anticipation of the elections of 1952. He refused to follow the standard nominating practices of the official party, however, and announced his own candidacy, prompting the PRI to expel him and his followers. The FPPM received its official registration as a political party and nominated Henríquez for president, and soon began to receive support from a wide range of groups, including *campesinos* and railroad workers, as well as prominent politicians and military leaders.[70]

Government authorities used a combination of tactics to defeat the *henriquista* challenge. The PRI candidate, Adolfo Ruiz Cortines, responded by incorporating elements of Henríquez's platform, including voting rights for women, while government auditors froze the assets of some of Henríquez's most profitable companies. The police and military helped by harassing and jailing FPPM activists and obstructing campaign rallies. The *henriquistas* did not shy away from violence; their armed attacks on PRI candidates and supporters resulted in the deaths of at least three people and earned the FPPM an official reprimand from the Federal Electoral Commission. The day after Henríquez lost the fraud-ridden election by two million votes, his followers organized a rally in the heart of Mexico City that dissolved into a bloody riot, pitting protestors against police and federal troops. Intelligence agents worried that the violence had only begun and that Henríquez intended to lead a rebellion.[71] This did not come to pass; the general was too busy trying to salvage his financial portfolio to spearhead a new revolution. Government leaders had managed to defend the PRI's stranglehold on elections, but they had also seen the inherent danger in populist movements that staked competing claims to revolutionary legitimacy.

---

[70] Elisa Servín, *Ruptura y oposición: El movimiento henriquista, 1945–1954* (Mexico City: Cal y arena, 2001).
[71] Navarro, *Political Intelligence and the Creation of Modern Mexico, 1938–1954,* 233, 248.

Discontent simmered in the countryside as well; another movement that concurrently laid claim to the legacy of the Mexican Revolution formed around a *campesino* organizer in the state of Morelos named Rubén Jaramillo. A veteran of the Mexican Revolution who had fought under Emiliano Zapata, Jaramillo led the residents of Morelos in a drawn-out struggle for the state support promised them in the nation's constitution. For years, Jaramillo and his followers alternated between trying to work within the Mexican legal framework to defend *campesino* interests and using other, more extreme, methods. They first took up the rifles that they had saved from the revolution and took to the hills in 1942, when state officials violently quashed a strike that the *jaramillistas* had led at a sugar cooperative. The federal government issued the group an official pardon a year later, and Jaramillo ran for state governor in 1946. The PRI candidate won and governmental repression forced the agrarian leader back into hiding to begin his second armed uprising. In 1951, the cycle repeated itself: the *jaramillistas* left the mountains, pursued the electoral path to reform in an alliance with the *henriquistas*, and eventually returned to clandestine armed struggle to escape repression. This third uprising lasted six years, until President López Mateos pardoned Jaramillo in 1959.[72]

In the 1950s, the government also faced its first significant threat in decades from students. A massive strike began in April 1956, when all twenty-five thousand students of the National Polytechnic Institute (*Instituto Politécnico Nacional*, or IPN) walked out, demanding more resources and educational reforms including increased student participation in the governance of the IPN and the removal of the rector and six other administrators. UNAM students declined to join the strike, but it quickly spread to other institutions, especially teacher training colleges (*normales*) and agricultural schools. Before long, it had drawn in more than one hundred thousand participants.[73] One aspect of this strike set it apart from earlier, less threatening, student activism: a heavy emphasis on direct action and confrontation. Peaceful tactics included informational brigades and *mítines relámpagos*, or lightning "hit-and-run" political rallies. The more confrontational strategies included hijacking buses, taking physical possession of buildings, and forming shock brigades to defend

---

[72] Tanalís Padilla, *Rural Resistance in the Land of Zapata: The Jaramillista Movement and the Myth of the Pax Priísta, 1940–1962* (Durham, NC: Duke University Press, 2008), 184.

[73] Gilberto Guevara Niebla, *La democracia en la calle: Crónica del movimiento estudiantil mexicano* (Mexico City: Siglo Veintiuno Editores, 1988), 16.

"liberated territories."[74] Articles in the U.S. press described rioting and other violent scenes in which groups of strikers roamed the streets of Mexico City stoning buses and beating drivers and passengers.[75]

Government leaders adopted a variety of measures to quash the protests in the National Polytechnic Institute. They orchestrated a press campaign to portray the strike as a communist conspiracy in order to curtail public sympathy; for the first time, the government and the media identified students as a "subversive threat to the nation."[76] President Ruiz Cortines negotiated a temporary truce, offering the students a greater role in policy making at their institution but refusing to fire any administrators. Agitation continued, however, and Ruiz Cortines responded to demands for a new rector by hiring an even more authoritarian figure than the last. The head of the police department, meanwhile, instructed his men to arrest all "subversive" students.[77] After six months of strikes and protests, the situation got so desperate that on September 23 the president called in the federal army to occupy the Polytechnic Institute. Nearly two thousand soldiers and four hundred police officers invaded the campus.[78] Authorities detained more than three hundred students and sent the leaders of the strike to prison for more than two years. In addition, the army continued to occupy the IPN until the end of 1958.

It was not long before the level of violence in university activism increased in response. Outraged by a hike in bus fares and inspired by labor unrest, hundreds of students from the National Autonomous University began a raucous, destructive protest known as the "bus movement" in August 1958.[79] They captured hundreds of vehicles, set fire to a terminal after violent confrontations with bus drivers, and painted slogans such as "Death to Bad Government" on the walls of the National

[74] Jaime Pensado, *Rebel Mexico: Student Unrest and Authoritarian Political Culture during the Long Sixties* (Stanford, CA: Stanford University Press, 2013), 89–93.
[75] "Striking Students Riot in Mexico City," *New York Times*, April 18, 1956.
[76] Pensado, *Rebel Mexico*, 84.
[77] "Se ordena a la policía detener a los estudiantes depredadores," *Excélsior*, August 22, 1956.
[78] Pensado, *Rebel Mexico*, 107.
[79] On the bus movement, see Raúl Jardón, *1968: El fuego de la esperanza* (Mexico City: Siglo Veintiuno Editores, 1998); Guevara Niebla, *La democracia en la calle*; Gerardo Estrada Rodríguez, *1968, estado y universidad: Orígenes de la transición política en México* (Mexico City: Plaza Janés, 2004); René Rivas O., *La izquierda estudiantil en la UNAM: Organizaciones, movilizaciones y liderazgos (1958–1972)* (Mexico City: Universidad Nacional Autónoma de México, Facultad de Estudios Superiores Aragón, 2007).

Palace.[80] The students also seized control of the UNAM campus, where they stashed the buses that they had commandeered. Soldiers surrounded the university, and police tried to recover the stolen vehicles, arresting various students in the process. A group of drivers armed with sticks and stones invaded the campus and recovered ten buses, leaving broken windows and disorder in their wake.[81]

What set this protest apart, in addition to its destructive nature, was its dedication to a cause outside the educational realm and its ability to connect with groups beyond the National University's campus. Those involved in the bus movement demanded an end to the private monopoly of city buses, improvement of the transportation system without increasing fares, and the immediate release of the arrested students.[82] They also defended bus drivers' rights to better working conditions and independent labor unions. The strikers organized a march to the Zócalo, which observers estimated brought together somewhere between thirty thousand and two hundred thousand participants. These included students from the National University, the Polytechnic Institute, and teacher training colleges. Teachers attended, as did railroad, petroleum, telegraph, and bus workers.[83] For the first time in Mexico's history, students from UNAM, IPN, and the Advanced Teachers College (Escuela Normal Superior) had formed an alliance.[84] Shortly after the march, President Ruiz Cortines spoke with the leaders and announced that he would meet some of their demands: fares would return to their original levels and all those arrested in connection with the events would be released from jail. The students returned the buses and the protest came to an end.

[80] Pensado, *Rebel Mexico*, 129.
[81] Comité 68 Pro Libertadores Democráticas and Fiscalía Especial para Movimientos Sociales y Políticos del Pasado [Special Prosecutor for Social and Political Movements of the Past, hereafter FEMOSPP], *Informe histórico presentado a la sociedad mexicana: Genocidio y delitos de la humanidad, documentos fundamentales, 1968–2008* (Mexico City: Comité 68 Pro Libertades Democráticas, 2008), 59.
[82] On issues of transportation in Mexico City in this period, see Diane E. Davis, *Urban Leviathan: Mexico City in the Twentieth Century* (Philadelphia: Temple University Press, 1994); Michael Joseph Lettieri, "Wheels of Government: The Alianza de Camioneros and the Political Culture of PRI Rule, 1929–1981," PhD diss., University of California San Diego, 2014.
[83] Guevara Niebla, *La democracia en la calle*, 22; Jardón, *1968*, 15; Pensado, *Rebel Mexico*, 139.
[84] Donald J. Mabry, *The Mexican University and the State: Student Conflicts, 1910–1971* (College Station: Texas A&M University Press, 1982), 211.

At the same time that the students were testing the limits of their oppositional power, various groups of workers were doing the same. The laborers who had made the Mexican Miracle possible found themselves increasingly excluded from the benefits of the economic boom, as their frozen wages kept production costs low for the government's policy of import substitution industrialization. When the CTM and charro union leaders refused to take action even after a devaluation of the peso further reduced workers' buying power in 1954, dissatisfaction spread. As U.S. Ambassador Robert Hill observed: "Failure of [the] 40-year old revolution to provide more substantial benefits in income, education, health facilities, and housing has left large numbers in [a] state of expectancy for [a] way to show their resentment."[85]

One of the largest strike movements in decades emerged among primary school teachers in Mexico City. Beginning in July 1956, Othón Salazar and Encarnación Pérez led a movement among teachers in Section IX of the National Union of Educational Workers that demanded a salary increase and new union leadership. Conflict between Salazar's supporters and the official leadership escalated until there were two unions competing for control of Section IX. The majority of the teachers sided with Salazar and joined his Revolutionary Teachers' Movement (Movimiento Revolucionario del Magisterio, or MRM), which grew in strength as the months passed. In April 1958, riot police broke up a demonstration in the Zócalo, prompting Salazar and the MRM to declare a citywide strike and occupy the patios of the Ministry of Education. The government then responded with a two-pronged approach: the educational authorities awarded a raise to the teachers of Section IX to meet the less institutionally threatening of their demands, but refused to recognize Salazar's union as their legitimate representative. When these peaceful methods failed to contain the MRM, police violently dispersed another demonstration and arrested Salazar and Pérez.[86]

Though these various political, social, and economic movements arose in Mexico in the early years of the global Cold War, they were not yet connected to that geopolitical confrontation. The *henriquista*, *jaramillista*, and student movements began almost exclusively as domestic developments with national- and local-level goals. International events did not

---

[85] Robert Hill, "Telegram from the Embassy in Mexico to the Department of State," August 29, 1958, in *FRUS, 1958–1960, American Republics*, Vol. 5, 840.

[86] Olga Pellicer de Brody and José Luis Reyna, *Historia de la Revolución Mexicana, periodo 1952–1960: El afianzamiento de la estabilidad política*, Vol. 22 (Mexico City: El Colegio de México, 1978).

play a significant role in inspiring these movements, nor did so-called foreign ideologies such as Marxism. They were independent responses to specific conditions in Mexico, to the stifling political system and the corrupt institutions that regulated the lives of *campesinos*, students, and workers. For the most part, Mexican authorities perceived these movements as isolated, and as a result, were confident of their own power and ability to defeat any opposition.

THE MEXICAN COMMUNIST MOVEMENT

Mexican communists were occasionally influential actors throughout the first half of the twentieth century, but more frequently they suffered government repression and served as bogeymen and scapegoats. Though the Mexican government usually maintained normal diplomatic relations with the Soviet Union, Mexican authorities and their security forces shared the U.S. government's anticommunist bent. Intelligence agents in Mexico, like those in the United States, labeled most oppositional activity as "communist" or "subversive." Over the course of the twentieth century and especially during the Cold War, a vicious cycle evolved in which agents' paranoia both fed upon and, in turn, increased the fears of their superiors. Some of the so-called communists who abounded in the national press and the pages of the U.S. and Mexican intelligence reports were actually members of Marxist organizations, but many were not. Fact and myth blended together, creating a climate of suspicion and uncertainty.[87]

The first Mexican organization to be affiliated with the Soviet Comintern, the Mexican Communist Party (Partido Comunista Mexicano, or PCM), emerged in November 1919 from what had previously been called the Mexican Socialist Party. The new party had a rocky first few years thanks to low membership, scarce funds, and bouts of governmental repression, but by the end of the 1920s it had established important ties with railroad workers, miners, and *campesino* groups. Railroad activist Valentín Campa, who along with Demetrio Vallejo

---

[87] Both participants in and observers of the Mexican communist movement frequently confused, ignored, and blurred the distinctions between the terms *Marxist*, *Communist*, and *Socialist*. People jumped from one party to another and groups changed names; meanwhile, observers frequently lumped them all together into the catchall category of "communists." This book makes an effort both to represent faithfully the historical actors as they would have described themselves and to examine how Mexico's leaders and their intelligence agents perceived communists and other leftists.

would lead the railroad workers' movement in the late 1950s, joined the party in 1927. During the 1920s the Mexican Communist Party also established close connections with a group of influential young muralists including Diego Rivera, David Álfaro Siqueiros, Xavier Guerrero, and José Clemente Orozco. However, by the end of the 1920s and the beginning of the 1930s, the Comintern's new sectarian policies and ultraleftism impelled the Mexican branch to drive out many of its members and cut its ties with noncommunist allies. At the same time, the Mexican government broke relations with the Soviet Union and conducted a domestic campaign of repression that forced the PCM to move underground and nearly disappear.[88] The press, especially the newspapers *Excélsior* and *El Universal*, helped contain the communist movement by conducting a disinformation campaign that blamed social upheavals on Bolshevik infiltrators.[89]

The Mexican Communist Party recovered from the lows of the early 1930s and reached the height of its power and popularity during Lázaro Cárdenas's presidency. Upon entering office in 1934, Cárdenas lifted the restrictions on the communist press and ordered the release of political prisoners who belonged to the party. The PCM, in turn, played an important role in the worker and *campesino* mobilizations of the 1930s, helped organize the Confederation of Mexican Workers, and supported the government's program of socialist education. The organization also massively broadened its overall membership and gained influence among workers, *campesinos*, and intellectuals.

The communists' day in the sun did not last long, however, and by the late 1930s the PCM was once again in trouble. Turmoil within the organization culminated in an extraordinary congress in March 1940, during which the group ousted many of its top leaders. Further waves of expulsions took place throughout the following decade, as the communists struggled to respond to the repression of Miguel Alemán's administration and the creation of Vicente Lombardo Toledano's Popular Party in 1948. Under Alemán, communists and other leftists were purged from their positions in the government and unions, and the police and army attacked them with greater audacity.

The Mexican Communist Party continued to lose clout throughout the 1950s, as the group dwindled in numbers and struggled against infighting

---

[88] Barry Carr, *Marxism and Communism in Twentieth-Century Mexico* (Lincoln: University of Nebraska Press, 1992), 16–31.
[89] Daniela Spenser, *The Impossible Triangle: Mexico, Soviet Russia, and the United States in the 1920s* (Durham, NC: Duke University Press, 1999), 53.

and government repression. In 1951, a member of the PCM wrote a
memorandum to his fellow communists describing the two fundamental
forms of attack that their "enemies" used to weaken the self-proclaimed
leaders of the proletariat. From outside the party, the methods consisted
of "containing every manifestation of our party to the point of declaring
it illegal and isolating it from the masses, [and] pursuing its leaders and
assassinating them in order to sow fear and dread among the ranks."
Attacks from within involved infiltrating police agents into the party
and taking advantage of the weakness of some members to turn them
into "lackeys and spies." In order to defend against the second form of
attack, the author of the memo recommended that "cell leaders interest
themselves and become familiar with the lives of each comrade – their
interests, weaknesses, vices, defects, and daily life – because that consti-
tutes excellent material with which to discover a spy or traitor."[90] In an
intriguing addition to the web of espionage, the Mexican Communist
Party's defensive measures even extended to keeping watch over the government's intelligence agents.[91]

The Mexican Communist Party was not the only group in Mexico
to espouse Marxist principles and goals. In 1948, Vicente Lombardo
Toledano founded the Popular Party, which flirted with Marxist theory
and officially adopted Marxism-Leninism in 1960, when it changed its
name to the Popular Socialist Party.[92] Historian Stephen R. Niblo has
described the party as Lombardo Toledano's attempt to "find a formula
by which he could oppose the PRI without offending the government."[93]
Lombardo Toledano established the group as the embodiment of his
long-standing goal of creating a unified leftist front, and the new party
initially attracted the support and participation of many former members
of the Mexican Communist Party and unaffiliated leftists. It grew rapidly
in its early years, with a core of intellectuals and *campesinos*. This party
played an inconsistent role in Mexican politics: Lombardo Toledano and
other leaders made occasional independent and even radical gestures,
but generally toed the government line on matters of domestic policy.

[90] Edelmiro Maldonado L., "La lucha contra la provocación y el espionaje," February 22,
     1951, Mexican Communist Party, Box 5, Folder 49, Columbia University Rare Book and
     Manuscript Library.
[91] Partido Comunista Mexicano, "[PCM report on activities of intelligence agencies]," June
     6, 1956, Mexican Communist Party, Box 5, Folder 49, Columbia University Rare Book
     and Manuscript Library.
[92] Rosendo Bolívar Meza, *Lombardo: Su pensamiento político* (Mexico City: Universidad
     Obrera de México, 2006), 157–67.
[93] Niblo, *Mexico in the 1940s*, 229.

This ambivalence increased the divisions within the Popular Party, and many members resigned in disgust, especially over the issue of Lombardo Toledano's conciliatory attitude toward the national government.

Another communist group, the Trotskyists, also took part in Mexican politics but, like the other Mexican communists, had trouble maintaining unity in their ranks and stability in their organizations. The followers of Leon Trotsky engaged in constant competition and struggle with adherents of the predominant branch of Stalinist communism. Prominent members of Mexican society including writer José Revueltas, muralist Diego Rivera, and labor leader Vicente Lombardo Toledano occasionally associated with or defended the Trotskyist movement.[94] During the Cárdenas administration, the Trotskyists had enough pull in government circles to convince the president to grant their leader asylum in Mexico in late 1936. The Mexican members took upon themselves the responsibility of protecting Trotsky during his exile, sharing the work with his followers from the United States and Germany. Despite their best efforts, a second assassination attempt succeeded in Mexico City in 1940. The movement enjoyed a revival in the late 1950s, and a new Trotskyist party called the Revolutionary Workers' Party (Partido Obrero Revolucionario, or POR) emerged in 1959.[95] The Trotskyist revival lasted through the 1960s and early 1970s, chiefly among students, but constantly suffered from internal strife among its members.[96]

In 1950, yet another communist party emerged in Mexico as a result of the Mexican Communist Party's infighting and expulsions. The Mexican Worker-Campesino Party (Partido Obrero-Campesino Mexicano, or POCM) incorporated many of the most effective leaders ousted from the PCM during the 1940s, including railroad unionists Campa and Vallejo.[97] Campa, much more interested in Marxist doctrine and ideology than Vallejo, was even on the governing board of the communist splinter party.[98] The POCM was never very large; nonetheless, it occasionally managed to play an important role in worker and student activism.

[94] Robert J. Alexander, *Trotskyism in Latin America* (Stanford, CA: Hoover Institution Press, 1973), 179–84.

[95] CIA, "International Communist Trends and Patterns: The Sino-Soviet Controversy in Cuba and Other Latin American Countries," February 1, 1961. CIA-RDP78-00915R001300280001-6, CIA Records Search Tool (CREST), NARA.

[96] On Trotskyist student groups, see René Rivas O., *La izquierda estudiantil en la UNAM*.

[97] Carr, *Marxism and Communism in Twentieth-Century Mexico*, 189.

[98] Robert F. Alegre, *Railroad Radicals in Cold War Mexico: Gender, Class, and Memory* (Lincoln: University of Nebraska Press, 2013), 182, 191.

The history of the communist movement in Mexico was also one of people, in addition to parties. Rank-and-file members of the organizations frequently disobeyed their leaders' directives. Members of the Mexican Communist Party cooperated with those of the Mexican Worker-Campesino Party, even when the directors of the two groups were in bitter conflict. Many individuals on the left wing of society bounced between parties or avoided affiliation with them entirely. José Revueltas, for example, was a member of the Mexican Communist Party from 1932 until he was expelled in 1943. He then helped Vicente Lombardo Toledano found the Popular Party in 1948, rejoined the PCM in 1956, and was expelled again in 1960. He later briefly joined the Mexican Worker-Campesino Party before forming the Leninist Spartacist League.[99] Diego Rivera joined the Mexican Communist Party in 1922, resigned in 1925, was readmitted in 1926, and was then expelled in 1929. In 1936, the muralist joined the Trotskyists. He helped persuade Cárdenas to grant refuge to Trotsky, who lived with Rivera and his wife Frida Kahlo for a little more than a year until Rivera discovered Kahlo's affair with their houseguest. In 1939, Rivera broke with the Trotskyist party, and for the next decade he repeatedly applied to rejoin the Mexican Communist Party (with a brief interlude as a member of the Popular Party in 1948) until he was readmitted to the PCM in 1954.[100] Frida Kahlo, Rivera's wife and a world-renowned artist in her own right, joined the Mexican Communist Party in 1928. She flirted (quite literally) with Trotskyism in the late 1930s and rejoined the PCM in 1949.[101]

U.S. officials believed that the Mexican government was not sufficiently worried about communism. A background paper prepared by the State Department for President Eisenhower in 1953 contended, "The Communist danger is not fully appreciated in Mexico."[102] A National Intelligence Estimate from 1957 went into more detail on how "the tolerant attitude of the Mexican government has permitted the use of the country as a center for [Soviet] Bloc activities in Latin America." The report noted that the Soviet Embassy in Mexico City was second in size only to

[99] Roberto Simon Crespi, "José Revueltas (1914–1976): A Political Biography," *Latin American Perspectives* 6, no. 3 (July 1, 1979): 93–113.

[100] Patrick Marnham, *Dreaming with His Eyes Open: A Life of Diego Rivera* (New York: Knopf, 1998).

[101] Hayden Herrera, *Frida, a Biography of Frida Kahlo* (New York: Perennial Library, 1983).

[102] "Memorandum by the Secretary of State to the President," October 13, 1953, in *Foreign Relations of the United States, 1952–1954, Volume IV: The American Republics* (Washington, DC: U.S. Government Printing Office, 1983), 1349–52.

that of the United States.[103] The Mexican government's tolerant attitude did, in fact, allow the Soviets to use their embassy as a central hub to collect information and coordinate activities with communists from across Latin America.[104] In a prescient letter to Senator Lyndon B. Johnson in November 1958, Assistant Secretary of State Roy Rubottom reflected, "It is almost as though Mexico hopes to mediate some day between the free world and the Communist world."[105]

Mexican Marxist organizations may not have been large, coherent, or stable, but they could be influential. Communists and socialists occasionally played important roles in Mexico's political and cultural life throughout the twentieth century. Sometimes they enjoyed a clear influence on politics, as in the case of Cárdenas's socialist educational program. Other times Marxists' influence took more indirect or ambiguous forms and their energies turned toward self-defense. Security officials, the media, and the nation's leaders struggled to understand the goals and capabilities of communists throughout the twentieth century, but one thing all these observers did grasp was the opportunity to use communists as scapegoats for any outbreak of political or social unrest.

THE RAILROAD MOVEMENT

Communists played an unclear – and much debated – role in one of the most important instances of activism in twentieth-century Mexico: the railroad movement of 1958–9. Under the leadership of Demetrio Vallejo and Valentín Campa, the workers of the most important company, the state-owned National Railroads of Mexico (Ferrocarriles Nacionales de México), demanded higher salaries, better benefits, and democratic unions. The railroad workers took advantage of the 1958 presidential elections to gain a significant wage hike from departing president Ruiz Cortines, who was determined to maintain stability for the political transition. In August 1958, Vallejo won a special election for the position of secretary general of the railway union, ousted the previous *charro* leaders, and pulled the union out of the national Worker Unity Bloc (Bloque de

[103] "National Intelligence Estimate," August 13, 1957 in *FRUS 1955–1957, Volume VI: American Republics*, 752–65.
[104] Michelle Reeves, "Extracting the Eagle's Talons: The Soviet Union in Cold War Latin America," PhD diss., University of Texas, Austin, 2014, 36, 54–5.
[105] Roy R. Rubottom, "Letter from the Assistant Secretary of State for Inter-American Affairs (Rubottom) to Senator Lyndon B. Johnson," November 11, 1958 in *FRUS 1958–1960, Volume V: American Republics*, 848–9.

Unidad Obrera).[106] The union undertook negotiations with the managers of
the national rail line, but when the effort failed it announced a systemwide
strike beginning February 25, 1959. The strike had been in effect for little more than twenty-four hours when President López Mateos stepped in,
making concessions on wages, medical benefits, and housing funds. Workers
on privately owned lines of Mexico's railroads demanded the same concessions, and Vallejo reluctantly agreed to continue the movement. The railroad workers scheduled a strike on the Ferrocarril Mexicano, Ferrocarril
del Pacífico, Ferrocarriles de Yucatán, and Terminal del Veracruz lines for
March 25, right in the middle of Holy Week, the most important week of
travel and tourism in Mexico.

The railroad strikes were the most dangerous labor movement since the
Mexican Revolution, prompting the nation's leaders to switch from negotiation to repression. Not only did the strikes threaten to shut down the
national economy, but the train workers' previous successes, as well as their
independence from the government-led Worker Unity Bloc and CTM, also
set a dangerous example that threatened the system of institutionalization
and co-optation so crucial to Mexico's economic stability. Other groups of
workers, including members of electrical, telegraph, petroleum, and teachers' unions had already begun demonstrating support for the railroad oper-
ators and in turn receiving assistance for their own strikes. Minister of the
Interior Gustavo Díaz Ordaz declared, "Our destiny and our history as a
country are at stake."[107]

Communist involvement in the railroad movement served as a lightning
rod for government and media attention. Intelligence agents and reporters alike were quick to blame the unrest on communist subversion.[108]
Conservative ideologue Mario Guerra Leal asserted in his memoirs that, on

---

[106] On the railroad strikes, see Evelyn Stevens, *Protest and Response in Mexico*
(Cambridge: Massachusetts Institute of Technology, 1974); Alegre, *Railroad Radicals in
Cold War Mexico*.
[107] Krauze, *Mexico: Biography of Power*, 634.
[108] Robert Alegre argues that it is impossible to determine the exact extent of communist
influence on the railroad movement, because many of the leaders embraced communism but most of the rank-and-file did not. Likewise, Alegre observes that "there is
no way to know for certain how sincere opponents of the movement were in label-
ing activists communists." Alegre, *Railroad Radicals in Cold War Mexico*, 95, 193.
Examples of newspaper articles that blamed communists for the movement include
Ponce, "Perspectiva: Táctica comunista," *Excélsior*, March 26, 1959; Raul Beethoven
Lomeli, "Reconquista sindical por los comunistas," *Excélsior*, March 27, 1959; "La
agitación comunizante," *Excélsior*, March 28, 1959; Alfonso Serrano I., "Obedecían
consignas internacionales en su labor de agitación, Vallejo y sus adictos," *Excélsior*,
March 30, 1959.

orders from President López Mateos, he accepted one hundred thousand pesos from the secretary of defense to write articles about communist influence in the movement.[109] The obliging ideologue would submit his work to the president's secretary for approval and then give the articles to the press, using money from the government to pay the newspapers to publish his incendiary accusations.[110]

The articles that the Mexican government likely planted blaming the communists for the railroad strikes illustrate the circuitous flow of information in Mexico. Government officials knew that many of the leaders of the railroad strikes, including Vallejo and Campa, were members of the Mexican Worker-Campesino Party. They drew the conclusion, or at least promoted the idea, that because Vallejo and Campa were communists, the strikes resulted from foreign subversion rather than from problems in the nation's labor system. Government officials told the media to propagate the theory of communist – and Soviet – interference in Mexico's railroad industry, and the newspapers complied.[111] Intelligence agents then culled the news for reports about communism – the papers, after all, were one of their primary sources of information – and read the articles that other government collaborators had planted about the strikes.

Mexico's leaders decided that a massive show of force was the best way to end the railroad movement. The Federal Conciliation Board declared the strike illegal, and on March 28, army troops seized control of all the railroads in the country, while soldiers, police, and secret service agents forced striking laborers to return to work at gunpoint. Within a few days, authorities had arrested and dismissed thousands of railway workers, including Vallejo and Campa, charging them with social dissolution.[112] Most of the strikers were set free shortly thereafter, but Vallejo, Campa, and other leaders would remain in prison for years, becoming some of Mexico's most renowned political prisoners. Finally, after the movement came to its abrupt end, the Mexican government expelled two Soviet diplomats in April 1959. Police told reporters that the diplomats had given Vallejo financial support and helped him travel around

---

[109] Mario Guerra Leal, *La grilla* (Mexico City: Editorial Diana, 1978), 144–5. One hundred thousand pesos were equivalent to $1,250 U.S. dollars in 1959. Banco de México, www.banxico.org.mx (accessed March 13, 2015).

[110] Ibid., 141.

[111] On the print media's role in spreading anticommunist information, see Elisa Servín, "Propaganda y Guerra Fria: la campaña anticomunista en la prensa mexicana del medio siglo," *Signos Históricos*, no. 11 (2004): 9–39.

[112] Alfonso Serrano I., "Vallejo y centenares de líderes y revoltosos, aprehendidos," *Excélsior*, March 29, 1959.

the country fomenting unrest.[113] The latter claim was especially ridiculous given the fact that railroad workers were among the most mobile of Mexican citizens and did not need foreign help to travel around their own country. CIA agents described the expulsion of the Soviet diplomats as "an attempt to rally national feeling behind the government's decision to curb Communist influence in the labor movement."[114]

In general, U.S. observers were uncertain about the role that the communists played in the railroad and other labor movements of the late 1950s. Ambassador Robert Hill wrote to the State Department that the known communist affiliations of leaders of the railroad and student movements as well as their organizational efficiency and "astute planning" indicated that communist methods were "principally though not exclusively responsible for [the] success of [the] disturbances."[115] U.S. intelligence agents recognized that problems within the Mexican labor system were the main source of the unrest. CIA analysts wrote that the widespread strikes resulted from "pressures from long overdue wage increases" and "workers' resentment against many corrupt, dilatory leaders in the government-dominated labor movement." In the CIA's view, these conditions had created opportunities for "militant leftist and Marxist dissident leaders" to seize control of key unions.[116] In their reports, intelligence agents criticized President Ruiz Cortines for his reluctance to deal firmly with the strikers and predicted that a strong, possibly violent, stand by the López Mateos administration would curtail the growing influence of Marxist leaders in the labor movement.[117]

MEXICO AS HAVEN

At the same time that the Mexican government repressed local communists and other activists, it offered a safe haven for foreigners seeking

---

[113] Alfonso Serrano I., "Decide México la expulsión de dos diplomáticos soviéticos: Estaban implicados en la conjura Vallejista," *Excélsior*, April 1, 1959.

[114] CIA, "Current Intelligence Weekly Summary: Communist Activities in Mexican Labor," April 9, 1959. CIA-RDP79-00927A002200050001-4, CREST Database, NARA.

[115] Hill, "Telegram from the Embassy in Mexico to the Department of State," *FRUS* Vol. 5, 843.

[116] CIA, "Current Intelligence Weekly Summary: The New López Mateos Administration in Mexico," November 20, 1958. CIA-RDP79-00927A002000040001-6, CREST Database, NARA.

[117] CIA, "Current Intelligence Weekly Summary: Mexican Labor Troubles," September 4, 1958. CIA-RDP79-00927A001900030001-0, CREST Database, NARA; CIA, "Daily Brief," February 26, 1959. CIA-RDP79T00975A004300140001-8, CREST Database, NARA.

shelter from even worse political conditions. In numerous moments throughout its history, Mexico had accepted political refugees from other countries. Thousands of political exiles fled there over the years, especially during Cárdenas's presidency and the Cold War. Mexico provided a new home for such luminaries as José Martí and Leon Trotsky, as well as for tens of thousands of Spanish Republican refugees, numerous U.S. writers, artists, and filmmakers, and exiles from Central America and the Southern Cone.[118] When the Mexican government provided haven to Fidel Castro, however, it unwittingly supported the revolution that would ignite Mexico's Cold War.

Though the Mexican government did little to prevent or protest the U.S.-supported coup that ousted Guatemalan president Jacobo Arbenz in 1954, it did provide refuge for many people fleeing that country.[119] In doing so, it rejected requests from Washington that all Latin American countries deny political asylum to Arbenz supporters.[120] Among the refugees were the Argentine firebrand Ernesto "Che" Guevara and Antonio "Ñico" López Fernández, a participant in Fidel Castro's July 26, 1953, assault on the Moncada barracks who had fled from Cuba to Guatemala. These two men had become friends in Guatemala, where Ñico regaled Che with tales of Castro's quest and the horrible political and social conditions in Cuba. Witnessing firsthand the events in

---

[118] On Mexico's tradition of offering political refuge, see Alfonso Herrera Franyutti, *Martí en México: Recuerdos de una época* (Mexico City: Consejo Nacional para la Cultura y las Artes, 1996); Robert Service, *Trotsky: A Biography* (Cambridge, MA: Belknap Press of Harvard University Press, 2009); Sebastian Faber, *Exile and Cultural Hegemony: Spanish Intellectuals in Mexico, 1939–1975* (Nashville, TN: Vanderbilt University Press, 2002); Rebecca Mina Schreiber, *Cold War Exiles in Mexico: U.S. Dissidents and the Culture of Critical Resistance* (Minneapolis: University of Minnesota Press, 2008); Pablo Yankelevich, *México, país refugio: La experiencia de los exilios en el siglo XX* (Mexico City: Plaza y Valdés, 2002). For a contrasting interpretation of Mexico's stance on exile, see Daniela Gleizer, *Unwelcome Exiles: Mexico and the Jewish Refugees from Nazism, 1933–1945*, trans. Susan Thomae (Leiden, The Netherlands: Brill, 2014).

[119] On the Mexican government's reaction to the coup in Guatemala, see Pellicer de Brody and Mancilla, *Historia de La Revolución Mexicana 1952–1960*, 103. Members of the Mexican public, especially student and workers' groups, did hold large demonstrations protesting the coup, and Mexican students laid a black-draped wreath at the entrance to the U.S. embassy "in memory of the Good Neighbor Policy." CIA, "Current Intelligence Weekly: Latin American Reactions to the Guatemalan Crisis," July 9, 1954. CIA-RDP79-00927A000300110001-8, CREST Database, NARA.

[120] CIA, "Current Intelligence Weekly: Latin American Reactions to the Guatemalan Crisis."

Guatemala further convinced Guevara of the need to fight imperialism across Latin America.[121]

Mexico's status as political haven became even more important to world history when Fidel Castro decided to take refuge there a year later in July 1955. By then, his brother Raúl had already struck up a friendship with Che, and the Argentine doctor soon met Fidel in the home of a Cuban woman whose Mexican husband was a *lucha libre* wrestler. According to Guevara's fiancée at the time, Hilda Gadea, the two men talked for almost ten straight hours upon first meeting each other. Che told her that he had "found in Fidel a deep conviction that in fighting against Batista he was fighting the imperialist monster that kept Batista in power."[122] He immediately enlisted in Castro's plan to organize a rebel army and liberate the island.

Three Mexican citizens played key roles in Castro's invasion. Arsacio Vanegas Arroyo, another *lucha libre* wrestler and printer whose grandfather had aided José Martí, opened his home to the Cubans and helped Fidel print fundraising bonds and propaganda.[123] The wrestler also figured out how to smuggle Castro's first manifesto into Cuba: taking advantage of a commission to print *Don Quijote de la Mancha*, Vanegas used the cover and some illustrations from the classic novel and printed a "new" edition with Fidel's manifesto camouflaged inside.[124] In addition, he trained Castro's group in hand-to-hand combat in a gymnasium in the working-class neighborhood of Tepito and supervised their physical conditioning in long walks along the Avenida Insurgentes, rowing exercises on Chapultepec Lake, and hikes in the hills surrounding Mexico City.

Vanegas was so enthusiastic about the Cuban Revolution that he composed and printed a *corrido*, or popular ballad, about Castro shortly after his victory in 1959. In the beginning of the song, Vanegas drew a connection between Mexico and Cuba's revolutionary histories, declaring: "I, as a good Mexican / Do not tolerate tyrants / And those who overthrow them / I esteem as brothers." The rest of the ballad recounted the history of Castro's early years, the cruelties that the Cubans suffered

---

[121] Hilda Gadea, who would later marry Guevara, introduced him to Ñico in Guatemala in January 1954. Hilda Gadea, *Ernesto: A Memoir of Che Guevara*, trans. Carmen Molina and Walter I. Bradbury (New York: Doubleday & Company, 1972), x.

[122] Ibid., 99.

[123] Mario Mencía, "La insurreción cubana y su tránsito por México," in *México y Cuba: Dos pueblos unidos en la historia*, Vol. 2 (Mexico City: Centro de Investigación Científica Jorge L. Tamayo, 1982), 279–301 and 416–19.

[124] Concepción Guillo Deza, "Cómo financió Castro la Revolución Cubana," in *México y Cuba*, 416–19.

under Batista's dictatorship, and the origins and eventual triumph of the 26th of July movement. Vanegas concluded the song: "For this I salute you / Beautiful land of Martí / And I salute Fidel Castro / Who forges your future" (see Figure 2).[125]

Another Mexican, Antonio del Conde Pontones, or "El Cuate," obtained supplies for the revolutionaries. Fidel bought most of his weapons from del Conde's arms shop and eventually shared his plans with his "buddy."[126] El Cuate then traveled to the United States in order to obtain more weapons for the Cubans and made uniforms for them in a factory behind his shop.[127] He also purchased the *Granma* for Fidel and watched from the shore as the overloaded yacht departed on its historic voyage.

On board was another Mexican citizen, Alfonso Guillén Zelaya, son of Honduran exiles and a member of the Mexican Socialist Youth group. Guillén happened to overhear Fidel giving a speech while strolling through Mexico City's Chapultepec Park and felt inspired to join the Cubans. Only twenty years old, he was the youngest member of the

---

[125] The complete lyrics to the corrido in the original Spanish are as follows: "Señores, voy a cantar/ porque me pega la gana,/ el triunfo de Fidel Castro/ allá en la tierra cubana./ Yo como buen mexicano/ no tolero a los tiranos/ y a aquellos que los durrumban/ los estimo como hermanos./ Por eso soy partidario/ de don FIDEL CASTRO RUZ;/ de su lucha y su calvario,/ de su triunfo y de su cruz./ Nació en Satiago [sic] de Cuba/ el año de veintiseis/ y fue a estudiar a La Habana/ en el Colegio 'Belén'./ Candidato a diputado/ el año cincuenta y dos/ vió frustrados sus anhelos/ por un cuartelazo atroz./ El diez de marzo de ese año,/ un sargento asaltó/ al campamento 'Columbia'/ y su tiranía implantó./ Siete años de dictadura/ impia, tremenda y cruel/ en que el furor de Batista/ mucha sangre hizo correr./ FIDEL fue superviviente/ del cuartelazo a traición;/ y a luchar contra el tirano/ desde entonces empezó./ El día veintiseis de julio/ del año cincuenta y tres,/ atacó el cuartel 'Moncada'/ sufriendo un serio revés./ Los con él confabulados,/ fueron hechos prisioneros/ y cruelmente asesinados/ por esbirros testa-ferros./ Hasta el presidio de Pinos/ fue luego bien confinado;/ más, por la acción popular,/ al año fue libertado./ Se pasó a Estados Unidos/ y luego a México vino;/ aquí empezó a conspirar/ y halló del triunfo el camino./ Fundó una organización/ dinámica en grado sumo;/ movimiento al que llamó/ el 'veintiseis de julio'./ Aquí en México reunió/ ochenta y un combatientes,/ en su mayoría cubanos/ decididos y valientes./ Veinticinco de noviembre/ del año cincuenta y seis,/ el yate 'Gramma' [sic] zarpaba/ de Tuxpan a Cabo Cruz./ Llegó a la Sierra Maestra;/ en ella se atrincheró,/ y desde entonces el trono/ de Batista tambaleo./ Dos años y un mes bastaron/ para poder derrocar/ al cruel tirano Batista/ al que Trujillo acogió./ Los esbirros del tirano/ han caido sin piedad/ y sobre charcos de sangre,/ se finca la libertad./ Por eso yo te saludo,/ linda tierra de Martí;/ y saludo a FIDEL CASTRO/ que forja tu porvenir./ Viva Cuba bella y libre/ con su cielo siempre azul;/ y así terminó el Corrido/ del Dr. FIDEL CASTRO RUZ./ El diecisiete de Enero/ del año cincuenta y nueve,/ les escribo este corrido/ aunque la trampa me lleve."

[126] "Cuate" is Mexican slang for friend or buddy.

[127] *De Tuxpan a la Plata* (Havana: Editora Política, 1985), 40–42. Mencía, "La insurreción cubana y su tránsito por México," 291–2.

FIGURE 2. Corrido by Arsacio Vanegas Arroyo in celebration of Fidel Castro and the Cuban Revolution. "Corrido de un mexicano a Fidel Castro Ruz."
Source: Taller de Gráfica Popular, 1959. Courtesy of the Center for Southwest Research, University Libraries, University of New Mexico, Taller de Gráfico Popular Collection.

expedition. Guillén was captured and imprisoned when the *Granma* landed. The Cuban authorities deported him to Mexico at the end of 1957, and he continued to raise funds for Fidel's movement.[128]

Two Cubans who decades earlier had taken advantage of Mexico's tradition of offering political refuge also assisted Castro's efforts. Alberto Bayo Giroud, a native of Cuba who had fought on the Republican side in the Spanish Civil War and then sought asylum in Mexico, provided Fidel's group with military training. Drawing on his previous experiences in battle, Bayo instructed the Cubans in guerrilla warfare and urban combat.[129] Teresa Casuso, a famous student activist in Cuba in the 1930s who had moved to Mexico in the 1940s, provided additional aid to Castro's group. Casuso had read about Fidel in the newspaper and sought him out, telling him "her house was his." Two days later, Castro awaited Casuso in her parlor; the next day he asked if he could store a few things in her house. Casuso agreed, and Fidel and his men returned with seven carloads of munitions – "a veritable arsenal."[130] She also rented the house next door at Castro's urging. It became another arms depot, as well as a home for Pedro Miret, a Cuban comrade of Fidel's who came to Mexico to train the revolutionaries in the handling, care, and repair of weapons. Casuso used her political connections to find powerful allies for Castro. She traveled to Miami to arrange a meeting between Fidel and her "dear friend," former president of Cuba Carlos Prío Socarrás (1948–52). Castro went to the border at Brownsville, Texas, and swam across the Rio Bravo to meet with Prío Socarrás. There, Prío agreed to help cover the expenses of Castro's movement, including the purchase of the *Granma*.[131]

Mexican authorities nearly derailed Castro's plans when they arrested him and the rest of his group in June 1956. The Cubans confessed that they were organizing a revolution against Fulgencio Batista, in clear violation of Mexican immigration law. They described their entire operation in exacting detail to their interrogator in the Department of Federal Security, Fernando Gutiérrez Barrios, who later became the head of Mexican intelligence in the 1960s.[132] Castro, Che, and the rest of the

---

[128] Roberto Álvarez Quiñones, "Entrevista con el internacionalista mexicano Guillén Zelaya Alger, expedicionario del 'Granma,'" in *México y Cuba*, Vol. 2, 420–5.

[129] *De Tuxpan a la Plata*, 39.

[130] Ibid., 105.

[131] Teresa Casuso, *Cuba and Castro* (New York: Random House, 1961), 89–90.

[132] Fernando Gutiérrez Barrios, "Investigación sobre conjura contra el gobierno de la república de Cuba," June 24, 1956, DFS, Versión Pública de Fidel Castro, Leg. 1, Hoja 3, AGN.

group of revolutionaries languished in Mexican prison, waiting to see whether they would be freed or turned over to Batista.

The man who would soon become Castro's greatest champion in Mexico, Lázaro Cárdenas, stepped forward. At the end of June, the former president read in the newspaper that Mexican police had arrested a group of Cuban exiles for plotting against Batista's government. "It is not strange," Cárdenas noted in his journal that evening, "that there is agitation in the heart of a nation like Cuba, which has seen bloody repression in recent years and that wants to be ruled by a non-military system."[133] Throughout the following month he received requests from various acquaintances to intercede on behalf of Castro's group. On August 1, Cárdenas visited President Ruiz Cortines and convinced him to free the prisoners. The president had been considering extraditing the group to Cuba at Batista's urging, but instead agreed to Cárdenas's request. Officials immediately released the group of revolutionaries, and the next day Castro went to the ex-president to express his gratitude.[134] Impressed with Castro's demeanor and dedication, Cárdenas described him in his journal as "a young intellectual of vehement temperament, with the blood of a fighter."[135] Thanks to Cárdenas, the Cubans were able to finish their preparations and launch their revolutionary expedition from the shores of Veracruz.

This collection of Mexican citizens and foreign residents – Arsacio Vanegas, Antonio del Conde, Alfonso Guillén, Alberto Bayo, Teresa Casuso, and Lázaro Cárdenas – all provided critical aid to the Cuban Revolution when it was at its weakest. In Mexico, Castro and his compatriots found housing, training, weapons, manpower, and political connections. By granting Castro's group asylum, the Mexican government unwittingly made possible the revolution that would spark Mexico's Cold War.

CONCLUSION

In the first decade of the global Cold War, it appeared that Mexico had managed to escape the political, social, and economic upheaval that gripped much of the rest of Latin America. Through a policy of

---

[133] Lázaro Cárdenas, *Apuntes: Una selección* (Mexico City: Universidad Nacional Autónoma de México, 2003), 795.

[134] "Se desistieron del ámparo, los 23 cubanos," *Excélsior*, August 3, 1956.

[135] Cárdenas, *Apuntes: Una selección*, 803.

"institutionalizing" the Mexican Revolution, the nation's leaders had developed a firm yet flexible web of organizations and practices that encouraged economic growth and kept the masses in check. Mexico's revolution still lent the government a great deal of symbolic legitimacy as the only "successful" Latin American revolution of the twentieth century. At the same time, the U.S. government helped solidify the rule of its southern neighbors by tolerating Mexican leaders' nationalist rhetoric and strengthening their intelligence capabilities.

Yet behind the façade of the *pax PRIista*, trouble was stirring. Throughout the 1940s and 1950s, politicians, *campesinos*, students, and workers began organizing movements that demanded that their government live up to the promises of the Mexican Revolution. Though these movements coincided with the early years of the global Cold War, they were mostly national and local in origin and had little to do with international ideologies or power struggles. A communist movement existed in Mexico, but it was small and divided, and communists served more often as scapegoats than instigators. The railroad movement and the Cuban Revolution, however, marked the beginning of the transition to a heightened Cold War atmosphere, in which Mexico's leaders began to fear that foreign influences were subverting the national order.

2

Responding to the Cuban Revolution

The news of Fidel Castro's triumph over Fulgencio Batista immediately caught the attention of the Mexican nation. In just the first week after Batista fled Cuba, Mexico's leading newspaper, *Excélsior*, published close to one hundred articles about the Cuban Revolution. While much of the early coverage was positive and celebrated the defeat of a tyrant, there were quite a few instances of condemnation as well.[1] In the immediate aftermath of the Cuban Revolution, Mexicans across the political spectrum debated the significance of the events.

Mexicans' responses to the Cuban Revolution grew out of the international, national, and local political climates. They interpreted the events in Cuba through the lens of their own struggles, and vice versa. As *Excélsior* columnist Aldo Baroni explained, "[E]very American Republic is no more than a mirror in which we can see reflected, if our instinct for self-preservation has not abandoned us, events that at any moment will disturb us."[2] Worker and student groups that had already begun challenging the government seized upon the Cuban example for inspiration and validation. Conservative groups, the media, and members of Mexico's intelligence organizations immediately started blaming Mexican unrest on Cuban subversion. U.S. officials watched the situation closely, alert for signs of instability, while the Cubans continued using Mexican territory for their own purposes. New alliances, both overt and covert, formed, while old ones were tested. As local and national struggles took

[1] Aldo Baroni, "Catástrofe en Cuba," *Excélsior*, January 2, 1959; "Tribuna libre del pensamiento fue ayer la embajada cubana en México," *Excélsior*, January 3, 1959.
[2] "La danza de las horas," *Excélsior*, January 3, 1959.

on increasingly international and transnational dimensions, they escalated into Mexico's Cold War.

ENTHUSIASM FOR THE CUBAN REVOLUTION

The segments of the Mexican population that demonstrated the greatest enthusiasm for the Cuban Revolution were those that had already begun to challenge the revolutionary legacy of their own government. Workers, artists, intellectuals, students, and even former president Lázaro Cárdenas embraced the events in Cuba and compared them to their own country's "institutionalized" revolution.

Their responses were in some ways part of a transnational development: the emergence of the New Left. This was a "movement of movements" that began in the 1950s and 1960s, "sharing certain common frames of reference: support for the Cuban Revolution, condemnation of the U.S. war in Vietnam, and the universal goal of socialism (whether Marxist-Leninist or Christian Democratic)."[3] In contrast to the so-called Old Left that looked to the Soviet Union for inspiration, participants in this new wave admired the youth, irreverence, and radicalism of the Cuban revolutionaries. According to Alexander Aviña, "the Cuban Revolution helped crystallize the beginnings of an elastic, diverse, and tension-filled New Left that generally advocated direct action, confrontation with state power, antiauthoritarianism, direct democracy, and/or the undermining of traditional patriarchal norms."[4]

When a group of young veterans of the Cuban Revolution traveled to Mexico City for five days in February 1959 as part of an international tour called Operation Truth, Mexicans from various walks of life cooperated to organize tributes. The largest took place at the end of the visit, when a crowd of two thousand railroad workers, electricians, and teachers from the unions that had recently fought for their independence joined students, politicians, and journalists, filling the seats of a newly built theater. Speakers included Mexican Supreme Court justice Franco Carreño, who laid out a legal rationalization for the controversial public executions that Castro's government had been

---

[3] Zolov, "Expanding Our Conceptual Horizons," 53; Van Gosse, *Where the Boys Are: Cuba, Cold War America and the Making of a New Left* (London: Verso, 1993).

[4] Alexander Aviña, "The New Left in Latin America," *Oxford Bibliographies Online*, www.oxfordbibliographies.com (accessed March 13, 2015). On the New Left, see also Staughton Lynd, "The New Left," *Annals of the American Academy of Political and Social Science* 382 (March 1969): 64–72.

undertaking.[5] The head of intelligence in the Department of Federal Security reported that when other speakers described the lack of liberty and justice that the Cubans had suffered under Batista, "the group began shouting insults against the regime of Don Adolfo López Mateos and cheers for the Russian and Cuban Revolutions." The insults continued when a representative from Demetrio Vallejo's railroad union spoke up, claiming that Castro had sent Vallejo congratulations when the union had seen its first victories. The railroad workers wanted to return the compliment, the representative reportedly stated, telling the Cuban visitors "We wish you success in the defense of the sovereignty of the Cuban people and hope that there never appears in Cuba the syndical terrorism that is currently destroying Mexico."[6]

Cuban diplomats were extremely pleased with the results of the tour. In a memorandum to his superiors, Ambassador Salvador Massip called the visit a "complete success in all respects." He described how a crowd of Mexican workers and students, along with Cubans, Spaniards, Dominicans, and Nicaraguans gathered at the airport to give the delegation a warm welcome. On the third day of the visit, the Cubans hosted a press conference at their embassy, where they gave more than fifty journalists, photographers, and cameramen firsthand accounts of the events on the island and showed them photographs of the atrocities that Batista's henchmen had committed. In the ambassador's opinion, the other highlight of the trip was the "extremely stimulating" reception that Lázaro Cárdenas offered to the visitors and the supportive words that he and his son, Cuauhtémoc, expressed.[7]

During and after the tour, numerous Mexican groups and individuals wrote directly to the new Cuban government to express their excitement about the revolution. In a "message of friendship and fraternity with the people of Cuba," a group called the Organization of American

[5] On Castro's public executions of Batista supporters, see Michelle Chase, "The Trials: Violence and Justice in the Aftermath of the Cuban Revolution," in *A Century of Revolution: Insurgent and Counterinsurgent Violence during Latin America's Long Cold War*, ed. Greg Grandin and Gilbert M. Joseph (Durham, NC: Duke University Press, 2010), 163–98.

[6] Manuel Rangel Escamilla, "Homenaje a la delegación cubana con sindicatos mexicanos," February 16, 1959, DFS, Exp 12-9-1959, Leg 3, Hoja 150, AGN.

[7] "[Memorandum from Salvador Massip to Ministro del Estado Roberto Agramonte y Pichardo]," March 2, 1959, Colección América Latina, México, 1959–62, Box Ordinario 6, Folder 1959, Colección América Latina, México, 1959–62, Box Ordinario 6, Folder 1959, Archivo del Ministerio de Relaciones Exteriores, Havana, Cuba [hereafter MINREX].

University Students attested that "all the Mexicans and Americans of good faith consider your liberating movement our own."[8] Daniel García Martínez, a veteran of the Mexican Revolution who had fought under Francisco "Pancho" Villa in the División del Norte and later supported Miguel Henríquez in his failed campaigns for the presidency, contacted the Cuban embassy and sent an article that he had written in case a newspaper in Cuba wished to publish it. The article, titled "This Is How It Should Be!" praised the Cuban revolutionaries for immediately eliminating their opponents and posited that if the fallen leaders of the Mexican Revolution, including Francisco Madero and Venustiano Carranza, had done the same then perhaps Mexico would not find itself "in a situation of oblivion and misery half a century later."[9]

Mexican and U.S. authorities resented the fact that some more prominent Mexican citizens were also expressing enthusiasm for the Cuban Revolution. World-renowned Mexican muralist David Álfaro Siqueiros, a leader of the Mexican Communist Party, made headlines for his verbal and artistic condemnation of the government's repression of the recent workers' movements.[10] Outraged with the imprisonment of the railroad union leaders, he became president of the National Committee for the Freedom of Political Prisoners and in Defense of Constitutional Guarantees and made several speeches criticizing the government. In January 1960, Siqueiros traveled to Cuba, where he publicly praised the Cuban Revolution and condemned the corruption of the Mexican Revolution, then went on to Venezuela to make similar speeches.[11] The muralist's denunciations of the Mexican government, and especially his criticism of President López Mateos, infuriated Mexican authorities. In the aftermath of a riot among students, teachers, and police, Siqueiros was arrested and charged with the crime of social dissolution. CIA agents reported that he "apparently" had Cuban support for his subversive

[8] Organización de Estudiantes Universitarios de América, "Mensaje de amistad y confraternidad al pueblo cubano," February 16, 1959, Colección América Latina, México, 1959–62, Box Ordinario 6, Folder 1959, MINREX.

[9] "[Letter from Teniente Daniel R. García Martínez to Cuban Embassy]," February 18, 1969, Colección América Latina, México, 1959–62, Box Ordinario 6, Folder 1959, MINREX. Madero was assassinated in 1913 on the orders of General Victoriano Huerta, whom he had summoned to put down a rebellion, while Carranza also suffered a violent death in 1920 at the hands of assassins likely hired by his former ally and later rival, Alvaro Obregón. Joseph and Buchenau, *Mexico's Once and Future Revolution*, 53, 85.

[10] Paul P. Kennedy, "Mexican Actors Tilt with Artist: Ring Down Curtain on Mural by Siqueiros before Final Political Scene Is Done," *New York Times*, April 25, 1959.

[11] Anthony White, *Siqueiros: A Biography* (Encino, CA: Floricanto Press, 1994), 347–8.

activities and had helped obtain weapons from the Cuban embassy to arm students, railroad workers, and teachers.[12] Siqueiros remained in prison for the next four years, convicted of the very crime of social dissolution that he had so often denounced.

The Cubans found an even more powerful ally in Lázaro Cárdenas. Accepting the invitation that they had extended to him during their Operation Truth tour, the former president visited Havana on July 26, 1959, for the celebration of the anniversary of the attack on the Moncada Barracks. "Faced with the campaign developed abroad by enemies of Cuba's revolution, authorized voices make themselves heard, asking for comprehension and moral support on her behalf," Cárdenas declared to a crowd of thousands, including journalists from around the world.[13] Photographers snapped pictures of the famous Mexican revolutionary general standing shoulder to shoulder with his younger Cuban counterpart (see Figure 3).

On the flight back to Mexico, Cárdenas explained his enthusiasm for the Cuban Revolution to Mexican writer Elena Poniatowska. He described his sympathy for the difficulties that the Cuban leaders were encountering and reminisced about how Mexican revolutionaries had faced the same animosity, criticism, and false accusations. "They are passing through the same thing that we did," he recounted, "we were also attacked ... and accused of serving foreign governments."[14] Cárdenas had not forgotten the negative U.S. reaction to both the Mexican Revolution and to his nationalization of the oil industry. He saw the events of 1959 as a repetition of the same process, the same powerful bully trying to prevent a weaker neighbor from seizing a chance at political and economic liberation.

U.S. ambassador to Mexico Robert Hill was quick to conclude that Cárdenas's enthusiasm for Castro played a critical role in shaping Mexican policy. In September 1959, he spoke to members of President López Mateos's cabinet about Cárdenas's visit to Havana. The ambassador learned that Cárdenas had spent five hours meeting with López Mateos the night before his trip to Cuba, at the conclusion of which the

[12] CIA, "International Communist Trends and Patterns," February 1, 1961. CIA-RDP78-00915R001300280001-6, CREST Database, NARA.

[13] Lázaro Cárdenas, "Discurso con motivo del VI aniversario de la iniciación del movimiento revolucionario '26 de julio,'" in *Palabras y documentos públicos de Lázaro Cárdenas, 1928–1970*, n.d., 86.

[14] Elena Poniatowska, *Palabras cruzadas* (Mexico City: Editorial Era, 1961), 31.

FIGURE 3. Lázaro Cárdenas and Fidel Castro stand together in front of Havana's capitol to celebrate the anniversary of Castro's July 26, 1959 attack on the Moncada army barracks. "Mexico's former president Lázaro Cárdenas waves to crowds outside of Havana's capitol, accompanied by Fidel Castro."
Source: Dr. Otto Bettmann and the United Press International, July 28, 1959. Courtesy of Corbis Images, Bettmann Collection, Stock Photo ID BE071243.

president had adopted a "hands off" attitude of neither approving nor interfering with Cárdenas's plans. In a message to Assistant Secretary of State Roy R. Rubottom, Hill explained that López Mateos had adopted that attitude because he "recognized that Cárdenas still enjoys a considerable following in Mexico." Hill also reported that the former president's influence "could be such as to make the president hesitate to follow a program which would arouse the opposition of Cárdenas and his followers."[15]

Lázaro Cárdenas had indeed become frustrated with the conservative turn of Mexican politics and was inspired by the events in Cuba. In a journal entry from February 1959, in which he reflected upon the fact that the

[15] "Letter from the Ambassador in Mexico (Hill) to the Assistant Secretary of State for Inter-American Affairs (Rubottom)," September 3, 1959, *FRUS, 1958–1960, American Republics*, Vol. 5, 880.

Mexican Revolution had been "detained," Cárdenas wrote: "an anguish
has overwhelmed my spirit ... Cuba, with its revolution in the Sierra
Maestra, led by Dr. F. Castro, provides hope."[16] Cárdenas began focusing
more and more on the need to revive and transform Mexico's revolution.
He was especially dismayed by the government's repression of the railroad
movement; he visited Vallejo and the other imprisoned workers in jail and
raised the subject in multiple conversations with López Mateos.[17] In April
1959, Cárdenas wrote in his journal "in order for Mexico to become an
integrally revolutionary country, to attain that status, it must make the
step from the current revolution to a socialist one."[18]

In addition to confiding in his journal and holding long private meetings with López Mateos, Cárdenas used public forums to broadcast his
opinions about Cuban and Mexican politics. On June 6, 1960, he presided
over a gathering of small business owners and *campesinos* in Apatzingán,
Michoacán, to protest the monopolistic practices of U.S. businessman
and local landowner William O. Jenkins.[19] The North American capital-
ist symbolized, in the ex-president's eyes, the betrayal of the Mexican
Revolution to imperialist foreign interests. According to a front-page
article in the next day's edition of *Excélsior*, Cárdenas declared amid
the enthusiastic applause of his audience, "Mexico is not exempt from a
revolution."[20]

Cárdenas's words to a small crowd in a local schoolhouse produced a powerful impact across the country. The secretary-general of
the National Campesino Confederation responded a week later at the
group's yearly convention, stating "We do not purport to correct our
agricultural deficiencies by organizing a new revolution."[21] At the same
meeting, the head of the PRI denounced the *vendepatrias* (traitors) who
misunderstood the meaning of the Mexican Revolution. Many of those
present interpreted his remark as a thinly veiled attack upon Cárdenas.
The ex-president's statement provoked such a strong and immediate
response because it undermined one of the Mexican government's
central justifications for its continuation in power: that the government *was* the Mexican Revolution in an institutionalized form. Now

---

[16] Cárdenas, *Obras: Apuntes 1957/1966*, Vol. 3, 90–1.
[17] Ibid., 122.
[18] Ibid., 104–5.
[19] On Jenkins, see Andrew Paxman, "William Jenkins, Business Elites, and the Evolution of
the Mexican State: 1910–1960," PhD diss., University of Texas, 2008.
[20] Eliseo Ibañez Gonzalez, "Cárdenas clamó contra latifundio y monopolio," *Excélsior*,
June 8, 1960.
[21] "Agrarismo: Una nueva revolución?," *Política*, July 1, 1960.

Cárdenas was suggesting that simply maintaining the old revolution was not enough.

U.S. sociologist C. Wright Mills reinforced Cárdenas's warnings about a new revolution in his landmark 1960 book *Listen, Yankee.* Prior to writing the book, Mills had spent three months in Mexico City during which time he delivered lectures at UNAM and become close to leading left-wing writers including Carlos Fuentes.[22] A Mexican publishing house produced a Spanish translation of Mills's book shortly after the English edition appeared.[23] In *Listen, Yankee,* Mills authored a series of "letters" to U.S. leaders about the problems of imperialism, colonialism, and monopolistic ownership, adopting the voices of protagonists of the Cuban Revolution.[24] He cautioned that the same problems that led to Castro's uprising in Cuba were to be found across Latin America. "What the Cubans are saying and doing today, other hungry peoples in Latin America are going to be saying and doing tomorrow," Mills warned.[25] Mexico was no exception. "And Mexico?" Mills asked rhetorically, "Her great revolution of 1910 has stalled … [but] the wind that once swept Mexico may yet sweep it again. Despite everything, which today is quite a lot, Mexico is a windy place."[26]

Excitement for the Cuban Revolution was also widespread among Mexican intellectuals. In May 1960, journalist Manuel Marcué Pardiñas began publishing a magazine called *Política*, which quickly established itself as the vanguard voice of the New Left in Mexico. The magazine printed twenty five thousand copies twice a month, selling fifteen thousand in Mexico City, five thousand across the rest of the country, and the remainder abroad.[27] By the 1960s, Marcué Pardiñas had worked his way into the center of much of Mexico's political life. He had a long history of collaborating with various leftist political organizations, including the Mexican Communist Party and the Popular Socialist Party, and helped organize demonstrations in support of the striking teachers and railroad workers. Marcué maintained contact with important leftist leaders including Demetrio Vallejo, David Álfaro Siqueiros, Lázaro Cárdenas, and Carlos Fuentes.

---

[22] Daniel Geary, *Radical Ambition: C. Wright Mills, the Left, and American Social Thought* (Berkeley: University of California Press, 2009); Pensado, *Rebel Mexico*, 164.

[23] Geary, *Radical Ambition*, 214–15.

[24] C. Wright Mills, *Listen, Yankee: The Revolution in Cuba* (New York: McGraw-Hill Book Company, 1960).

[25] Ibid., 7.

[26] Ibid., 172.

[27] Fernando Gutiérrez Barrios, "Revista 'Política,'" March 11, 1966, IPS Caja 2959A, AGN.

Manuel Marcué Pardiñas used his magazine and his political connections to promote the Cuban Revolution and to pressure the Mexican government to live up to its own revolutionary promises. *Política* lauded the accomplishments of the Cuban Revolution and cheered the island nation in its confrontation with the United States. The first edition carried a story about a declaration of solidarity with Cuba signed by leaders from across Latin America, including Cárdenas, and nearly every subsequent issue in the magazine's seven-year run included at least one article about the island. Headlines declared: "Cuba Is the Current Example of America," "Cuba Is Not Alone," and "The Duty of the Moment: Defend Cuba."[28] Marcué Pardiñas and the contributors to *Política* provided in-depth analysis of Mexico's policy toward Cuba, advertised pro-Castro events, printed texts of statements about Cuba from important political figures, and described pro-Cuba meetings and congresses in Mexico and across the Americas. Political cartoons by the famous cartoonist and comic book writer Eduardo del Río, or "Rius," abounded, including one that depicted Fidel Castro as an angel of revolution, sent from the heavens to blow the dust and cobwebs off the decrepit Mexican Revolution (see Figure 4).[29] In pursuit of the goal of imitating the Cuban Revolution, *Política* published documents of Cuban origin that government leaders would have preferred to keep out of the public eye, such as Che Guevara's guide to guerrilla warfare.[30]

Mexican students were also among the most enthusiastic supporters of the Cuban Revolution. The Cuban embassy in Mexico City received admiring letters from young people all over the country, including the Federation of University Students of Michoacán, a high school student in Tampico, the Front of Latin American Students Residing in Mexico, and a young man studying economics at the National Polytechnic Institute.[31]

---

[28] "Cuba es el ejemplo actual de América," *Política*, May 15, 1960; "Cuba no está sola: Manifiesto del National Liberation Movement," *Política*, January 15, 1962; "El deber del momento: Defender a Cuba," *Política*, September 15, 1962.

[29] On Rius, see Chuck Tatum and Harold Hinds, "Eduardo Del Río (Rius): An Interview and Introductory Essay," *Chasqui* 9, no. 1 (November 1, 1979): 3–23.

[30] Ernesto Guevara, "La guerra de guerrillas: Un método. Una interpretación de la Segunda Declaración de La Habana," *Política*, October 1, 1963.

[31] "[Letter from the Federación de Estudiantes Universitarios de Michoacán to Ambassador Salvador Massip]," March 17, 1960; "[Letter from Máximo Garza Sánchez to Ambassador Salvador Massip]," May 15, 1960; "[Letter from the Frente de Estudiantes Latinoamericanos Residentes en México to Cuban Ambassador José Antonio Portuondo]," July 12, 1960; "[Letter from Gregorio Jiménez García to the Cuban Embassy]," August 30, 1960. Colección América Latina, México, 1959–62, Box Ordinario 6, Folder 1960, MINREX.

FIGURE 4. Political cartoon by Eduardo del Río, or Rius, depicting Fidel Castro as a revolutionary angel sent from the heavens to awaken the Old Left and revive the Mexican Revolution.

Source: *Política* magazine, February 1, 1966. Courtesy of the Biblioteca Lerdo de Tejada and the U.S. Library of Congress, Historic Newspapers.

The 1960 graduating class from the National University of Agriculture named Fidel Castro their *padrino* and invited the Cuban ambassador to their closing ceremonies.[32] Young members of the Mexican Communist Party and the Popular Socialist Party began a campaign in December 1960 to form volunteer brigades to send to Cuba in case of an attack upon the island.[33] A month later, nine student organizations in the state of Nuevo León organized a five-hundred-person demonstration of solidarity with the Cuban Revolution and sent a telegram to López Mateos asking him to defend the island.[34]

In the months immediately following the Cuban Revolution, it was clear to all observers that a large swath of the Mexican population had aligned themselves with their Cuban neighbors. Castro and his compatriots had already found economic, political, and logistical support in Mexico that proved critical to the success of their insurrection; now they enjoyed widespread enthusiasm for their new government. Students, workers, intellectuals, and even influential political leaders like Lázaro Cárdenas seized upon the Cuban Revolution for hope and inspiration; for them, Castro's success demonstrated the possibility of new – or renewed – revolutions everywhere.

LÓPEZ MATEOS EMBRACES THE CUBAN REVOLUTION

President López Mateos had to decide how to respond to both the Cuban Revolution and Mexican citizens' enthusiasm for Castro. In these early years of his presidency, he was under a great deal of pressure to define the tone of his administration. The repression of the railroad strikes in the first months of his term had injured López Mateos's reputation as a moderate leftist and conciliator. The fiftieth anniversary of the Mexican Revolution loomed, and the president needed to find a way to restore his own political legitimacy and that of his government.

During a tour of Latin America in January 1960, López Mateos made a number of statements to foreign journalists that indicated that he had decided to embrace the spirit of the Cuban Revolution, at least in public. When Chilean reporters asked about Cuba's agrarian reforms, López Mateos pointed out that because Mexico was the first country in Latin

---

[32] "Educación: Chapingo y Cuba," *Política*, December 1, 1960. A *padrino*, or godfather, is the symbolic leader of a graduating class.

[33] "El Pueblo, con Cuba," *Política*, January 15, 1961.

[34] "Nuevo León: En apoyo de Cuba," *Política*, February 1, 1961.

America to take such measures, "it could not watch with anything other than positive eyes as another country with similar problems resolves them according to the interests of its own people."[35] He made statements along those same lines to Venezuelan and Brazilian journalists, repeatedly praising the Cuban Revolution and comparing it to Mexico's.

At the same time that he commended the Cuban Revolution, López Mateos tried to make his own government appear more leftist and revolutionary. Evoking the nationalist ethos of the Mexican Revolution, he told reporters at the National Press Club in Washington, D.C., in October 1959 that "for Mexico, as for the majority of Latin American countries, the greatest problem is the United States."[36] In the same press conference he denied that the new Cuban government was communist or that it posed a threat to the hemisphere. In July 1960, López Mateos addressed the question of his political leanings directly, telling a crowd in Guaymas, Sonora: "My government is, within the Constitution, of the extreme left."[37] This "Declaration of Guaymas" triggered an explosion of debate within and beyond Mexico, as commentators struggled to parse the meaning of the president's words. After Mexico's Congress called a special meeting to discuss and define the new "extreme left" policy, the president of the permanent commission of the Mexican Congress, Emilio Sánchez Piedras, explained that "the declaration is a message and a summons to those in power to carry out with fidelity the postulates of the Mexican Revolution."[38]

López Mateos used the occasion of another presidential tour to further embrace the Cuban Revolution, this time playing enthusiastic host to Cuban president Osvaldo Dorticós Torrado. A visible outpouring of popular and official excitement greeted Dorticós when he arrived in Mexico in June 1960 on the last stop of a tour of Latin America. Telegraphers, sanitation workers, china factory employees, and electricians published welcoming advertisements. "The cause of Cuba is the cause of Latin America," the workers declared, "because the crucial problems of our twenty sister countries are the same, and Cuba shows us, with her example, the path to the true and effective solution to the most grave of those problems."[39] Mexico City newspapers also carried paid advertisements signed by Minister of the Interior Gustavo Díaz Ordaz and Mayor

---

[35] *Presencia Internacional de Adolfo López Mateos*, 225.
[36] Ibid., 39.
[37] "Política Interior: Izquierda, centro y derecha," *Política*, July 15, 1960.
[38] Ibid.
[39] "¡Bienvenido a México!," *Excélsior*, June 9, 1960.

Ernesto P. Uruchurtu urging Mexicans to give a cordial welcome to the Cuban leader. The half-page announcement described Cuba as a "sister country, united with Mexico by traditional ties of friendship" and provided information about the date and time of Dorticós's arrival.[40]

Not everyone was enthusiastic about the visit, however. A group called the Youth Confederation of the Mexican Republic published a quarter-page ad in *Excélsior* in which they claimed that "the dictatorial Cuban regime that Dorticós represents is every day increasingly proposing the integration of a totalitarian state, of the sort of red fascism that reigns in Soviet Russia and communist China."[41] Another advertisement, possibly planted by the U.S. embassy, compared the Cuban and Mexican Revolutions and criticized the former for failing to consecrate itself in a democratic constitution as the latter had done. "We have seen other foreign political personalities parade down the streets of Mexico, who exercised authority in their countries and then fell from power," the ad warned.[42] Mexican intelligence agents reported that leaders of the conservative PAN party worried that Dorticós's visit would strain relations between Mexico and the United States.[43] Nonetheless, a subsequent security report indicated that the PAN intended to live up to its nickname of "loyal opposition"; a journalist for the party's magazine told intelligence agents that "the PAN is disposed to give support to any act that takes place related to Dr. Oswaldo Dorticós's arrival."[44] Even conservative groups were willing to swallow, or at least tone down, their misgivings about the Cuban government in order to ensure a smooth visit.

President Dorticós's visit turned out to be everything the Cuban and Mexican governments could have hoped. President López Mateos awaited his arrival at the Mexico City airport, as did some fifteen thousand other people who chanted, cheered, and hoisted colorful signs. A group from the National School of Agriculture displayed a banner that read: "If Cuba needs agricultural soldiers, [we] can provide them!" Railroad and

[40] Gustavo Diaz Ordaz and Ernesto P. Uruchurtu, "El gobierno de la república y las autoridades de la ciudad reiteran su invitación al pueblo a recibir con toda cordialidad al Señor Doctor Osvaldo Dorticós," *Excélsior*, June 6, 1960.

[41] "Cuba Libre," *Excélsior*, June 10, 1960.

[42] "Está Usted en su casa, Señor Dorticós," *Excélsior*, June 10, 1960. *Política* claimed that the anti-Cuban ads in *Excélsior* were planted by the U.S. embassy under the cover of fake anticommunist groups. See "Dorticós en México," *Política*, June 15, 1960, 5–7.

[43] Manuel Rangel Escamilla, "[PAN leader's reaction to Dorticós's visit]," June 4, 1960, DFS, Exp 48-2-960, Leg. 13, Hoja 65, AGN.

[44] Manuel Rangel Escamilla, "[PAN will cooperate with Dorticós's visit]," June 7, 1960, DFS, Exp 48-2-960, Leg. 13, Hoja 66, AGN.

telephone workers, teachers, electricians, and members of various polit-ical parties bore welcoming signs as well.[45] Thousands of students fol-lowed Dorticós from the airport to his hotel, where they obliged him to give a short speech. Lázaro Cárdenas led a group of distinguished Mexican intellectuals that visited the Cuban president at his hotel to pay their respects.[46]

López Mateos took advantage of the visit to draw more parallels between the Mexican and Cuban Revolutions. "I am pleased to receive on our soil," he declared, "the representative of a friendly nation with whom Mexico is bound not only by longstanding and fraternal ties, but also by similar aspirations of justice." López Mateos went on to tell Dorticós that he would find in Mexico examples of dedication to agrar-ian reform as well as social, cultural, and economic improvement. "We trust that the Cuban Revolution will be, like the Mexican Revolution has been, one step more toward the greatness of America," he concluded.[47] López Mateos also issued a joint declaration with Dorticós, in which the two presidents celebrated the fact that the visit had allowed them to "confirm the understanding of their reciprocal interests and the depth of the affection that so happily unites Mexico and Cuba."[48]

The reception that the Cuban president received in Mexico was the highlight of his multicountry tour and stood in stark contrast to his expe-rience in most of the rest of Latin America. The Argentine ambassador to Cuba, Julio Amoedo, had accompanied Dorticós throughout his travels and afterward shared his impressions with the U.S. ambassador to Cuba, Phillip Bonsal. According to Amoedo, the visit to Argentina earlier in the tour was "a frost" due to lack of popular interest, while the Brazilian visit was "no more than officially correct." CIA investigators reported that Dorticós cut his time in Venezuela from four days to thirty-six hours after receiving minimal official attention.[49] The Argentine ambassador told Bonsal that "the Mexican reception greatly heartened Dorticós and his group" and was "much more than they had expected." Bonsal, who at that point was trying to develop what he called a "continental point of view" about the threat that the Cuban Revolution posed to the

---

[45] "México respeta la autodeterminación, dijo ayer López Mateos: Dorticós es desde ayer huésped de nuestro país," *Excélsior*, June 10, 1960.

[46] "Relaciones Exteriores: Dorticós en México," *Política*, June 15, 1960.

[47] *Los presidentes de México: Discursos políticos 1910–1988*, 82–4.

[48] *Presencia internacional de Adolfo López Mateos*, 10.

[49] CIA, "Current Intelligence Weekly Summary," June 9, 1960. CIA-RDP79 – 00927A002700110001-2, CREST database, NARA.

hemisphere, was not happy to hear about Mexico's posture.[50] In a message to Assistant Secretary of State Rubottom, Bonsal posited that the warm welcome for Dorticós was most likely the Mexican government's way of avoiding internal trouble. The U.S. ambassador described López Mateos's decision as a "regrettable ... shortsighted form of expediency."[51]

The CIA seconded Bonsal's conclusion that Mexican leaders had used Dorticós's visit as a way to maintain domestic peace. Minister of the Interior Gustavo Díaz Ordaz told a CIA source that the rousing reception "was planned by the Mexican Government as a means of frustrating the efforts of local leftist groups to exploit the visit and embarrass the government." The CIA report claimed that Mexico's leaders had received information prior to the visit that indicated that "Communist and Marxist political parties, front groups, and left-wing labor organizations were going to use the occasion to attack the Mexican and U.S. governments."[52] Mexican intelligence agents had indeed submitted reports about leftist plans in the days leading up to the Cuban president's visit, lending credence to the CIA's contention that Mexican leaders were afraid of domestic unrest.[53]

Upon his return to Cuba, President Dorticós described his stay in Mexico in glowing terms. He told reporters in a televised interview "the Mexican government demonstrated great interest in our visit ... we were greeted with an official reception replete with military and diplomatic honors, full of human warmth on the part of President López Mateos." The Cuban president, in a rare – and unintentional – instance of agreement with U.S. observers, also attributed his treatment in part to public pressure. "A government that is not afraid to show solidarity and sympathy with the Cuban Revolution has a great opportunity to win the sympathy of its people," he remarked. Dorticós told Cuban reporters that everywhere he went in Mexico, he was met with spontaneous applause and cheers for Cuba, the revolution, and Fidel Castro. "It was truly moving," he recalled.[54]

[50] Philip W. Bonsal, "Letter from Philip W. Bonsal to Roy R. Rubottom Jr.," May 14, 1960, Philip W. Bonsal Papers, Box 2, Folder 1, Manuscript Collection, Library of Congress.

[51] Philip W. Bonsal, "Letter from Philip W. Bonsal to Roy R. Rubottom Jr.," June 16, 1960, Philip W. Bonsal Papers, Box 2, Folder 1, Manuscript Collection, U.S. Library of Congress.

[52] CIA, "Mexico Gives Visiting Cuban President Warm Welcome," June 15, 1960, Declassified Documents Reference System.

[53] Manuel Rangel Escamilla, "[Activities planned by leftist groups to celebrate Dorticós's visit]," June 1, 1960, DFS, Exp 11-4-60, Leg. 10, Hoja 104, AGN.

[54] Ministerio de Relaciones Exteriores de Cuba, Departamento de Relaciones Públicas, "La revolución cubana es un fenómeno histórico que se impone ante todos los pueblos,"

Dorticós was not the only Cuban grateful for the warm welcome that he had received in Mexico. Fidel Castro gave a televised speech thanking the Mexican people and their government for the hospitable reception and the "generous attitude" that they had adopted toward Dorticós.[55] Castro also took the opportunity to praise the people of Mexico for their proud history of resistance, referring specifically to Mexico's venerated "*niños héroes*," or boy heroes, who had chosen death over surrender in defense of the Castle of Chapultepec in 1847 during the Mexican-American War.[56] By reminding his audience of the wrongs that Mexico had suffered at the hands of the United States, Castro implied that Cuba and Mexico had a common enemy.

Less than a month later, a speech by the leader of Mexico's Congress prompted further displays of gratitude from the Cubans. When the United States cut the island's sugar quota in July 1960, the president of the permanent commission of the Congress, Emilio Sánchez Piedras, declared that even though the United States was "closing the doors of friendship and comprehension on Cuba," the Mexican people never would.[57] In response, Castro expressed eternal gratitude to the people and government of Mexico for their solidarity.[58] Foreign Minister Raúl Roa personally delivered a message to Mexican ambassador Gilberto Bosques in which he promised that Cuba "would never forget Mexico's valiant gesture."[59] Trucks decorated with the Cuban and Mexican flags circled the streets of Havana, and four thousand Cubans gathered in front of the Mexican embassy, waving flags and signs that read "Viva México" and "Thank You to Our Mexican Brothers." The most important

Boletín 117, June 16, 1960. Expediente 28, Embajada de Cuba en Panamá, 1959, Recortes de Periódicos, Boletines, Revistas y Publicaciones de Cuba, Archivo del Ministerio de Relaciones Exteriores, Panama City, Panama. Many thanks to Aaron Moulton for sharing this document.

55 "Castro TV Speech on Havana Channel 2," June 11, 1960, LANIC Castro Speech Database, http://lanic.utexas.edu/project/castro/db/1960/19600611.html (accessed March 13, 2015).

56 On the *niños héroes* and the Mexican-American War see Cecil Robinson, ed., *The View from Chapultepec: Mexican Writers on the Mexican-American War* (Tucson: University of Arizona Press, 1989); Paul W. Foos, *A Short, Offhand, Killing Affair: Soldiers and Social Conflict during the Mexican-American War* (Chapel Hill: University of North Carolina Press, 2002); José Manuel Villalpando César, *Niños héroes* (Mexico City: Planeta, 2004).

57 "Líderes de la revolución mexicana contra los EEUU," *Revolución*, July 8, 1960.

58 Fidel Castro Ruz, "Optimistic Castro Interviewed on TV," July 9, 1960, LANIC Castro Speech Database, http://lanic.utexas.edu/project/castro/db/1960/19600711.html (accessed March 13, 2015).

59 "Gratitud de Cuba al pueblo mexicano," *El Mundo*, July 9, 1960.

organizations in Cuba, including the Confederation of Cuban Workers, the 26th of July Movement, the Federation of University Students, and the Popular Socialist Party all signed a letter to the Mexican ambassador, thanking him for his country's support. "The people and government of Mexico have once again demonstrated their devotion to defending the age-old principles of independence, the right to non-intervention, and social progress that were the basis of the Mexican Revolution," the letter read.[60]

The Mexican congressman's statements in favor of Cuba threatened to upset his country's relations with the United States. U.S. ambassador Robert Hill was sick with a fever on the day of the speech, so he sent embassy councilor Raymond G. Leddy to demand answers from the subminister of foreign relations, José Gorostiza. Waving a copy of *Última Noticias* in Gorostiza's face, Leddy asked whether the news of the speech was correct and promised that it would have a significant impact in the United States. "Relations between Mexico and the United States are at their highest level in many years and constitute an example for the entire world of excellent relations, and it would be a shame if they suffered as a consequence of the declaration by Sánchez Piedras," the councilor warned.[61] During the meeting, Ambassador Hill called to repeat the message of concern and requested that the Mexican government make a declaration about the situation. When Leddy's warning failed to produce quick enough results, Hill roused himself from his sickbed the next day to hold an hour-long meeting with Mexican Foreign Minister Manuel Tello, which he left looking grim.[62] President Dwight Eisenhower reportedly telephoned the State Department from his vacation headquarters in Rhode Island to find out what was going on in Mexico.[63]

The U.S. press and business community also reacted strongly to Sánchez Piedras's pro-Cuba speech. The Mexican consul in New York reported that radio and television stations were running special news bulletins about the speech every half hour and connecting it with President López Mateos's policy toward Cuba. Headlines in the *New York Times* and the *New York Herald Tribune* announced: "Mexican Backs Cuba"

---

[60] "Cuba: 'Gracias, México,'" *Política*, July 15, 1960; Harold K. Milks, "Cubanos felices por lo que dijo Sánchez Piedras: Para demostrarlo hacen en La Habana manifestaciones," *Excélsior*, July 9, 1960.

[61] "Memorandum," July 7, 1960, III-5591-11, Archivo de la Secretaría de Relaciones Exteriores, Mexico City [hereafter SRE].

[62] "Hill Is Grim in Mexico," *New York Times*, July 9, 1960.

[63] "U.S. Fails to Get Official Statement," *El Paso Times*, July 9, 1960.

and "Mexico Backs Castro, Top Spokesman Says."[64] Furthermore, numerous Wall Street investors and bankers had contacted the consulate demanding to know whether the congressman's statements represented the official position of the Mexican government. Mr. Arthur McCusker of Amott Banker and Co. called on behalf of a group of financiers and warned "they had many millions of dollars invested in [Mexico] and naturally found this news enormously alarming." The presidents of the First National City Bank of New York, the Mexican Chamber of Commerce, the New York State Chamber of Commerce, and the U.S. Chamber of Commerce also called the Mexican embassy for clarification.[65]

After a few days of pressure on these multiple fronts, the Mexican government finally conceded to the requests for explanation. Foreign Minister Tello issued a press release in which he minimized the importance of Sánchez Piedras's remarks, stating that only Mexico's president could determine foreign policy. "The statements of the members of Congress do not compromise the executive, nor do they necessarily reflect the opinion of it," Tello explained. He also took the opportunity to clarify the government's position on Cuba. "There exists in Mexico a profound affection for Cuba," he recognized, "and we understand and share their longing for economic improvement and social justice." But Tello disagreed with Sánchez Piedras's depiction of U.S.-Cuban relations. "The Foreign Ministry does not share the opinion that the doors have closed on a solution to the differences that exist between the United States and Cuba." He proposed that the mechanisms of the inter-American system be put to use to resolve the conflict between Mexico's neighbors.[66]

The Mexican government was especially anxious to resolve the escalating conflict between Cuba and the United States because these external problems were causing internal unrest. Mexican students' responses to the U.S. cuts in the Cuban sugar quota showed that the international confrontation could destabilize Mexico. On July 12, some four thousand students held a pro-Cuba demonstration in Mexico City (see Figure 5). They

[64] "Mexican Backs Cuba," *New York Times*, July 8, 1960; "Mexico Backs Castro, Top Spokesman Says," *New York Herald Tribune*, July 8, 1960.

[65] Raúl Reyes Spindola, "Reacción en esta ciudad sobre el discurso del Sr. Diputado Emilio Sánchez Piedras, ante nuestras Cámaras de Diputados y Senadores," July 8, 1960, III-5591-11, SRE.

[66] "La política exterior la marca el ejecutivo: Tello se refiere a las palabras de los legisladores," *Novedades*, July 12, 1960, p. 1; "Government Sources in Mexico Reject Idea of Pro-Cuban Policy: Envoy in Conference," *Washington Post*, July 10, 1960, A7. See also CIA "NSC Briefing: Cuba," July 14, 1960. CIA-RDP79R00890A001200070021-4, CREST Database, NARA; "[Press release]," July 11, 1960, III-5591-11, SRE.

FIGURE 5. "Mexican student Antonio Tenorio Adame holds aloft a U.S. flag which a group of student demonstrators tried to burn in demonstration in support of Cuban premier Fidel Castro, in Mexico City, July 13, 1960. Police rescued the flag before it was damaged by demonstrators shouting anti-U.S. slogans. Sign says students are with Cuba and with teachers of Mexican Revolutionary Movement."
Source: AP Photo. Courtesy of AP Images, image ID number 439348253359.

marched through the streets of the city center, trailed by fifty intelligence agents. The demonstration ended in a bloody confrontation between the students and the police and grenadiers who were waiting at the entrance to the National Palace after the demonstrators announced their intention to burn a U.S. flag. The police's violent response only prompted further protests. Three days later, twice as many students held another pro-Castro demonstration. They demanded that the Mexican government take the Cuban side in the conflict with the United States and that the head of the police department be forced to resign for his role in the recent violence. Close to a thousand police, grenadiers, secret agents, and firefighters awaited their arrival in the Zócalo. They dispersed the crowd, but one thousand protestors then went to the offices of two conservative newspapers and pelted them with stones.[67]

U.S. observers paid close attention to the ways that international tensions could affect Mexico's domestic politics. A background paper prepared by the State Department for the August 1960 meeting of the Organization of American States in San José, Costa Rica, went into great detail about Mexico's internal politics. "Because of the domestic situation in Mexico," the report began, "the present Cuban situation presents an extremely delicate problem to the Government of Mexico." The State Department was aware of the demonstrations and riots among students, workers, and *campesinos* as well as rumors that Lázaro Cárdenas was starting a new, leftist political party. "In an effort to counter this development a number of PRI members, including the president himself ... have made statements asserting that the PRI and the López Mateos administration is leftist and not opposed to the economic and social aims of the Castro regime," the report explained.[68] The CIA concurred with the State Department's conclusions about the connections between Mexico's foreign and domestic policy. Agents predicted that "While many government leaders privately deplore the excesses of the Castro regime, it is unlikely that they will show open hostility to it, since a large number of Mexicans – perhaps led by Lázaro Cárdenas – still find a close parallel between the goals of the Cuban and Mexican revolutions."[69]

President Eisenhower was so worried about Mexican stability that he decided to delay OAS actions against Castro until after he had spoken with López Mateos. In October 1960, Eisenhower had a conversation with various State Department and army officials about Cuba, in which he expressed concern that OAS sanctions against Castro might cause trouble. "If Mexico were to become disgruntled and if we were to see the Communists come to power there, in all likelihood we would have to go to war about all this," he brooded. Eisenhower described the sanctions as

[67] "Homenaje a Cuba," *Política*, August 1, 1960.

[68] "Meeting of Foreign Ministers, San José, August 1960: Bilateral Paper–Mexico," August 12, 1960, RG 59, Entry A1 3148, ARC 2363836, Box 6, NARA. CIA reports from the previous years had also repeatedly warned about labor unrest threatening Mexico's stability. See CIA, "Growing Labor Unrest in Mexico," June 26, 1958, CIA CREST Database, NARA; CIA, "Mexican Labor Troubles," September 2, 1958, CIA CREST Database, NARA; CIA, "The New López Mateos Administration in Mexico," November 20, 1958, CIA CREST Database, NARA.

[69] CIA, "Current Intelligence Weekly Summary: Leftist Pressures in Mexico," August 4, 1960. CIA-RDP79-00927A002800080001-5, CREST Database, NARA.

a very difficult move so far as Mexico was concerned. Undersecretary of State C. Douglas Dillon agreed, acknowledging that the Mexican government was "under great pressure from the Cárdenas Leftists."[70]

President López Mateos felt concerned enough to make an oblique reference to student activism in the State of the Union address that he delivered a little more than a month after the conflict between Cuba and the United States had sparked violent confrontations in Mexico. "There is a noble restlessness among the young generation to take part in national life outside the sphere of their specific activities," he observed. "But some of their worries," he continued, "tend to be erroneously directed against the revolutionary effort or driven by examples of distant struggles and peoples distinct from our own." He explained that some countries in the world were currently fighting for goals that the Mexican Revolution had already achieved.[71] Although the president did not specifically criticize students' enthusiasm for the Cuban Revolution, he made it clear that they should not seek to follow Castro's example, especially because Mexico's earlier revolution had supposedly made such actions unnecessary.

López Mateos's embrace of the Cuban Revolution, while crucial to Mexico's international and domestic politics, was superficial. In addition to repressing and admonishing popular demonstrations of support for Castro, the Mexican government secretly cooperated with U.S. efforts to spy on Castro's government. Cuba officially became the top intelligence priority of the CIA's Mexico City station when Chief of Station Winston Scott returned from a White House regional conference in May 1960.[72] The CIA tapped every telephone line in the Cuban embassy and in the official residences of its diplomats, while photographic surveillance recorded everyone who entered and exited the embassy. Agents sorted through the Cubans' trash and mail for information. They installed hidden microphones throughout the embassy, including inside walls, love seats, and the leg of a coffee table in the ambassador's office.[73]

The CIA coordinated many of its anti-Cuban operations with Mexican officials, especially those in the Department of Federal Security. For example, the surveillance of travel between Mexico and Cuba required

---

[70] *FRUS, 1958–1960. Cuba*, Vol. 6 (Washington, DC: U.S. Government Printing Office, 1991), 1085.

[71] "El Lic. Adolfo López Mateos, al abrir el Congreso sus sesiones ordinarias, el 10 de septiembre de 1960," in *Los presidentes de México ante la nación*, Vol. 4 (Mexico City: Cámara de Diputados, 1966).

[72] Goodpasture, "Mexico City Station History."

[73] Ibid.

cooperation between U.S. and Mexican agencies. A CIA technician, along with two local agents, installed a concealed passport camera in the Mexico City airport to photograph everyone traveling to or from Havana. The technician would periodically service the camera and pick up the film during meetings with the Mexican chief immigration inspector. After a few years, the Department of Federal Security took over the operation, while still giving the film to the CIA for processing.[74] According to press reports, Mexico's Federal Judicial Police also operated a camera at the airport to photograph everyone who traveled to Cuba and provided names and photos to foreign governments that were trying to trace their own citizens.[75] This collaboration helped Mexico, the United States, and other countries keep track of Castro's international connections.

Another way the Mexican government restricted travel between Cuba and the mainland was by tightening controls over visas. In September 1960, Mexican visa regulations for Cuban nationals changed to conform to the U.S. State Department's policy. Under the new rules, all requests for travel had to go through the Ministry of the Interior in Mexico City, leading to long delays and a backlog of requests. Meanwhile, the CIA used a special channel in the ministry to expedite visas for certain Cuban dissidents.[76] The stricter limits on travel permissions hampered the Cubans' ability to take advantage of their air connection with Mexico. Grateful, U.S. leaders in Washington carefully avoided any public comment on Mexico's cooperation in "using its key political and geographic position to help control Castro."[77]

These and other quiet measures that the Mexican government took against Cuba produced low-level tensions between the two countries. Cuban and Mexican officials frequently argued over whether Cuban diplomats could carry weapons in Mexico's airports. On at least four occasions, the conflicts escalated into scuffles, arrests, and seizures.[78] The

---

[74] Ibid.

[75] Gerry Robichaud, "Cuba Travel Spotlighted by Mexico," *Washington Post*, March 27, 1963.

[76] Willard C. Curtis, "Processes for Cubans to Obtain Mexican Visas," October 25, 1963, RG 233 Box 72 /32 JFK/CIA RIF 104-10092-10135, NARA.

[77] Dean Rusk, "Memorandum to President Johnson," February 18, 1964, National Security Files [hereafter NSF], Mexico, Box 61, Folder 2, Document 9, Lyndon Baines Johnson Presidential Library, Austin, TX [hereafter LBJ Library].

[78] Gilberto Bosques, "[Telegram from Mexican Embassy in Havana to Foreign Ministry about complaints that travelers in Cuba are being photographed in Mexico]," December 17, 1960, Folder III-5591–9, SRE; "[Prensa Latina employee arrested for carrying weapons in Mexico City airport]," August 19, 1961, DFS, Exp 65-92-61, Leg. 2, Hoja 29, AGN; Daniel Ramos Nava, "Incidente con 2 diplomáticos de Cuba desarmados en el

director of Cuba's National Fishing Institute complained that Mexican officials on the Isla Mujeres refused to accept Cuban pesos in payment for repairs and "treat[ed] us as though we were not citizens of a sister country."[79] Numerous Cubans seeking to leave the island protested that employees of the Mexican embassy in Havana charged for exit visas.[80] Negative articles in the Mexican press accusing the Cuban government of espionage and propagandizing also contributed to a strained relationship between the two countries.[81]

In the two years immediately following the Cuban Revolution, the Mexican government developed a multivalent response to the actual and potential domestic turmoil that events in the neighboring country had unleashed. Publicly, President López Mateos embraced the Cuban Revolution and its leaders, seizing every opportunity to compare it to Mexico's own revolution. In so doing, he strengthened both the myth of the Mexican Revolution and the government's control over its legacy. At the same time, the president and his assistants in the intelligence services and other security forces struggled to contain the rise of the New Left and the spread of Mexico's bourgeoning Cold War. They violently repressed worker and student activism wherever it arose and cooperated with U.S. operations against Castro.

aeropuerto," *Novedades*, December 9, 1961; José Gorostiza, "Diplomáticos cubanos desarmados en el aeropuerto de esta ciudad," December 14, 1961, Folder III – 2867 – 16, SRE; Luis Echeverría, "[Reply from Luis Echeverría to José Gorostiza about conflict between Cuban and Mexican officials in the airport]," January 29, 1962, Folder III – 2867 – 16, SRE; "Diplomáticos cubanos que cargaban pistola, desarmados en el aeropuerto," *Excélsior*, August 4, 1962; Secretaría de Relaciones Exteriores, "[Telegram to Mexican Embassy in Havana about Cuban diplomats bringing weapons to Mexican airports]," August 17, 1962, Folder III – 2867 – 16, SRE.

[79] Letter from Porfirio Alaria Mondón to Francisco Brey, "Problema existente en Islas Mujeres," August 4, 1960. Box América Latina, México, 1959–62, Ordinario 6, Folder 1960, MINREX.

[80] Secretaría de Relaciones Exteriores, "[Memorandum to Mexican Embassy in Caracas about Mexican Embassy in Havana charging Cubans for exit visas]," February 4, 1961, Folder III – 2852 – 5, SRE; Gilberto Bosques, "[Telegram from Mexican Embassy in Havana to Foreign Ministry about accusations of charging for exit visas]," February 6, 1961, Folder III – 2852 – 5, SRE; E. Rafael Urdaneta, "Cargos que formula un exlider obrero cubano contra personal de nuestra embajada en La Habana, Cuba," March 21, 1962, Folder III – 2852 – 5, SRE; E. Rafael Urdaneta, "Denuncia formulada por el Señor Eduardo E. Sotolongo M., ex-asilado en la embajada de México en La Habana," August 30, 1962, Folder III – 2852 – 5, SRE; Secretaría de Relaciones Exteriores, "[Report to Mexican President about ambassador to Cuba's activities]," July 24, 1967, SPR 540-Bis5, SRE.

[81] Ministerio de Relaciones Exteriores de la República de Cuba, "México: Relación de agresiones perpetradas contra nuestra embajada que han podido poner en peligro nuestras relaciones con ese país," July 1961, América Latina, México, 1959–62, Ordinario: 1961, MINREX.

THE CUBANS MAKE USE OF MEXICO

Mexico played a crucial role in Fidel Castro and Che Guevara's efforts to encourage revolution throughout the rest of Latin America. Though they consistently rejected accusations that they "exported" revolution, Cuban leaders did inspire and support groups in other countries that sought to overthrow their own governments. The Cuban "*foco*" (focal point) theory of revolution was highly formulaic and based on the belief that their experience of starting from a small group of dedicated fighters could serve as a blueprint for other rebellions.[82] They also saw support for foreign revolutions as a way to protect their own regime by gaining new allies and weakening old adversaries, including the United States.[83] Just as they had used Mexican territory as a safe haven from which to launch their own crusade in 1956, Castro and his followers tried to use the same fertile ground to assist revolutions in other countries and start a new Latin American news service. Mexican and U.S. officials also believed that Cuban agents occasionally crossed the line and intervened in Mexico's internal affairs, contrary to Castro's public declarations of mutual respect.[84]

Castro made no secret of his conflict with the leaders of many other Latin American countries and his encouragement of opposition movements in those nations. Supporting foreign revolutions was not particularly unusual; as historian Carla Anne Robbins observes, "[P]lotting the overthrow of dictators is a well-respected tradition among Latin America's democratic left."[85] In 1959, Cubans took part in three failed

[82] Matt D. Childs, "An Historical Critique of the Emergence and Evolution of Ernesto Che Guevara's Foco Theory," *Journal of Latin American Studies* 27, no. 3 (October 1995): 593–624.

[83] Domínguez, *To Make a World Safe for Revolution*, 113–14.

[84] The question of Cuban involvement in Mexico's internal politics remains a sensitive subject. Works on Mexican history that deny Cuban support for opposition groups in Mexico include Castañeda, *Utopia Unarmed*; Sergio Aguayo Quezada, *1968: Los archivos de la violencia* (Mexico City: Editorial Grijalbo, 1998); Donald Hodges and Ross Gandy, *Mexico under Siege: Popular Resistance to Presidential Despotism* (London: Zed Books, 2002); Sergio Aguayo Quezada, "El impacto de la guerrilla en la vida mexicana: Algunas hipótesis," in *Movimientos armados en México, siglo XX*, ed. Verónica Oikión Solano and Marta Eugenia García Ugarte, Vol. 1 (Zamora: El Colegio de Michoacán, 2006), 91–8; Fernando Herrera Calderón and Adela Cedillo, "Introduction: The Unknown Mexican Dirty War" in *Challenging Authoritarianism in Mexico: Revolutionary Struggles and the Dirty War, 1964–1982*, ed. Fernando Herrera Calderón and Adela Cedillo (New York: Routledge, 2012).

[85] Carla Anne Robbins, *The Cuban Threat* (New York: McGraw-Hill, 1983), 12. On transnational revolutionary networks in Latin America prior to the Cuban Revolution,

revolutions against the governments of Panama, Haiti, and the Dominican Republic.[86] Revolutionaries from Nicaragua received money and supplies from the Cubans, in addition to training on the island.[87] The hundreds, perhaps thousands, of guerrillas who traveled to Cuba for instruction in the decade after the Cuban Revolution had to take indirect routes after their home countries cut relations, and many of them went through Mexico.[88]

Mexican and U.S. government officials believed that the Cubans were using their connections with Mexico to export revolution to the rest of Latin America. U.S. embassy officials described Mexico as "a major overseas base for Castroist subversion and terrorism in the other Latin American countries."[89] Mexican security officers contended "the Cuban embassy in Mexico is in charge of directing the diverse movements throughout Latin America against the so-called Central American dictatorships."[90] In July 1960, Mexican agents reported that the Cuban embassy was providing instruction and financial support to various groups of Nicaraguan political exiles that sought to overthrow the dictatorial Anastasio Somoza.[91] An employee of the Cuban embassy who defected in Mexico City accused the cultural attaché of providing weapons and money to Guatemalan and Nicaraguan exiles.[92] According to CIA reports, members of the Cuban diplomatic staff in Mexico began providing assistance to the Guatemalan guerrilla movement as early

see Aaron Coy Moulton, "Building Their Own Cold War in Their Own Backyard: The Transnational, International Conflicts in the Greater Caribbean Basin, 1944–1954," *Cold War History*, Advanced Access, published February 3, 2015, DOI: 10.1080/14682 745.2014.995172 (accessed February 5, 2015).

[86] Robbins, *The Cuban Threat*, 9.

[87] Carlos Fonseca, *Obras, Vol. I: Bajo la bandera del sandinismo* (Managua: Editorial Nueva Nicaragua, 1982); Tomas Borge, *The Patient Impatience: From Boyhood to Guerrilla: A Personal Narrative of Nicaragua's Struggle for Liberation* (Willimantic, CT: Curbstone Press, 1989).

[88] Subcommittee on Inter-American Affairs U.S. Congress, House of Representatives, "Communist Activities in Latin America, 1967" (U.S. Government Printing Office, July 3, 1967); Ulises Estrada, *Tania: Undercover with Che Guevara in Bolivia* (Melbourne, Australia: Ocean Press, 2005).

[89] US Embassy–Mexico, "Effect in Mexico of Severance of Mexican-Cuban Relations," June 8, 1964, RG 59, Entry P2, ARC 602903, Box 1, NARA.

[90] Manuel Rangel Escamilla, "Actividades de asilados políticos nicaraguenses residentes en nuestro país que en forma constante tratan de efectuar una conjura en contra del gobierno actual de la república de Nicaragua que preside el Gral. Anastasio Somoza," July 11, 1960, DFS, Exp 11-56-60, Leg 1, Hoja 123, AGN.

[91] Ibid.

[92] "[Interview of a Cuban Embassy official]," September 22, 1960, DFS, Exp 76-3-60, Leg. 1, Exp 229.

as 1962.[93] The Cubans reportedly sent thousands of weapons through Mexican territory to Guatemala.[94]

Disaffected Cuban officials claimed that their embassy in Mexico City was the center of an international web of espionage and revolution. When commercial representative Pedro L. Roig defected, he told agents in Mexico's Department of Political and Social Investigations that the Cuban embassy was a hotbed of undercover activities. He declared that embassy officials "were required to learn the secrets of the Mexican Government."[95] In a book that he later published, Roig depicted the Cuban embassy in Mexico as both a "trampoline" for the distribution of tons of communist propaganda and as the center point of a vast network of espionage, arms trafficking, and contraband.[96] A former Cuban intelligence agent who had operated in Paris seconded Roig's claims that Cuban diplomats in Mexico supported clandestine operations throughout Latin America.[97] A third, who had escaped and sought asylum in Canada, described Mexico as the base of operations for other regions of Latin America and the "route through which everything moves between Cuba and the rest of the continent."[98]

In September 1966, Mexican officials finally gained hard evidence of Cuban involvement in smuggling weapons and money to Guatemala. On September 15, a box labeled "electrical supplies" fell off a truck headed from Mexico City to Chiapas. Inside, police discovered guns, ammunition, canteens, and syringes. The discovery led to a series of arrests, culminating with that of Julian Lopez Díaz, the press secretary of the Cuban embassy, who was caught delivering $6,000 in U.S. twenty-dollar bills to the house of the Guatemalan in charge of the Mexico City end of the smuggling ring.[99] Mexican authorities later released Lopez Díaz

---

[93] Central Intelligence Agency, "The Communist Insurgency Movement in Guatemala," September 20, 1968, NSF, Latin America–El Salvador and Guatemala, Box 54, LBJ Library.

[94] Central Intelligence Agency, "Guatemala–A Current Appraisal," October 8, 1966, NSF, Latin America–El Salvador and Guatemala, Box 54, LBJ Library.

[95] "Declaraciones de Pedro L. Roig," June 12, 1962, IPS Caja 1456-A, Exp. 1, Hoja 56, AGN.

[96] Pedro L. Roig, *Como trabajan los espías de Castro: Como se infiltra el G2* (Miami: Duplex Paper Products of Miami, 1964), 64, 72.

[97] Orlando Castro Hidalgo, *Spy for Fidel* (Miami: E. A. Seemann Pub, 1971), 104.

[98] "Dirección General de Inteligencia," May 1966, SPR – 540 – BIS5, SRE.

[99] CIA, "Arrests of Arms Smugglers; Arrest of Julian Lopez Díaz, Third Secretary in Charge of Press at Cuban Embassy in Mexico City," September 27, 1966, Declassified Documents Reference System; Policía Judicial Federal and Agente #430, "[Deterioration of relations between Cuba and Mexico]," November 16, 1966, Presidential Collection

and forced him to leave the country, declaring him *persona non grata*. Despite this attempt to limit Cuban activities, CIA documents suggested that Cuba's embassy in Mexico remained an important supply depot for the Guatemalan rebels. One guerrilla group in particular, the FAR, reportedly received up to $15,000 per month through this channel.[100]

It appeared that Mexico was not only a transit point, but also may have been the final destination for many "subversive" Cubans and their tools of the trade. Even before Fidel Castro declared that his regime was socialist in April 1961, Mexican intelligence agents lumped the Cuban government and its representatives into the Soviets' international communist conspiracy and suspected the Cubans of involvement in Mexican affairs. In September 1960, the air attaché of the Cuban embassy told security officials that some of his co-workers were involved in numerous subversive movements within Mexico. The Cubans supposedly provided opposition groups with encouragement, economic help, and communist orientation. He claimed that students from his country who were members of the Communist Youth traveled to Mexico to agitate among students there and explained that his embassy had close ties to its Soviet counterpart and received instructions from the Russians.[101] The last part of the attaché's statement contained an element of truth: Cuban ambassador to Mexico Salvador Massip and his wife did in fact meet with the Soviet ambassador to Mexico on multiple occasions, and the first high-level contacts between Cuban and Soviet officials took place in Mexico City at the end of 1959.[102]

Mexican officials also believed that the Cubans created new student organizations within Mexico. The head of the Department of Federal Security submitted a series of reports in which he claimed that the Cuban embassy, in cooperation with Mexican leftist leaders including Lázaro Cárdenas, had organized a new student group called the Latin America Movement.[103] According to the intelligence director, the Cubans provided instruction on agitation, communist propaganda, and guerrilla manuals.[104] The embassy also reportedly covered the costs of the student

of Gustavo Díaz Ordaz [hereafter GDO] 206 (125), AGN; Policía Judicial Federal and Agente #430, "[U.S. Press coverage of communism in Mexico]," December 1, 1966, GDO 206 (125), AGN.

[100] CIA, "The Communist Insurgency Movement in Guatemala."
[101] "[Interview of a Cuban embassy official]," September 22, 1960, DFS, Exp 76-3-60, Leg. 1, Exp 229, AGN.
[102] Reeves, "Extracting the Eagle's Talons," 79–89.
[103] Manuel Rangel Escamilla, "Movimiento América Latina," May 18, 1961, DFS, Exp 63-1-61, Leg. 14, Hoja 74, AGN.
[104] Manuel Rangel Escamilla, "Movimiento América Latina," July 10, 1961, DFS, Exp 63-1-61, Leg. 14, Hoja 178, AGN.

leaders' "constant trips" to Cuba.[105] The group's members supposedly spent their meetings concocting sinister plots to stir up trouble among the students and *campesinos* of Jalisco and Baja California.[106] Adding insult to injury, the Cuban-sponsored Latin America Movement also distributed propaganda "attacking the minister of the interior, saying that he was a deaf and dumb accomplice to the clergy's violation of the constitution."[107] The Cuban embassy's investments in the Latin America Movement paid noteworthy dividends, in the view of the intelligence director. Among its activities, the student organization held pro-Cuba rallies and showed movies about the amazing technical, scientific, and cultural advances that the socialist countries had made.[108] In November 1960, the group issued a call to the "progressive men of Mexico," including Lázaro Cárdenas, Emilio Sánchez Piedras, and numerous other groups and individuals, to unite their efforts and defend Cuba more effectively.[109] Though the Cuban embassy in Mexico City did indeed collect copies of the Latin America Movement's propaganda, it is unclear whether the Cubans were actually supporting or training the members of the organization.[110]

Mexican intelligence agents considered all Cuban promotional materials propaganda; they submitted numerous reports claiming that the Cubans were spreading communist ideology and filed away copies of any pamphlet or magazine they could get their hands on. In order to counter some of the bad press that they were receiving in Mexico, the Cuban embassy in Mexico City and the consulates in Mérida, Tampico, and Veracruz produced news bulletins such as the *Bulletin of the Cuban Embassy* and the *Informative Bulletin of the Cuban Consulate in Mérida* and distributed copies of magazines published in Havana like *Bohemia*.[111] Cuban diplomats held

---

[105] Manuel Rangel Escamilla, "Algunos aspectos de la situación que prevalece en la Universidad Nacional Autónoma de México," February 21, 1962, DFS, Exp 63-1-62, Leg. 16, Hoja 189, AGN.

[106] Manuel Rangel Escamilla, "Movimiento América Latina," May 18, 1961, DFS, Exp 63-1-61, Leg. 14, Hoja 74, AGN.

[107] Manuel Rangel Escamilla, "Movimiento América Latina," July 8, 1961, DFS, Exp 63-1-61, Leg. 14, Hoja 177, AGN.

[108] Manuel Rangel Escamilla, "Movimiento América Latina," November 28, 1961, DFS, Exp 63-1-61, Leg. 16, Hoja 1, AGN.

[109] Movimiento América Latina, "Atención: Hombres progresistas de México: Un llamado del Movimiento América Latina en pro de la Revolución Cubana," November 1960. América Latina, México, 1959–62, Ordinario 6, Folder 1961, MINREX.

[110] Movimiento América Latina, "Carta de Principios" September 1960, América Latina, México, 1959–62, Ordinario 6, Folder 1961, MINREX.

[111] "[Letter from Ambassador Salvador Massip to Roberto Agramonte, asking for money to buy a mimeograph machine]," April 7, 1959. América Latina, México, 1959–62, Ordinario 6, Folder 1959, MINREX; General Francisco Ramírez Palacios, "[Cuban

screenings of movies produced on the island and in the socialist countries of
Europe.[112] The "José Martí" Mexican-Cuban Institute of Cultural Relations
housed a bookstore, news library, music store, and film club.[113]

The content of the publications that Cubans distributed in Mexico did
at times contain a clear political agenda. One bulletin from Mérida, in
the southern state of Yucatán, included a letter from a young woman in
Havana. "In spite of all the calumnies and lies, victory will be ours because
fighting for socialism is fighting for a great step forward in the history of
humanity," she boasted.[114] Describing how Cuba had gone from a bour-
geois state that represented an exploitative minority to a nation governed
by the common people, the author of the letter painted a rosy picture of
her country's socialist revolution. When John F. Kennedy visited Mexico
in 1962, the Cuban consulate in Veracruz published a supplement to its
cultural bulletin titled "Mexico Invaded in a Visit by Mercenaries Who
Wish to Buy It." The head of the Department of Federal Security wrote a
report about this pamphlet, claiming that the Cuban consul in Veracruz
who authored it also practiced communist proselytism among local students and paid for their trips to Cuba.[115]

While intelligence agents considered Cuban publications subversive
propaganda, other Mexican officials saw them as a form of public diplomacy and sometimes helped distribute such materials. In March 1961,
Mexican ambassador to Cuba Gilberto Bosques sent samples of a pamphlet from the National Railroad Federation of Cuba to the Mexican
Railroad Syndicate.[116] The publication, a booklet titled *Workers,
Syndicates, and Production*, advertised itself as "an orientation guide to
the principles of combat organizations."[117] It exhorted railroad workers

propaganda]," February 7, 1962, IPS Caja 1456 A, AGN; Joaquin Morales Solis,
"[Cuban propaganda]," May 2, 1968, IPS Caja 2958 E, AGN; Manuel Rangel Escamilla,
"[Investigation of Cuban Consul in Yucatán]," April 27, 1962, DFS, Exp 12-9-962, Leg
11, Hoja 241, AGN; Oscar Treviño Ríos, "Se informa y se solicita su intervención,"
March 14, 1962, Leg. III – 2873 – 24, SRE.

[112] "[Activities of Cuban Consuls]," n.d., IPS Caja 2958 D, AGN.

[113] "El Instituto Mexicano-Cubano de Relaciones Culturales 'José Martí,'" *Boletín de
Información de la Embajada de Cuba*, September 1961.

[114] Estrella Rubio Bernal, "La revolución socialista y los estudiantes," *Boletín informativo
del consulado de Cuba en Mérida*, November 23, 1961.

[115] "México invadido en una visita de mercenarios para comprarlo" and Manuel
Rangel Escamilla, "Consulado General de Cuba en Veracruz," August 18, 1962, Leg.
III-5663-3, SRE.

[116] Gilberto Bosques, "Se remiten folletos," March 2, 1961, Leg. III – 2522 – 19, SRE.

[117] *Los trabajadores, los sindicatos, y la producción* (Havana: Comisión Nacional de
Cultura y Propaganda de la Federación Nacional Ferroviaria de Cuba, 1960), 3.

to band together to fight against the oppression of national and foreign capitalism. It appears that Bosques, a senior government official who had worked in the foreign service since the Cárdenas years, shared Cárdenas's sympathy for the railroad workers and wanted to use the Cuban example to help revive their movement.[118]

Mexico also played an important role in Castro's efforts to seize control over information on a hemispheric and global scale. Castro began planting the seeds mere days after taking command of Cuba's government when, in January 1959, he hosted a gathering of hundreds of journalists from across Latin America. The conference, part of Operation Truth, aimed to counteract the negative publicity that the Cuban leaders had been receiving for their executions of Batista's collaborators. Castro exhorted his audience to challenge the dominant U.S. and European news agencies. "The press of [Latin] America should take control of the means that will permit them to know the truth and not be victims of lies," he proposed.[119] Six months later, in June 1959, Prensa Latina was officially inaugurated in Havana and began its first transmissions to subscribers abroad.

The new wire service showed great promise. It expanded quickly, opening offices in nearly every country of the Americas by the end of 1959. Within a year, the directors of Prensa Latina had signed contracts with news agencies across Europe, Asia, and Africa as well.[120] By that time, the wire service was sending more than four hundred messages a day on average to more than two hundred newspapers, magazines, and radio stations, including *L'Express* in France, the *New Statesman* in England, and the *New York Times*, *The Nation*, and the *New Republic* in the United States.[121] Prensa Latina worked with partners both large

---

[118] Gilberto Bosques, Mexican ambassador to Cuba from 1953 to 1964, was a self-described democratic leftist who had helped Castro gain asylum in Mexico. Though he did not openly criticize his government's repression of the railroad movement, in his memoirs he described López Mateos's response as "a result of circumstances that forced the president to contradict his 'revolutionary attitudes.'" Graciela De Garay, ed., *Gilberto Bosques: Cuba 1953–1964* (Jalisco: El Colegio de Jalisco, 2007), 57.

[119] CIA, "Cuba: Castro's Propaganda Apparatus and Foreign Policy," November 1984, Central Intelligence Agency FOIA Electronic Reading Room, www.foia.cia.gov/docs/DOC_0000972183/DOC_0000972183.pdf (accessed March 14, 2015); "Prensa Latina: Al servicio de la verdad–Antecedentes," *Prensa Latina* (Havana, 2009), http://www.prensa-latina.cu/Dossiers/Dossier50AnosPL/Antecedentes.htm (accessed March 14, 2015).

[120] "Prensa Latina: Al servicio de la verdad."

[121] "Un Año de 'Prensa Latina,'" *Política*, July 1, 1960; Conchita Dumois and Gabriel Molina, *Jorge Ricardo Masetti: El Comandante Segundo* (Havana: Editorial Capitán San Luis, 2012), 170.

and small; in Mexico, the wire service provided information to provincial papers such as *El Dictámen* of Ciudad Obregón, Sonora, as well as national magazines like *¡Siempre!* and *Política*.[122] Observers in the United States and Mexico suspected that Prensa Latina offered its service for free in order to increase its subscriptions.[123]

Before long, however, Mexico became one of the few countries in Latin America to allow Prensa Latina to operate. The governments of Paraguay, the Dominican Republic, and Nicaragua quickly banned the news agency. General Miguel Ydígoras Fuentes of Guatemala accused Prensa Latina of following a "Marxist ideology" and publishing stories that embarrassed the government and canceled the wire service's permission to operate in his country.[124] Prensa Latina had to close its offices in Peru and Argentina at the end of 1960, Venezuela in 1961, and in other countries across the Americas soon thereafter.[125] Frequently, the eviction of the news agency coincided with the host government's severance of diplomatic relations with Cuba.

As both Prensa Latina and its parent country became increasingly isolated in the Americas, their ties to Mexico became ever more important. Mexico City was a central point of communication between Prensa Latina's main offices in Havana and its employees spread across the rest of the hemisphere. Intelligence agents claimed that communist leaders in Nicaragua, Ecuador, and Chile used the Mexican offices of the wire service to transmit their secret correspondence with Cuba. Revolutionaries in the Dominican Republic and Peru also reportedly sent messages to Havana through Mexico.[126]

Though the wire service was primarily a Cuban undertaking, it relied upon support from other countries. Friendly news articles about Prensa Latina claimed that it received money from Mexican and Venezuelan investors.[127] The first president of the news agency was Mexican

---

[122] Manuel Rangel Escamilla, "Investigación acerca de la agencia noticiosa 'Prensa Latina,'" December 26, 1962, DFS, Exp 65-92-62, Leg. 2, Hoja 216, AGN; CIA, "Current Intelligence Weekly Summary: Prensa Latina: Cuban-Backed News Agency," September 3, 1959. CIA-RDP79-00927A002400050001-2, CREST Database, NARA.

[123] "Prensa Latina informe," November 25, 1968, DFS, Versión Pública de Fidel Castro, Leg. 1, Hoja 295 and Exp 65-92-69, Leg. 3, Hoja 132, AGN; "How Castro Pushes 'Hate U.S.' All Over Latin America," *U.S. News and World Report*, May 2, 1960.

[124] "Un Año de 'Prensa Latina.'"

[125] Manuel Rangel Escamilla, "[Prensa Latina offices closed for serving Soviet interests]," December 29, 1960, DFS, Exp 65-91-60, Leg. 1, Hoja 15, AGN; "Prensa Latina: Al servicio de la verdad"; Domínguez, *To Make a World Safe for Revolution*, 269.

[126] "Prensa Latina informe."

[127] "Un Año de 'Prensa Latina.'"

industrialist Guillermo Castro Ulloa, a former president of his country's chamber of commerce.[128] According to an overview of Prensa Latina that the CIA provided to Mexican intelligence officers, Castro Ulloa was in charge of funneling money to and from Cuba to cover the operating costs. In October 1959, the arrangement soured when he pocketed $100,000.[129] Thereafter, funding began coming directly from Havana, frequently through more reliable channels in the Cuban embassies across Latin America.[130] The Soviet and Chinese governments also provided financial and technical support to Prensa Latina.[131]

The international character of Prensa Latina's leadership supported the news agency's claims that it was more than just a Cuban propaganda machine. Among the founders were Argentine journalists Jorge Ricardo Masetti, Jorge Timossi, Rogelio García Lupo, Carlos Aguirre, and Rodolfo Walsh. Colombian writer Gabriel García Márquez, who would later win the Nobel Prize for literature, helped create Prensa Latina and represented the news agency in Bogotá and New York.[132] Peruvian activist Hilda Gadea, Che Guevara's one-time wife, worked for a magazine published by Prensa Latina called *Latin American Economic Panorama*. Mexican journalist Armando Rodríguez Suárez served as a coordinator of the news agency first in Cuba and then in Mexico.[133]

The first director of Prensa Latina, Jorge Masetti, lent significant international prestige to the news agency. The Argentine journalist had traveled to Cuba in 1958 to interview Fidel and Che in the Sierra Maestra. He accepted Che's invitation to return to Cuba for Operation Truth in 1959 and remained on the island in order to help launch Prensa Latina. Masetti's experience working in a similar organization – Juan Domingo Perón's Agencia Latina – made him the ideal person to run Castro's wire service.[134] Masetti recruited such illustrious intellectuals as Jean

---

[128] "Prensa Latina informe"; CIA, "Cuba: Castro's Propaganda Apparatus and Foreign Policy."

[129] "Prensa Latina informe." On the CIA origins of the "Prensa Latina informe" see Enrique Condés Lara, *Represión y rebelión en México (1959–1985)*, Vol. 3 (Mexico City: Miguel Ángel Porrúa, 2009), 173.

[130] CIA, "Agencia Informativa Latinoamericana (Prensa Latina)," April 1960, CIA CREST Database, NARA; Manuel Rangel Escamilla, "[Prensa Latina receiving money from Cuba]," January 30, 1961, DFS, Exp. 12-9-61, Leg. 8, Hoja 39, AGN.

[131] Dumois and Molina, *Jorge Ricardo Masetti*, 51.

[132] "Prensa Latina: Al servicio de la verdad."

[133] "Prensa Latina informe."

[134] Gabriel Rot, *Los orígenes perdidos de la guerrilla en la Argentina: La historia de Jorge Ricardo Masetti y el Ejército Guerrillero del Pueblo* (Buenos Aires: Ediciones El Cielo por Asalto, 2000), 24. Che Guevara had also worked for Agencia Latina during his time

Paul Sartre, Simone de Beauvoir, C. Wright Mills, Carleton Beals, Waldo Frank, and Miguel Ángel Asturias as collaborators.[135] Masetti worked as the general director of Prensa Latina until 1961, when he resigned as a result of political divisions within the organization and decided to dedicate his full attention to revolutionary activities.[136]

Jorge Masetti's career after leaving the news agency illustrates the possible connections between Prensa Latina and Cuba's involvement in foreign revolutions. In early 1961, Masetti began working full-time for Cuba's General Intelligence Department (*Dirección General de Inteligencia*, or DGI).[137] He traveled to Africa soon thereafter, bearing a message from Castro offering aid to the rebel leaders of the Algerian National Liberation Front. They accepted, and the Argentine journalist supervised the delivery of a shipload of weapons from Cuba – the first military aid that Castro sent to Africa. Masetti used his time in Africa to gain training in urban guerrilla warfare, which he intended to put to use in his home country.[138] In 1963, he returned to Argentina with Che's blessing and became "Comandante Segundo," the leader of the People's Guerilla Army operating in the northern province of Salta. Unfortunately for the aspiring revolutionary, his small guerrilla *foco* was no match for the Salta rural police.[139] The first director of Prensa Latina died in April 1964, his uprising a complete failure.

---

in Mexico. Jon Lee Anderson, *Che Guevara: A Revolutionary Life* (New York: Grove Press, 1997), 158.

[135] "Prensa Latina: Al servicio de la verdad." Sartre and de Beauvoir both attended a funeral rally in Havana in 1960 after the explosion of the French freighter Le Coubre in Havana's harbor killed dozens of people. This was the rally where a photographer captured the shot that immortalized Che's image. Gabriella Paolucci, "Sartre's Humanism and the Cuban Revolution," *Theory and Society* 36, no. 3 (May 2007): 245–63. On Prensa Latina's extensive list of collaborators, see also Dumois and Molina, *Jorge Ricardo Masetti*.

[136] It is also possible that Masetti resigned out of frustration with the increasingly large role that the Cuban communist party was assuming in the direction of Prensa Latina, as his son, also named Jorge Ricardo Masetti, later claimed. Jorge Masetti, *In the Pirate's Den: My Life as a Secret Agent for Castro* (San Francisco: Encounter Books, 2002), 9. On the question of Masetti's motivations for resigning, see also Rot, *Los orígenes perdidos de la guerrilla en la Argentina*, 61–5; Dumois and Molina, *Jorge Ricardo Masetti*, 173–81.

[137] Gleijeses, *Conflicting Missions*, 31.

[138] "Prensa Latina: Al servicio de la verdad"; Gleijeses, *Conflicting Missions*, 52; Rot, *Los orígenes perdidos de la guerrilla en la Argentina*, 84.

[139] Gleijeses, *Conflicting Missions*, 101. Masetti used the title "Comandante Segundo" because Che Guevara was supposed to join the group and become "Comandante Primero." Rot, *Los orígenes perdidos de la guerrilla en la Argentina*, 100. On Masetti's

Mexican and U.S. intelligence agents claimed that Jorge Masetti was not the only employee of Prensa Latina involved in clandestine activities. Reports about the news agency's ties to subversion, propaganda, and revolution abounded. Mexican security agents monitored the telegrams that the wire service sent from Mexico to Cuba about such politically sensitive topics as meetings between heads of state, arrests of protestors, and student activism.[140] The director of the Department of Federal Security claimed that the head of the Mexican office of Prensa Latina controlled a radio station at UNAM. Furthermore, he asserted that employees of Prensa Latina were directing a smear campaign against the federal government, agitating the public on behalf of political prisoners.[141] An in-depth CIA report about the organization began: "Prensa Latina is not only a news agency but also an instrument of Castro's government, used to spread propaganda and undertake illicit political activities in foreign countries while at the same time dedicating itself to espionage and other clandestine missions."[142] The report went on to trace connections between Prensa Latina and Cuba's spy apparatus. A disaffected DGI agent declared in his memoirs that the intelligence organization had "virtually taken over" Prensa Latina.[143]

Another Cuban refugee also claimed that the news agency was a cover for spy operations. Pedro L. Roig asserted that the training school for the foreign services – including Prensa Latina – was actually a "school for spies."[144] He described the pivotal day during his own training when Comandante Manuel Piñeiro Losada or "Redbeard," the head of Cuba's intelligence services, visited the training center and shared a state secret with Roig and the other students. "The truth," Piñeiro supposedly confided, "is that you will receive classes to graduate as officials of state security, officials of the glorious G2." According to Roig, many of his

---

guerrilla expedition in Argentina, see also Daniel Jacinto Avalos, *La guerrilla del Che y Masetti en Salta – 1964: Ideología y mito en el Ejército Guerrillero del Pueblo*, 2nd ed. (Salta: Ediciones Política y Cultura, 2005).

[140] Manuel Rangel Escamilla, "[Prensa Latina sending information to Cuba]," October 24, 1960, DFS, Exp 65-92-60, Leg. 1, Hoja 6, AGN; Manuel Rangel Escamilla, "[Prensa Latina sending information about Latin America to Cuba]," July 19, 1961, DFS, Exp 65-92-61, Leg. 1, Hoja 234, AGN. The CIA also monitored Prensa Latina's mail pouch and correspondence. Agee, *Inside the Company*, 531.

[141] Rangel Escamilla, "Investigación acerca de la agencia noticiosa 'Prensa Latina.'"

[142] "Prensa Latina informe."

[143] Castro Hidalgo, *Spy for Fidel*, 106.

[144] Roig, *Como trabajan los espías de Castro*, 45.

fellow students at the so-called spy school went on to join Prensa Latina's "extensive web of espionage."[145]

U.S. politicians expressed a great deal of anxiety about Prensa Latina. In a hearing before the U.S. Senate, the deputy director of the CIA, General C. P. Cabell, fielded a number of questions about the news agency. The Chairman of the Judiciary Committee, James O. Eastland of Mississippi, repeatedly asked whether Prensa Latina was under communist control. While Cabell hesitated to call it a communist organization, he did affirm that "[t]he communists undoubtedly encouraged or even inspired the organization of Prensa Latina, have infiltrated the organization, and have aided it both by providing news and utilizing its services." Attempting to calm the senators' worries about the news agency, the CIA deputy director reassured them, "We are watching it like a hawk."[146]

Similar concerns about Prensa Latina prompted Mexican officials to try to curtail the news service's activities. In March 1960, secret service agents raided the wire service's offices and interrogated the employees.[147] In August 1961, officials arrested a "very dangerous" member of Prensa Latina's staff for carrying weapons in the Mexico City airport.[148] Police detained a man carrying a Prensa Latina credential when they caught him painting "Viva Cuba" in lipstick on public walls immediately following the Cuban Missile Crisis.[149] A Costa Rican man who worked for the news agency accused agents in the Department of Federal Security of apprehending him illegally in front of Prensa Latina's offices in Mexico City. The officials reportedly took the foreigner to a hotel room where they tortured him and told him to confess to illicit activities like arms smuggling and organizing subversive movements. When the Costa Rican journalist refused, the department of immigration deported him.[150]

---

[145] Ibid., 47. The term "G2," copied from the United States, is commonly used to refer to Cuba's intelligence services. Juan Antonio Rodríguez Menier, *Cuba Por Dentro: El MININT* (Miami: Ediciones Universal, 1994), 35.

[146] *Communist Threat to the United States through the Caribbean* (Washington, DC: U.S. Government Printing Office, 1959).

[147] Francisco Tapia Navarro (Agente 83) and Ismael Arciniega Rivera, "Informe sobre la revista 'Prensa Latina,'" March 28, 1960, DFS, Exp 65-92-60, Leg. 1, Hoja 1, AGN.

[148] "[Prensa Latina employee arrested for carrying weapons in Mexico City airport]."

[149] "[Prensa Latina employee detained]," November 3, 1962, DFS, Exp 65-92-62, Leg. 2, Hoja 153, AGN.

[150] "Atormentado y deportado," *Política*, September 15, 1963.

Prensa Latina was one of Fidel Castro's most effective weapons in his war with the United States. It provided newspapers, magazines, and radio stations around the world with an alternative source of news, challenging the United States' and Europe's control over information. In addition, the wire service also operated as a propaganda machine. Favorable news about Cuba and negative portrayals of the United States emanated from Prensa Latina's offices. And finally, the fungibility between the activities of reporting the news and passing along intelligence information meant that the agency likely supported Cuban espionage. The Mexican office of Prensa Latina, in particular, served as an important bridge between the wire service's home in Havana and the rest of its affiliates throughout Latin America. Mexican and U.S. officials believed that Prensa Latina's news network was just one of the many ways that Fidel Castro used Mexican territory as a base for subversive activities in the rest of the Americas.

CONCLUSION

The widespread, though not unanimous, excitement for the Cuban Revolution in Mexico forced the country's leaders to stake out a position. They watched as workers, intellectuals, students, and powerful politicians praised Castro and compared Cuba's revolution to that of Mexico. In order to preempt unfavorable comparisons, President López Mateos seized the initiative and tried to promote the idea that the Cuban Revolution was pursuing goals that the Mexican Revolution had already accomplished. He also adopted a posture of solidarity toward Cuba's leaders, especially President Dorticós.

However, the friendship between the Mexican and Cuban governments was superficial, more performance than substance. At the same time that López Mateos used his country's relations with Cuba to shore up his revolutionary legitimacy and gain leftist support, his intelligence agents were assisting U.S. operations against Castro. Mexican leaders were eager to cooperate with the United States because they believed that the Cubans were creating trouble in Mexico and using their country as a bridge to export revolution to the rest of the continent. Cuban policy toward Mexico was equally utilitarian, and Castro's public statements of friendship with Mexico proved just as superficial as those of López Mateos. While Castro and his collaborators were genuinely grateful to the many Mexicans who enabled and subsequently embraced the

Cuban Revolution, they also were aware of the Mexican government's cooperation with the United States. In addition, Castro, Che, and others had spent time in Mexico, and they had personal connections with groups and individuals there who were separate from, and in some cases opposed to, the government. But most importantly, Castro had higher priorities than developing a true friendship with Mexico's leaders: his quest to protect the Cuban Revolution by expanding it.

3

Mexico's Cold War Heats Up

As the Cuban Revolution became increasingly radical, it polarized Mexico. Castro's success inspired admiration among some sectors, and fear among others. Castro's turn to the Soviet Union, his conflict with the United States, and other Cuban political events had a significant impact on life in Mexico.

Some members of the Mexican population sought to emulate the Cuban Revolution, while others sought to contain it. Leftist groups marveled at Cuba's agrarian reforms, literacy campaigns, and challenges to U.S. imperialism. Conservative groups watched in horror as Castro embraced communism and nationalized all businesses and properties within his reach. New organizations sprang up across Mexico, and protestors took to the streets. Meanwhile, government officials sprang into action to prevent the conflagration that had begun in Cuba from spreading to Mexico. Combatants on all sides of Mexico's Cold War adopted a variety of strategies to build alliances and prepare for battle.

LÁZARO CÁRDENAS AND THE LATIN AMERICAN
PEACE CONFERENCE

Lázaro Cárdenas decided to capitalize upon the popularity of the Cuban Revolution in order to call the world's attention to the problems facing Mexico and the rest of Latin America. In March 1961, he convened the World Peace Movement's Latin American Conference for National Sovereignty, Economic Emancipation, and Peace (or Latin American Peace Conference) in Mexico City.[1] Cárdenas and the other organizers

---

[1] On the founding and objectives of the Word Peace Movement/Council, see *The World Peace Council: What It Is and What It Does* (Helsinki: Information Centre of the

intended to draw international attention to economic conditions in Latin America, denounce the United States' imperialist activities in the region, and defend the Cuban Revolution. "We understand that the defense of Cuba is the defense of Latin America," the announcement of the peace conference declared.[2]

The popular response to the Latin American Peace Conference exceeded the organizers' expectations. The day the meeting began, more than 2,500 delegates from twenty Latin American nations as well as Europe, Asia, and Africa crowded into an auditorium, and at least a thousand additional people listened to the proceedings on loudspeakers installed outside the building.[3] Journalists from around the world attended to provide newspaper and television coverage, and Soviet leader Nikita Khrushchev and Zhou Enlai, Premier of the People's Republic of China, sent telegrams congratulating the organizers. The delegates, most of whom were not officially affiliated with their national governments, spent four days discussing the importance of international solidarity, proclaiming the right of the nations of Latin America to defend their sovereignty, and denouncing the imperialist practices of the United States.

Multiple pro-Cuban speeches set the tone for the rest of the conference. In his welcoming address, Cárdenas lauded the Cuban Revolution and praised its "incorruptible" leaders.[4] Cuban revolutionary veteran Vilma Espín gave a rousing speech about the liberation of her people in which she compared Fidel Castro to Abraham Lincoln and said that the Cuban Revolution demonstrated the vulnerability of imperialism.[5] Espín

---

World Peace Council, 1978); Frederick C. Barghoorn and Paul W. Friedrich, "Cultural Relations and Soviet Foreign Policy," *World Politics* 8, no. 3 (April 1956), 323–44; Bernard S. Morris, "Communist International Front Organizations: Their Nature and Function," *World Politics* 9, no. 1 (October 1956): 76–87; U.S. Department of State, "Soviet Active Measures: The World Peace Council" (Washington, DC: U.S. Department of State, 1985); Patrick Iber, "The Imperialism of Liberty: Intellectuals and the Politics of Culture in Cold War Latin America," PhD diss., University of Chicago, 2011.

[2] "Convocatorio de la Conferencia Pro-Paz," *La Prensa*, January 28, 1961.

[3] Manuel Arvizu, "Dió comienzo la junta de carácter pacifista," *La Prensa*, March 6, 1961; "Nuestra América se reúne," *Política*, March 15, 1961; "[Conferencia Pro-Paz documents]," March 1961, IPS Caja 1475-B, Exp 40–43, AGN; Manuel Rangel Escamilla, "Conferencia Pro-Paz," May 5, 1961, DFS, Exp. 11-6-61, Leg. 2, Hoja 311, AGN.

[4] "Documentos de la Conferencia Latinoamericana por la Soberanía Nacional, la Emancipación Económica y la Paz," *Política*, April 1, 1961.

[5] Espín had worked with Frank País, the urban coordinator of Castro's movement, to help prepare the Cuban Revolution; upon his death, she had taken over command of the urban organization, which served as the second front of the rebel army in the island's eastern cities. Less than a month after the success of the Cuban Revolution, she married

declared that although her country did not export revolutions, it was impossible to contain the power of the island's example. Other delegates lent weight to Vilma Espín's claims. One of Cárdenas's co-presidents of the conference, Argentine professor of engineering Alberto T. Casella, called the Cuban experience an important lesson and inspiring example. Ramón Danzós Palomino, a prominent Mexican agrarian leader, stated that all people and nations could benefit from studying the profound reforms undertaken by the Cubans. Vicente Lombardo Toledano ended his speech with the hope that "the light of the Cuban Revolution may illuminate all of America."[6]

Conference attendees vowed to follow the example of the Cuban Revolution and to defend Cuba from attack. The delegates produced a final declaration, which Cárdenas read at the closing ceremony. "In energetically reaffirming that they will defend Cuba against all aggression," the ex-president stated, "the Latin American people know that they defend their own destiny."[7] The final resolutions of the conference went into further detail on how to protect Cuba. They contained promises to fight all enemies of Castro's government – counterrevolutionaries, mercenaries, and North American imperialists – wherever they were found. The declaration also defended the Cuban people's rights to determine their own government and to seek and accept help from any country of the world.[8]

Conference attendees devoted a similar amount of attention in their speeches and resolutions to the related theme of U.S. imperialism. "Yankee imperialism has returned to the most aggressive forms in its history in its relations with Latin America," Vicente Lombardo Toledano declared. The representative from Paraguay protested her country's "official and permanent intervention" in recent years by the U.S. State Department. The Peruvian delegate denounced his own nation's role as a "peon of Yankee imperialism."[9] Delegates accused the United States of a wide range of crimes, including economic exploitation, military intervention, territorial

---

Raúl Castro, and in August 1960 she founded and became president of the Federation of Cuban Women. Carolina Aguilar Ayerra, *Por siempre Vilma* (Havana: Editorial de la Mujer, 2008).

[6] "Documentos de la Conferencia Latinoamericana por la Soberanía Nacional, la Emancipación Económica y la Paz."

[7] "Declaración de la Conferencia pro Soberanía," *Excélsior*, March 9, 1961.

[8] "Documentos de la Conferencia Latinoamericana por la Soberanía Nacional, la Emancipación Económica y la Paz." "North America" is common Latin American shorthand for the United States. References to "North America" very rarely include Mexico and Canada. "Yankee" is another popular substitute.

[9] Ibid.

conquest, cultural penetration, and support of tyrants. The final declaration of the conference put it plainly: "The fundamental force that blocks the development of Latin America is North American imperialism." The declaration denounced the Monroe Doctrine, the OAS, and the U.S. policies of hemispheric defense and Pan Americanism. It concluded, "North American imperialism has compromised Latin America in the politics of the Cold War."[10]

Cárdenas led some of the delegates in a weeklong tour of Mexico after the conference's closing ceremonies in order to convey their messages to the public. He also wanted to demonstrate to his government that he intended to carry out the conference resolutions. Participants in the tour, including Mexican writer Carlos Fuentes and a number of Cuban visitors, traveled to the states of Querétaro, Guanajuato, Jalisco, and Michoacán. They held meetings and demonstrations attended by thousands of eager listeners. In an article in *Política*, Fuentes described how in Pénjamo, Guanajuato, the "entire city emptied out into the plaza." As Cárdenas descended from his vehicle, the schoolchildren, women, and *campesinos* shouted in a thousand voices, "Viva Cárdenas, who gave us land and freedom!"[11]

Cárdenas told the crowds about the accomplishments of the Cuban Revolution, denounced U.S. imperialism, and criticized the conservative turn that the Mexican government had taken since his time in office. Fuentes wrote that the audience listened fervently to Cárdenas's words and embraced his message. The writer quoted a *campesino* in Pénjamo: "We do not read the press. We only know that in Cuba people are fighting for the same thing we have fought for here in Mexico and that they fight against the same exploiters. That is what we know." According to Fuentes, the mere mention of Cuba was enough to set off enthusiastic ovations and choruses of "Viva!" from the crowds. He described Cárdenas's tour as a "renaissance of the Mexican people."[12] The ex-president spread the energy and message of the conference to his followers across the country, connecting with areas outside the reach of the government-controlled press and inspiring admiration for the Cuban Revolution wherever he went.

President López Mateos did he everything he could to dampen the effects of the Latin American Peace Conference. He did not attend any

[10] "Declaración de la Conferencia pro Soberanía."
[11] Carlos Fuentes, "Siete días con Lázaro Cárdenas," *Política*, April 1, 1961.
[12] Ibid.

part of the conference, nor did he lend his name to any of the documents that it produced. Two months before the opening ceremonies, the president welcomed CIA chief Allen Dulles into his home for a frank conversation about Cuba, communism, and the peace conference. When Dulles observed that Cuba's government was "definitely communist" and thus a problem for all of Latin America, López Mateos heartily agreed. According to a CIA memorandum, the Mexican president described Cárdenas's gathering as "a communist tool." Though López Mateos rejected Dulles's suggestion that he shut down the peace conference, he did promise to do "whatever he could to help the CIA disrupt and hamper" it. He also bragged that Mexico had better facilities for coverage and control than many other Latin American countries.[13]

As López Mateos saw it, U.S. officials could look at the Cuban communist problem as a strictly international matter because there was little chance of "Castroism" having any effect within the United States. In Mexico, by contrast, Castroism was "a domestic political problem" because of a large body of sympathy for Castro and his revolution. Mexicans' emotional identification with the Cuban Revolution, López Mateos explained, "had to be weighed in all actions concerning Cuba." The Mexican president added that even though he personally would like to see Castro overthrown, the Cuban leader's popularity in Mexico was such that he could take no overt action.[14]

Dulles and his subordinates in the CIA found López Mateos's arguments about domestic pressures convincing. A month after the conversation, the CIA produced a special working paper on the attitudes of Latin American countries toward Cuba that reflected the president's remarks. The report put Mexico in the category of "countries that for domestic reasons [appear] either unwilling or unable to come out openly against Castro." The CIA contended that "leading officials in Mexico [who] would like to see the Cuban dictator done away with" were hindered by "Mexico's leftist revolutionary heritage, the nation's traditional policy of staying out of inter-American disputes, the extreme political liability of seeming to follow the U.S. lead, and the strong sympathy of a few weight-swinging politicians for things Cuban and Communist."[15]

---

[13] "Meeting between López Mateos and Dulles," January 14, 1961, RG 263 CIA Miscellaneous Files JFK -M-7 (F1) to JFK -M-7 (F3) Box 6. JFK-MISC 104-10310-10001, NARA.

[14] Ibid.

[15] CIA, "Attitudes of Other Latin American Governments toward Cuba," February 13, 1961, CIA CREST Database, NARA.

While López Mateos expressed his concerns in private, the president of the PRI was publicly dismissive of Cárdenas's peace conference. In a meal with foreign journalists immediately following the gathering, PRI president Alfonso Corona del Rosal described the sectors represented at the conference as an absolute minority of the Mexican population. When asked about Cárdenas's role, the party spokesman stated: "I respect General Cárdenas as an ex-president of our party, but regarding his behavior in this congress I leave all judgment to what his own conscience dictates as a citizen and as a Mexican."[16] By minimizing the conference to the press and implying that its chief organizer would have to answer to his conscience for his actions, Corona del Rosal attempted to limit its impact both in Mexico and abroad. Indeed, the PRI leader's statements might have been an element of President López Mateos's promises to "disrupt and hamper" the peace conference.

Mexico's main newspaper chains refused to print paid publicity for the peace conference, much to Cárdenas's disgust. In his journal, Cárdenas wrote in January 1961 that the organizers had sent the program for the conference to *Excélsior* and *Novedades* to be printed as a paid advertisement. The secretary to the editor of *Novedades* had promised to print it, but the next day informed the conference organizers that the editing chief had ordered the suspension of the advertisement. Cárdenas remarked cynically: "So this is how the owners of newspapers such as *Novedades* and *Excélsior* honor freedom of the press."[17] None of the biggest newspapers – *Excélsior, Novedades,* and *Universal* – ever published any of the documents produced by the conference. Journalists from the leftist magazine *Política* promoted the theory of a government-imposed blanket of silence. They reported learning that the major press outlets had received orders from López Mateos's private secretary to publish nothing about the conference, neither in favor nor against it.[18]

Cárdenas and the other organizers of the conference did not blame the Mexican government, however. In a meeting with the international press, Cárdenas stated that the pressures of "imperialism" were impeding the coverage of the major newspapers. Journalist Jorge Carrión reportedly said that the U.S. State Department spent more money silencing the press than the organizers had spent putting on the conference.[19] Carlos Fuentes

[16] "El PRI anhela tener un rival poderoso, no importa si es de izquierda o derecha," *Excélsior*, March 10, 1961.
[17] Cárdenas, *Obras: Apuntes 1957/1966*, Vol. 3, 186.
[18] "Soberanía Nacional y Paz," *Política*, March 1, 1961.
[19] "[Conferencia Pro-Paz documents]."

blamed the members of the press, accusing them of "criminally abstaining from informing the public."[20] It is likely that the conservative interests of the wealthy owners of the major newspapers coincided with those of the Mexican and U.S. governments, and that the press was all too willing to limit coverage of the conference. An agreement based on shared interests rather than force is especially likely because the Mexican government's control over the press, while significant, was not complete. Other newspapers and magazines such as *Política, La Prensa, El Popular, El Diario de México, El Diario de la Tarde, ¡Siempre!,* and *El Fígaro* provided neutral or positive coverage of the gathering. However, with the exception of *La Prensa,* these newspapers and magazines had a much smaller readership and circulation than *Excélsior, El Universal,* and *Novedades.*

At the same time that the Mexican government was limiting the public's knowledge of the Latin American Peace Conference, it was collecting vast amounts of information for its own benefit. Agents from both the Department of Federal Security and the Department of Political and Social Investigations composed hundreds of pages of reports on the events, which they submitted to Minister of the Interior Gustavo Díaz Ordaz. One fifteen-page memorandum written by IPS agents provides vivid evidence of the fear and hostility that Mexican security forces felt toward the peace conference. The report stated that all of the foreign delegates were of the extreme left and fervent followers of the Soviet Union, "red China," and Fidel Castro. The agents claimed that the Cuban government had contributed "extremely large" quantities of money to finance the meeting; Cuban contributions reportedly included a 150,000 peso payment from the Cuban ambassador in Mexico to conference organizers and unspecified "large sums" paid directly to Lázaro Cárdenas by a special emissary from Havana.[21]

Mexican intelligence agents depicted the peace conference as a significant threat to Mexico's stability. The authors of the IPS memorandum warned that the Cuban participants were taking advantage of the conference to encourage subversion and revolution throughout Latin America. The report claimed that the twenty-eight Cuban delegates exhorted the other foreign and Mexican attendees "to work, each in his own country, to <u>OVERTHROW</u> governments of the bourgeoisie and <u>substitute them</u> with Fidel-style regimes."[22] The Cubans supposedly promised moral and

---

[20] "Nuestra América se reúne."
[21] "[Conferencia Pro-Paz documents]."
[22] Ibid. Emphasis in original.

material aid to fellow revolutionaries. Intelligence agents also submitted a summary of a so-called Secret Agreement signed by Lázaro Cárdenas and all the presidents of the various delegations. The conference leaders reportedly agreed to "the initiation of SABOTAGE ON A GRAND SCALE, ON A PERMANENT BASIS, IN EVERY COUNTRY OF LATIN AMERICA, AGAINST BUSINESSES, PROPERTIES AND GENERAL INTERESTS OF NORTH AMERICAN IMPERIALISM."[23]

What worried the writers of the memo even more than Cuban machinations, however, was the growing power of Lázaro Cárdenas. At least half of the IPS report was devoted to the former president and his role in the proceedings, describing him as the "indisputable and undisputed" central figure of the conference. According to the IPS agents, "The Congress, in spite of the silence of the press and other media, WAS A HUGE SUCCESS. The figure of CÁRDENAS HAS NOW REACHED GIGANTIC PROPORTIONS." The authors of the report also speculated about Cárdenas's plans to start a new political party in Mexico to rival the PRI. The agents described Lázaro Cárdenas as extremely powerful, popular, and dedicated to the "Fidelization of [Latin] America."[24]

According to Mexico's intelligence services, the Latin American Peace Conference did not in reality seek peaceful, nonviolent ways to pursue national sovereignty and economic emancipation. The agents portrayed the gathering as a meeting of communists and other extreme leftists, coming together to plot revolution, subversion, and destruction. They spared no ink in their efforts to elucidate the threat that conference attendees, especially Lázaro Cárdenas, could pose to the Mexican government if they so desired.

Intelligence agents were not the only ones worried about Cárdenas and the leftist threat. The Mexican National Anticommunist Party held its first convention in Mexico City on the same four days as the peace conference. The leaders of the group even changed the dates of their gathering so as to coincide.[25] The president of the Anticommunist Party claimed in his memoirs that the idea for the rival conference came directly from President López Mateos.[26] *Excélsior* reported that hundreds of people from across Mexico, mostly of humble origins, gathered for the anticommunist meeting.[27] Writers from *Política* retorted that most of the

[23] Ibid. Emphasis in original.
[24] Ibid.
[25] Manuel Rangel Escamilla, "Conferencia Pro-Paz," May 5, 1961, DFS, Exp. 11-6-61, Leg. 2, Hoja 311, AGN.
[26] Guerra Leal, *La grilla*, 156.
[27] "Comenzó ayer la junta del Partido Anticomunista: Atacaron a Cárdenas e hicieron un desfile sobre las banquetas," *Excélsior*, March 6, 1961, 4–5.

attendees "of the humble class" were only there because they were paid to attend.[28]

Multiple conservative groups launched vitriolic attacks against the Latin American Peace Conference. The speakers at the anticommunist convention criticized Cárdenas and other "bad Mexicans who allow communism to enter our country and corrode our customs and traditions."[29] Advertisements in *La Prensa* and *Atisbos* signed by "a group of Latin American delegates to the [peace] conference" mocked Cárdenas's gathering and demanded national sovereignty for the nations within the Soviet orbit.[30] The ads denounced the "peace" that reigned in Hungary and Tibet (areas occupied by the Soviet Union and the People's Republic of China), along with the "peace" of Soviet concentration camps, Chinese communes, and Cuban "*paredones*."[31]

Church leaders also joined in the efforts to malign the peace conference. On the first day of the conference, clergy in Mexico City churches distributed religious images on cards with a message on the back. The cards described the Latin American Peace Conference as "a communist farce that seeks to destroy Mexican sovereignty" and exhorted Mexicans to open their eyes to the betrayal and deceit. The message concluded with a prayer. "Sacred Virgin of Guadalupe, Queen of Peace, Empress of America: Defend us from the enemy!"[32]

The reaction in the United States to an international conference that denounced U.S. imperialism was also decidedly negative. Shortly after the closing ceremony, the U.S. Senate Judiciary Committee held a hearing to investigate and invited Dr. Joseph F. Thorning, a professor of Latin American history, associate editor of *World Affairs*, and author of multiple books on communism and Latin America, to provide testimony. Thorning called the conference a propaganda show and accused the organizers of attempting to promote the "political enslavement of all the American Republics under a Soviet regime, economic thralldom as a part of the Soviet economic juggernaut, and internecine warfare throughout the Western Hemisphere." He warned the Senate that the Latin American Peace Conference sought

---

[28] "Nuestra América se reúne," 15.

[29] "Comenzó ayer la junta del Partido Anticomunista: Atacaron a Cárdenas e hicieron un desfile sobre las banquetas," 4–5.

[30] "Conferencia Latinoamericana por la Soberania Nacional, por la Emancipacion Económica y por la Paz," *La Prensa*, March 5, 1961, 8.

[31] In the Cuban context, *paredón* (literally, "large wall") was shorthand for the wall against which victims of firing squads stood to be executed. Castro's government received a great deal of international criticism for sending prisoners to the *paredón*.

[32] "Nuestra América se reúne," 15.

to stir up "Fidel Castro-type revolutions" through active Soviet intervention. Thorning claimed that Lázaro Cárdenas had proven himself "most
effective" in carrying out Soviet directives and policies.[33]

The CIA also suspected that the Soviets were the driving force behind the
Latin American Peace Conference. The agency considered the World Peace
Council one of the most important and comprehensive "Soviet-sponsored
international communist fronts."[34] A CIA memo tied the Latin American
Peace Conference to a proposal for a People's Congress for Latin America
that emerged from the 1959 international communist party congress in
Moscow. According to the CIA, the Soviets planned to have prominent
leftist figures in the region – including Cárdenas – overtly sponsor the
gathering in order to camouflage communist participation. "Cárdenas's
reputation may give the conference a substantial anti-U.S. propaganda
impact," the intelligence agency warned.[35] In the CIA's view, the peace
conference aimed to take advantage of Latin American nationalism in
order to spread anti-U.S. and pro-Soviet sentiment.

Fidel Castro, meanwhile, responded to the Latin American Peace
Conference with what would turn out to be excessive enthusiasm. In late
March, he gave a speech at a banquet in Havana in which he praised
the meeting that had just taken place in Mexico. In an attempt to warn
U.S. leaders that an invasion of Cuba would risk igniting a continental
war throughout the Americas, Castro claimed that Lázaro Cárdenas had
sworn that peasants across Mexico were ready to take to the mountains
to defend the Cuban Revolution.[36]

Castro's claim about the Mexican *campesinos* provoked an immediate backlash in Mexico. Headlines blared: "Castro Ruz Threatens Total
War" and "Castro Believes He Has the Support of Spanish America."[37]

[33] U.S. Senate Committee on the Judiciary, *Cuban Aftermath – Red Seeds Blow
South: Implications for the United States of the Latin American Conference for National
Sovereignty and Economic Emancipation and Peace* (Washington, DC: U.S. Government
Printing Office, 1961), 3.

[34] CIA, "The World Peace Council: A Soviet-Sponsored International Communist Front,"
December 1971. CIA-RDP78-02646R000600220001-7, CREST Database, NARA.

[35] CIA, "Pro-Communist 'Peace' Conference to Meet in Mexico," February 23, 1961, CIA
CREST Database, NARA.

[36] Fidel Castro Ruz, "Castro Warns against Hemispheric War" (LANIC Castro Speech
Database, March 25, 1961), http://lanic.utexas.edu/project/castro/db/1961/19610325
.html (accessed March 14, 2015).

[37] Robert Berrellez, "Castro Ruz amenaza con 'guerra total': Dice que en México cuenta
con el apoyo del General Cárdenas," *Excélsior*, March 27, 1961; "Castro cree tener
el apoyo de Iberoamérica: Los campesinos irán a la montaña si EU lo ataca, afirma,"
Excélsior, March 26, 1961.

Editorialists described his statements as ravings, and leaders of *campesino* organizations called Castro a liar and his statements absurd.[38] The head of the Mexican Federation of Agricultural Organizations accused Castro of interfering in Mexico's internal politics. The president of the Mexican Anticommunist Party filed a complaint with the attorney general about Cárdenas, using Castro's speech as evidence that the ex-president had committed treason.[39] The furor grew so great that Cárdenas had to step in. He sent a statement to *Excélsior* condemning the disproportionate reaction to Castro's speech and explaining that Castro's claims were not the ravings of a madman, but rather were firmly rooted in the final declarations of the Latin American Peace Conference. Furthermore, Cárdenas attested that during his postconference tour of Mexico, he had indeed heard avowals of support for Cuba from various sectors of the population. There was therefore nothing wrong with Castro's statement; the negative news coverage consisted of "speculations at the margins of reality." Cárdenas dismissed the Anticommunist Party's accusations as well, describing them as false charges that would self-destruct.[40]

Cárdenas's defense of Castro elicited palpable gratitude in Cuba. The Cuban embassy in Mexico City forwarded a signed copy of his declarations to the Ministry of International Relations in Havana, and newspapers across the island reprinted the text of the ex-president's letter to *Excélsior*.[41] The semiofficial newspaper *Revolución* accompanied Cárdenas's declaration with a four-page photo spread of his tour of the Mexican interior following the peace conference. The text and images displayed the Mexican public's admiration for both their ex-president and for Cuba. The subtitle to a photograph of a group of *campesinos* proclaimed: "In these young people the significance of our revolution acquires extraordinary dimensions: they become excited at the mere mention of Cuba or Fidel Castro."[42] The newspaper's editors tried to use Cárdenas's words and images to reinforce Castro's claims that Mexicans would defend Cuba from attack.

[38] "Los desvaríos de Fidel Castro," *Excélsior*, March 28, 1961; "Califican de absurdo la declaración de Castro, de que en México será defendido," *Excélsior*, March 28, 1961.
[39] "Consignación del General Cárdenas a la Procuraduría," *Excélsior*, March 27, 1961.
[40] "Habla Lázaro Cárdenas," *Excélsior*, March 31, 1961.
[41] [Letter from José Antonio Portuondo to MINREX], April 7, 1961, América Latina, México, 1959–62, Ordinario: 1961, MINREX; "Latinoamérica defendería a Cuba, ratifica Cárdenas: Riposta a ataques de lacayos contra Fidel," *Revolución*, April 1, 1961; "Difusión a la declaración de Lázaro Cárdenas," *Novedades*, April 2, 1961.
[42] Lisandro Otero, "Con tata Lázaro por los caminos de México," *Revolución*, April 1, 1961.

In addition, Castro decided to soften his declarations about the loyalties of the Mexican *campesinos*. Less than two weeks after his controversial speech, he granted a predawn interview to a Mexican journalist, during which he clarified his relationship with the Mexican government and people. "I said that the Mexican campesinos would rise against imperialism," Castro explained, "never against the government of Mexico, for whose president we feel all the respect he deserves." He maintained that he had no reason to interfere in Mexico's internal affairs, because the two governments enjoyed friendly relations. Castro reiterated his gratitude for the warm welcome that President Dorticós had received in Mexico the previous year and called President López Mateos "the most dedicated defender of the principle of nonintervention."[43] The Cuban leader did everything he could to smooth the feathers he had ruffled with his impulsive statements.

Ironically, Lázaro Cárdenas's peace conference helped escalate the tensions and the violence of the Cold War in Mexico, Cuba, and the United States. The conference's bold demonstration of both nationalism and solidarity, and the attendees' vows to defend the Cuban Revolution, demanded a response. The Mexican government, the host but not the target, was able to answer with a combination of repression and condemnation. U.S. leaders, however, as the object of the vast majority of the criticism, believed that they had to respond more forcefully. The conference called attention to the desires of many Latin Americans to emulate the Cuban Revolution and impelled the U.S. and Mexican governments to recognize the popularity – and danger – of Castro's example.

MEXICO AND THE BAY OF PIGS INVASION

By the time that the Latin American Peace Conference came to a close, the CIA and White House were already committed to their most forceful response yet to the Cuban Revolution – the Bay of Pigs invasion. During the 1960 presidential elections, John F. Kennedy had campaigned as a dedicated Cold Warrior, promising the American public that he would eliminate the Castro-communist threat from the hemisphere. Upon entering office, he inherited plans for an invasion of Cuba that the CIA had drawn up and begun implementing under Dwight Eisenhower. Kennedy found himself under a tremendous amount of pressure to approve the ill-conceived scheme; the potential for reward was too great, as was the

---

[43] Fernando F. Revuelta, "Semana Santa en La Habana," *Novedades*, April 5, 1961.

fear of appearing weak if he backed out. When weighing the risks of the invasion, Kennedy and the other U.S. officials who approved the plan ignored warnings that their actions would have a significant impact on third-party countries, including Mexico. Undersecretary of State Chester Bowles cautioned Secretary of State Dean Rusk that if the invasion went forward, "there will be riots and a new wave of anti-Americanism throughout Latin America."[44]

At one point, Mexico's president had secretly considered aiding the Bay of Pigs invasion. When the CIA realized that the air base that it had constructed in Retalhuleu, Guatemala, was too far from Cuba to serve for tactical air operations by B-26 aircraft, they began looking elsewhere. According to a memorandum composed by the CIA, President López Mateos had "indicated a willingness" to allow the invasion forces to use the air field at Cozumel, an island off the coast of Mexico's Yucatán Peninsula, for limited staging operations over a forty-eight-hour period. The organizers considered this offer unsatisfactory for their purposes and eventually found more willing collaborators in Nicaragua.[45] López Mateos might have predicted that his minimal offer of cooperation would be rejected; it is possible that his indication of willingness was merely a hollow gesture of appeasement rather than genuine enthusiasm.

As the U.S.-trained troops began landing on Cuban shores, the Mexican government publicly condemned the violation of Cuba's national sovereignty. López Mateos initially tried to avoid taking sides by calling for national unity in Mexico and describing the events in Cuba as a "civil war," but he soon clarified his position after witnessing the public's outrage. A few days after the invasion began, he reminded a group of academic and artistic leaders that his government had already defended Cuba on numerous occasions. "I want to declare," he promised them, "that for the rest of my time in office, this posture will not change."[46] The Ministry of Foreign Relations issued a statement that "the government of Mexico reiterates its firm adhesion to the principle of nonintervention."[47]

---

[44] Bowles to Rusk, March 31, 1961, FRUS 1961–3, X: 178–81. Rusk expressed his opposition to the plan to Kennedy in the days leading up to the invasion, as did Senator J. William Fulbright and Arthur Schlesinger Jr.

[45] CIA, "Record of Paramilitary Action Against the Castro Government of Cuba," May 5, 1961. CIA-RDP85-00664R000700150001-8, CREST Database, NARA.

[46] "México contra toda ayuda a una guerra civil en Cuba," *El Nacional*, April 19, 1961, 1; "La nación: Cuba en México," *Política*, May 1, 1961.

[47] "Ningún mexicano podrá ir a pelear," *Excélsior*, April 19, 1961.

López Mateos's stance won the respect not only of his own citizens, but also that of the wider Latin American community. Telegrams of support flooded into his office by the hundreds. The leadership of the Popular Socialist Party "warmly supported the international policy of the regime," while faculty from UNAM congratulated the president on his declarations in defense of Cuba. The authors of another telegram wrote that this was the first time that they had felt moved to contact their government "in order to congratulate you very warmly for your vibrant and clear declaration of support for our brother country of Cuba."[48] President Miguel Ydígoras Fuentes of Guatemala and President Rómulo Betancourt of Venezuela also sent messages to López Mateos, asking him to intercede with the Cuban government to prevent the execution of prisoners captured during the invasion.[49]

Mexico's delegate to the United Nations, Luis Padilla Nervo, went a step further than the rest of his government in his defense of Cuba. Padilla Nervo proposed that the global assembly bypass the OAS and call upon all UN member states to avoid letting their territories be used to foment civil war in Cuba.[50] U.S. Ambassador to Mexico Thomas C. Mann remarked in a message to Dean Rusk that Padilla Nervo was "a Cárdenas man," and had probably pushed for the resolution in defiance of direct orders from the Foreign Ministry to support a different proposal from seven other Latin American countries that would send the Bay of Pigs matter to the OAS. "Our estimate is that Padilla is probably playing up to Mexican public opinion and that Adolfo López Mateos's fear of Cárdenas is such that he will not take decisive action to bring Padilla into line on this issue," Mann explained.[51]

Cuban observers also concluded that the Mexican government's protests against the invasion had more to do with domestic concerns than international principles. The Department of Latin American Affairs (Dirección de Asuntos Latinoamericanos) in Havana composed a report about the response in Mexico, observing, "Mexico's position, without

---

[48] "[Telegrams of Support for Mexico's Defense of Cuba]," April 1961, IPS Caja 1456 A, AGN.

[49] Miguel Ydígoras Fuentes, "[Telegram from President of Guatemala to López Mateos]," April 26, 1961, Gallery 3, Presidential Collection of Adolfo López Mateos [hereafter ALM] 559.1/2, AGN; Rómulo Betancourt, "[Telegram from the President of Venezuela to López Mateos]," September 29, 1961, Gallery 3, ALM 559.1/2, AGN.

[50] "Iniciativa de México sobre Cuba en la ONU: Pide al mundo que no se fomente la guerra civil," *Excélsior*, April 19, 1961.

[51] Thomas Mann, "Mann to SecState," April 21, 1961, U.S. State Department Files Microfilm (24,461), 712.00/4-2161, Nettie Lee Benson Latin American Collection.

doubt, is extremely favorable to the [Cuban] Revolution." The percep-
tive author or authors of the report cautioned that the Mexican declarations about nonintervention were, however, a double-edged sword that
could later be used to condemn any aid that the socialist countries might
offer to Cuba. The report concluded that Mexico's government "adopts
this posture of conditional support for the [Cuban] Revolution because
it fears that if a direct attack of imperialism against Cuba did occur
and if [the Mexican government] made statements criticizing socialist
aid, the people would accelerate their process and a revolution would
explode in Mexico."[52]

The Bay of Pigs invasion did in fact ignite a political conflagration
in Mexico. Thousands of people, including Lázaro Cárdenas and David
Álfaro Siqueiros, requested permission to travel to Cuba to defend the
island from attack. From his cell in Lecumberri Prison, the famous muralist sent a telegram to López Mateos in which he explained that his experience as a soldier in the Mexican Revolution and the Spanish Civil War
"demands that I leave now for Cuba, the country that leads the current
democratic revolution of Latin America and that is today assaulted by
Yankee imperialism."[53] Members of the Popular Socialist Party and the
Mexican Communist Party signed a list of volunteers who were ready
to go to Cuba, calling themselves the Francisco Villa Brigade after the
Mexican revolutionary hero.[54] Recruitment centers to send volunteers to
Cuba sprang up around the country, from the UNAM campus in Mexico
City to Ciudad Madero in Tamaulipas to Tuxpan, Veracruz.[55]

When President López Mateos threatened to revoke the citizenship of anyone who left to fight in Cuba, members of the public found
other ways to express their solidarity. The head of the Department of
Federal Security reported that the PCM was printing pro-Castro propaganda for distribution across the country.[56] Numerous groups and

[52] Dirección de Asuntos Latinoamericanos, Departamento "A," "México: Posición favorable en los círculos oficiales ante la agresión," April 25, 1961. América Latina, México,
1959–62, Ordinario: 1961, MINREX.

[53] "Ningún mexicano podrá ir a pelear."

[54] Cap. Lemuel Burciaga, "Informe relativo a actividades pro-Castristas," April 21, 1961,
DFS, Exp 100-6-3-61, Leg. 2, Hoja 5, AGN; Fernando Gutiérrez Barrios, "PPS Semana
de Homenaje a la Revolución Cubana," July 20, 1967, DFS, Exp 11-2-67, Leg. 19, Hoja
1, AGN.

[55] Francisco Rabatte, "[Telegram from Jefe de Migración in Tampico to Secretaría de
Gobernación]," April 22, 1961, IPS Caja 1456 A, AGN.

[56] Manuel Rangel Escamilla, "Información sobre el estado de Coahuila," April 21, 1961,
DFS, Exp 100-6-3-61, Leg. 2, Hoja 1, AGN.

individuals followed Cárdenas's example and issued declarations to the
national media. A broad coalition of organizations including Othón
Salazar's Revolutionary Teachers' Movement, the University Student
Federation (Federación Estudiantil Universitaria), the National Council
of Railroad Workers (Consejo Nacional Ferrocarrilero), the Mexican
Peace Movement, the Latin America Movement, the Democratic Union
of Mexican Women, and the PCM published an ad in *Novedades* that
expressed their desire "to support the valiant people of Cuba, in their
unequal battle against the greatest imperial power in history."[57] A group
of seventy-eight professors in UNAM's School of Economics issued a declaration that called upon the Mexican government and public to continue
their support of Cuba, concluding "The Cuban cause is also our own."[58]

Of course, not everyone in Mexico condemned the Bay of Pigs invasion. *Excélsior* ran an editorial on April 18 that portrayed the exile troops
as an army of liberators sent to free the island from the "communist tyr-
anny of Fidel Castro." The author of the piece predicted:

If the Cuban people triumph in the glorious enterprise of reestablishing in their
homeland the rule of liberty and law, and extract the claw that has thrust red
imperialism into their midst, then the threatening presence of the totalitarian
monster in America will have passed like a horrible nightmare; but if, on the contrary, the liberation attempt that has just begun in Cuba fails, then the horizon of
all the countries of our hemisphere will darken and turn red.[59]

The PAN issued a statement that said that the Cuban exiles were acting within their rights to use violent methods to overthrow the regime
that was oppressing their country. The National Sinarchist Union (Union
Nacional Sinarquista) criticized groups like the PPS that were organizing contingents to send to Cuba. "Young Mexicans are not meat for
exportation," they declared. The head of the National Anticommunist
Party called upon all "good Mexicans" to resist the lure of foreign doctrines, reminding them they had their own principles clearly engraved in
Mexico's constitution.[60]

Cuban exile groups in Mexico resorted to prayer in their efforts to
assist the invasion. The women's section of the Revolutionary Democratic
Front organized a special mass on the night of April 21 at the Saint
Augustine Church in Mexico City to pray for the speedy recovery of their

---

[57] Círculo de Estudios Mexicanos et al., "¡Solidaridad con la Revolución Cubana!,"
   Novedades, April 22, 1961, 12.
[58] "Profesores universitarios con Cuba," *Novedades*, April 22, 1961, 12.
[59] "Cuba en su hora de crisis," *Excélsior*, April 18, 1961, sec. Editorial.
[60] "Opiniones en Pro," *Novedades*, April 18, 1961, 10.

homeland. An overflow crowd of a thousand people attended the event, where they received copies of the U.S. State Department's White Book on Cuba.[61] A week later, Cuban exiles worked with the Sinarquist Union to organize a procession that ended at the Basilica of Guadalupe. Some two thousand people participated in the march, singing hymns and carrying a banner that pleaded: "Virgin of Guadalupe, intercede for us. Save Cuba and all of America from communism."[62]

These events were overshadowed, however, by the vastly larger and louder demonstrations denouncing the Bay of Pigs invasion. Somewhere between thirty thousand and eighty thousand people participated in a protest march in downtown Mexico City on April 18, which culminated with a speech by Lázaro Cárdenas in the Zócalo.[63] Prior to Cárdenas's arrival, the marchers reportedly burned an effigy of Uncle Sam while chanting "Cuba Sí, Yankees No!"[64] Campesino leader Rubén Jaramillo and his wife Epifania Zúñiga spoke at a rally in Cuernavaca, where they denounced the invasion and praised Castro's economic reforms.[65] General Heriberto Jara presided over a gathering of more than two hundred people in Veracruz; at the back of the room hung a banner that read: "People of Veracruz, do not forget that the Yankees invaded us twice and stole half our national territory. They want to do the same thing to Cuba that they did to us."[66] According to the magazine *Política*, more than one million people across the country, in large cities and small towns alike, participated in protesting the invasion.[67]

Many of the demonstrations escalated into riots and vandalism, as the violence in Cuba spread to Mexico. Three thousand soldiers armed with bayonets stood by as police in Mexico City used tear gas and clubs to break up a demonstration of thirty thousand students who threatened to burn U.S. flags and a swastika-bedecked effigy of Kennedy.[68] Groups

---

[61] Manuel Rangel Escamilla, "Exiliados políticos cubanos," April 21, 1961, DFS, Exp 12-9-61, Leg 8, Hoja 125, AGN.

[62] "Política interior: Mitin en la Basílica," *Política*, May 15, 1961.

[63] "La nación: Cuba en México."

[64] Manuel Rangel Escamilla, "Manifestación estudiantil de apoyo a Cuba," April 18, 1961, DFS, VPLC, Leg. 2, Hoja 168, AGN.

[65] Padilla, *Rural Resistance in the Land of Zapata*, 199.

[66] Consulado General de la República de Cuba en Veracruz, "Acto de solidaridad del pueblo veracruzano en pro de Cuba," April 19, 1961, América Latina, México, 1959–62, Ordinario 6: 1961, MINREX.

[67] "El país, con Cuba," *Política*, May 1, 1961.

[68] "Para impedir que quemaran la bandera de EEUU, la policía disolvió la manifestación estudiantil," *Novedades*, April 22, 1969, 1; Leddy, "Mexican Police Break up Bay of Pigs Demonstrations," April 22, 1961, U.S. State Department Files Microfilm, 712.00/4-2261, Nettie Lee Benson Latin American Collection.

of students in Nuevo León, Jalisco, and Michoacán attacked buildings
associated with the United States, including newspaper offices, consulates, and cultural exchange institutes.[69] In Puebla and Chihuahua, clashes
between pro-Castro and anti-Castro groups intensified into drawn-out
battles in which numerous participants were injured and even killed.
Política accused the bishop of Chihuahua of fomenting the violence
by arming high school students with sticks, stones, bottles of acid, and
Molotov cocktails.[70] In Puebla, police intervention in a protest against
the Bay of Pigs invasion sparked rioting and a university reform movement. The students split into two factions that expanded outward beyond
the university, sharply polarizing local society.[71] The CIA claimed that
communist university students had led the attacks in Michoacán and that
a pro-Castro group behind the agitation in Puebla had issued a manifesto proclaiming "the Socialist Republic of Puebla."[72] The manifesto
also supposedly announced that the student movement was the first step
toward the establishment of a "26th of July Movement" in Mexico.[73]
The army eventually had to occupy the city to put an end to the conflict.

Cuban officials were overjoyed with the outpouring of public outrage that they witnessed in Mexico. The Department of Latin American
Affairs carefully documented the many manifestations of support for
Cuba that they witnessed, describing the student demonstrations, the declarations by workers' groups and Rubén Jaramillo, the efforts on the part
of Vicente Lombardo Toledano to recruit people to send to the island,
and the actions taken by Lázaro Cárdenas.[74] The Cuban Consulate in
Veracruz composed a memorandum about a demonstration that the
Committee of Solidarity with Our Sister Republic of Cuba had organized, in which the author or authors recounted the kind messages that

[69] Eric Zolov, "¡Cuba Sí, Yanquis No! The Sacking of the Instituto Cultural México-
Norteamericano in Morelia, Michoacán, 1961," in *In from the Cold: Latin America's
New Encounter with the Cold War*, ed. Gilbert M. Joseph and Daniela Spenser
(Durham, NC: Duke University Press, 2008), 214–52; "Mitin estudiantil de apoyo a
Castro, en Monterrey N.L." *Novedades*, April 20, 1961, 11.
[70] "Chihuahua: Agresión sinarquista," *Política*, May 15, 1961.
[71] "La nación: Y detrás de Puebla ... ?," *Política*, May 15, 1961. See also Nicolás Dávila
Peralta, *Las santas batallas: El anticomunismo en Puebla* (Puebla: Litografía Magno
Graf, 2001), 107–17; Pansters, *Politics and Power in Puebla*, 97–124.
[72] CIA, "Pro-Castro Demonstrations by Mexican Students," June 2, 1961, CIA CREST
Database, NARA.
[73] CIA, "Mexico," June 2, 1961, CIA CREST Database, NARA.
[74] Dirección de Asuntos Latinoamericanos, Departamento "A," "México: Posición favorable en los sectores populares ante la agresión," April 25, 1961. América Latina, México,
1959–62, Ordinario: 1961, MINREX.

numerous speakers had sent to the people of Cuba and the audience's cheers of "Cuba Sí, Yankees No!"[75]

Ultimately, the Bay of Pigs invasion did much more damage to Mexico and the United States than Cuba. The failed attack on Castro backfired by strengthening Kennedy's enemies and weakening his allies. Widespread outrage in Mexico prompted thousands, possibly millions, of people to take to the streets to protest the United States' violation of Latin American sovereignty. Disagreement between those opposed to the Cuban Revolution and those inspired by it flared into violent confrontations that took their toll in lives and property. The Bay of Pigs invasion deepened preexisting divisions in Mexican society and prompted people on both sides to take action.

NEW LEFTIST ORGANIZATIONS: THE NATIONAL
LIBERATION MOVEMENT, THE INDEPENDENT
CAMPESINO CENTER, AND THE NATIONAL CENTER
OF DEMOCRATIC STUDENTS

The Latin American Peace Conference and the Bay of Pigs invasion that followed on its heels inspired Mexicans on both ends of the political spectrum to begin organizing in earnest. Just as the government had "institutionalized" the Mexican Revolution, members of civil society tried to create new institutions to solidify the alliances that they had formed in response to international and domestic pressures. Observers in the Mexican government watched anxiously as new leftist organizations threatened to upset Mexico's vaunted stability.

Government leaders' fears of leftist cooperation began to materialize with the formation of the National Liberation Movement (Movimiento de Liberación Nacional, or MLN) in 1961. Participants in the Latin American Peace Conference, including Lázaro Cárdenas and Vicente Lombardo Toledano, formed the MLN to enact the gathering's resolutions. Their wide range of goals encompassed electoral transformation, rejection of North American imperialism, liberation of political prisoners, economic emancipation of *campesinos* and workers, and defense of the Cuban Revolution. Nearly two hundred founding members from across the country met in August 1961 in Mexico City, where they formed a national committee and agreed on a program of action.

[75] Consulado General de la República de Cuba en Veracruz, "Acto de solidaridad del pueblo veracruzano en pro de Cuba."

The members of the National Liberation Movement worked to unite
all of the scattered leftist groups in Mexico under the umbrella of their
organization. They reached out to intellectuals, *campesinos*, workers, students, artists, communists, socialists, and moderates. They held educational sessions and demonstrations, papered the country with pamphlets
and posters, and published their own magazine called *Liberación*, which,
one intelligence agent claimed, "[had] a magnificent reception in political circles, student groups, workers' associations, and among the general
public interested in the political development of the country."[76] One year
after the formation of the MLN, another intelligence agent reported that
the group had more than sixty thousand members distributed in 230
local committees across the nation.[77] The head of the movement, Alonso
Aguilar Monteverde, claimed that the MLN had more than three hundred thousand members in six hundred committees.[78]

However, the National Liberation Movement's greatest claim to
power was not its numbers, but its leadership – especially that of Lázaro
Cárdenas. The former president spoke at the founding meeting of the
movement, exhorting the members of the audience to unite and defend
their interests in an organization that would help achieve the goals of
the Mexican Revolution.[79] *Política* magazine published an interview with
Cárdenas in which he avowed: "I am in complete solidarity with the
National Liberation Movement, and I will be as long as I live."[80] The
ex-president delivered the closing address before a thousand people at
the MLN's first national convention in October 1963, declaring that the
movement would take part in the civic battle to reform Mexico's electoral system. He also took the opportunity to reiterate his support for
"Cuba's glorious revolution."[81]

Cárdenas declared that he was a member of the movement, not a
leader; but any level of association between the former president and
the MLN was enough to attract affiliates.[82] More than eight hundred

[76] José Jiménez García, "[MLN magazine]," September 2, 1965, DFS, Exp 11-6-65, Leg. 15,
Hoja 94, AGN.
[77] Hector Fierro García, "[MLN meeting]," July 10, 1962, DFS, Exp 11-6-62, Leg. 7, Hoja
178, AGN.
[78] Gastón Martínez Rivera, *La lucha por la democracia en México*, 57.
[79] "La nación: Liberación nacional," *Política*, August 15, 1961.
[80] Roberto Blanco Moheno, "Comunista: Una palabra que no debe espantarnos," *¡Siempre!*,
December 13, 1961.
[81] "El MLN se reúne," *Política*, October 15, 1963.
[82] Manuel Rangel Escamilla, "[L. Cárdenas's connections to MLN]," January 21, 1963,
DFS, VPLC, Leg. 3, Hoja 24, AGN.

campesinos and workers gave Cárdenas a warm ovation when he spoke at the opening ceremonies of the movement's regional assembly in Zamora, Michoacán.[83] The director of the Department of Federal Security wrote a report about an MLN meeting in Mexico City in which a member described Cárdenas as the head of the organization. At the same meeting, a representative from Xochimilco attested: "General Lázaro Cárdenas instills us with courage, and we are at his orders."[84]

Security agents worried that Cárdenas would use his connections with the National Liberation Movement to create trouble for the government. Military intelligence reported that the former president gave movement leaders in Baja California instructions for agitation.[85] The director of the Department of Federal Security claimed that Cárdenas promised to aid a strike movement in a metal factory, on the condition that the union members join the MLN.[86] Lázaro Cárdenas's relationship with the National Liberation Movement was mutually beneficial; his status attracted members and attention to the movement, and in return he gained the manpower necessary to push for the causes close to his heart.

Cárdenas had multiple contentious conversations with López Mateos about the National Liberation Movement. In October 1961, toward the end of a meeting with the president, Cárdenas raised the subject of police hostility toward MLN members in Jalisco. "From what do they seek liberation?" López Mateos inquired. Cárdenas tried to defend the group's aims but confided to his journal: "In reality, Licenciado López Mateos does not sympathize with the organization."[87] At another meeting two months later, Cárdenas tried again to defend the MLN. He explained that the movement was neither a political party nor an enemy of López Mateos's administration. Finally, the president gave his word that as long as the members of the organization stayed within the limits of the nation's constitution, no one would bother them. "I hope so, Mr. President," Cárdenas replied as he left.[88]

---

[83] "Don Lázaro habló en la asamblea del Movimiento de Liberación en Zamora," *La Voz de Michoacán*, May 29, 1962. See also Manuel Rangel Escamilla, "[Cárdenas's involvement with the MLN], May 31, 1962, DFS, VPLC, Leg. 2, Hoja 336, AGN.

[84] Manuel Rangel Escamilla, "[National Liberation Movement]," December 3, 1961, DFS, Exp 11-6-61, Leg. 5, Hoja 194, AGN.

[85] General de División Comandante Hermenegildo Cuenca Díaz, "Actividades del MLN en Baja California," July 1962, IPS Caja 1475-A, Exp 27, AGN.

[86] Manuel Rangel Escamilla, "[National Liberation Movement]," December 19, 1961, DFS, Exp 11-6-61, Leg. 6, Hoja 1, AGN.

[87] Cárdenas, *Obras: Apuntes 1957/1966*, Vol. 3, 243–6.

[88] Ibid., 255.

One of the many causes that the National Liberation Movement shared with Lázaro Cárdenas was defense of the Cuban Revolution. Members led educational seminars about the achievements of the Cuban Revolution, held large celebrations to celebrate the anniversary of Castro's assault on the Moncada Barracks every 26th of July, published manifestos and articles about Cuba, and organized rallies whenever Castro's government came under verbal or physical attack. Cuban diplomats and Mexican intelligence agents alike attended these events and submitted detailed reports and photographs to their superiors.[89]

In fact, the Mexican government kept a close watch on all of the National Liberation Movement's activities. Intelligence agents monitored the movement's mail, telegrams, and telephones.[90] They collected samples of the group's posters, fliers, press bulletins, and newspapers. They photographed the movement's offices and compiled biographical information about its leaders. They assembled lists of people who attended meetings or made financial contributions to the MLN.[91] Other government functionaries aided the surveillance efforts: a member of Congress reported to Minister of the Interior Díaz Ordaz on the movement's activities, as did prominent employees of the Ministry of Defense.[92] Intelligence agents also tried to bribe employees of the MLN. In late October 1962, officials

---

[89] Consul Marián García Pérez to Director of Dirección de Asuntos Latinoamericanos, "Enviando fotografías de la celebración del 26 de Julio en este consulado," August 7, 1962, América Latina, México, 1959–1962, Ordinario 6: 1962, MINREX; Manuel Rangel Escamilla, "[MLN gathering in support of the Cuban Revolution]," November 15, 1962, DFS, Exp 11-6-62, Leg. 9, Hoja 85, AGN; Fernando Gutiérrez Barrios, "[MLN conference about Cuba]," July 19, 1965, DFS, Exp 11-6-65, Leg. 14, Hoja 287, AGN; Manuel Rangel Escamilla, "[MLN meeting about the Cuban Missile Crisis]," October 23, 1962, DFS, Exp 11-6-62, Leg. 8, Hoja 243, AGN; "Elementos del MLN que forman parte del Comité Pro-Solidaridad con Cuba elaborando el perioódico mural en el local que ocupa el Movimiento de Liberación Nacional," October 10, 1961, DFS, Exp. 11-6-62, Leg. 6, Hoja 85, AGN.

[90] For examples of surveillance, see DFS, Exp 11-6-62, Leg 6. More evidence of phone tapping is available in MLN leader Jorge L. Tamayo's letters to the DFS, in Jorge L. Tamayo, *Obras de Jorge L. Tamayo*, Vol. 9: Cartas (Mexico City: Centro de Investigación Científica Jorge L. Tamayo, 1986).

[91] "Personas que apoyan al MLN," November 14, 1963, DFS, Exp 11-6-63, Leg. 11, Hoja 143, AGN.

[92] Dip. Lic. Arturo Moguel Esponda, "Actividades del MLN," September 20, 1963, IPS Caja 1475-A, Exp 1, AGN; Francisco Ramírez Palacios, "Organización del MLN en Durango," October 11, 1961, IPS Caja 2964 C, AGN; General de División Comandante Hermenegildo Cuenca Díaz, "Informe sobre las actividades que ha desarrollado en la Entidad el Lic. Jorge Moreno Bonet, miembro destacado del Movimiento de Liberación Nacional," February 2, 1963, IPS Caja 2963 A, AGN. Cuenca Díaz became Minister of Defense in 1970.

from the Department of Federal Security went to the house of Ricardo Martínez Tapia, a typist for the movement. They offered to pay him twice his monthly wages from the MLN for information. Martínez answered evasively, saying he did not want to complicate his life, and the agents concluded that the typist was lazy and lacked ambition. They held out hope that with a little more work and persuasion, they could eventually convince him to spy on his employers. The agents resolved to continue cultivating their potential informant and following his activities.[93]

Members of the public also displayed concern about the liberation movement. In 1962, the League of Agrarian Communities and Campesino Syndicates of Zitácuaro, Michoacán, wrote to López Mateos complaining about the MLN. "Allow me to communicate to you the great labor of agitation that has been taking place within the Agrarian Communities of this region by the party of National Liberation," read the letter. "[The movement] has been causing disorientation, confusion, and, as a consequence, division among the *campesinos* that later may become a serious problem."[94] According to the outraged agrarian league of Zitácuaro, the MLN was spreading propaganda and inviting *campesinos* to meetings and gatherings, all with the collusion of the town mayor. A year later, the Federation of Workers and Campesinos of the Region of Chietla wrote to López Mateos to denounce the activities of the National Liberation Movement and Mexican Communist Party in Puebla. The letter warned that the MLN and PCM, in cooperation with Lázaro Cárdenas and functionaries from the Department of Agrarian Affairs, were "undertaking a labor of disorientation" against the government's agrarian program.[95] According to the federation, the subversive groups were organizing demonstrations and fabricating census documents. These letters and others indicated to Mexican leaders that concern about the MLN was not limited to government officials and employees but was widespread among the public as well.

Another former president of Mexico, Emilio Portes Gil (1928–30), added to the chorus when he publicized his misgivings about Cárdenas and the National Liberation Movement. The two ex-presidents exchanged a heated series of open letters in 1962 and 1963, beginning when Portes Gil accused the MLN of following orders from the Kremlin

[93] Juan Varas Buere and Luis Ramirez López, "Contacto con miembro del MLN," November 8, 1962, DFS, Exp 11-6-62, Leg. 9, Hoja 71, AGN.
[94] "[Letter to López Mateos complaining about MLN in Michoacán]," June 19, 1962, ALM 433/408, AGN.
[95] "[Letter about MLN agitation in Puebla]," February 7, 1963, ALM 542.2/210(3), AGN.

to deviate the course of the Mexican Revolution.[96] After Cárdenas published his own letter defending the movement, Portes Gil responded by charging him with attacking the Mexican regime at the Latin American Peace Conference.[97] An editorial in *Excélsior* the following day praised Portes Gil and claimed that the country was divided into two fronts: "the patriotic front, purely Mexican and constitutional, over which presides Dr. Adolfo López Mateos, possessing as its principle the ideology of the Mexican Revolution; and the communist front, over which, exactly as Portes Gil describes, Cárdenas reigns."[98] In a third and final letter, Portes Gil called Cárdenas an instrument of international communism and accused him of trying to undermine the regime and stage a new revolution.[99]

Meanwhile, intelligence agents speculated that the National Liberation Movement was the first step in a leftist plan to form a new political party. The head of the Department of Federal Security reported that the leaders of the MLN were holding meetings with other leftists to discuss the possibility of creating a new electoral coalition.[100] Another agent simply referred to the movement as "Alonso Aguilar Monteverde's newly formed party."[101] A commander in the Ministry of Defense claimed that the goal of the MLN was to "form a party in open opposition to the legally formed government."[102] Lázaro Cárdenas's involvement with the MLN added fuel to the fire, as government agents already suspected the ex-president of harboring electoral designs. Intelligence officers relayed rumors that his son, Cuauhtémoc Cárdenas, was preparing to run for president with the support of the MLN.[103] A member of the movement in Acapulco reportedly told his companions that if Cuauhtémoc decided to

---

[96] Emilio Portes Gil, "El cuarto informe presidencial y el Movimiento de Liberación Nacional," *Política*, October 1, 1962. Reprinted from *El Universal*, September 14, 1962.

[97] "Portes Gil pide a Lázaro Cárdenas que rectifique su actitúd," *Ovaciones*, January 10, 1963.

[98] "La carta de Portes Gil," *Excélsior*, January 11, 1963.

[99] Emilio Portes Gil, "Portes Gil lanza otra andanada de graves cargos a Cárdenas," *Ovaciones*, January 24, 1963.

[100] Manuel Rangel Escamilla, "[MLN discussing possibility of forming new leftist party]," April 5, 1963, DFS, Exp 11-6-63, Leg. 10, Hoja 10, AGN.

[101] Capitán de la Barreda, "[National Liberation Movement]," December 13, 1961, DFS, Exp 11-6-61, Leg. 5, Hoja 291, AGN.

[102] Cuenca Díaz, "Actividades del MLN en Baja California."

[103] "[Rumor that Cuauhtémoc Cárdenas might run for president]," March 31, 1963, DFS, Exp 100-6-3-63, Leg. 1, Hoja 90, AGN; "[Rumor that Cuauhtémoc Cárdenas might run for president]," August 27, 1963, DFS, Exp 11-141-63, Leg. 3, Hoja 62, AGN.

run, they would have to unite and "battle physically to raise him to that high post."[104]

Other Mexican government officials worried that the liberation movement was involved in even more insidious activities. An army general in Baja California sent a report to the Secretary of National Defense claiming that the MLN was distributing guerrilla manuals to students in a deliberate effort to incite an armed movement against the government.[105] A congressman sent Díaz Ordaz a report from the chief of Special Services of Pemex about subversion within Mexico's state-owned petroleum company. The report warned that a local MLN leader in Reynosa, Tamaulipas, was an engineer in Pemex's Department of Security and Hygiene. The petroleum intelligence chief suspected the engineer of distributing communist propaganda and organizing opposition to the government amongst the workers.[106] The Chief of the Presidential Guard of the Ministry of National Defense submitted a report to Díaz Ordaz about MLN activities in the state of Sinaloa in 1962, claiming that a local newspaper called *El Liberal* was practicing "agitation and social dissolution." The newspaper of "communist tendencies" was supposedly trying to drive a wedge between the public and the army according to the dictates of a preconceived plan. An informant had seen the local head of the MLN and owner of *El Liberal* meeting with the MLN's national leaders in the editorial offices of the paper. The source also suspected that the newspaper owner was receiving propaganda from the movement as well as instructions on the formation of shock brigades and the fabrication of Molotov cocktails.[107] The Chief of the Presidential Guard claimed in his report that the Sinaloa newspaper's acts of "social dissolution" had caused "throughout the region, a climate of agitation and antagonism between people and organizations." He attributed tensions between various local workers' groups to the news of "insidious slander" and calls for dissolution printed on a regular basis in *El Liberal*.[108] The security chief painted a frightening picture of unbridled leftist agitation in Sinaloa. By

104 "[Rumors that Cuauhtémoc Cárdenas might run for president]," September 8, 1963, DFS, Exp 100-10-3-63, Leg. 1, Hoja 78, AGN.
105 General de División Comandante Hermenegildo Cuenca Díaz, "Actividades del MLN en Baja California," July 1962, IPS Caja 1475-A, Exp 27, AGN.
106 Dip. Antonio García Rojas, "[MLN activities in Reynosa, Tamaulipas]," August 1, 1962, IPS Caja 1475-A, Exp 27, AGN.
107 Miguel Hernández Palacios, "[Subversive activities in Sinaloa]," November 10, 1962, IPS Caja 2898 A, AGN.
108 Hernández Palacios, "[Subversive activities in Sinaloa]."

specifically warning about social dissolution in his report, he also provided the government with legal grounds for prosecuting the owner of
the newspaper.

U.S. officials were also worried about the National Liberation
Movement and its impact on Mexico's domestic politics and international relations. Observers in the U.S. embassy and the CIA consistently referred to the MLN as a "rabidly anti-United States, pro-Cuba
Communist front."[109] A CIA memorandum described Lázaro Cárdenas
as the secret head of the organization.[110] U.S. intelligence agents believed
that the MLN received support from the Cuban and Soviet embassies and
consulates.[111]

When leftist leaders associated with the National Liberation
Movement began forming a new agrarian organization in 1963 called
the Independent Campesino Center (Central Campesina Independiente,
or CCI), they sparked a nationwide uproar.[112] In January 1963, more
than a thousand people from across the country, claiming to represent
five hundred thousand previously unaffiliated *campesinos*, gathered in
Mexico City for the CCI's constitutional congress.[113] A newspaper article quoted one of the leaders of the CCI who stated that the organization would unite more than a million people who were not members
of the National Campesino Confederation.[114] Over the course of three
days, the founders of the new organization hammered out their goals
and composed a "Call to the Nation," exhorting the *campesinos* to seize
control over their own destinies. The center set out to reinvigorate the
agrarian aims of the Mexican Revolution as exemplified by Cárdenas's

---

[109] E.g., see CIA, "National Liberation Movement Plans in Connection with Approaching
Visit of President Kennedy," June 9, 1962, National Security Files, Trips and Conferences,
Box 237, John F. Kennedy Presidential Library, Boston, Massachusetts [hereafter JFK
Library].

[110] CIA, "Communist Plan to Protest the Visit of President Kennedy," May 26, 1962. Papers
of President Kennedy, National Security Files, Trips and Conferences, Box 237, JFK
Library.

[111] "Castro's Subversive Capabilities in Latin America," November 9, 1962, National
Security Files, National Intelligence Estimates, Box 9, LBJ Library.

[112] The CCI was affiliated with the MLN and many of the same people led both groups,
but it was not a tool of the movement, as many critics claimed at the time. "La Central
Campesina Independiente y el Movimiento de Liberación Nacional," *Política*, January
15, 1963.

[113] DFS agents estimated that one thousand people attended, while *Política* maintained that
more than two thousand participated. Manuel Rangel Escamilla, "[Lázaro Cárdenas
and the CCI]," January 6, 1963, DFS, Exp 11-136-63, Leg. 1, Hoja 1, AGN; "Nace una
Central," *Política*, January 15, 1963.

[114] "Constitución de la Central Campesina Independiente," *Ovaciones*, January 7, 1963.

presidency. Their demands included landownership, improved access to water and credit, unionization of agricultural workers, and improved education and social security. "Through the independent and combative unification of the campesinos and the alliance of the working class," they declared, "we will continue forward, in spite of the obstacles and the attacks and WE WILL TRIUMPH for the good of the campesinos and of Mexico."[115]

Cuban officials kept a close watch on the new *campesino* group from the beginning. At the request of Foreign Minister Raúl Roa, diplomats collected copies of the CCI's "Call to the Nation" and another pamphlet titled "The Independent Campesino Center: What It Is and What It Fights For" and sent them back to Havana.[116] The person in the Cuban embassy who processed the CCI's documents underlined various sections, including one that read, "With fifty years of distance from the armed battle for land, the land is once again concentrated in the hands of a few individuals."[117] Rather than seeing Mexico's revolution as an example to emulate, the Cubans looked to their neighbors for lessons in what not to do.

Lázaro Cárdenas's involvement with the Independent Campesino Center drew particular attention from all observers. When he arrived to speak at the group's constitutional congress, the entire audience rose to their feet, applauding deliriously. A chant of "Cár-de-nas! Cár-de-nas! Cár-de-nas!" filled the air. The former president spoke to the assembly, declaring his support for the CCI and describing the organizers' motivations as noble and patriotic.[118] The CCI plastered a quote from Cárdenas on all of its publications and posters: "Campesino: If the organization to which you belong does not defend your interests, abandon it."[119] A member of the Popular Socialist Party who wrote a letter to the Cuban ambassador about the CCI and other matters called Cárdenas the "leader of the campesinos" and "our Fidel."[120]

The announcement of the formation of the Independent Campesino Center prompted a tidal wave of criticism in Mexico. Editorials in *Excélsior* called the organization a "pro-Soviet communist trap" and

---

[115] "Nace una Central." Emphasis in original.
[116] Ramón Sinobas to Ministro de Relaciones Exteriores Raúl Roa, February 5 1963, América Latina, México, 1963–7 Ordinario 7: 1963, MINREX.
[117] CCI, "Que es y porque lucha el Central Campesina Independiente," América Latina, México, 1963–7 Ordinario 7: 1963, MINREX.
[118] "Nace una Central."
[119] E.g., see "[CCI letterhead]," n.d., DFS, Exp 11-136-64, Leg. 4, Hoja 350, AGN.
[120] Macario González Mireles to Mexican Ambassador and Consuls and Radio Habana, April 1, 1963, América Latina, México, 1963–7 Ordinario 7: 1963, MINREX.

described its leaders as "extremist Castro-communist militants."[121] The editorialist claimed that many of the speeches at the convention were subversive and frank challenges to the national government. The *Excélsior* writer also called the CCI "political blackmail" and asserted "its leaders are trying to submit us to a 'peasant' dictatorship."[122] The conservative newspaper *El Sol de Monterrey* claimed that most of the *campesinos* who attended the CCI's convention were indigenous people who did not speak Spanish and thus could not have understood what they were doing.[123]

Many of the critics of the Independent Campesino Center directed their venom at Lázaro Cárdenas, the symbolic head of the organization. A congressman from Puebla called the ex-president "ungrateful, Machiavellian, and unpatriotic."[124] An editorial in *Excélsior* contended that as the chief organizer of the National Campesino Confederation, Cárdenas was betraying his legacy by supporting the new group.[125] Ex-president Emilio Portes Gil, who had published a series of letters to Cárdenas criticizing his participation in the National Liberation Movement, returned to his soapbox. Portes Gil said that his fellow ex-president was destroying his own prestige, claimed that he was attacking President López Mateos, and called him "an instrument of international communism."[126]

The chorus of critics included other groups and leaders who had their own connections to the Mexican Revolution. General Heriberto Jara, one of Cárdenas's closest friends, spoke out against the new *campesino* group. *Excélsior, Ovaciones,* and *El Nacional* published a declaration by the Agrarian Old Guard, a group of many of the founders of the National Campesino Confederation, which accused the CCI of being antiagrarian and unpatriotic.[127] "Cárdenas is dedicated to drawing away power and

---

[121] "Trampa comunista para campesinos: Futurismo político prosoviético," *Excélsior,* January 8, 1963; "La nueva Central Campesina, guiada por Cárdenas, se perfila como partido político," *Excélsior,* January 7, 1963.

[122] "El gran chantaje político; Quién da el dinero a los 'campesinos'?," *Excélsior,* January 9, 1963.

[123] "Termina hoy asamblea de izquierdistas mexicanos," *El Sol de Monterrey,* January 8, 1963.

[124] "Nace una Central."

[125] Luis Chavez Orozco, "Cárdenas, negación de sí mismo?," *Excélsior,* January 11, 1963.

[126] Emilio Portes Gil, "Portes Gil lanza otra andanada de graves cargos a Cárdenas," *Ovaciones,* January 24, 1963.

[127] Vieja Guardia Agrarista de México, "A la clase campesina," *Excélsior,* January 9, 1963; "Declaración de la Vieja Guardia Agrarista de México," *El Nacional,* January 9, 1963; Homero Bazan Viquez, "La Vieja Guardia contra los que apoyan la nueva central: Que se trata de dividir al pueblo en una maniobra de ocultos fines," *Ovaciones,* January 9, 1963.

fomenting divisions," claimed Rafael Carranza, a senator from Coahuila and the son of revolutionary hero Venustiano Carranza.[128] Emiliano Zapata's son, head of the Zapatista Front of the Republic, exhorted the *campesinos* to ignore the CCI.[129]

The leading leftist political party in the country also opposed the new *campesino* organization. By the time that the CCI came onto the scene, Vicente Lombardo Toledano had withdrawn his Popular Socialist Party from the National Liberation Movement and returned to the government fold. As a result, he did not respond favorably to the attempt to create a new organization that would challenge the government's control over the peasantry. Lombardo Toledano sent a statement to the national press, calling the CCI "a new act of division inspired in the old and sick sectarianism of the Communist Party."[130]

Government leaders took a dismissive approach to the Independent Campesino Center – at least, in public. Gustavo Díaz Ordaz told reporters that the members of the new *campesino* group were simply making use of their constitutional right to free assembly.[131] The editors of government-mouthpiece *El Nacional* advised their readers not to worry about the CCI, because it would soon become obvious that the group was unnecessary and ineffective.[132] President López Mateos publicly belittled the CCI when, during a trip to France, he faced questions from journalists about the new *campesino* group. "The CCI is not at all important," he responded, "the small grouping could be considered the 'Battalion of Loose Pieces.'"[133] The trivializing nickname was a reference to the center's claims that they were not trying to steal members away from the National Campesino Confederation but merely providing an organization for those *campesinos* that did not yet belong to any other group. The leaders of the CCI did not appreciate López Mateos's slight and, at a celebration of the twenty-fifth anniversary of Cárdenas's nationalization of the petroleum industry, proudly declared that their so-called Loose-Piece Battalion counted more than 1.3 million members.[134]

---

[128] "Nace una Central."

[129] Ibid. On Nicolás Zapata's betrayal of his father's revolutionary legacy, see John Womack, *Zapata and the Mexican Revolution* (New York: Vintage Books, 1970), 379–85.

[130] "Rojo Gómez y Lombardo contra los cismáticos: El PPS dice que la CCI es obra del enfermizo sectarismo del PC," *Excélsior*, January 9, 1963.

[131] "Los integrantes de la CCI hacen uso de un derecho," *Ovaciones*, January 8, 1963.

[132] "La política de la realidad agraria," *El Nacional*, January 14, 1963.

[133] *Presencia internacional de Adolfo López Mateos*, Vol. 1, 431.

[134] "El 'Batallón de sueltos'," *Política*, April 15, 1963, 9–10.

The Independent Campesino Center used its large membership to influence the government on political and economic issues. The organization frequently organized public demonstrations as a pressure tactic. One of the largest took place in Puebla in 1964 on behalf of a union of milk producers against a new law of obligatory pasteurization. Three thousand people gathered to protest the law and local police responded violently, arresting more than one hundred people. The next day, students gathered to denounce the repression and again the authorities interfered. Intelligence agents reported that the activist students followed the direct orders of "rabid communists."[135] Street demonstrations and confrontations between police and protestors continued for the next two weeks, until the army stepped in, the state governor resigned, and the interim governor revoked the controversial pasteurization law.[136] This victory and others demonstrated the CCI's ability to mobilize opposition to the government.

Security forces' surveillance of the Independent Campesino Center reveals the fear that the group inspired. A description of a CCI meeting in Coahuila from the Ministry of National Defense related numerous quotes from members of the center. One of the speakers reportedly told the 150 people assembled that "the Independent Campesino Center is an organization of combat." A female speaker exhorted the *campesinos* to "stop behaving so meekly and start behaving like men." If weapons were being used to enslave them, she argued, they could also be used to liberate them. Another speaker foretold the overthrow of the government and the installation of a socialist republic, a mission, he claimed, which the CCI was born to fulfill. One of the national leaders of the CCI, Ramón Danzós Palomino, reportedly swore to lead his followers in arms against the "government of the bourgeoisie." A *campesino* leader called López Mateos's program of agrarian reform "pure falsehood and lies" and maintained that it "would never equal the agrarian work of Lázaro Cárdenas." Another speaker contrasted the Mexican government's expenditures of public monies to widen avenues in Mexico City with the Cuban government's support of agriculture.[137] It was clear that the Cuban Revolution had overtaken and replaced the Mexican one in the eyes of the CCI's members.

---

[135] "Universidad Autónoma de Puebla," June 8, 1964, IPS Caja 444, Exp 1, AGN.

[136] "Puebla: Victoria del pueblo," *Política*, November 1, 1964.

[137] General Francisco Ramírez Palacios, "[CCI meeting]," November 9, 1963, IPS Caja 2851 A, AGN.

At the end of the report about the *campesino* meeting, the author, a general in the Mexican army, laid out his conclusions and recommendations regarding the Independent Campesino Center:

The communist leaders [of the CCI] are practicing frank, subversive agitation against the Government, the Army, and other Institutions, and are the real cause of the land invasions in different States of the Republic; for which, in the opinion of this Superiority, they should be consigned to the Judicial Authorities and punished according to the Law, which would serve as an example to correct this dangerous agitation among campesinos and workers whom this Center is trying to unify.[138]

Other members of the government's security services corroborated this claim that the CCI was dangerous. Agents of the Department of Federal Security attributed land invasions to CCI leadership and reported on the organization's efforts to provide legal defense for imprisoned *campesinos*.[139] They also read the group's mail and told their superiors about meetings between Lázaro Cárdenas and leaders of the organization.[140] The intelligence that López Mateos and Díaz Ordaz received about the Independent Campesino Center corroborated what they read about the group in the press. In their eyes, the CCI was a communist-dominated organization determined to undermine the government's control over the nation's *campesinos*.

The same year that agrarian activists created the Independent Campesino Center, the city of Morelia hosted the first congress of the National Center of Democratic Students (Central Nacional de Estudiantes Democráticos, or CNED), a new organization that would become one of the most important student groups in 1960s Mexico. It united young activists from across the country, encouraging them to engage in political protests and coordinating their efforts. Intelligence agents kept a close watch on the CNED and blamed the organization for much of the activism among students.

The Mexican Communist Party spearheaded the effort to create the CNED when its leaders saw a need for a broad coalition in the universities. Members of the Mexican Communist Youth group began organizing

---

[138] Ibid.

[139] "[List of invasiones de tierras]," February 29, 1964, DFS, Exp 11-136-64, Leg. 4, Hoja 290, AGN; Manuel Rangel Escamilla, "[CCI efforts on behalf of arrested campesinos]," October 31, 1963, DFS, Exp 11-136-63, Leg. 4, Hoja 73, AGN.

[140] Manuel Rangel Escamilla, "[CCI letter to Cárdenas]," October 30, 1963, DFS, Exp 11-136-63, Leg. 4, Hoja 70, AGN; "[CCI activities]," May 7, 1963, IPS Caja 2935 A, AGN.

the CNED in Mexico City in 1961. One of the leaders of the effort from outside the capital was a member of the MLN from Baja California named Rafael Aguilar Talamantes. Prior to the founding conference in 1963 in Morelia, Aguilar Talamantes spent two or three months canvassing the Pacific coast of Mexico to spread the word to some seventy schools.[141]

The conference of the CNED that took place in Morelia in 1963 marked the organization's debut on the political scene. Two hundred and fifty delegates attended, claiming to represent one hundred thousand students across the country.[142] They hammered out a "Declaration of Morelia" in which they demanded "popular and scientific education" based on "concrete humanism, which sees the real person, the worker, the campesino, the laborer subjugated to the exploitation of his daily tasks … the humanism that tends to transform the socioeconomic structure to the benefit of the masses."[143] Their call to arms exhorted students across the nation to unite in a democratic, pluralist organization independent of government control. Perhaps some of the authors of the CNED's "Declaration of Morelia" had been inspired by the Students for a Democratic Society's "Port Huron Statement," produced the previous year.[144] Despite the shared emphasis on democracy and humanism, the Mexican student group was significantly more militant than the U.S. student group, as illustrated by the CNED's slogan – "fight while studying."

Although the CNED originally purported to be an ideologically pluralist coalition, the communists soon used their numerical majority to dominate the organization. According to one student leader, "the Communist Party of Mexico, instead of reinforcing consensus, instead of negotiating, applied the old rule of imposition, ruling by majority to present its own point of view as the official stance of the organization."[145] As a result, most of the other members withdrew from the CNED and the group essentially became a student wing of the Communist Party.

Intelligence agents and police connected the CNED to student activism across the country. Reports from the Judicial Police claimed that

[141] Raúl Álvarez Garín and Gilberto Guevara Niebla, *Pensar el 68* (Mexico City: Cal y arena, 1988), 27. Álvarez Garín was one of the leaders of the CNED and helped write the group's Declaration of Morelia.

[142] Rivas O., *La izquierda estudiantil en la UNAM*, 282.

[143] Ibid. Annex 9, 779–84.

[144] Jeremi Suri, ed. *The Global Revolutions of 1968: A Norton Casebook in History* (New York: W. W. Norton, 2007), 40.

[145] Guevara Niebla, *1968: Largo camino a la democracia* (Mexico City: Cal y arena, 2008), 167. See also Jardón, *1968*, 17; Carr, *Marxism and Communism in Twentieth-Century Mexico*, 230.

members of the organization planned to stir up trouble in Veracruz. They also blamed CNED organizer Rafael Aguilar Talamantes for directing a student movement in the northern part of the country.[146] Agents from the Department of Political and Social Investigations tied Aguilar Talamantes to student uprisings in Puebla and Michoacán, as well as agitation within the National Autonomous University and the National Polytechnic Institute.[147] The head of the Department of Federal Security relayed a student leader's claim that the CNED "controlled twenty-two schools or faculties of the UNAM, that is, seventy-five percent of the student body."[148] Another intelligence agent noted that the CNED cooperated with a group called the Federation of Socialist Campesino Students of Mexico (Federación de Estudiantes Campesinos Socialistas de México, or FECSM) in the rural teaching colleges across the country.[149]

The MLN, CCI, and CNED were three of the most significant efforts in decades to challenge the government's hold over the country. They all attracted members by capitalizing upon widespread discontent with Mexico's institutionalized revolution and enthusiasm for Cuba's genuine revolution. Though the organizations used peaceful methods to pursue their quests for reform, observers in the media and the security forces suspected that the leftists were preparing to take more drastic measures. However, it was actually conservative groups and agents of the government who were the first to resort to calculated violence.

CONSERVATIVE BACKLASH

Conservative sectors of the Mexican population also responded to the Cuban Revolution by forming new organizations. Religious groups, politicians, businessmen, and conservative students across Mexico created their own public and clandestine groups. Though some of these organizations limited themselves to peaceful methods of influence, others embraced the use of violence.

---

[146] Policía Judicial Federal and Agente #383, "[Communist student agitation]," March 16, 1965, GDO 203 (122), AGN; Policía Judicial Federal, "Central Nacional de Estudiantes Democráticos," April 5, 1965, GDO 203 (122), AGN.

[147] "Antecedentes de elementos del Partido Comunista Mexicano: Rafael Aguilar Talamantes," April 19, 1965, IPS Caja 2892 A, AGN.

[148] Fernando Gutiérrez Barrios, "[PCM connections with students]," June 15, 1966, DFS, Exp 11-4-66, Leg. 16, Hoja 293, AGN.

[149] "[CNED activities, plans to control students]," September 15, 1966, DFS, Exp 11-142-66, Leg. 2, Hoja 190, AGN.

Naturally, the Catholic Church was one of the leaders of the anticommunist charge. The Church's opposition to Marxist ideology predated the Cold War; Pope Leo XIII had rejected communist solutions to the problems of poverty and inequality in his 1891 papal encyclical *Rerum Novarum*, and over the years his successors continued to develop and deepen the Church's opposition to communism.[150] Most Church leaders in Mexico embraced the doctrinal line set out in Rome as they gradually recovered from the anticlericalism of the Mexican Revolution and the violence of the Cristero Rebellions.[151] Following President Manuel Ávila Camacho's (1940–6) confession of his Catholic beliefs in 1940, the Church began taking a more active role in Mexican politics and reasserting its position at the center of Mexican society. A shared dedication to anticommunism helped bridge the divisions between Church and state and served as the basis for cooperation.[152]

The Cuban Revolution and Castro's subsequent alignment with the communist bloc appalled Mexican religious leaders: conflicts between Church and state in Cuba stirred painful memories of the Mexican Revolution at the same time that they demonstrated the threat that the Cold War posed to the Catholic Church in Latin America. Events in Cuba gave new urgency to the preexisting fight against communism, and Catholic leaders sought to prevent the spread of Castro's godless revolution. Mexican archbishop Miguel Darío Miranda Gómez held the presidency of the Latin American Episcopal Council (Consejo Episcopal Latinoamericano, or CELAM) at the time that Castro came to power. When the bishops participating in the council held a gathering in November 1959 in Colombia, they issued a declaration stating, "Catholicism and communism are two openly incompatible

---

[150] John C. Super, "'Rerum Novarum' in Mexico and Quebec," *Revista de Historia de América*, no. 126 (January 1, 2000): 63–84.

[151] Articles 3 and 130 of the Constitution of 1917 rescinded the government's recognition of the Catholic Church as a legal entity, denied clergy various rights, forbade religious education, declared all church buildings property of the nation, and outlawed public religious rituals outside of churches. On the Church in revolutionary and postrevolutionary Mexico, see Roberto Blancarte, *Historia de la Iglesia Católica en México* (Mexico City: Fondo de Cultura Económica, 1992); Matthew Butler, *Popular Piety and Political Identity in Mexico's Cristero Rebellion: Michoacán, 1927–29* (Oxford: Oxford University Press, 2004); Ben Fallaw, *Religion and State Formation in Postrevolutionary Mexico* (Durham, NC: Duke University Press, 2013).

[152] Dávila Peralta, *Las santas batallas*, 76; Soledad Loaeza, "Notas para el estudio de la Iglesia en el México contemporáneo," in *Religión y política en México*, ed. Martín de la Rosa and Charles A. Reilly (Mexico City: Siglo Veintiuno Editores, 1985), 42–58, see p. 52.

doctrines."[153] In October 1960, the Mexican Episcopal council composed a pastoral letter in which the bishops warned of the dangers of communism and sent a special message of support to Church leaders in Cuba. "We share with them their fears and anxieties," the Mexican bishops attested.[154]

When the Bay of Pigs invasion touched off spontaneous, tumultuous protests across Mexico, the Church scrambled to formulate a response. On May 15, the president of the Mexican Episcopal council, Archbishop of Puebla Octaviano Márquez y Toriz, published a pastoral letter in which he claimed, "The directors of these social convulsions are the instruments of materialist and atheist communism, that spreads from Russia and attempts to take over the entire world." The archbishop reminded his readers and the audiences who listened to the letter at mass that his warning was not an idle one. "It would be enough to look at one example, extremely sad and close," he told them: "everything that is happening in our sister nation of Cuba."[155]

The crowds that had gathered to protest the Bay of Pigs invasion had chanted "Castro Sí, Yankees No." Church leaders adopted the same format and changed the words to "Christianity Sí, Communism No." Anticommunist crusaders plastered the slogan across banners, posters, fliers, and walls. An announcement advertising a gathering to commemorate the seventieth anniversary of *Rerum Novarum* in the Basilica of Guadalupe in Mexico City read: "Mexicans: Fight for your Fatherland and your ideas. Christianity Sí, Communism No."[156] The magazine *Política* published a photograph of a dog in Contla, Tlaxcala, wearing a banner on his back that bore the anticommunist phrase; in the article beneath the photo, the author noted that the "noble animal's political opinion had not been consulted" (see Figure 6).[157]

One of Mexico's most prominent politicians proposed a more violent way to combat the communist menace. At the beginning of June 1961, newspapers leaked a private letter that ex-president Abelardo L. Rodríguez (1932–4) had written to nineteen of the nation's leaders of commerce, industry, banking, and agro-business. Rodríguez claimed that

---

[153] Blancarte, *Historia de la Iglesia Católica en México*, 172.
[154] Ibid., 180.
[155] Dávila Peralta, *Las santas batallas*, 121.
[156] "La balanza inclinada," *Política*, June 15, 1961, 5–20.
[157] "También él tuvo que manifestar sus 'ideas!,'" *Política*, August 1, 1961, 10.

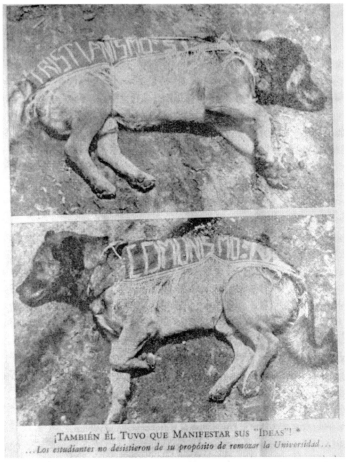

¡TAMBIÉN ÉL TUVO QUE MANIFESTAR SUS "IDEAS"! *
...Los estudiantes no desistieron de su propósito de remozar la Universidad...

FIGURE 6. Photograph of a dog wearing a banner that proclaims "Christianity, Sí, Communism, No." The original caption below reads: "He also had to express his 'ideas!'"
Source: *Política* magazine, August 1, 1961, p. 10. Courtesy of the Biblioteca Lerdo de Tejada and the U.S. Library of Congress, Historical Newspapers.

the unrest occurring throughout the country had its origins in foreign doctrines and urged the most powerful men in Mexico to undertake a coordinated effort to create shock brigades to protect their country. He envisioned the new organizations as "well-prepared and well-organized groups of citizens, especially young men who have completed their military service, who are capable of materially rejecting the acts of vandalism, social subversion, and provocation that unsanctioned agents of

Russian-Chinese-Cuban communism are executing."[158] The former president clearly believed that the government was doing an insufficient job of defending Mexico against communism.

President López Mateos could not tolerate this open challenge to the government's monopoly over the use of force. The police and military had just finished subduing the country after the Bay of Pigs invasion had ignited protests and rioting, and now they faced a new threat. Less than a week after Rodríguez's letter went public, López Mateos responded in a vigorous speech to an assembly of Mexican journalists. He called once again for national unity; then, the president warned his audience "my government will suppress the excesses of demagogic individuals or groups of the right or left who outside the limits of the Constitution attempt to disassemble national life and violate the constitutional order."[159]

Heeding this warning, some conservative leaders decided to form a legal political organization to advocate for their position. Less than a month after the National Liberation Movement made its debut, a manifesto appeared in the national newspapers signed by a group calling itself the Mexican Civic Front of Revolutionary Affirmation (*Frente Cívico Mexicano de Afirmación Revolucionaria*), or Civic Front for short. The signatories of the manifesto, men associated with the politically moderate and conservative administrations of Ávila Camacho, Alemán, and Ruíz Cortines, repeatedly affirmed that they were acting within their constitutional rights and pursuing democratic ends. "We do not believe that in order to solve our problems the catastrophe of a new revolution of communist tint should be necessary," the document read, in a clear response to the references that Lázaro Cárdenas, C. Wright Mills, and others had been making to new revolutions.[160]

Rumors swirled that Abelardo Rodríguez, Miguel Alemán, and even President López Mateos were the masterminds behind the creation of the Civic Front. *Política* claimed that the Civic Front's manifesto was written at the suggestion of López Mateos.[161] U.S. ambassador Thomas Mann claimed that reliable sources had told him that the Mexican president had informally green-lighted the creation of the Civic Front.[162] Half a

---

[158] "Abelardo, fascista," *Política*, June 15, 1961, 21.
[159] "Discurso del Presidente López Mateos el 'Día de la Libertad de Prensa,'" *Política*, June 15, 1961, 16–17.
[160] "Política interior: Tres manifiestos y dos ideas," *Política*, September 1, 1961, 6.
[161] "Tres fuerza políticas se definen," *Política*, September 1, 1961, inside back cover.
[162] Mann to Secretary of State, June 29, 1961. National Security Files, Countries Box 141, JFK Library.

year later, López Mateos had reportedly begun to regret his initial support of the front and was starting to see the anticommunist organization as a threat to his control.[163] A memorandum for National Security Advisor McGeorge Bundy seconded the rumors about López Mateos's misgivings and explained that Alemán was the recognized, though unofficial, leader of the Civic Front. According to the memo, the goal of the group was to "provide organized and effective opposition to the pro-Castro and communist MLN."[164]

Other conservative members of Mexican society ignored López Mateos's warning and remained dedicated to the idea of meeting the leftist threat with force. Businessmen, journalists, Church leaders, participants in secret societies, and the most conservative members of the PAN and PRI parties cooperated covertly to organize violent student groups in universities across Mexico.[165] In Puebla, they helped strengthen the Anticommunist Student Front (Frente Universitario Anticomunista); they played a key role in the expansion of a fascist, militant student organization in Guadalajara called TECOS or "The Owls" (Tarea Educativa y Cultural hacia el Orden y el Síntesis); and in Mexico City, a loose alliance of conservatives sponsored a violent student group that went by the initials MURO (Movimiento Universitario de Renovadora Orientación, or the University Movement of Renovating Orientation).[166]

MURO quickly became one of the most influential conservative student groups in Mexico. Though the exact origins of the organization remain murky, it appears that a violent confrontation between pro-Castro and anticommunist groups on the campus of the national university on July 26, 1961 precipitated the creation of MURO, which made its first public appearance in March 1962.[167] The members of this militant,

---

[163] Mann to Secretary of State, January 19, 1962. National Security Files, Countries Box 141, JFK Library.

[164] L. D. Battle, "Proposed Call on the President by Former President of Mexico Miguel Alemán," March 30, 1962, National Security Files, Countries, Box 141, JFK Library.

[165] On one of the most influential secret societies, El Yunque (The Anvil), see Álvaro Delgado, *El Yunque: La ultraderecha en el poder* (Mexico City: Editorial Grijalbo, 2003).

[166] On the various student groups, see Edgar González Ruiz, *MURO: Memorias y testimonios, 1961–2002*, 2nd ed. (Puebla: Gobierno del Estado de Puebla: Benemérita Universidad Autónoma de Puebla, 2004); Jaime Pensado, "'To Assault with the Truth': The Revitalization of Conservative Militancy in Mexico during the Global Sixties," *The Americas* 70, no. 3 (January 2014): 489–521; Fernando Herrera Calderón, "Contesting the State from the Ivory Tower: Student Power, Dirty War and the Urban Guerrilla Experience in Mexico, 1965–1982," PhD diss., University of Minnesota, 2012.

[167] Manuel Rangel Escamilla, "Algunos aspectos de la situación que prevalece en la Universidad Nacional Autónoma de México," February 21, 1962, DFS, Exp 63-1-62, Leg. 16, Hoja 189, AGN.

semisecret Catholic organization dedicated themselves to waging three battles: excising leftist politics from the campuses of UNAM and its affiliated high schools, removing liberal U.S. values from Mexican society, and defending the nation against the threat of *cardenismo*.[168] Though most of the participants were students, its financial backers included conservative ideologues Jorge Prieto Laurens and Agustín Navarro Vázquez and wealthy businessman Hugo Salinas Price. In his memoirs, Salinas Price described MURO as "a shock brigade of young people," and fondly recalled watching members of the group burn an effigy of Fidel Castro on the campus of the national university.[169] Some of the organization's other activities were more peaceful; MURO issued political manifestos and published a newspaper called *Puño* that bore the slogan "To Assault with the Truth." However, as Salinas Price indicated, the group did not shy away from violence. Intelligence agents reported that the members attended secret training camps where the young men learned the arts of sabotage, guerrilla warfare, and self-defense while the women received training in espionage.[170] MURO's activities became increasingly violent and confrontational throughout the 1960s, while its ties with the government grew ever closer.[171]

At the same time, Mexico's government also began using more violent tactics to silence leftist opponents. Campesino leader Rubén Jaramillo, who had returned to public life after López Mateos pardoned him in 1959, was once again posing a challenge to authorities. He and six thousand *campesinos* initiated proceedings to establish a community on vacant *ejido*, or communal, territories in western Morelos and requested land, loans, roads, housing, and electricity. Unfortunately for them, powerful entrepreneurs in Mexico City coveted the same location for an industrial project. In February 1961, the *jaramillistas* "invaded" the land while the ownership was still under dispute, built interim houses, and began planting crops. The government sided with the entrepreneurs and rescinded the approval it had granted Jaramillo's group. Soldiers intervened to remove the *campesinos* a year after they had settled the land.[172]

In response, Jaramillo's group began radicalizing its strategies and building broad alliances. They offered solidarity to railroad workers

---

[168] Pensado, "'To Assault with the Truth,'" 490.
[169] Hugo Salinas Price, *Mis Años Con Elektra: Memorias* (Mexico City: Editorial Diana, 2000), 122.
[170] Pensado, "To Assault with the Truth," 498.
[171] Ibid., 497–8.
[172] Padilla, *Rural Resistance in the Land of Zapata*, 194.

and teachers, and Jaramillo joined the Mexican Communist Party in 1961 and participated in rallies organized by the National Liberation Movement.[173] The head of the Department of Federal Security reported that Jaramillo received help from local MLN leaders in Cuernavaca and from the Cuban ambassador to Mexico.[174] Authorities knew that Jaramillo was planning a trip to Cuba and worried that he would receive training in guerrilla warfare.[175]

Some *jaramillistas* were in fact advocating a strategy of clandestine organization. Their plans included political education and the creation of a "socialist region" and a "people's revolutionary army."[176] A growing faction argued for the formation of cells, or small groups, that would secretly receive training and instructions from Jaramillo for use in their own local communities. The cells could expand into cooperatives, which would then slowly establish a socialist region with a revolutionary consciousness. The political education would come from Jaramillo. By sharing his knowledge, he could "create many Rubéns," as one *jaramillista* explained, and thus decrease the movement's dependence on a single leader.[177] This radical sector of the movement anticipated governmental repression and planned to form a revolutionary army for self-defense. Intelligence agents were probably aware of at least some of these incipient plans.

Mexican authorities decided to put a definitive end to Rubén Jaramillo's "subversive" activities. On May 23, 1962, some sixty soldiers and several armed civilians surrounded Jaramillo's house and seized him along with his pregnant wife and three sons. His family displayed the official pardons from López Mateos, but the officer in charge stuffed the paper into his pocket and continued with his assignment. In the confusion, Jaramillo's stepdaughter escaped. Rubén and the rest of his family were not so lucky. Their bodies turned up riddled with bullets a few hours later beside an archaeological site known as the Xochicalco ruins, near Cuernavaca.[178]

Conservative sectors of Mexican society, both within the government and without, were largely responsible for escalating the violence of

---

[173] Ibid., 10, 198; "La nación: La matanza de Xochicalco," *Política*, June 1, 1962; Laura Castellanos, *México armado, 1943–1981* (Mexico City: Ediciones Era, 2007).

[174] Manuel Rangel Escamilla, "[Agitation in Morelos]," October 12, 1961, DFS, Exp 100-15-3-61, Leg. 1, Hoja 1, AGN.

[175] Hodges and Gandy, *Mexico under Siege*, 53.

[176] Padilla, *Rural Resistance in the Land of Zapata*, 201–2.

[177] Ibid., 202.

[178] Ibid., 1.

Mexico's Cold War. They responded to the increasing amount of leftist activism with their own organizations, many of which embraced the use of force. At the same time, the military's brazen assassination of Rubén Jaramillo demonstrated that the government was willing to use ever more violent methods to silence its critics.

CONCLUSION

Little more than two years after Castro's bearded army marched into Havana, the Cuban Revolution began to have a visible impact on Mexico's domestic politics. Groups and individuals who before had limited themselves to verbally supporting the Cuban Revolution began taking action to emulate it. After formulating organizational strategies at the Latin American Peace Conference, leftists from all sectors of Mexican society gained further motivation from the Bay of Pigs invasion. In those few days, they not only witnessed the Cuban nation's ability to resist an attack organized by the most powerful country in the world; they also experienced their own power to influence their country's politics. Inspired by Castro and emboldened by the outburst of public activism during the Bay of Pigs invasion, they created ambitious new groups including the National Liberation Movement, the Independent Campesino Center, and the National Center of Democratic Students, which sought to revive the original aims of the Mexican Revolution.

These same events redoubled the anxieties that were already building within Mexico's government and conservative groups. The peace conference, the Bay of Pigs invasion, and the creation of the new leftist groups all provided ample evidence to support their fear that the Cuban Revolution could spread to Mexico. Conservative politicians, students, religious leaders, and businessmen responded in kind by creating their own new organizations, such as the Civic Front and MURO, but they also raised the stakes. In resorting to force, the Mexican government and the conservative sectors of society introduced a new, violent aspect to Mexico's Cold War.

4

Negotiating Relations with Cuba and the United States

At the same time that Mexican leaders were trying to respond to the increased domestic activism that the Cuban Revolution had sparked, they also had to fend off a renewed U.S. effort to push them into a harder line on the issue of Cuba. Officials in the Eisenhower administration had adopted a tolerant attitude regarding Mexico's relations with Castro, because they understood the important role that Mexico's foreign policy played in shoring up the country's tenuous stability. However, John F. Kennedy came into office in January 1961 determined to use all available means to remove the communist presence from Cuba. Both Kennedy and the man he appointed as ambassador to Mexico, Thomas C. Mann, repeatedly tried to make Mexican leaders cut relations with Cuba. The U.S. press, investors, and tourists provided additional sources of pressure, as did such events as the Cuban Missile Crisis and Kennedy's assassination. In response, President López Mateos secretly adjusted some aspects of his policy toward Castro while publicly refusing to break relations.

U.S. PRESSURE

In the early 1960s, Mexico's defense of Cuba threatened to derail its relations with the United States. Kennedy found López Mateos's response to the Bay of Pigs invasion especially vexing. On April 20, 1961, Kennedy summoned Richard Nixon to a meeting at the White House and mentioned that he was sending Vice President Lyndon Johnson down to Mexico to try to gain support on the Cuba issue. "I have just told him to tell the Mexicans they owe us a vote. Don't you think we should be tough with them?" the president remarked to Nixon, who was quick to agree. According to Nixon, he advised Kennedy that "the Mexicans often take the soft line where the communists are concerned, because of the Cárdenas influence, but they need us as much or more than we need them today, and this is one time when I think we should insist that they stand with us."[1]

The U.S. press was also critical of Mexico's position on the Cuba issue. Newspapers across the United States provided detailed coverage of the riots and violence that erupted in Mexico in response to the Bay of Pigs invasion.[2] The *Tri-State Defender* in Memphis, Tennessee, and the *Chicago Defender*, apparently ignorant of Mexican geography, published an article with the ludicrous claim that a communist in Morelia, Michoacán, had incited mobs to "go into the bars and nightclubs and drag out the American tourists and throw them into the sea."[3] A writer for the *Los Angeles Times* described remarks that López Mateos made about nonintervention as an "indignant attack" and "an obvious dig at the United States."[4] When two Cuban diplomats in Mexico City defected and accused their countrymen of printing communist propaganda and spreading it throughout Mexico and the rest of Latin America, an editorial in the *Chicago Tribune* speculated that "maybe the deeds and words of Cuban diplomats will impress their fellow Latin Americans more than repeated warnings from the United States. If so, their governments will realize that the real danger is not internal, but external."[5]

Bad press in the United States took its toll by reducing tourism, one of Mexico's most important sources of foreign revenue. In the early 1960s, tourism accounted for almost a quarter of Mexico's foreign exchange earnings.[6] Graphic accounts in U.S. newspapers of mobs throwing tourists into the sea and burning American flags did not portray Mexico as an enticing destination. When President López Mateos summoned

---

[1] Richard M. Nixon, "Cuba, Castro, and John F. Kennedy," *Readers' Digest*, November 1964.
[2] "Mobs Spread Violence in Latin America Cities: Mexico City, Caracas and La Paz Scenes of Wild Rioting by Castro Followers," *Los Angeles Times*, April 19, 1961; "Riots in Latin Cities Rap U.S. Over Cuban Invasion," *Chicago Tribune*, April 20, 1961; "Red-Led Mobs Protest 'U.S. Role' in Cuban War," *Washington Post*, April 20, 1961.
[3] Geraldine Hawley, "Memo from Mexico," *Tri-State Defender*, May 12, 1961; Geraldine Hawley, "Memo from Mexico," *Chicago Defender*, May 6, 1961. Morelia is landlocked – nowhere near any sea.
[4] Ruben Salazar, "Mexico President Slaps U.S. on Intervention," *Los Angeles Times*, May 23, 1961.
[5] "The Red Plot Confirmed," *Chicago Tribune*, May 27, 1961.
[6] Secretaría de Industria y Comercio, *Anuario estadístico de los Estados Unidos Mexicanos, 1962–1963* (Mexico City: Talleres Gráficos de la Nación, 1965), 109. See also Laura Bergquist, "Mexico: The Big Puzzle Next Door," *Look Magazine*, July 18, 1961.

Lázaro Cárdenas to his office two weeks after the Bay of Pigs invasion, he complained that the revenues from tourism were already down and an "intense campaign" in the United States was only making the situation worse.[7] Journalist Paul Kennedy of the *New York Times* reported in June 1961 that tourism had dropped significantly, thanks in part to bad publicity about anti-American protests in Mexico.[8] A writer from the *Los Angeles Times* relayed statements from the Mexico City hotel association that in the two months after the Bay of Pigs invasion hotels were operating at 30 percent capacity and losing money daily; an airline official told the reporter that incoming traffic was down as much as 60 percent.[9]

The Mexican government lashed out after the Latin American edition of *Time* magazine published a particularly offensive article about Mexico and its relations with Cuba. The article, titled "Mexico: Castro's Champion" claimed that the main reason the Mexican government defended Cuba was because López Mateos was afraid to challenge Cárdenas, "Castro's number one hero and the number one hero of the Mexican masses."[10] Mexico's government responded to the *Time* article immediately and angrily. The state-mouthpiece newspaper *El Nacional* ran an editorial on its front page titled "The Difficult Talent of Soiling Everything." The editorial denied that the Mexican government supported Castro, that its leaders feared Cárdenas or any other leftists, that López Mateos prevented the ex-president from flying to Cuba, or that personal sentiments of any nature dictated the government's policy toward Cuba. It insisted, "It is principles, and only principles, which inspire Mexico's conduct in the present case."[11] The editorial's vehemence suggested that the claims in the *Time* article had hit a little too close to home.

Mexico's government also had to deal with pressure from the U.S. State Department. As ambassador to Mexico from 1961 to 1963, Thomas Mann repeatedly tried to push Mexican leaders to cut diplomatic ties with Cuba.[12] Before arriving at his post in Mexico, he received

---

[7] Cárdenas, *Obras: Apuntes 1957/1966*, 212.

[8] Paul P. Kennedy, "Mexico Entering a Crucial Period: Political Conflicts Causing an Economic Slowdown," *New York Times*, June 11, 1961.

[9] "Is Anti-Americanism Increasing in Mexico? Not Noticeably, Claim U.S. Citizens Living There, but Tourism Sags Sharply," *Los Angeles Times*, June 1, 1961.

[10] "México: El campeón de Castro," *Time Latin América*, May 12, 1961, IPS Caja 1456 A.

[11] "El difícil talento de ensuciarlo todo," *El Nacional*, May 16, 1961.

[12] For conflicting views on Mann, see Thomas Tunstall Allcock, "Becoming 'Mr. Latin America': Thomas C. Mann Reconsidered," *Diplomatic History* 38, no. 5 (2014): 1017–45; Walter LaFeber, "Thomas C. Mann and the Devolution of Latin American Policy: From the Good Neighbor to Military Intervention," in *Behind the Throne: Servants of Power to Imperial Presidents, 1898–1968*, ed. Thomas J McCormick

a memorandum from the interim charge d'affaires of the U.S. embassy that recommended making a more concerted effort to bring Mexico into line on the subjects of Cuba and communism. "In spite of extraordinary efforts to win Mexico's confidence and support, the United States can count on neither in international organizations," the memo reported. It listed the many ways that Mexico had supported Castro and thumbed its nose at U.S. efforts to halt the spread of communism. The embassy official recommended that the United States abandon its tactic of "ardent wooing" and instead deliberately delay any friendly move in Mexico's direction.[13] Mann agreed with the recommendations, and spent much of his time in Mexico testing different tactics to pressure his hosts to change their foreign policy.

A month after the Bay of Pigs invasion, Mann requested a meeting with Mexico's minister of foreign relations, Manuel Tello; the two men debated at length over the nature of the Cuban threat and the measures that the countries of Latin America should take to protect themselves. When Mann said that his government had decided that direct force was the only way to dislodge Castro, Tello disagreed vehemently on international and domestic grounds, arguing that "external attacks against Cuba's revolutionary government would do nothing but strengthen it and its sympathizers in Latin America."[14] Tello also dismissed Mann's warnings that Castro could spread his revolution to neighboring countries, observing that the Cuban government had enough internal problems to occupy its attention. Without any apparent sense of irony or self-reflection, the Mexican foreign minister argued that communism was making inroads in Latin America because too many governments were turning their backs on the needs and aspirations of their own people. When Mann ran through a laundry list of sanctions against Cuba that the United States wanted the OAS to pursue, including breaking commercial and diplomatic relations and creating a joint air and naval patrol, Tello refused and pointed out that the sanctions went against Mann's earlier argument that force was the only effective strategy. Tello offered instead

and Walter LaFeber (Madison: University of Wisconsin Press, 1993), 166–203. See also "Thomas C. Mann Oral History Interview," March 13, 1968, Oral History Interview, Thomas C. Mann, JFK Library.

[13] Letter from Edward G. Cale to Thomas C. Mann, "The Tactical Handling of Relations with Mexico," February 14, 1961. DOS, CF, 611.12/2–1461. *FRUS, 1961–1963: American Republics*, Vol. 12 Microfiche Supplement (Washington, DC: U.S. Government Printing Office, 1996), Doc. 179.

[14] "Memorandum estríctamente confidencial para el Señor Presidente de la República," May 19, 1961, SPR-400-9, SRE.

to mediate between Cuba and the United States, but Mann insisted that he would rather see Mexico abstain from any involvement in actions against Castro than try to lead new reconciliation efforts. By the end of the meeting, Mann had failed to make any progress with the foreign minister.

Mann likely had Tello's intransigence in mind when in January 1962, before a meeting of the OAS in Punta del Este, Uruguay, the ambassador telegraphed Secretary of State Dean Rusk to warn him that the Mexican government would probably oppose an anti-Cuba resolution. He asked whether Mexico's policy of "simply acquiescing" to communism would send the message that the OAS was incapable of defending itself against subversion. In his opinion, the consequences of the Mexican government's decision were so far-reaching as to be "unacceptable" to the United States. Mann believed that representatives of the U.S. government had to steady their nerves and demonstrate to Mexico – privately and tactfully – that defense of Castro did not pay. He recommended that Washington use its political and economic leverage to influence Mexico's policy and suggested indefinitely postponing a state visit that Kennedy planned to make in order to send the message that the United States did not approve of its neighbor's independent foreign policy. He also proposed that the U.S. government delay action on any loans and encourage international lending institutions to do the same.[15] He had made similar recommendations earlier that year in cables to the State Department about Mexico's "equivocal" stand on communism.[16]

Shortly after writing to Rusk, Mann began putting his plan into action during a private meeting with López Mateos. The ambassador told the president that given Mexico's anticipated defense of Cuba in the OAS, it would be problematic for Kennedy to visit immediately thereafter. Mann also inquired whether López Mateos had considered that siding with Cuba might cause "a further weakening of confidence which is essential to Mexican economic growth."[17] After the conversation, Mann reiterated his recommendations to the State Department to postpone

[15] Thomas Mann, "Telegram 1634 from Mann to Secretary of State," December 6, 1961, Papers of Arthur M. Schlesinger Jr., White House Files, Classified Subject File, WH-41, JFK Library.

[16] Thomas Mann, "Mexico City to Secretary of State," June 13, 1961, NSF, Countries, Box 141, JFK Library; Thomas Mann, "Mexico City to Secretary of State," July 17, 1961, NSF, Countries, Box 141, JFK Library.

[17] Thomas Mann, "Mexico City to Department of State," December 17, 1961, NSF, Countries, Box 141, JFK Library.

Kennedy's trip and delay action on loans. Washington took his advice and delayed the visit.[18]

In response to U.S. pressure, López Mateos showed only a partial willingness to adjust his country's stance at the January OAS meeting. He told Mann that he could not abandon Mexico's traditional defense of nonintervention. However, he suggested that the U.S. ambassador consult with Mexico's foreign minister before the Punta del Este gathering "to reconcile U.S. and Mexican points of view," thereby opening the door for negotiation.[19] The Mexican government eventually adopted an ambiguous position on the question of Cuba at the OAS meeting. Mexican foreign minister Manuel Tello abstained from voting on resolutions that expelled Cuba from the OAS and applied economic sanctions against the island. In so doing, he claimed that Mexico was maintaining its traditional defense of the principles of self-determination and nonintervention.[20] At the same time, however, Tello's speech to the rest of the ministers laid the juridical groundwork for Cuba's expulsion from the inter-American system. "There is a radical incompatibility," he declared, "between belonging to the Organization of American States and a Marxist-Leninist political avowal."[21] His words signaled a shift in Mexico's earlier unmitigated defense of Cuba.

Mexico's ambivalent position at the OAS conference was not enough to smooth its rocky relations with the United States. The same day that Tello gave his speech about incompatibility, Mann sent a cable from Mexico City to the State Department using the Punta del Este conference as evidence that López Mateos was "going out of his way to be friendly with Communists." The ambassador recommended that the State Department arrange for the Inter-American Development Bank to "put a slow man" on the job of processing loans to Mexico in order to demonstrate that the United States expected cooperation to be a two-way street.[22] The British Ambassador to Mexico, Sir Peter Garran, speculated in a dispatch to his

---

[18] George Ball, "Telegram from State Department to Embassy in Mexico City," December 19, 1961, Papers of Arthur M. Schlesinger Jr., White House Files, Classified Subject File, WH-41, JFK Library.

[19] Mann, "Mexico City to Department of State."

[20] "Punta del Este," *Política*, February 1, 1962.

[21] Manuel Tello, "Address by his Excellency Manuel Tello, Secretary of Foreign Affairs of Mexico, before the First Plenary Session of the VIII Meeting of Consultation of Foreign Ministers of the American Republic Being Held in Punta del Este, Uruguay," January 24, 1962, NSF, Countries, Box 54, JFK Library.

[22] Thomas Mann, "Mexico City to Secretary of State," January 24, 1962, NSF, Countries, Box 141, JFK Library.

home office a month later that if the Mexican government had hoped that Tello's declaration at the OAS would put the U.S.-Mexican relationship on easier footing, it must have been disappointed. "The mutual distrust between the Administration and business and banking circles goes too deep to admit of the restoration of confidence by a single policy statement," he reported, "and this goes also for the restoration of confidence in the United States-Mexican political and economic relations."[23]

Mann grew more and more frustrated with Mexico's foreign policy during his time as ambassador. When a State Department official asked whether the "slow man technique" was enough to stop the so-called leftist drift of Mexican policy, Mann let loose a barrage of criticism.[24] He complained that the principle objective of Mexico's foreign policy was the advancement "in a short-sighted way, of narrow, nationalistic, selfish Mexican interests." Mann claimed that for many years, the general direction of Mexican policy had been toward the type of leftism that was harmful to basic U.S. interests, and that those in control of the government planned to continue this trend in the future. He recommended that the United States make silent use of its economic leverage to push Mexican leaders to amend their "selfish" ways.[25]

A more powerful official than Thomas Mann – President Kennedy – also tried to influence Mexican policy. In June 1962, Kennedy and his wife Jacqueline made their long-awaited state visit to Mexico, where they received an extravagant welcome complete with a ticker-tape parade. The government gave public employees the day off from work and cancelled classes at schools across Mexico City to encourage attendance at the parade. Mexican officials went to great lengths to ensure the success of the visit, and intelligence services kept their U.S. counterparts abreast of all security measures. Agents compiled lists of dangerous people to "watch and control" during Kennedy's stay, including at least forty-five members of the Mexican Communist Party, the Popular Socialist Party, and the National Liberation Movement.[26] According to a memo by the counselor for political affairs of the U.S. embassy, the Mexican security

[23] Sir Peter Garran, "Meeting at Punta Del Este of Foreign Ministers of the American Republics, January 1962, to Consider the Problem of Cuba," February 27, 1962, Archives Direct UK.

[24] "Telegram from State Department to Mexico City," April 12, 1963, Papers of Arthur M. Schlesinger Jr., White House Files, Classified Subject File, WH-41, JFK Library.

[25] Thomas Mann, "Mexico City to Secretary of State," April 16, 1963, NSF, Countries, Box 141, JFK Library.

[26] Luis Ramirez López et al., "[List of people to watch and control during Kennedy's visit]," May 17, 1962, DFS, Exp 30-3-62, Leg. 2, Hoja 23, AGN.

agencies reassured them that they planned to round up known "troublemakers and Communist agitators" throughout the country prior to Kennedy's arrival.[27] Mexican officials told Ambassador Mann that they planned to raid places where pamphlets and other propaganda denouncing the visit were stored and offered to search any other locations that the U.S. embassy wished.[28] They also reportedly asked the leadership of the conservative Mexican Civic Front of Revolutionary Affirmation to provide "thousands of its members and sympathizers to be deputized as special security agents along Kennedy's march route."[29] Cuban observers reported that seven hundred Mexican "secret agents" joined police and military forces to guard the visiting president.[30]

The Mexican security services kept their promise to protect Kennedy. In a telegram to Rusk after the visit, Mann reported that Mexican police had arrested and incarcerated a considerable number of possible troublemakers, especially communist students and leaders, and had kept a much larger number of people under surveillance. Police and intelligence agents also watched over possible trouble areas such as universities, Soviet bloc embassies, and the U.S. embassy. In addition, they destroyed derogatory signs and prevented groups of students from leaving the grounds of the National University. Mexican police dispersed four truckloads of students attempting to leave the UNAM campus, as well as a group of demonstrators along the parade route.[31]

The public aspects of Kennedy's visit proceeded smoothly, and both presidents took the opportunity to make declarations of support for each other and for the recently launched Alliance for Progress. After acknowledging that the Alliance's objectives for social, economic, and political reform were ambitious, Kennedy pointed out to reporters that "the Mexican Revolution has helped demonstrate that it is possible ... and even though the revolution is far from complete in Mexico, we should now work together to bring that hope and opportunity to all of the Americas."[32]

[27] Robert W. Adams, "Communist Activity Related to Forthcoming Visit by President Kennedy," May 31, 1962, NSF, Trips and Conferences, Box 237, JFK Library.

[28] Thomas Mann, "Presidential Visit," June 25, 1962, NSF, Trips and Conferences, Box 237, JFK Library.

[29] Pensado, *Rebel Mexico*, 183.

[30] Dirección de Asuntos Latinoamericanos, "Informe especial de México," July 10, 1962, América Latina, México, 1959–1962, Ordinario 6, 1962, MINREX.

[31] Thomas Mann, "Kennedy Visit Security Measures," July 2, 1962, NSF, Trips and Conferences, Box 237, JFK Library.

[32] "La décima entrevista," *Política*, July 1, 1962, 7. On the Alliance for Progress, see Stephen G. Rabe, *The Most Dangerous Area in the World: John F. Kennedy Confronts*

With these words, Kennedy not only validated the Mexican government's claim that it was still pursuing revolutionary goals, but also argued that the Mexican Revolution, not the Cuban one, should serve as a model for the rest of Latin America.

Behind closed doors, however, tensions between the U.S. and Mexican heads of state ran high. In a private meeting with López Mateos, Kennedy raised the issue of Cuba. "What does Mexico think should be done to prevent the spread of Communism in other American Republics?" he inquired.[33] López Mateos replied that economic growth was the best way to combat the threat and pointed to the Alliance for Progress as a promising initiative. Attempting to push López Mateos into a harder line, Kennedy returned again and again to his chief concern: What was Mexico doing to fight communism? López Mateos's foreign minister, also present at the meeting, reminded the U.S. president that Mexico had contributed the doctrine of incompatibility to the debates over Cuba at the OAS conference in Punta del Este. López Mateos kept reiterating his argument that economic development and social progress were the answers. By the end of the meeting, Kennedy had settled for promises of future discussions of measures to combat the communist threat.

The Cubans monitored Kennedy's visit as best they could, searching through press releases and newspaper accounts for indications of any change in Mexican policy. Analysts in the Department of Latin American Affairs celebrated the fact that "Kennedy failed in his objective of bringing about a radical change in the Mexican posture of nonintervention and self-determination, especially with relation to our country." They did note, however, that the visit and the agreement to new loans under the auspices of the Alliance for Progress had served to deepen Mexico's "economic compromises with imperialism."[34]

In another private meeting at the end of Kennedy's visit, López Mateos tried one final time to make amends for his position on Cuba. He explained that he recognized that his relations with Castro had created doubts "in some parts of United States' opinion" about Mexico's loyalties, but told Kennedy that he wished to reassure him and his people

Communist Revolution in Latin America (Chapel Hill: University of North Carolina Press, 1999); Jeffrey F. Taffet, *Foreign Aid as Foreign Policy: The Alliance for Progress in Latin America* (New York: Routledge, 2007).

33 "Communism in Latin America," June 29, 1962, NSF, Trips and Conferences, Box 236, JFK Library.

34 Dirección de Asuntos Latinoamericanos, "Informe especial de México," July 10, 1962, América Latina, México, 1959–1962, Ordinario 6, 1962, MINREX.

that "in case any conflict should arise, Mexico would be glad to guard the United States' rear with its 35 million people."[35] The Mexican president was not willing to cut relations with Cuba, but he vowed that his country's fundamental ties and loyalties were with the United States. An unprecedented international event would soon force López Mateos to live up to this promise.

MEXICO AND THE CUBAN MISSILE CRISIS

On October 22, 1962, President Kennedy revealed to the world that the Soviet Union had installed missiles in Cuba with offensive capabilities. He announced a "quarantine" of the island and demanded that the weapons be removed.[36] The Cuban Missile Crisis put Mexico's ambiguous foreign policy to the test. When it counted the most, would Mexico side with Cuba or the United States?

In the weeks leading up to the crisis, President López Mateos had maintained his noncommittal defense of Cuba. On October 3, during a layover in Los Angeles on his way to Asia, the president told U.S. reporters that his sources indicated that Castro possessed only defensive weapons. "If the arms are defensive, we do not consider [Cuba to have] a dangerous arsenal," he stated. However, López Mateos opened the door for a change in policy, explaining that if the weapons were offensive, "the situation would be different."[37]

Even after Kennedy's television broadcast on October 22, López Mateos avoided making any formal commitments. He told reporters in the Philippines that his position was the same as always: if Cuba was arming itself defensively, it presented no threat. This time, his audience pressed for clarification. What was the difference between offensive and defensive weapons? The president responded that anti-aircraft missiles were acceptable, while ground-to-ground ones constituted a threat to world peace. He insisted that he would do nothing until the OAS and the United Nations had seen proof and decided upon a course of action.[38]

---

[35] "Salinity and Other Problems," June 30, 1962, NSF, Trips and Conferences, Box 236, JFK Library.

[36] Kennedy deliberately used the term *quarantine* rather than *blockade* to describe the action in order to avoid accusations that he was breaking the international law of freedom of the seas. Larman C. Wilson, "International Law and the United States Cuban Quarantine of 1962," *Journal of Inter-American Studies* 7, no. 4 (October 1, 1965): 485–92.

[37] *Presencia internacional de Adolfo López Mateos*, Vol. 1, 296.

[38] Ibid., 391–2; Carlos Denegri, "Nueva actitud si Cuba tiene poder ofensivo," *Excélsior*, October 23, 1962.

The White House demanded a clearer answer: Would Mexico approve an OAS resolution condemning the missiles? Kennedy was determined to have unanimous support for the quarantine. López Mateos's airplane was en route from the Philippines to Mexico during the crucial hours of debate in the OAS. The man who worked as director of information in the Ministry of the Interior at the time, Luis M. Farías, recalled in his memoirs that his supervisor, Gustavo Díaz Ordaz, had to make the decision. Farías recounts how his "good friend" Thomas Mann contacted him and asked to see the minister of the interior. "You can tell President Kennedy," Díaz Ordaz told Mann, "that we have always supported Cuba's right to have defensive weapons but not offensive ones. In this case you are right. The weapons are foreign, controlled by the Russians, who want to take advantage of Cuban territory to threaten the United States."[39] After giving Mexico's answer to the U.S. ambassador, the minister of the interior called López Mateos during his layover in Hawaii to tell him what had happened. A conflicting account suggests that López Mateos made the final decision about Mexico's position during the Cuban Missile Crisis. According to the U.S. ambassador to the OAS at the time, Delesseps S. Morrison, Kennedy spoke with López Mateos twice over the phone after announcing the presence of offensive missiles, when the latter was first in Manila and then in Hawaii.[40] It is thus possible that López Mateos, rather than Díaz Ordaz, decided that Mexico would stand beside the United States.

When López Mateos returned to Mexico, he immediately demonstrated where his country's loyalties lay. Speaking from the balcony of the national palace, he declared: "We are in the ranks of democracy. We will fight for peace and for liberty."[41] The ranks of which he spoke were those of the United States. Defending Cuba on principle was one thing, but defending Castro's right to possess nuclear weapons capable of reaching Mexico City or Washington was another matter. Mexico approved the OAS resolution demanding that the missiles be removed from Cuba, though it did not go so far as to support an invasion if the Soviets or Cubans refused to comply.[42]

---

[39] Luis M. Farías, *Así lo recuerdo: Testimonio político* (Mexico City: Fondo de Cultura Económica, 1992), 236.

[40] Delesseps S. Morrison, *Latin American Mission: An Adventure in Hemisphere Diplomacy* (New York: Simon and Schuster, 1965), 244.

[41] *Presencia internacional de Adolfo López Mateos*, Vol. 1, 399.

[42] On the Cuban Missile Crisis and regional politics, see Renata Keller, "The Latin American Missile Crisis," *Diplomatic History*, Advanced Access, published on March 17, 2014 at

In reality, "fighting for peace" entailed clamping down on public protests regarding the missile crisis; Mexican officials had learned from their experiences during the Bay of Pigs invasion that international events could spark domestic unrest. Intelligence agents and army officials monitored the actions of any group suspected of harboring sympathies for Cuba. Different branches of the security forces cooperated and shared information; for example, on October 25, the Ministry of National Defense sent a report to Minister of the Interior Díaz Ordaz warning of leftist plans for informal, "lightning," protest meetings.[43] On November 4, riot police arrived two hours before a coalition of leftist groups planned to hold a meeting criticizing the U.S. quarantine of Cuba. The police ripped signs and banners from the walls and ordered the organizers to vacate the premises.[44]

This firm governmental response combined with a relative lack of popular activism to keep violence to a minimum. No problems arose when a thousand students at UNAM held a peaceful protest denouncing the quarantine.[45] Lázaro Cardenas, the Mexican Communist Party, the Popular Socialist Party, and the National Liberation Movement all limited their actions to nonviolent forms of protest: organizing meetings, sending telegrams, and issuing declarations.[46] Once the crisis had passed, *Política*'s director Manuel Marcué Pardiñas bemoaned the lack of activism in his country. "In all the countries of Latin America," Marcué Pardiñas wrote, "there occurred popular manifestations of support for Cuba and rejection of the aggressive plans of the United States; in all, except Mexico." He accused leftist groups of negligence and irresponsibility, claiming that their silence afforded the president with no option but to support the United States. He argued "even if President López Mateos had wanted to resist U.S. pressure, on the basis of a united and powerful leftist opposition, he would not have been able because the left was neither united nor mobilized."[47]

DOI: 10.1093/dh/dht134; James G. Hershberg and Christian F. Ostermann, eds., "The Global Cuban Missile Crisis at 50," *Cold War International History Project Bulletin*, no. 17–18 (Fall 2012).

[43] General de División Agustin Olachea Aviles, "[M.L.N. activities in Mexico City during Missile Crisis]," October 25, 1962, IPS Caja 1475-A, Exp 27, AGN.

[44] Manuel Rangel Escamilla, "[MLN act supporting Cuba prevented by police]," November 4, 1962, DFS, Exp 11-6-62, Leg. 9, Hoja 47, AGN.

[45] "Apoyo de la juventud mexicana," *Revolución*, October 27, 1962.

[46] Movimiento de Liberación Nacional, "[MLN poster about Cuban Missile Crisis]," October 23, 1962, DFS, Exp 11-6-62, Leg. 9, Hoja 18, AGN; "Lázaro Cárdenas escribe a 'N.Y. Times' sobre la situación," *El Nacional*, November 2, 1962.

[47] Manuel Marcué Pardiñas, "La política internacional del gobierno del Presidente Adolfo López Mateos," *Política*, December 1, 1962.

Leftist groups had remained mostly quiet because more Mexicans supported the quarantine than opposed it; Mexico, after all, was well within range of the missiles in Cuba. The U.S. consulates in Mérida, Tampico, Tijuana, Matamoros, and Monterrey reported widespread approval of the United States during the crisis. As the consul in Mérida put it, "All in all, the U.S. had overwhelming support from this area and the only dissenting voice came from the local Cuban consul himself."[48] A group calling itself the Mexican Federation of Agricultural Organizations petitioned López Mateos "on behalf of half a million campesino families" to break relations with "a government that has subdued and enslaved the Cuban people and out of vanity and narcissism has delivered its democratic and autonomous homeland to Soviet imperialism."[49] Students at the University of Morelos in Cuernavaca burnt an effigy of Fidel Castro.[50]

U.S. leaders appreciated Mexico's stance during their time of crisis. A year and a half later, Secretary of State Dean Rusk wrote a memorandum to President Johnson about López Mateos. "At times his foreign policy has been too independent – for example on Cuba," Rusk acknowledged, "but when fundamental issues are at stake we have usually found him understanding and willing to be helpful."[51] Johnson expressed the same sentiment more colloquially in a subsequent meeting with López Mateos, saying he knew that "when the chips were down, Mexico would be on the side of the United States."[52] The Mexican president confirmed Johnson's impression. López Mateos's successor, Díaz Ordaz, used the exact same turn of phrase when he reminded Johnson of Mexico's position during the Cuban Missile Crisis. He explained that it was proof that "the United States could be absolutely sure that when the chips were really down, Mexico would be unequivocally by its side."[53]

Mexican support for the United States during the missile crisis led to a subtle but important shift in the relationship between the two countries. Before October 1962, Mann, Kennedy, and other U.S. officials had

---

[48] "Reactions to Missile Crisis," November 1962, U.S. State Department Files Microfilm (24,461), 712.00/10–3162, Nettie Lee Benson Latin American Collection, Austin, TX.

[49] "Medio millón de campesinos mexicanos piden se rompan relaciones con Fidel Castro," *Novedades*, Managua, Nicaragua, November 8, 1962.

[50] "Clamor mundial conduz á trégua," *Última Hora*, October 26, 1962.

[51] Dean Rusk, "Memorandum for the President," February 18, 1964, NSF, Mexico, Box 61, Folder 2, Document 9, LBJ Library.

[52] "Meeting between President Johnson and President López Mateos," February 21, 1964, NSF, Mexico, Box 61, Folder 2, Document 34b, LBJ Library.

[53] "Mexican-Cuban Relations," November 12, 1964, NSF, Mexico, Box 61, Folder 5, Document 39b, LBJ Library.

worried that the Mexicans were not taking the communist threat seriously and tried to use diplomatic and economic pressure to compel them to break relations with Castro's government. However, when Kennedy presented the world with indisputable proof of Soviet nuclear warheads in the Caribbean, the Mexican government had to choose a side. By supporting the United States in that crucial moment, López Mateos demonstrated where his true loyalties lay and gained U.S. acceptance of his foreign policy toward Cuba.

OSWALD IN MEXICO

When Lee Harvey Oswald caught a bus from the Texas border to Mexico City on September 26, 1963, he set into motion yet another series of events that would strain relations between Mexico, Cuba, and the United States. After arriving in the Mexican capital the next morning, Oswald checked into a cheap hotel and then went to the Cuban embassy. He told a Mexican woman who worked there, Silvia Durán, that he wanted a visa to go to Cuba en route to the Soviet Union. Durán sent him away, explaining that he would have to go to the Soviet embassy nearby to get permission from them before the Cubans could issue a transit visa. Oswald then went to the Soviet embassy, where they informed him that he would have to wait as long as four months while they sent his request to their main office in Washington. Undeterred, Oswald returned to the Cubans and told Durán that the Soviets had approved his request. She called the other embassy to verify his story, only to learn that Oswald had lied about receiving approval. When she confronted Oswald, he stormed out of the building.[54] Over the next few days, he returned to both embassies and tried again to obtain a visa to travel to Cuba, with no success. Through their systems of surveillance surrounding the embassies, the FBI and CIA took note of all these interactions and sent reports back to Washington.[55] Oswald left Mexico City on October 2 and returned to the United States.[56] A month and a half later, on November 22, he killed President Kennedy in Dallas.

The news of Kennedy's assassination appalled Mexicans. President López Mateos declared three days of mourning and ordered that flags

---

[54] Morley, *Our Man in Mexico*, 181–2.

[55] CIA, "Mexico City Chronology Covering Period 27 Sept 63–3 Feb 68," n.d., RIF 104-10522-10085, Mary Ferrell Foundation Digital Archive.

[56] Peter Kihss, "Oswald's Trip to Mexico in September Was a Lonely Venture, Inquiry Shows," *New York Times*, December 3, 1963.

on all public buildings be lowered to half-mast. Visibly shaken, he told reporters at a press conference that he hoped that Kennedy's death would not endanger world peace.[57] Gustavo Díaz Ordaz took a break from his presidential campaign to issue a statement condemning the murder and lamenting the fact that "the United States lost a great president of just and progressive spirit, a defender of the Negroes like Abraham Lincoln, and like Lincoln, also assassinated."[58] All of Mexico's political parties issued declarations about Kennedy and dozens of businesses and organizations published announcements in the nation's newspapers expressing their condolences. The National Institute of Fine Arts cancelled its shows for three days and the Church held a special mass in the Basilica of Guadalupe, which Kennedy had visited during his stay in Mexico.[59]

It took U.S. and local officials in Mexico only a few hours to realize that Kennedy's assassin was the same man who contacted the Cuban and Soviet embassies, and they immediately began cooperating to investigate whether Oswald had been part of an international communist conspiracy. At 5 P.M. on the afternoon of November 22, the CIA station in Mexico City cabled headquarters in Washington to point out that Oswald had been in recent contact with Cuban and Soviet officials in Mexico.[60] After headquarters replied that they wanted all information available about Oswald's time in Mexico, CIA Chief of Station Winston Scott sent a message the next morning to Luis Echeverría, Mexico's interim minister of the interior, requesting that the Mexicans arrest and interrogate Silvia Durán.[61] He also asked one of his best officers, Anne Goodpasture, to investigate the actions of Valeriy Kostikov, a KGB operative involved in assassination operations and the Soviet embassy official with whom Oswald had met during his stay in Mexico.[62] At the same time, Mexican officials did their own review of the Soviet embassy wiretaps and, discovering Oswald's contacts with Kostikov, put the KGB agent under

[57] José Manuel Jurado, "Decreta ALM tres días de duelo nacional; Expresa deseos de que no se altere la paz," *Excélsior*, November 23, 1963.

[58] "Indignado, El Lic. Díaz Ordaz reprobó el sacrificio de JFK," *Excélsior*, November 23, 1963.

[59] "Anuncio del Instituto Nacional de Bellas Artes," *Excélsior*, November 23, 1963.

[60] Senate Select Committee to Study Governmental Operations with Respect to Intelligence Activities, *The Investigation of the Assassination of President John F. Kennedy: Performance of the Intelligence Agencies*, Vol. 5 (Washington, D.C.: U.S. Government Printing Office, 1976), 24.

[61] "Sylvia Duran," November 23, 1963, RIF 104-10195-10358, Mary Ferrell Foundation Digital Archive.

[62] Morley, *Our Man in Mexico*, 208.

physical surveillance. President López Mateos called Scott to inform him that Mexican agents had located the transcript of a call that Oswald had made to the Soviet embassy.[63]

Officials in Washington feared that the response in Mexico was spinning out of their control. On the afternoon of November 23, the Mexico desk chief from CIA headquarters contacted Scott to instruct him to call off Durán's arrest. Scott reported that it was too late; he had just received a call from Echeverría promising to "get the woman." CIA headquarters tried sending Scott an urgent telegram: "Arrest of Silvia Durán is [an] extremely serious matter which could prejudice [U.S.] freedom of action on [the] entire question of [Cuban] responsibility." CIA headquarters instructed Scott to ensure that Durán's arrest was "kept absolutely secret, that no information from her is published or leaked, that all information is cabled to us, and [the] fact of her arrest and statements not spread to leftists." A few hours later, Echeverría again contacted Scott to report that Mexican authorities had arrested Durán and a number of her family members; López Mateos had instructed his agents to "proceed and interrogate forcefully." Though the Mexicans promised to try to keep the arrest secret, Scott expected that the Cuban embassy would find out before long.[64]

Winston Scott was right: The Mexican government was only able to keep Durán's arrest a secret for a few days before the Cubans launched a public protest. On the morning of November 26, President Osvaldo Dorticós called Ambassador Joaquín Hernández Armas in the Cuban embassy in Mexico and the two men discussed the arrest.[65] That night, Cuba's foreign minister Raúl Roa summoned Mexican ambassador Gilberto Bosques and gave him a note of protest. The Cuban government also provided the text of the message to the media. Roa's note described Durán's arrest and protested that she had been subjected to a "violent and coercive interrogation" during which the agents had "despicably insinuated that she had personal, even intimate, relations with Oswald." The foreign minister claimed that the conduct of the Mexican police demonstrated that they were complicit in a reactionary plot to kill Kennedy and blame Cuba, concluding, "The unpunished perpetration of these actions damages the friendly relations between our governments."[66] Mexico's

[63] CIA, "Mexico City Chronology," 9–11.
[64] Ibid.
[65] Ibid., 22.
[66] Raúl Roa, "Texto de la nota entregada el día 26 de noviembre de 1963 por el Ministro de Relaciones Exteriores de Cuba, Doctor Raúl Roa, al embajador de México en aquel país, Profesor Gilberto Bosques," November 26, 1963, Leg. III-5714-2, SRE.

foreign minister Manuel Tello fired back; he vehemently rejected the note, calling it unacceptable, and told reporters that because Durán was a Mexican citizen, her arrest did not represent a violation of diplomatic immunity.[67]

Though news of Durán's interrogation went public and caused tension between the Cuban and Mexican governments, U.S. and Mexican authorities managed to keep the existence of another potentially dangerous witness top secret. On November 25, a Nicaraguan man named Gilberto Alvarado contacted U.S. officials in Mexico City to report that during a visit to the Cuban embassy on September 18 he had seen a black man with red hair pass $6,500 to Oswald.[68] Alvarado originally claimed that he was a member of a group of leftist Nicaraguan exiles and was in the process of getting false travel papers from the Cuban embassy to go to Havana for guerrilla training, but later admitted that he had been an agent of the Nicaraguan government sent to spy on exile groups in Mexico. Even though Alvarado had the dates of Oswald's visit wrong and kept changing his back story, his claim that Oswald had received money from the Cubans before assassinating Kennedy was alarming enough to set off a frenzy of activity at the top levels of the U.S. government.

The man who had to step into Kennedy's place, Lyndon Johnson, was especially horrified by the claim that Castro had paid off Kennedy's killer. Johnson had been keeping close track of the investigations in Mexico; on the morning of November 23, he asked FBI director J. Edgar Hoover whether he had established any more information about Oswald's visit to the Soviet embassy in Mexico City, and he appeared to have the issue of Mexico very much on his mind when he met with CIA director John A. McCone the next day.[69] Johnson had been equivocating about how to respond to the assassination until Alvarado's claims about Cuban bribery convinced him that he needed to form a special commission. On November 29, he summoned a reluctant Chief Justice Earl Warren to the Oval Office to convince him to chair the investigation. When Warren resisted, Johnson told him that the situation was dire and read to him from a report describing Alvarado's allegations to show him how close the United States was to nuclear war.[70] Warren relented and, later that evening, Johnson used the same tactic on his old friend and mentor

---

[67] José Manuel Jurado, "Los términos de la queja, inaceptables," *Excélsior*, November 29, 1963.
[68] CIA, "Mexico City Chronology," 19.
[69] Max Holland, *The Kennedy Assassination Tapes* (New York: Knopf, 2004), 72, 82.
[70] Ibid., 160.

Senator Richard Russell to get him to join the commission. "This is a question that has a good many more ramifications than [are] on the surface," Johnson told Russell. "We [have] got to take this out of the arena where they're testifying that Khrushchev and Castro did this and did that, and that [could end up] kicking us into a war that can kill 40 million Americans in an hour."[71]

At the same time that Johnson was using Alvarado's story to terrify people into joining the special commission, U.S. officials in Mexico were working with their local counterparts to resolve the situation with the Nicaraguan. Ambassador Mann was particularly aggressive in his pursuit of answers and sent a message to Washington through CIA channels asking for permission to tell López Mateos about Alvarado's story so that the Mexicans could interrogate him and possibly arrest Durán again to ask her more questions. Mann suggested that the Mexicans be instructed to "go all out" to make Durán confess; he wanted them to tell her that "her only chance for survival is to come clean with the whole story."[72] As had happened a few days before, CIA headquarters told their people in Mexico to hold off on arresting Durán or anyone else only to learn that Mexican police had already hauled her in again.[73]

Officials in Washington were desperate to keep the investigation in Mexico from dragging them into a war with Cuba. After Mann wrote yet another telegram recommending the arrests of more employees of the Cuban embassy, CIA headquarters sent an urgent message to Winston Scott. "For your private information, there is a distinct feeling in all three agencies [CIA, FBI, and the State Department] that Ambassador [Mann] is pushing this case too hard and that we could well create [a] flap with Cubans which could have serious repercussions."[74] The FBI recommended that the CIA station in Mexico City turn Alvarado over to Mexican authorities for interrogation, which they did on November 28. Fernando Gutiérrez Barrios of the Department of Federal Security submitted the Nicaraguan to multiple rounds of questioning and within twenty-four hours got him to sign a statement recanting his entire tale of seeing Oswald receive money in the Cuban embassy. In a meeting with an FBI agent the next day, however, Alvarado reverted to his previous story and claimed that he had only signed the confession because his interrogators had threatened to hang him by his testicles. By then it was too late;

---

[71] Ibid., 197.
[72] CIA, "Mexico City Chronology," 23–4.
[73] Ibid., 27.
[74] Ibid., 29–33.

the White House, State Department, FBI, and CIA had already turned their attention to other aspects of the assassination and sent their official thanks to Mexican officials for discrediting the Nicaraguan's story.[75]

While Alvarado's claim that Oswald had collected money in the Cuban embassy received a great deal of attention, there were other potential leads in Mexico that U.S. officials failed or declined to follow. On December 1, CIA headquarters received a report of unusual activities in the Mexico City airport on the day that Kennedy was murdered; a Cubana Airlines flight had delayed its departure from Mexico until ten at night waiting for an important passenger who arrived on a private airplane and then traveled directly to Havana without passing through Mexican customs.[76] A year later, an "untested" source passed along related information that he claimed to have received from a well-known Cuban scientist. The scientist said that he had been at the Havana airport on the afternoon of Kennedy's death and had seen two Cuban "gangsters" exit a plane with Mexican markings that had arrived from Dallas through Tijuana and Mexico City. A CIA report on the matter noted that they had been unable to follow up with the source because he had died since furnishing the information.[77]

A Mexican writer, Elena Garro de Paz, provided further evidence of a cover-up when she told her story to a political officer in the U.S. embassy a few years later. Garro, the wife of novelist Octavio Paz and famous in her own right, told Charles Thomas in 1965 that she had seen Lee Harvey Oswald at a "twist" party in Mexico City in September 1963. She reported that her cousin's wife, Silvia Durán, whom she despised and considered a whore, was also at the party and had been Oswald's mistress during his stay in Mexico. Garro claimed that she had seen Cuban consul Eusebio Azcue at the twist party and at a different party in the company of a "Latin American negro man with red hair." At the other party, Garro had overheard Azcue and others discussing Kennedy; "they came to the conclusion that the only solution was to kill him," she told Thomas. Garro also claimed that when she found out that Oswald had murdered Kennedy, she and her daughter immediately went to the Cuban embassy and started shouting "assassin" and other insults at the staff. Shortly afterward, a friend from the Mexican interior ministry visited her with orders to escort her to a small, obscure hotel where she was

---

[75] Ibid., 40–2.
[76] Ibid., 41.
[77] Ibid., 90.

kept silent for eight days under the pretext of protection. When Garro asked for permission to go to the U.S. embassy to report what she knew of Oswald's Cuban connections, Mexican officials told her that it would not be safe to do so.[78] Thomas apparently believed Elena Garro's story and wanted to investigate it, but his superiors did not.[79]

Mexican and U.S. responses to Kennedy's assassination reveal that the governments of both countries were more interested in maintaining peace than solving the mystery of his murder. Johnson, López Mateos, and others worried that the assassination would drag the United States and its neighbors into the nuclear war that they had only recently escaped during the Cuban Missile Crisis. Officials in Mexico and the United States were also reticent to launch a full probe because they did not want any details about their surveillance activities to leak out and endanger future operations. Both governments worked together to give the appearance of investigating the murder while actually discarding or hiding evidence that the Cubans might have been involved.

SECURING THE ELECTIONS

Kennedy's tragic and mysterious death could occupy Mexico's leaders for only so long; they had their own country to run. The presidential election of 1964 was approaching and they had every reason to expect some difficulty in managing the political theater of democracy. By that time, it had become customary for groups across the political spectrum to agitate in order to influence the outgoing president's choice for his successor or to gain favors in exchange for acquiescence. The year proceeding López Mateos's election and inauguration in 1958 had seen an outbreak of workers' and student strikes, and that was at the end of a relatively peaceful *sexenio*. It was reasonable for the nation's leaders to fear that the increasing amount of activism and violence that had seized their country with the spread of the Cold War would lead to even worse problems surrounding the 1964 elections.

Mexico's leaders made sure that U.S. officials understood that the need to maintain stability as the elections approached would have implications for their foreign policy. A full two years before the elections, Mexican

---

[78] Ibid., 92–3.

[79] On Garro and her story of the twist party, see Philip Shenon, *A Cruel and Shocking Act: The Secret History of the Kennedy Assassination* (New York: Henry Holt and Company, 2013).

ambassador Antonio Carrillo Flores told Secretary of State Dean Rusk that López Mateos could not change his country's position on Cuba because he was "trying to find a solution that would not boomerang." The ambassador explained that Mexico "was limited by its own political situation and upcoming presidential election ... steps by Mexico on the Castro regime would have serious political consequences."[80] López Mateos gave a similar answer about electoral necessities to U.S. Assistant Secretary of State Edwin Martin when questioned on the subject of Cuba. He reiterated his willingness to give public support to any action against Castro necessary to prevent a serious threat, as during the Cuban Missile Crisis, but added that he would not join in symbolic measures. López Mateos explained that he was especially concerned about the domestic impact of public actions against Castro because he was trying to secure the support of all elements of his party for his upcoming designation of the PRI's next presidential candidate. "With tensions increasing each year between the left and right wings of the party, these objectives can only be secured by avoiding public positions which would tend to alienate either group," he argued.[81]

However, conflict was unavoidable; when López Mateos designated his conservative, repressive minister of the interior, Gustavo Díaz Ordaz, as his successor at the beginning of November 1963, there was an immediate outcry on the left wing of Mexico's political spectrum. Just a few months before, the magazine *Política* had called Díaz Ordaz a reactionary and declared that he "should not and can not become president."[82] In *Política's* coverage of Díaz Ordaz's presidential campaign, the magazine's journalists maintained that the crowds that the government gathered to greet the official candidate responded coldly and indifferently. The magazine claimed that the radio producers who broadcasted Díaz Ordaz's campaign speeches had to splice in applause from other recordings to compensate for the crowds' lukewarm response.[83] The same month that López Mateos designated Díaz Ordaz, the cover of *Política* consisted of a cartoon of the presidential candidate wearing Catholic vestments with a Nazi swastika, carrying a bludgeon in one hand, and stone tablets in the other. The tablets contained a quote from the *Wall*

[80] "Memorandum of a Conversation, Washington, September 18 1962," in *FRUS, 1961–1963: American Republics*, Vol. 12, 320.

[81] "Memorandum from Acting Secretary of State Ball to President Kennedy, Washington, May 24 1963," in *FRUS, 1961–1963: American Republics*, Vol. 12, 346.

[82] José Felipe Pardiñas, "'Política' y la sucesión presidencial," *Política*, May 15, 1963.

[83] "La gira de GDO," *Política*, December 15, 1963.

FIGURE 7. A cover of *Política* magazine with a political cartoon by Rius of Gustavo Díaz Ordaz wearing Catholic vestments with a Nazi swastika, carrying a bludgeon in one hand and stone tablets in the other. The caption below reads: "The candidate and his professional political ballast."

Source: *Política* magazine, November 1, 1963. Courtesy of the Biblioteca Lerdo de Tejada and the U.S. Library of Congress, Historical Newspapers.

Street Journal that described him as "a vehement anti-communist who commands the powerful support of ex-president Miguel Alemán and of the Catholic Church" (see Figure 7). A pamphlet containing a copy of the cartoon and the accompanying article protesting Díaz Ordaz's candidacy made its way into the files of the government's Department of

Political and Social Investigations.[84] The president-to-be was fully aware of *Política*'s criticism.

In addition to denouncing the official candidate, Mexican leftists also decided to create a new political party. Government leaders' fears of an electoral challenge became a reality in April 1963 with the formation of the People's Electoral Front (Frente Electoral del Pueblo, or FEP). On April 22, the leaders of the FEP held a press conference, confirming the rumors about a new, leftist party.[85] They distributed a manifesto that read: "The hour has arrived for the people to choose sides, to unite and organize, to steel themselves to defend, in the electoral battle that approaches, their interests and those of the nation."[86] The FEP leaders described the dangers of demobilizing the Mexican masses, as the PRI had done, and denounced the politicians that "call themselves revolutionaries but deep down agree with the policies of the government." The new party drew support from numerous leftist organizations, including Demetrio Vallejo's National Railroad Workers Council, Othón Salazar's Revolutionary Teachers' Movement, the Independent Campesino Center, and the Mexican Communist Party. The FEP aimed to participate in the 1964 elections, and its leaders hoped that under a new electoral reform law they could at least obtain a few positions in the Congress, as well as in local offices.[87]

The FEP's platform called for the reinvigoration of the Mexican Revolution and defense of the Cuban Revolution. Its candidates demanded political and social democratization, independent economic development, full sovereignty and national liberation, immediate and substantial improvement in the quality of life of Mexican citizens, and respect for self-determination.[88] The leaders of the new party celebrated Cuba as an example of a country that had already achieved many of those goals. At the FEP's national assembly, its presidential candidate, Ramón Danzós Palomino, read a resolution of solidarity with Cuba and called the Cuban Revolution "an example of the emancipatory battle in

---

[84] "['Política' pamphlet]," November 1, 1963, IPS Caja 2851 A, AGN.

[85] Rogelio Cárdenas, "En los frentes políticos: Junta organizadora del FEP," *Excélsior*, April 23, 1963.

[86] "Nace el FEP," *Política*, May 1, 1963.

[87] The Electoral Law of 1962 reformed the constitutionally prescribed electoral allotments, and guaranteed five congressional seats to any party polling at least 2.5 percent of the vote (up to a maximum of twenty seats) even if it did not actually win in any constituencies.

[88] "Convocatoria del FEP," *Política*, October 15, 1963.

the Latin American sphere."[89] A member from the state of Nayarit stated on the same occasion: "We consider the enemies of Cuba our own enemies ... the Cuban Revolution is our revolution, which we must defend and support."

Cuba's ambassador, Joaquín Hernández Armas, must have appreciated the new party's expressions of support, but he was not optimistic about its chances for electoral success. In a report that he sent in June 1963 to Foreign Minister Raúl Roa about Mexico's internal politics, the ambassador observed that even though the FEP purportedly wanted to unite Mexico's leftist forces, it was actually dividing them. The report related opinions of the FEP from various other leftist groups that contained more criticism than praise. Hernández Armas withheld final judgment, but hazarded a guess that "perhaps [the FEP] does not have enough resources to be able to organize such a great mobilization in such a short time."[90]

The Cuban ambassador was right: the creation of the FEP did lead to a great deal of confusion and disagreement among Mexico's leftists. Vicente Lombardo Toledano's Popular Socialist Party rejected the FEP outright. Many of the leaders of the FEP were prominent members of the National Liberation Movement, but the MLN took pains to make clear that the group as a whole would refrain from endorsing any parties or candidates. The MLN tried to preemptively distinguish itself from the new political party by publishing a declaration about the 1964 elections twelve days before the official announcement of the FEP.[91] The declaration affirmed that the National Liberation Movement was not a political party and would not endorse any candidates. It was a coalition of a wide range of liberal groups and individuals, and its leaders believed that supporting the electoral designs of any one of its parts would be a disservice to the whole. When *Política*'s coverage of the formation of the FEP claimed that the MLN had created the new party, the movement's leaders were quick to correct the error in a strongly worded letter to the editor.[92] The National Liberation Movement decided to take a different approach to the electoral process and in November 1963 began preparing propaganda for distribution across the country. Its pamphlets, some of which ended up in the hands of intelligence agents, exhorted voters to

[89] Felix L. Alvahuante et al., "[FEP asamblea nacional day 2]," June 27, 1963, DFS, Exp 11-141-63, Leg. 2, Hoja 148, AGN.
[90] Ambassador Joaquín Hernández Armas to Foreign Minister Raúl Roa, "Política interna," June 28, 1963, América Latina, México, 1963–1967 Ordinario 7: 1963, MINREX.
[91] "El MLN y la campaña electoral," *Política*, May 1, 1963.
[92] Movimiento de Liberación Nacional, "Aclaración del MLN," *Política*, May 15, 1963.

get wise to the government's electoral deception and demonstrate their political consciousness by casting blank ballots.[93]

The FEP's relationship with Lázaro Cárdenas was also ambiguous and controversial. The former president had shown his willingness to support leftist groups when he spoke out in favor of the National Liberation Movement and the Independent Campesino Center. The question on everyone's mind in 1963 and 1964 was: Whom would Cárdenas endorse for president? The counselor of the U.S. embassy in Mexico, Robert W. Adams, told his superiors in July 1963 that Cárdenas's influence on the elections and his relationship with the FEP was "an enigma."[94] Agents of Mexico's Federal Police reported that leftist leaders were observed discussing instructions from Cárdenas to form a *campesino* army. According to the report, "General Lázaro Cárdenas had told them to form brigades of armed campesinos in all of the States of the Republic, as well as here in the Federal District, so that at the necessary moment they can confront the Army and the Police."[95] The head of the Department of Federal Security reported in February 1964 that Cárdenas had been seen meeting with FEP leaders.[96] FEP candidates added to the confusion by invoking Cárdenas's name and legacy in their campaign. The FEP's presidential nominee, Danzós Palomino, told the crowd at a rally in Cuautla, Morelia, that after Cárdenas's departure from office, the government had suffered a marked regression.[97] In Cárdenas's birthplace of Jiquilpan, Michoacán, the FEP candidate called his administration "the only revolutionary and progressive regime."[98] In Zamora, Michoacán, Danzós led a crowd of three hundred *campesinos* in a round of cheers for the FEP, the CCI, and Lázaro Cárdenas.[99] All these events generated extensive reports from the Mexican security agencies. Cárdenas broke his sphinxlike silence shortly before the elections, and his decision struck

[93] José Jiménez García, "[MLN propaganda encouraging people to cast blank votes]," November 29, 1963, DFS, Exp 11-6-63, Leg. 11, Hoja 171, AGN.

[94] Robert W. Adams, "Progress Report on the Presidential Race," July 30, 1963, NSF, Countries, Box 141, JFK Library.

[95] Jefatura de Policía del DF Secretaría Particular, "[Lázaro Cárdenas is organizing a campesino army]," September 6, 1963, DFS, Exp 11-6-63, Leg. 10, Hoja 264, AGN.

[96] Manuel Rangel Escamilla, "[Cárdenas meeting with FEP leaders]," February 26, 1964, DFS, VPLC, Leg. 3, Hoja 139, AGN.

[97] Manuel Rangel Escamilla, "[FEP campaign–Morelia]," April 10, 1964, DFS, Exp 11-141-64, Leg. 8, Hoja 59, AGN.

[98] Manuel Rangel Escamilla, "[FEP campaign–Michoacán]," February 27, 1964, DFS, Exp 11-141-64, Leg. 7, Hoja 59, AGN.

[99] Manuel Rangel Escamilla, "[FEP campaign–Michoacán]," February 26, 1964, DFS, Exp 11-141-64, Leg. 7, Hoja 55, AGN.

a blow to his friends in the FEP. "Gustavo Díaz Ordaz has the recognized honesty and character to govern, and will protect the weak against the strong," Cárdenas declared on June 9, 1964, ending the debate over his political loyalties.[100]

Even without Cárdenas's endorsement, the leaders of the People's Electoral Front worked tirelessly to organize a grassroots challenge to the PRI's political machine. They held assemblies in states across the nation in order to get the seventy-five thousand signatures required to gain official recognition as a party. They organized a national registration assembly in Mexico City, attended by members of the National Liberation Movement, Independent Campesino Center, Mexican Communist Party, and workers' unions, as well as by numerous police and intelligence agents.[101] Less than three months after the FEP's leaders announced the creation of their new party, they presented the Ministry of the Interior with a petition for recognition containing more than eighty-four thousand signatures.[102] Díaz Ordaz denied the FEP official recognition, however, claiming that it did not hold the required number of registration assemblies and that many of the signatures on the petition were falsifications or repetitions.[103] The leaders of the FEP resolved to maintain the fight and participate in the elections, regardless of Díaz Ordaz's response. In November an intelligence agent told his superiors that the FEP's presidential candidate was about to begin his tour of the Yucatán Peninsula, "where he is said to count on the support of seventy-five percent of the population."[104] The intelligence report suggested that the lack of official recognition had not dampened public enthusiasm for the FEP.

It was easy enough to prevent the FEP from coming to power through legal elections; what worried Mexican authorities much more was the possibility that leftist groups and individuals might use more insidious tactics to cause instability and seize power. The head of the Department of Federal Security reported in September 1963 that leaders of the Independent Campesino Center and the People's Electoral Front were

[100] "Díaz Ordaz visitó la Cuenca del Balsas acompañado de Cárdenas: Al darle bienvenida a la región, el ex presidente expresó su confianza en que el candidato del PRI sabrá gobernar," *El Nacional*, June 10, 1964.

[101] Manuel Rangel Escamilla, "FEP asamblea de registro," June 16, 1963, DFS, Exp 11-141-63, Leg. 1, Hoja 133, AGN.

[102] "Partido habemus," *Política*, July 15, 1963; Manuel Rangel Escamilla, "[FEP petitions to become a political party]," July 5, 1963, DFS, Exp 11-141-63, Leg. 2, Hoja 197, AGN.

[103] "El FEP, sin registro," *Política*, November 1, 1963.

[104] "[FEP candidate begins campaign]," November 7, 1963, DFS, Exp 11-141-63, Leg. 4, Hoja 81, AGN.

purchasing weapons to distribute among *campesinos* and railroad workers in Baja California. He also claimed that the FEP was forming shock brigades that would bring weapons to demonstrations in order to repel the grenadiers and secret police.[105] A few months later, another intelligence agent submitted an even more appalling report. He claimed that the National Liberation Movement, upon orders from Cuauhtémoc Cárdenas, had called a secret meeting about forming a militia. Members of the Independent Campesino Center, the People's Electoral Front, the Popular Socialist Party, the Mexican Communist Party, and railroad workers who followed Demetrio Vallejo supposedly attended. These militias would be in charge of managing the opposition to Díaz Ordaz's presidential candidacy through sabotage and assassination. At the secret meeting, the leftist groups also reportedly agreed to accelerate the training of guerrilla troops, equipping them with weapons that were soon to arrive from Cuba.[106]

Numerous intelligence reports claimed that the Cubans and Soviets had connections with leftist organizations and parties within Mexico. One agent, in a report about the FEP, informed his superiors about "communist activities" in the states of Veracruz, Chiapas, and Oaxaca; according to the official, a clandestine guerrilla group in possession of Czechoslovakian weapons had installed itself in those three states. The weapons supposedly came from Cuba. The intelligence agent suspected that the guerrillas were receiving instructions from communist members of the PPS in Mexico City and from a naturalized Spaniard of Czech origin, Alfredo Hirsch Bumenthal. Hirsch, in addition to working for various Mexican insurance companies, was also rumored to be a Soviet spy who operated in worldwide espionage circles under the alias "Mink." The intelligence report described him as "the most dangerous and important communist agent in Mexico." It claimed that he "directly serves the Czechoslovakian and Soviet embassies, from which he receives instructions." The report explained that Hirsch's work in the field of insurance facilitated his labors of espionage and subversion. In the margins, someone scrawled: "*Se investiga*" – under investigation.[107] The intelligence officer's superiors might not have believed his claims automatically, but they were willing to take them into consideration.

[105] Manuel Rangel Escamilla, "[FEP and CCI acquiring weapons]," September 9, 1963, DFS, Exp 11-141-63, Leg. 3, Hoja 93, AGN.
[106] "[MLN militias]," December 4, 1963, DFS, Exp 11-6-63, Leg. 11, Hoja 180, AGN.
[107] Ricardo Ruiz Hidalgo, "Asunto: FEP," September 3, 1963, DFS, Exp 11-141-63, Leg. 3, Hoja 112, AGN.

As the elections approached, the warnings about violent opposition and guerrilla groups increased. The head of the Department of Federal Security reported in February 1964 that leaders of the FEP had been overheard bragging about how many followers they had ready to go to the mountains. One leader reportedly claimed that he had twenty-five thousand men in Chihuahua prepared to stage guerrilla warfare against the government. Another said that he planned to gather ten thousand men to take to the hills around Mexico City. They would operate there for about five to six weeks, "just like the guerrillas of Fidel Castro," in order to pressure the government to provide more support to *campesinos* and workers.[108] Another DFS agent reported that members of the CCI in the state of Colima were receiving training in the methods of guerrilla warfare from a retired veteran of the Mexican Revolution.[109] According to the CIA, President López Mateos and other Mexican officials were "greatly concerned over the success Communist agitators have achieved in winning influence among the peasants of north Mexico" and feared that communists might try to assassinate Díaz Ordaz.[110]

While some of these reports were obviously false or exaggerated, Mexican intelligence agents were not completely fabricating the existence of threats: outbreaks of violence surrounding the elections did actually occur. On April 6, 1964, the visit of presidential candidate Gustavo Díaz Ordaz provoked a riot in Chihuahua. After the speeches ended, a commotion broke out and the crowd of ten thousand people set fire to the front of the city hall and assaulted Díaz Ordaz's hotel. Díaz Ordaz suffered a minor injury when a piece of wood struck him on the head.[111] State officials across the country took measures to avoid further disturbances. A few days after the incident in Chihuahua, the governor of Guerrero sent a telegram to the interim minister of the interior, Luis Echeverría, to request advice on dealing with "extreme leftist" plans to agitate against the state government.[112] Two months later, on the eve of the elections, the same governor sent another telegram. This time, he passed along recommendations from a local authority that some

[108] Manuel Rangel Escamilla, "[FEP members ready to fight]," February 27, 1964, DFS, Exp 11-141-64, Leg. 7, Hoja 61, AGN.

[109] "[CCI guerrilla plans]," May 29, 1964, DFS, Exp 11-136-64, Leg. 6, Hoja 12, AGN.

[110] CIA, "Daily Brief: Mexico," May 1, 1964. CREST Database, CIA-RDP79T00975A007600380001-6, NARA.

[111] Ibid; "Leading Mexican Candidate Is Hurt in Campaign Riot," *New York Times*, April 8, 1964.

[112] Dr. Raymundo Abarca Alarcón, "[Extreme leftist agitators]," April 9, 1964, IPS Caja 2851 A, AGN.

recently active subversives be relocated to another state or part of the country until the elections had passed.[113]

The government's security measures worked: Gustavo Díaz Ordaz was elected president on July 5, 1964 with no significant opposition. Even *Política* admitted that Díaz Ordaz had won without recourse to fraud; the editors of the magazine attributed his victory instead to the public's low level of civic consciousness, calling it "a hard lesson for the Left."[114] The next day, the head of intelligence in the Department of Federal Security reported that the organizers of the People's Electoral Front were content to celebrate the three hundred thousand votes that their candidates had received in the states of Tamaulipas, Nuevo León, Jalisco, Sonora, Baja California, and Guerrero. "The FEP has thousands and thousands of sympathizers across the Republic," Danzós Palomino boasted to his fellow party leaders, "and whether the officials of this government like it or not, within a year our group will be registered as an official political party."[115] Instead of presenting a real challenge to the government, either at the ballot boxes or on the battlefield, most of the leftist opposition quietly accepted yet another imposed president.

MEXICO STANDS ALONE WITH CUBA

At the same time that Mexico's leaders were trying to orchestrate a smooth electoral process, they had to answer a pressing question of foreign policy: would Mexico join the hemispheric effort to isolate Cuba? Venezuela's government had accused Castro of providing weapons to guerrilla groups and had spent months petitioning the OAS to take action against Cuba. Mexico's responses to earlier situations involving Cuba provided little in the way of a clear precedent: at the January 1962 OAS meeting Mexico had abstained from the vote that expelled Cuba, but in October of that year Mexico had supported the international effort to pressure the Cubans to relinquish Soviet missiles. As Mexican leaders had warned their U.S. colleagues on multiple occasions, they were worried that the Castro issue would create domestic discord and rifts in the PRI's coalition during the crucial build-up to the elections. Mexico's

---

[113] Dr. Raymundo Abarca Alarcón, "[Electoral agitation]," June 29, 1964, IPS Caja 2851 A, AGN.

[114] "El triunfo electoral de Díaz Ordaz, dura lección para la izquierda," *Política*, July 15, 1964, back cover.

[115] Manuel Rangel Escamilla, "Frente Electoral del Pueblo," July 7, 1964, DFS, Exp 11-141-64, Leg. 10, Hoja 217, AGN.

ambassador to the OAS reportedly told the rest of the assembly that "the Mexican government may fall" if it abandoned its defense of Cuba.[116]

Ultimately, López Mateos decided to use his response to the Cuba question to shore up leftist support for the government ahead of the elections. Articles in the government's mouthpiece newspaper, *El Nacional*, began laying the groundwork a month before the July 1964 OAS meeting, highlighting Mexico's dedication to the principles of self-determination and nonintervention.[117] A few days before the July 5 presidential election, Foreign Minister José Gorostiza met with López Mateos and then held a press conference. Downplaying the inconsistencies in Mexico's policy toward Cuba, the minister declared: "Mexico's foreign policy is unchangeable ... its line has been traced with absolute clarity and firmness since a long time ago."[118] Rather than waiting a few weeks until the OAS meeting to make its position known, the Mexican government timed its announcement about Cuba to coincide with the elections.

Mexico's leaders were true to their word: when the rest of the countries of Latin America voted that all diplomatic and economic ties to Cuba should be severed, Mexico alone refused to comply. Mexico's representative to the OAS, Vicente Sánchez Gavito, told Mexican reporters that he didn't believe that the Venezuelans had provided adequate evidence for their accusations that Castro had threatened the peace and security of the Americas. He argued that the Rio Treaty regarding hemispheric defense should only be invoked in serious cases of threat and should not be used as a tool to further discord among the nations of the Americas.[119] Furthermore, he maintained, any "collective" sanctions would affect the OAS member countries unequally, because only four countries still maintained diplomatic relations with Cuba at that point and only Mexico still had air contact.[120] Sánchez Gavito made the same arguments in his speech to the OAS assembly, declaring "Our victory is

[116] Virginia Prewett, "Mexico Fights OAS Action against Cuba," *Washington Daily News*, June 24, 1964, CIA CREST Database, NARA.
[117] Carlos Villar-Borda, "La autodeterminación es la base de México y Chile, en la OEA," *El Nacional*, June 21, 1964.
[118] "Clara e inmutable, la doctrina internacional de México: Terminante declaración de Gorostiza sobre la Junta de Cancilleres de la OEA," *El Nacional*, July 2, 1964.
[119] On the Rio Treaty, see Hans-Joachim Leu and Freddy Vivas, eds., *Las relaciones interamericanas: Una antología de documentos* (Caracas: Universidad Central de Venezuela, 1975), 132–7.
[120] "Amplias declaraciones del delegado mexicano ante la OEA," *El Nacional*, July 23, 1964. The four countries that still had relations with Cuba were Mexico, Chile, Uruguay, and Bolivia. Mexico was the only one that refused to implement the OAS's resolutions after the July 1964 meeting.

in the imperturbable observance of our principles and in the constant invigoration of our democracy."[121]

Mexico's defiance of the OAS made front-page news. Editorialists praised the "international nobility" of their country's position, while political cartoons showed a Mexican cowboy bringing a message of fraternity, peace, and self-determination to the world (see Figure 8).[122] *El Nacional* explicitly celebrated the domestic benefits of Mexico's foreign policy. "All Mexicans Are with the Government in the Case of the OAS," one headline declared.[123] Other front-page articles described support for the government's Cuba policy on the part of workers, intellectuals, bureaucrats, and lawyers.[124] One reporter characterized the country's position in the OAS as the "express mandate of the people."[125] The coverage of the OAS meeting in the pages of *El Nacional* conveyed the impression that Mexico's foreign policy was so "unobjectionable" that the entire country had united around it.[126]

El Nacional's assessment of the domestic climate was correct: broad swathes of the population celebrated Mexico's policy toward Cuba. In a message to the head of Mexico's OAS delegation, Lázaro Cárdenas wrote that the "just interpretation of Mexico's international policy ... deserved the unanimous support of the people."[127] He sent similar letters to President López Mateos and Foreign Minister José Gorostiza.[128] Intelligence agents reported that the National Liberation Movement circulated a document praising Mexico's position in the OAS.[129] Leaders

---

[121] "Intervención del representante de México en la IX Reunión de Cancilleres de la OEA," *Política*, August 1, 1964.

[122] José Muñoz Cota, "Nobleza internacional de México," *El Nacional*, July 20, 1964, sec. Editorial; "México lucha por la dignidad de los pueblos," *El Nacional*, July 22, 1964, sec. Editorial.

[123] "Todos los mexicanos están con el gobierno en el caso de la OEA," *El Nacional*, July 19, 1964.

[124] "Respaldo a la política del régimen," *El Nacional*, July 29, 1964; "Pleno apoyo a la posición del gobierno," *El Nacional*, July 19, 1964; "Se exaltó el patriotismo de la obra del Presidente López Mateos," *El Nacional*, July 29, 1964; Luis Ernesto Cárdenas, "Se le da la razón a México en su política internacional," *El Nacional*, July 30, 1964; "Adhesión de los empleados de la SSA a la política internacional mexicana," *El Nacional*, July 25, 1964.

[125] "'No vamos a atacar ni a defender a ningún gobierno'–Sánchez Gavito," *El Nacional*, July 19, 1964.

[126] Pedro Guillen, "La inobjetable posición de México," *El Nacional*, July 18, 1964, sec. Editorial.

[127] Lázaro Cárdenas, *Epistolario de Lázaro Cárdenas* (Mexico City: Siglo XXI, 1975), 154.

[128] Ibid., 153, 155.

[129] Manuel Rangel Escamilla, "Se informa en relación con el Movimiento de Liberación Nacional," August 7, 1964, DFS, Exp 11-6-64, Leg. 12, Hoja 324, AGN.

FIGURE 8. A political cartoon by Salvador Pruneda from the officialista newspaper *El Nacional* showing a Mexican cowboy (or mariachi) bringing a message of fraternity, peace, and self-determination to the world. The title over the cartoon reads: "In the meeting of Chancellors," and the caption below reads: "Mexico firmly maintained its loyal posture in accordance with the doctrine of self-determination and the rejection of all interventionism in the internal affairs of nations."

Source: *El Nacional* newspaper, July 28, 1964. Courtesy of the Biblioteca Lerdo de Tejada.

of the Independent Campesino Center and the People's Electoral Front wrote celebratory letters to the press and the president.[130]

Many of these same groups held demonstrations to show their support for Mexico's foreign policy. Nearly two thousand people gathered in a theater in Mexico City to repudiate the OAS and show their dedication to Castro. A speaker from the National Liberation Movement praised the Mexican government's "virile defense of the Cuban people." Alonso Aguilar Monteverde, one of the founders of the MLN, affirmed: "This is how a government can win the support of its people." A leader of the Mexican Communist Party used the same evocative language when he told the audience members that they should support the government of López Mateos for its "virile and independent attitude in the meeting of ministers." Even muralist David Álfaro Siqueiros, who had been recently released after spending nearly four years as a political prisoner, congratulated the government on its foreign policy.[131]

Mexicans across the political spectrum showed approval of their government's OAS stance. Journalists, lawyers, businessmen, bankers, industrialists, revolutionary veterans, petroleum workers, *campesinos*, intellectuals, poets, senators, congressmen, governors, students, and teachers all expressed their support for Mexico's foreign policy. Even conservative ideologue Mario Guerra Leal praised the government's "dignified international posture."[132] Thomas Mann reassured those who worried about retaliation from the United States when he told reporters that he understood that Mexico's policy was a defense of principles, not of Castro, and said that it would not affect Mexico's relations with the United States.[133]

A leader of the People's Electoral Front best captured the significance of his country's stance in a speech entitled "Why Mexico Did Not Vote against Cuba." He told his audience that they should not be grateful

[130] "Apoyo al presidente," *Política*, July 15, 1964; Manuel Rangel Escamilla, "Se informa en relación con el Frente Electoral del Pueblo," July 23, 1964, DFS, Exp 11-141-64, Leg. 11, Hoja 9, AGN; "[FEP letter to López Mateos about OAS meeting]," July 29, 1964, DFS, Exp 11-141-64, Leg. 11, Hoja 72, AGN.

[131] Manuel Rangel Escamilla, "Mitin de apoyo a Cuba," July 26, 1964, DFS, Exp 11-141-64, Leg. 11, Hoja 22, AGN; "Distrito Federal: Mitin en el Teatro 'Lírico,'" July 26, 1964, IPS Caja 444, Exp 2, AGN; "Por México y por Cuba," *Política*, August 1, 1964. On Siqueiros's imprisonment and release, see "Siqueiros en libertad," *Política*, July 15, 1964.

[132] "Unidad Nacional," *Política*, August 1, 1964; "Solidaridad con el gobierno," *Política*, August 15, 1964.

[133] "Thomas Mann comprende la posición de México en la OEA," *El Nacional*, July 24, 1964.

to the Mexican representative in the OAS for refusing to vote against Cuba, but instead should "thank the diverse social sectors in the country that forced the government to act in this manner."[134] In one sentence, the speaker explained both the creation and the importance of Mexico's policy toward Castro. The Mexican government had decided to maintain relations with Cuba in response to pressure from domestic groups. Defense of the Cuban Revolution was a cause around which the disparate leftist groups could have united, had the government cut relations with Castro.

Instead, Mexico's leaders turned that threat into an opportunity and used their ties with Cuba to ingratiate themselves with same people who could have been dangerous opponents. After the Mexican government refused to break relations with Cuba, students joined the nationwide chorus of support. Professors and students from the School of Economics of the National University sent a telegram to President López Mateos commending the "practical attitude of your government in solidly opposing the subordination of Mexico's most precious interests to the provocative and interventionist politics of those who wish to set themselves up as governors of the Cuban people."[135] At a meeting of young members of the PCM and the FEP, one attendee stated that maintaining relations with Cuba was "the only thing for which we are grateful to the president."[136]

The decision to maintain relations with Cuba also placated another potential opponent: Fidel Castro. Castro responded to the OAS meeting by excoriating the rest of the nations of Latin America in his "Declaration of Santiago de Cuba," calling the hemispheric resolution "an unprecedented, cynical act in which the victimizers claim to be judges in order to impose illegal sanctions against the victim."[137] He warned that if the attacks and acts of sabotage did not cease, the people of Cuba would consider it their right to assist revolutionary movements in all the countries that practiced similar interference in Cuban affairs.

Castro showed equal passion when it came to praising Mexico for defying the OAS. "We understand with all sincerity," he proclaimed, "that the current president of Mexico, [Adolfo López Mateos], will go down in history, like the great president Lázaro Cárdenas, among the good and

---

[134] Manuel Rangel Escamilla, "Frente Electoral del Pueblo," August 6, 1964, DFS, Exp 11-141-64, Leg. 11, Hoja 83, AGN.

[135] "Unidad nacional," *Política*, August 1, 1964.

[136] Manuel Rangel Escamilla, "[PCM and FEP members praise Mexico's Cuba policy]," September 3, 1964, DFS, Exp 11-141-64, Leg. 11, Hoja 156, AGN.

[137] "Declaración de Santiago de Cuba," *Política*, August 1, 1964.

the great presidents that Mexico has had." Castro reiterated his respect
for López Mateos and admiration for his country's history of resistance
and revolution. "With the government of Mexico we are disposed to con-
verse and discuss," he said; "we are disposed to compromise, to maintain
a policy subject to norms, inviolable norms of respect for the sovereignty
of each country."[138] Mexico's defiance of the OAS resolution gave Castro
a chance to demonstrate his willingness to respect governments that
showed him the same courtesy.

The Cuban newspaper *Revolución* also celebrated Mexico's refusal to
comply with the rest of the OAS. Headlines praised Mexico's valor and
proclaimed "Mexico Repudiates the Sanctions against Cuba."[139] Articles
quoted numerous Mexican leaders expounding upon the "ties of friendship" between the two countries and the need to resist the OAS's "igno-
minious" actions. They published statements from writer Carlos Fuentes
that his country's defense of Cuba amounted to the greatest contribution that Mexico had made to the international order since the days of
Cárdenas.[140] The Cuban press dedicated pages and pages to the theme of
Mexican-Cuban solidarity.

Privately, Cuban officials had a much more cynical view of the Mexican
government and its response to the Cuban Revolution. A memorandum
composed by an official in the Ministry of Foreign Relations enumerated
the various factors that explained Mexico's policy toward Cuba, including the solidarity with the Cuban Revolution that multiple Mexican
organizations and political parties had demonstrated, and Mexico's own
history of revolution and foreign intervention. The memorandum also
pointed out the contradictions between Mexico's defense of Cuba on the
international stage and its repression of pro-Cuba demonstrations within
Mexico. It concluded:

As an analysis of the internal politics of President López Mateos would illustrate,
the various governments that Mexico has suffered from in more or less intense

---

[138] Fidel Castro Ruz, "Ninguna autoridad moral ni jurídica tiene la OEA para tomar medidas contra Cuba: Discurso del primer ministro y primer secretario del Partido Unido de
la Revolución Socialista Cubana, Fidel Castro, el 26 de Julio de 1964," *Política*, August
1, 1964; "México mantuvo la posición más firme en su oposición a este acuerdo cínico,"
Revolución, July 27, 1964.

[139] "México ha tenido el valor de mantener esa posición igual que Uruguay, Chile y
Bolivia," *Revolución*, July 27, 1964; "Rechazo a acuerdos de la OEA: Repudia México
las sanciones contra Cuba," *Revolución*, July 29, 1964.

[140] "Paro general obrero en Uruguay en apoyo a Cuba y contra la OEA: Líderes de
México elogían actitud de su gobierno contra el acuerdo anticubano," *Revolución*, July
31, 1964.

TABLE 1. *Mexico's imports from Cuba, 1959–1969*

Year	Mexico's Imports from Cuba (value in million pesos)
1959	8.15
1960	11.34
1961	2.69
1962	0.26
1963	0.08
1964	0.29
1965	0.14
1966	0.47
1967	0.71
1968	0.35
1969	0.28

Source: United Nations *Yearbook of International Trade Statistics* (New York: Department of Economic and Social Affairs, 1963, 1966, 1969).

ways have been maintained behind the backs of the Mexican public, limiting and violating in the majority of occasions the principles framed in their constitution. This contradiction between Mexico's external and internal policy results from the fact that the democratic-bourgeois revolution has been departing every day more from its original postulates; the bourgeoisie has been solidifying its position in power and in order to maintain itself there, it has been necessary to accentuate the methods of repressing the country's exploited classes.[141]

Though the author or authors of this memorandum composed it a year before the 1964 OAS meeting, little had happened in the intervening time to change the situation that they described.

Mexico's relations with Cuba were in fact very limited by 1964, and had more to do with political utility than revolutionary solidarity. Already in 1961, Mexico's imports from Cuba had dropped from eleven million pesos to a little under three million. Mexico's imports from Cuba continued to decline the following year and remained negligible for the rest of the decade (see Table 1). In this manner, the Mexican government quietly implemented the sanctions against Castro without officially approving them.[142] Controlling Mexican exports to Cuba proved a greater

[141] "Posición del gobierno mexicano con respecto a la revolución cubana," July 9, 1963, *América Latina, México, 1963–1967*, Ordinario 7: 1963, MINREX.

[142] On Mexico's opposition to sanctions at the VII Meeting of Foreign Ministers of the OAS in San José, Costa Rica, in August 1960, see Bobadilla González, *México y la OEA*, 75.

TABLE 2. *Mexico's exports to Cuba, 1959–1969*

Year	Mexico's Exports to Cuba (in million pesos)
1959	35.6
1960	18.37
1961	43.3
1962	9.9
1963	8.29
1964	31.19
1965	20.14
1966	6.56
1967	79.31
1968	50.12
1969	0.37

Source: *United Nations Yearbook of International Trade Statistics* (New York: Department of Economic and Social Affairs, 1963, 1966, 1969).

challenge. Throughout the 1960s, the volume of exports fluctuated (see Table 2). López Mateos told Ambassador Mann in December 1961 that Mexico had taken unilateral measures against Castro including refusing to sell petroleum products and preventing delivery of foodstuffs to the island. The two men also discussed cooperating to prevent the transshipment of U.S. goods to Cuba.[143] The latter effort apparently failed; in 1964 the Department of Commerce reported that Mexico was one of the three principle transshipment points in the world for U.S.-origin products going to Cuba. Most significantly, automobile parts and equipment from the United States entered the Caribbean island through this channel.[144]

By the time of the 1964 OAS meeting, Mexican authorities had already managed to apply unofficial sanctions against Cuba in other, more effective, ways. In 1962, Ambassador Mann observed that the Mexican government denied port facilities to ships engaging in trade between Cuba and the Soviet bloc.[145] Authorities in the international airport in Mexico City compiled lists and photographs of everyone traveling to and from

[143] Thomas Mann, "Mexico City to Department of State," December 17, 1961, NSF, Countries, Box 141, JFK Library.

[144] "Ninth Meeting of Foreign Ministers Pan American Union, Washington DC, July 21–24 1964 Background Paper: Cuban Foreign Trade," July 17, 1964, RG 59, Entry P2, ARC 602903, Box 1, NARA.

[145] Thomas Mann, "Mexico City to Secretary of State," December 31, 1962, NSF, Countries, Box 54, JFK Library.

Cuba, which they shared with the CIA.[146] They marked the passports of everyone arriving from Havana with a special "Entry from Cuba" stamp to prevent clandestine travel.[147] Cuban officials complained in internal documents "the Mexican Government lets its agents, under the direction of the U.S. embassy, commit discriminatory acts against nationals and foreigners who travel to Cuba."[148] U.S. authorities summed up Mexico's efforts in a briefing book for President Johnson: "Mexico has taken unpublicized measures to restrict travel to and from Cuba and has cooperated with the U.S. against Castro in other ways which do not draw public attention."[149]

What was more, Mexican and U.S. officials observed that their countries could actually benefit from the maintenance of relations between Mexico and Cuba. The State Department was well aware of the intelligence opportunities that Mexico's relations with Cuba presented. In a memorandum about the possible repercussions of a break between the two countries, U.S. embassy officials observed, "existing communications and travel between Mexico and Cuba provide an extremely useful intelligence channel used by U.S. agencies." The report described Castro's espionage operations in Mexico as relatively minor compared to those of the United States, concluding, "The severance of relations would affect U.S. intelligence collection capability far more adversely than it would the Cuban capacity in Mexico."[150]

Top officials in Mexico and the U.S. were more oblique when they spoke about the benefits of Mexico's ties with Cuba. Shortly after Mexico defied the OAS resolution, Mexican president-elect Díaz Ordaz remarked to U.S. ambassador Fulton Freeman at a dinner party that it could be useful to leave ajar the only remaining door from Cuba to Latin America.[151]

[146] On photographing operations at the Mexico City airport, see *FRUS, 1961–1963: American Republics*, Vol. 12, 245; "Cuban Airlists," December 19, 1963, RG 233 Box 90 Reel 46 JFK/CIA RIF 104-10516-10312, NARA; "Procuraduría: Los censores del aeropuerto," *Política*, August 1, 1962; Anne Goodpasture, "Mexico City Station History."

[147] Thomas Mann, "Mexico City to Secretary of State," April 3, 1963, NSF, Countries, Box 141, JFK Library.

[148] "Posición del gobierno mexicano con respecto a la revolución cubana," July 9, 1963, América Latina, México, 1963–1967, Ordinario 7: 1963, MINREX.

[149] "Meeting of Presidents Johnson and López Mateos in California, February 20–22 1964: Background Paper: U.S.-Mexican Cooperation on Cuba," February 1964, NSF, Mexico, Box 61, LBJ Library.

[150] U.S. Embassy–Mexico, "Effect in Mexico of Severance of Mexican-Cuban Relations," June 8, 1964, RG 59, Entry P2, ARC 602903, Box 1, NARA.

[151] Fulton Freeman, "Mexico City to Secretary of State," August 25, 1964, NSF, Mexico, Box 58, Folder 9, Document 75, LBJ Library.

Mexico's Cold War

Rusk seemed to have the same idea when he told the National Security Council that the United States did not push Mexico to break its connections with Cuba because it was the last remaining air link between Havana and the mainland.[152] He also advised Johnson not to pressure Díaz Ordaz on the Cuba issue. "During our foreign ministers meeting in late July, a number of us– Brazil and others – talked about the practical desirability of having one Latin American embassy [in Cuba] if possible ... and so the hemisphere is fairly relaxed about the Mexicans staying on there for a time," Rusk explained.[153]

This agreement about Mexico's ties to Cuba endured. In 1967, three years after Mexico became the only Latin American country to maintain relations with Castro, the U.S. deputy chief of mission in the embassy in Mexico cabled the State Department about the matter. He mentioned an "informal understanding" at the highest levels of the U.S. and Mexican governments that the latter should maintain relations with Castro so that "one OAS country can have [a] foot in the door which might sometime be helpful."[154]

One group that certainly benefited from the open door between Mexico and Cuba were U.S. citizens who sought repatriation to the United States from the island. On multiple occasions throughout the 1960s, Mexican officials facilitated the departure of U.S. nationals and their families from Cuba.[155] In December 1966, the Mexican ambassador to Cuba convinced Castro to authorize the repatriation of approximately two thousand U.S. citizens, who would return to their homeland through Mexico.[156] The U.S. ambassador to Mexico, Fulton Freeman,

[152] "Summary Record on National Security Meeting No. 536, July 28, 1964," July 28, 1964, NSF, NSC Meetings File, Box 1, LBJ Library.

[153] [Telephone conversation between Johnson and Rusk], Recordings of Telephone Conversations-White House Series (Tape WH6411.18: Dean Rusk, 9:40 a.m., PNO 6342, 1964), LBJ Library.

[154] Henry Dearborn, "Telegram from Henry Dearborn to the Secretary of State," June 28, 1967, RG 59, CFPF 67–69, POL Cuba-A, NARA. On the long history of U.S. communication with Castro through back channels, see William M. LeoGrande and Peter Kornbluh, *Back Channel to Cuba: The Hidden History of Negotiations between Washington and Havana* (Chapel Hill: University of North Carolina Press, 2014).

[155] Dirección General de Información, "[Repatriation of U.S. citizens]," December 5, 1968, IPS Caja 2958 E, AGN; Fernando Gutiérrez Barrios, "Estado de Yucatán," December 28, 1966, IPS Caja 2958 E, AGN.

[156] "Gracias a México, salen de Cuba cientos de norteamericanos: Puente aéreo entre La Habana y Mérida," *Excélsior*, December 29, 1966.

cautioned his superiors to keep this assistance in mind when deciding whether to try to push Mexico on Cuban matters in the OAS.[157]

CONCLUSION

President López Mateos managed to perform a difficult balancing act when conducting his international relations with Cuba and the United States. Numerous members of the U.S. government and public tried to pressure the Mexican government into cutting relations with Cuba. On multiple occasions – OAS meetings, the Cuban Missile Crisis, the Kennedy assassination – López Mateos had to take this factor into account when deciding how to approach the Cuba issue. At the same time, he was trying to maintain stability at home and the appearance of democratic rule. A large swath of domestic leftist groups unanimously demanded that their government defend the neighboring revolutionary regime.

López Mateos crafted an intricate, flexible foreign policy that allowed him to maintain his various domestic and international alliances. In public, Mexico's government defended Cuba's right to self-determination and nonintervention. This pleased not only Castro, but also the disparate leftist groups within Mexico that might otherwise have united around their shared enthusiasm for Cuba. However, the Mexican government also quietly implemented many of the same economic and political sanctions against Cuba that it was publicly protesting, which, combined with Mexico's assistance in intelligence collection, earned the gratitude of U.S. officials. As López Mateos's six years in office came to a close, the question became: Would the dogmatic, conservative Gustavo Díaz Ordaz manage to navigate the minefield of Mexico's Cold War as successfully as his predecessor?

---

[157] Fulton Freeman, "Mexico City to Secretary of State," September 1967, NSF, Mexico, Memos and Miscellaneous, Vol. 3, 3/67–11/67 (2 of 3), LBJ Library.

5

Insurgent Mexico

By the time that Gustavo Díaz Ordaz made the transition from minister of the interior to president, his predecessor Adolfo López Mateos had managed to resolve most of the international difficulties that the Cuban Revolution presented to the Mexican government; the internal aspects of Mexico's Cold War, however, would continue to prove a greater challenge. Díaz Ordaz wasted no time in strengthening his nation's defenses against what he perceived as the communist threat. The new president sent more than three hundred officers to U.S. military academies shortly after taking office in 1964 and insisted that the military onboarding process include training in guerrilla warfare.[1] Increasingly, his intelligence agents attributed domestic disturbances to foreign, communist subversion. Under Díaz Ordaz, Mexico's Cold War escalated into a vicious cycle in which the government's treatment of its own citizens prompted them to participate in domestic opposition groups and international solidarity efforts, which in turn inspired authorities to resort to further acts of repression and violence.

STUDENT UNREST

It was not long before Gustavo Díaz Ordaz faced his first challenge from the younger members of the Mexican population. Mere days before he entered the presidential office, a doctors' movement broke out among

---

[1] Jorge Luis Sierra Guzmán, "Armed Forces and Counterinsurgency: Origins of the Dirty War (1965–1982)," in Calderón and Cedillo, eds., *Challenging Authoritarianism in Mexico*, 182–197, 187.

medical residents and interns that disrupted hospital services in Mexico City for nearly a year. The participants in the movement went out on strike and composed a five-point petition requesting better wages and working conditions as well as opportunities to participate in the planning of training programs.[2] The Executive Committee of the Society of Students of the Faculty of Medicine, which represented the eight thousand medical students of UNAM, declared its support for the striking doctors.[3] For the duration of the protests, medical and dentistry students at the National University, the National Polytechnic Institute, and across the country held assemblies and rallies and formed propaganda brigades. They organized protest marches through the streets of the capital and stood for hours outside the National Palace.[4] Intelligence agents claimed that the strike was secretly directed and financed by leaders of the Mexican Communist Party and the National Liberation Movement.[5] Díaz Ordaz eventually resorted to force to put an end to the doctors' movement, calling in the riot police and arresting and firing some of the participants.

However, Mexican authorities did not always use violent methods to resolve student conflicts. Coinciding with the doctors' movement, in April 1965 ten thousand students from the majority of the nation's rural teacher training schools held a more successful month-long strike. Their demands were more limited than those of the doctors; they wanted an increase in scholarship money for food, better laboratory equipment and library books, and improved transportation. The students held demonstrations and public meetings across the country, finding particular support for their cause in the cities of Puebla, Zacatecas, and Cuernavaca.[6] Intelligence agents believed that the organization behind the strikes, the Federation of Socialist Campesino Students of Mexico, was under the control of the National Liberation Movement.[7] After resisting for

[2] Stevens, *Protest and Response in Mexico*, 131.

[3] Rivas O., *La izquierda estudiantil en la UNAM*, 437.

[4] "Fin del Conflicto Médico?," *Política*, June 1, 1965.

[5] "[MLN organization of the doctors' strike]," February 2, 1965, DFS, Exp 11-6-65, Leg. 14, Hoja 43, AGN.

[6] "Huelga en las Normales," *Política*, May 1, 1965.

[7] Manuel Rangel Escamilla, "[MLN controls the FECSM]," September 19, 1963, DFS, Exp 63-19-63, Leg. 1, Hoja 198, AGN; Manuel Rangel Escamilla, "[MLN and FEP control the FECSM]," February 27, 1964, DFS, Exp 63-19-64, Leg. 1, Hoja 280, AGN. On the FECSM's role in student politics, see Tanalís Padilla, "Rural Education, Political Radicalism, and *Normalista* Identity in Mexico After 1940," in Gillingham and Smith, *Dictablanda*, 341–59.

a month, the government granted the students' demands and classes resumed in the rural teaching colleges.

A massive strike at UNAM a year later caused Díaz Ordaz more trouble. In March 1966, a series of protests spread across the campus and the country and eventually forced the National University's rector, Dr. Ignacio Chávez, to resign. An outspoken leftist, Chávez had presided over a number of controversial reforms at the university during his five years at the helm. He told economist Jesús Silva Herzog that students from all ideological groups participated in the movement against him, from Trotskyists on the extreme left to members of MURO on the extreme right. The ousted rector also claimed that two employees of the U.S. embassy who were possibly CIA agents encouraged the movement.[8] Rumors circulated that Díaz Ordaz had secretly supported and even instigated the strike in order to remove the rector.[9] After Chávez resigned, leftist students seized control of the fragmented movement and demanded changes to the university's curriculum and governing system. One group of some thirty students who had barricaded themselves into a building on the UNAM campus showed writer Elena Poniatowska a collection of Molotov cocktails that they had assembled.[10] The students eventually managed to put an end to some of the more authoritarian and repressive elements of Chávez's administration, including the "vigilance corps" of university police that he had used to prevent student activism.[11]

President Díaz Ordaz became extremely frustrated with the frequency of student protests. In his state of the union address that September, Díaz Ordaz gave them a clear warning. "Adolescence is not an escape from reality nor does it grant immunity from the law," Díaz Ordaz admonished young Mexicans; "neither claims of social and intellectual rank, nor economic position, nor age, nor profession nor occupation grant anyone immunity. I must repeat: No one has rights against Mexico!"[12] Soon, the

---

[8] González Ruiz, *MURO: Memorias y testimonios*, 346.

[9] CIA, "Student Strike at the University of Mexico," May 6, 1966. CREST Database, CIA-RDP79-00927A005300010001-4, NARA; "El gobierno violó la autonomía universitaria: ¿Qué es, en realidad, lo que ha sucedido en la Universidad Nacional?," *Política*, May 1, 1966.

[10] Elena Poniatowska, "El punto de vista de los estudiantes: ¡Que vengan nuestros maestros! ¡Queremos dialogar con ellos! ¡No nos dejen solos!" *Política*, May 15, 1966, 25–7, and *¡Siempre!* May 18, 1966.

[11] Ignacio Chávez de la Lama, *La madre de todas las "huelgas": La UNAM en 1966* (Monterrey: Universidad Autónoma de Nuevo León, 2011).

[12] "El Lic. Gustavo Díaz Ordaz, al abrir el Congreso sus sesiones ordinarias, el 10 de septiembre de 1966," in *Los presidentes de México ante la nación*, Vol. 4.

president would demonstrate the sincerity of his threat: the Mexican government would no longer tolerate challenges to its authority.

A month after Díaz Ordaz's address, the students of Michoacán tested his resolve. The University of Michoacán of San Nicolás de Hidalgo was one of the oldest institutions of higher education in the Americas, and throughout its long history had developed a reputation for political activism. Students there enthusiastically embraced the spirit of the Cuban Revolution and had sacked the Mexican-North American Cultural Institute in 1961 to protest the Bay of Pigs invasion.[13] In 1965, the head of the Department of Federal Security reported that the rector of the University of Michoacán, Alberto Bremauntz, was trying to stir up agitation against the federal and state governments.[14] An agent of the Federal Police described Bremauntz as an "addict of Castro-communism" and claimed that he was trying to spread that philosophy throughout the university.[15]

Rector Bremauntz was indeed an enthusiastic supporter of Fidel Castro. At the beginning of 1966, he published the book *Mexico and the Socialist Revolution of Cuba*, in which he lavished praise upon Cuba's leaders and their educational reforms. "Castro is for me the most prominent figure in the Americas," Bremauntz wrote, describing Castro as "a valiant, dynamic, and experienced politician who has known how to resolve the great problems that on all fronts have affected his people."[16] Bremauntz's publication also contained the text of a speech that he had delivered in Havana when he visited in 1964 for the Week of Mexico celebrations. He had concluded his remarks with a pledge to the Cubans: "Whenever any sacrifice may be necessary, any contribution or aid of any Mexican, there are some, including myself, ready to collaborate with you in any way necessary in defense of the Socialist Revolution of Cuba."[17] Intelligence agents would remember Bremauntz's enthusiasm for socialist revolution when problems arose at his university shortly thereafter.

These concerns about communism and Bremauntz's connections with Cuba colored Mexican officials' interpretations of student activism

---

[13] Zolov, "Cuba sí, Yanquis no!"

[14] Fernando Gutiérrez Barrios, "[Student agitation in Michoacán]," March 26, 1965, DFS, VPLC, Leg. 3, Hoja 180, AGN.

[15] Policía Judicial Federal and Agente #450, "[Communist activities in Morelia]," September 29, 1965, GDO 204 (123), AGN.

[16] Alberto Bremauntz, *México y la revolución socialista cubana* (Morelia: Universidad Michoacana de San Nicolas de Hidalgo, 1966), 28–9.

[17] Ibid., 158.

in Michoacán. On October 2, 1966, the students of the University of Michoacán organized a public rally to protest an increase in bus fares, and police officers killed one of the participants.[18] That night, the new rector (Bremauntz had retired less than two months before the protests began), the faculty, and the students of the university went on strike, demanding punishment for those responsible as well as the removal of the state governor. Student organizations across the country declared their solidarity, leading agents from the Federal Police to conclude that the strike was the result of a nationwide conspiracy. They claimed that students from UNAM and members of the Independent Campesino Center and the Federation of Socialist Campesino Students of Mexico were involved in the strike.[19] They also reported that members of a group called the Communist Spartacus League planned to travel to Morelia in order to join the Mexican Communist Party in support of the protest. The Federal Police claimed that the communists wanted to keep the movement alive to serve as an example for agitation against other state governors.[20] Intelligence agents from the Railroad Special Services Department agreed that members of the PCM were directing the protests.[21] The CIA also reported evidence of communist involvement in the disorders, claiming that "the identification of agitators trained in the USSR, Cuba, and Communist China points up the central direction of the agitation as well as its national significance."[22]

Mexican and U.S. intelligence agents showed particular concern about the role that the National Center of Democratic Students played in the uprising at the University of Michoacán. The organization had, after all, held its first conference in Morelia and named its founding declaration after the city. Shortly after the strikes broke out, the CNED issued a manifesto, which agents of the Department of Political and Social Investigations read closely, marking the most damning sections with a red pen. The officials underlined the group's demands, including the removal of the governor of Michoacán. They also highlighted the CNED's battle cry: "We call upon all of the forces of the student movement, all the

[18] "Michoacán se onganiza," *Política*, October 1, 1966.
[19] Policía Judicial Federal and Agente #330, "[Student agitation in Morelia]," October 5, 1966, GDO 206 (125), AGN.
[20] Policía Judicial Federal, "[Communist agitation in Morelia]," October 7, 1966, GDO 206 (125), AGN.
[21] Nicolas Castillo Ibarra, "[PCM activities reports from Ferrocarriles Servicios Especiales]," October 11, 1966, GDO 206 (125), AGN.
[22] CIA, "Central Intelligence Bulletin," October 12, 1966. CREST Database, CIA-RDP79T00975A009300060001-2, NARA.

political personalities, all the responsible Mexicans, to fight along with the future of our country for these demands, to express their dissatisfaction with the present situation."[23] Mexican agents reported that the CNED was forming propaganda brigades in the Federal District and posting the manifesto on the walls of the National Polytechnic Institute and the national teacher training college.[24] The CIA claimed that leaders of the Mexican Communist Party were instructing the CNED to organize a nationwide student strike.[25]

While communists were indeed involved in the student movement at the University of Michoacán and elsewhere, their participation did not necessarily prove that student activism was the result of a vast communist conspiracy. On the contrary, much of the evidence that intelligence agents collected could have come from a secret effort within one section of the government's security forces to divide and discredit student movements. Historian Jaime Pensado found a report that agents of the Department of Political and Social Investigations wrote in 1966 detailing a step-by-step plan for the government to sponsor pseudopolitical organizations of violent provocateurs that would distribute spurious Trotskyite, Guevarist, and Maoist propaganda and pretend to be radical communists.[26] These instigators and their fake propaganda not only fooled the students and the public; they probably also deceived Mexican and U.S. government agents who were not involved in the plot. These multiple levels of deceit made it extremely difficult for all observers to understand the true goals and scope of student activism.

Díaz Ordaz responded forcefully to the uncertainty of the situation, fearing that the student movement in Michoacán would spread to other parts of the country. With complete disregard for the tradition of university autonomy, he ordered the army to seize control of the campus and directed his soldiers to arrest more than six hundred students and other participants.[27] Three of the students would remain in prison for years.[28] After the university had been subdued, the subminister of the interior

[23] CNED, "Manifiesto de la CNED," October 13, 1966, IPS Caja 2862 A Exp 15, AGN.
[24] IPS, "[CNED propaganda activities]," October 20, 1966, IPS Caja 2862 A Exp 15, AGN.
[25] CIA, "Central Intelligence Bulletin," October 15, 1966. CREST Database, CIA-RDP79T00975A009300090001-9, NARA.
[26] Pensado, *Rebel Mexico*, 188.
[27] "Michoacán se organiza."
[28] "Actividades de la Central Nacional de Estudiantes Democráticos," 1966, IPS Caja 2181 A, AGN; Lucio Rangel Hernández, *La Universidad Michoacana y el movimiento estudiantil, 1966–1986* (Morelia: Universidad Michoacana de San Nicolás de Hidalgo, 2009), 174.

explained to two political officers from the U.S. embassy that Díaz Ordaz had unilaterally made the decision to send in the army. According to the official, Díaz Ordaz believed in a Mexican version of the domino theory – if the governor of Michoacán fell, "the next week Guerrero, Yucatán, Oaxaca, Sinaloa, and Durango would go."[29]

The former rector of the University of Michoacán, Alberto Bremauntz, criticized Díaz Ordaz for his repression of the student movement. He stated prophetically that it set a "fatal precedent" for institutions of higher education in the country.[30] Bremauntz was correct: Díaz Ordaz was increasingly resorting to force to crush internal dissent, and it was this force that would in turn cause future unrest.

THE RED MENACE

Díaz Ordaz reacted so strongly to these student movements and other instances of agitation in part because he believed that Mexico was the target of an international communist conspiracy. He knew that members and leaders of the Mexican Communist Party had helped organize many of the new organizations that arose in the 1960s such as the National Liberation Movement, the Independent Campesino Center, and the People's Electoral Front. He knew that the PCM received thousands of dollars each month from the Soviet Union.[31] He also knew that the Communist Party had gained popularity among a new generation of students who had been radicalized by the Cuban Revolution and had helped create the National Center of Democratic Students. His intelligence agents told him that the communist embassies, especially those of the Soviet Union and Cuba, provided Mexican dissidents with propaganda, money, weapons, and guerrilla training. As Díaz Ordaz perceived it, he was defending the Mexican people from a dangerous foreign threat, not repressing them.

There could be no doubt that Mexican students cared about Cuba. Events on the island, such as the Bay of Pigs invasion, prompted widespread activism, as did important anniversaries like the 26th of July. In

---

[29] US Embassy–Mexico, "Conversation with Subdirector of Gobernación," October 14, 1966, RG 59, Entry P2, ARC 602903, Box 6, NARA. On the domino theory, see Campbell Craig and Fredrik Logevall, *America's Cold War: The Politics of Insecurity* (Cambridge, MA: Belknap Press of Harvard University Press, 2009), 220–3.

[30] Alberto Bremauntz, *Setenta años de mi vida: Memorias y anécdotas* (Mexico City: Ediciones Jurídico Sociales, 1968).

[31] On Soviet support for the PCM, see Condés Lara, *Represión y rebelión en México*, 261–8.

June 1966, police prevented a pro-Cuba demonstration organized by the Mexican Communist Party, the editors of the magazine *Política*, and leaders of the National Center of Democratic Students. Groups of students who tried to attend the demonstration held impromptu "lightning meetings" throughout the city instead, cheering for Cuba and yelling insults at the president like "Death to Díaz Ordaz!"[32]

Later that year, another intelligence report reinforced the message that Díaz Ordaz's position on Cuba had a strong impact on the way that the student population perceived him. An agent of the Judicial Police claimed that students at the National University, even those in circles traditionally opposed to the government, had been making favorable comments about Díaz Ordaz's denial of rumors that he was about to break relations with Cuba.[33] The report suggested that by defending Cuba, the president was able to gain some respect even from his most contentious, intractable critics.

Leftist Mexican students demonstrated their continued dedication to Cuba's heroes in 1967 when they learned that Che Guevara had been killed while trying to spark a revolution in Bolivia. On walls and fences across Mexico City, a grieving population painted signs declaring that Che was not dead and that he would always be on the front lines of battle. UNAM students held gatherings in which they mourned Guevara's death and recounted stories of his heroic deeds. They sang the "song of the guerrilla" in his memory: "I want them to bury me like a revolutionary, wrapped in a red flag and with my rifle by my side."[34] Members of an organization called the Revolutionary Leftist Student Movement (Movimiento de Izquierda Revolucionaria Estudiantil) decided to protest Che's execution at the hands of Bolivian soldiers by planting an explosive device in the Bolivian embassy in Mexico City.[35]

Many Mexican students avidly read and circulated literature about the Cuban Revolution. As one leading student activist, Oscar González, recalled, "We were all influenced by the same revolutionary figures, independent thinkers, and artists." González listed the books *Cuba For*

---

[32] Fernando Gutiérrez Barrios, "[PCM clashes with police over pro-Cuba acts]," June 10, 1966, DFS, Exp 11-4-66, Leg. 16, Hoja 279, AGN; Policía Judicial Federal, "[Students organizing pro-Cuba event]," June 9, 1966, GDO 205 (124), AGN.

[33] Policía Judicial Federal and Agente #430, "[Student approval of maintenance of relations with Cuba]," December 12, 1966, GDO 206 (125), AGN.

[34] "La presencia del Che en México," *Política*, October 15, 1967.

[35] Jorge Poo Hurtado, "Los protagonistas olvidados," in *Asalto al cielo: Lo que no se ha dicho del 68*, ed. Rogelio Carvajal Dávila (Mexico City: Editorial Océano, 1998), 121–30.

Beginners by Mexican political cartoonist Eduardo del Río or "Rius,"
Listen, Yankee by C. Wright Mills, *Revolution in the Revolution* by Régis
Debray, and the magazine *Política* among the canon of "required readings
for all student activists."[36] In the pages of the leftist magazine, students
could read the text of Fidel Castro's speeches and Che Guevara's guide
to guerrilla warfare.[37] Headlines on *Política*'s covers compared Mexico's
revolution unfavorably to the Cuban one (see Figure 9).

Díaz Ordaz and his intelligence agents kept a close watch on *Política*
and its director, Manuel Marcué Pardiñas. In 1966, the director of the
Department of Federal Security compiled a twenty-one-page report about
the journalist. The document contained a great deal of information about
Marcué Pardiñas's private and professional life, listing more than twelve
years' worth of his activities. The head of intelligence described Marcué
Pardiñas as "a radical communist ... a violent and temperamental individual ... with an irascible character." The journalist was "an immoral
person, especially in his intimate life," who tried to seduce the wives of
his best friends and business partners.[38] The intelligence report described
how Marcué Pardiñas organized and helped print propaganda for demonstrations in favor of Cuba, the Dominican Republic, Vietnam, workers,
students, political prisoners, and the Mexican Communist Party. He also
helped arrange the welcome for Cuban president Osvaldo Dorticós when
he visited Mexico, and promoted the creation of the José Martí Institute
of Mexican-Cuban Cultural Exchange. The report claimed that Marcué
Pardiñas had made eleven trips to Cuba in the years following the Cuban
Revolution and received money from the Cuban and Soviet embassies to
cover *Política*'s expenses.[39]

Manuel Marcué Pardiñas was not the only prominent Mexican citizen
suspected of communist connections. In 1966, Agent 430 of the Federal

---

[36] Pensado, *Rebel Mexico*, 168.

[37] Ernesto "Che" Guevara, "La guerra de guerrillas: Un método," *Política*, October 1, 1963.

[38] Gutiérrez Barrios, "Revista 'Política.'" While Marcué Pardiñas did little to hide his amo-
rous dalliances, including an affair with actress Beatríz Baz, he never admitted to seduc-
ing his friends' wives. Carlos Perzabal, *De las memorias de Manuel Marcué Pardiñas*
(Mexico City: Editorial Rino, 1997), 22–5.

[39] Members of the *Política* staff also speculated that a significant amount of the magazine's
funding came from Cuba and the Soviet Union. Marcué Pardiñas did indeed make frequent trips to Cuba and confessed to having an account for the magazine in the National
Bank of Cuba. Perzabal, *De las memorias de Manuel Marcué Pardiñas* 109, 130; Comité
68 Pro Libertadores Democráticas, *Los procesos de México 68: La criminalización
de las víctimas. México: Genocidio y delitos de lesa humanidad, documentos básicos
1968–2008* (Mexico City: Comité 68 Pro Libertades Democráticas, 2008), 358.

FIGURE 9. A cover of *Política* magazine with a photograph of Cuban Revolutionary heroes Camilo Cienfuegos and Fidel Castro. The text over the photograph reads: "Latin Americans! The Mexican Revolution is not the way...." *Source*: *Política* magazine, August 1, 1966. Courtesy of the Biblioteca Lerdo de Tejada and the U.S. Library of Congress, Historical Newspapers.

Police warned that the communists might be forming an alliance with three powerful men: Ernesto P. Uruchurtu, who had recently resigned from his position as mayor of Mexico City, Carlos A. Madrazo, who had renounced his post as president of the PRI, and Dr. Ignacio Chávez, who had resigned as rector of the national university. According to the police report, the three disaffected political leaders were working with the communists to "cause the most serious problems to the current regime of President Gustavo Díaz Ordaz and seize political control of the country in the next presidential term." The information came from "a prominent source in Congress who demonstrated, from various angles, that this alliance is not absurd, but actually has many reasons for being entirely viable." Agent 430 also referred to earlier reports in which he had warned that Uruchurtu possessed vast wealth and probably planned to use it to return to the political scene.[40] While it is unlikely that these prominent political figures were actually conspiring with communists, Uruchurtu, Madrazo, and Chávez had been involved in significant conflicts with Díaz Ordaz in 1966 that contributed to their resignations.[41] It would not have been entirely unreasonable, then, for the president to believe that three powerful men whom he had helped to drive out of office would have wished him harm.

Other intelligence agents claimed that Lázaro Cárdenas was involved in subversive communist activities. In 1965, the head of the Department of Federal Security reported that Cárdenas and other leftist leaders were using students in Michoacán to stir up agitation against the federal and state governments. The intelligence director claimed that various communist "elements" with indirect connections to Cárdenas had been seen holding meetings and had received instructions to travel around Mexico provoking unrest among students, teachers, workers, and *campesinos*. These communist student leaders reportedly obtained money from the Soviet and Cuban embassies, and many of them had traveled to Cuba and the Soviet Union.[42]

Mexican authorities believed that, in addition to collaborating with powerful politicians, foreign and local communists were using a variety of tactics to endanger domestic stability, including indoctrination, infiltration, subversion, and terrorist training. In 1965, Agent 399 of the

---

[40] Agent #430, "[Communist alliance with important politicians]," October 27, 1966, GDO 206 (125), AGN.

[41] Davis, *Urban Leviathan*, 186–8.

[42] Fernando Gutiérrez Barrios, "[Student agitation in Michoacán connected to Cárdenas and Cubans]," March 26, 1965, DFS, VPLC, Leg. 3, Hoja 180, AGN.

Federal Police reported that members of the Mexican Communist Party had been overheard discussing the success of their efforts to infiltrate police organizations. "They have managed to occupy posts in the different police organizations throughout the entire country, principally those of Mexico City," the agent stated.[43] The leaders of the PCM were reportedly satisfied with the information that they received from their spies in the police groups. The PCM leaders also said that they were having more trouble infiltrating the national army but were slowly making headway. The existence of internal reports detailing the activities of the Department of Federal Security and the Federal Police written by members of the Mexican Communist Party in the 1950s suggest that Agent 399 was correct, and that communists had been infiltrating Mexico's security organizations for years.[44]

Mexican officials also suspected that communists were sneaking into the government. An officer of the Federal Police reported in April 1965 that the leader of the CNED was "seeking the help of the communists that [had] infiltrated the different state governments." This assistance consisted of support for demonstrations and provision of money "with the premeditated goal of occupying an official post that would facilitate the spreading of Marxist-Leninist theories."[45] A few months later, Agent 399 of the Federal Police reported that communists had infiltrated sectors of the national government and were using their positions for subversive purposes. He claimed that leaders of the Mexican Communist Party had ordered their followers in the Department of Agrarian Affairs to incite divisions among their coworkers. These infiltrators were known agitators who had been jailed previously for participating in the railroad workers' movement.[46]

The PRI was another suspected target of communist subversion. In 1966, the head of the Department of Federal Security investigated claims made in an article in the newspaper *Última Noticias* titled "Communist Infiltration in the PRI." The article had named a few communists who were supposedly embedded in the youth wing of the party and planning to take over the organization at the upcoming national congress.

---

[43] Policía Judicial Federal and Agente #399, "[Communist infiltration of police]," July 21, 1965, GDO 204 (123), AGN.

[44] Partido Comunista Mexicano, "[PCM Report on Activities of Intelligence Agencies]."

[45] Policía Judicial Federal, "Central Nacional de Estudiantes Democráticos," April 5, 1965, GDO 203 (122), AGN.

[46] Policía Judicial Federal and Agente #399, "[Communists in the Agrarian Department]," July 15, 1965, GDO 204 (123), AGN.

In response, the intelligence agent wrote a report providing information about all of the suspected infiltrators identified in the article. He corroborated the claims that some of the leaders of the PRI's youth group were "radicals." He described one as a leftist agitator who traveled to Cuba and published a magazine funded by the National Liberation Movement. Another youth named in the article also collaborated with the MLN.[47]

According to intelligence agents, the Mexican Communist Party, obeying the dictates of the Soviets, had influenced a number of political developments in Mexico. A short biography that investigators composed in 1967 about the head of the PCM, Arnoldo Martínez Verdugo, claimed that he "served international communism as the coordinator of propaganda in Latin America." This "professional agitator" had reportedly received training in the Soviet Union in 1955 and 1959. Martínez Verdugo had, in fact, visited Moscow in February 1959 and then stopped in Cuba for three months on the way home, and he did frequently attend events in the Cuban and Soviet embassies in Mexico City.[48] Intelligence agents believed that Martínez Verdugo was drawing on this extensive training and contact with foreign communists to help direct the Independent Campesino Center and the People's Electoral Front and was playing a significant role in various student protest movements.[49] They attached his biography to a longer report about the CNED that claimed that it was an extremist, subversive organization that was affiliated with the Mexican Communist Party and received instructions from Prague and Havana.[50]

One of the Mexican government's greatest fears was that its citizens were traveling to Cuba and the Soviet Union for instruction in the art of guerrilla warfare. This fear was not completely unfounded; revolutionaries from around the world did go to Cuba and the Soviet Union to receive training. According to a former member of Cuba's intelligence department, in the early 1960s as many as 1,500 men and women matriculated through the guerrilla schools each year.[51] Another Cuban exile who had fought beside Che in Africa and Bolivia, Dariel Alarcón Ramírez or "Benigno," claimed in his memoirs that he had personally provided training to Mexicans who had come to Cuba for ideological orientation and

---

[47] Fernando Gutiérrez Barrios, "[Possible communist infiltration of the PRI]," February 11, 1966, DFS, Exp 48-4-66, Leg. 9, Hoja 245, AGN.

[48] Carr, *Marxism and Communism in Twentieth-Century Mexico*, 379n91.

[49] "Arnoldo Martínez Verdugo," July 4, 1967, IPS Caja 2892 A, AGN.

[50] "Central Nacional de Estudiantes Democráticos," May 4, 1968, IPS Caja 2892 A, AGN.

[51] Castro Hidalgo, *Spy for Fidel*, 94.

to learn the arts of sabotage and espionage.[52] Members of the Mexican Communist Party did in fact frequently enroll in one- to three-year programs of education in schools in Moscow.[53]

Mexican leaders received reports from multiple sources about Mexican nationals receiving revolutionary training in Cuba and the Soviet Union. In May 1966, Mexico's ambassador in Havana sent a message to the Foreign Ministry with a list of nine Mexicans who were about to return to the country, supposedly after having received guerrilla training in Cuba. Eight others were to remain on the island for additional instruction.[54] Later that year, the head of the Mexican Communist Party reportedly announced plans to send six members to Cuba for guerrilla training.[55] IPS agents claimed that the Independent Campesino Center was sending groups to the Soviet Union to learn subversive techniques.[56] The Judicial Police reported in 1966 that the leader of the CCI, Ramón Danzós Palomino, was about to leave for Havana to attend a worldwide peasant congress. There, the Cubans would give him a "revolutionary orientation" with regard to *campesino* activism.[57] DFS agents compiled a list of eight members of Mexican "radical leftist groups" who were in Cuba and about to depart for Moscow, where they would study guerrilla warfare before returning to Mexico.[58] A general intelligence summary composed in 1968 mentioned that a Mexican couple had spent time on the island receiving instruction in so-called revolutionary work. "Mexico is not exempt from Castro's goals to provoke disorder," the author of the report maintained.[59]

Of course, guerrilla training could take place on Mexican soil as well. Agent 399 of the Federal Judicial Police reported in 1966 that members of the youth wing of the Mexican Communist Party were planning a trip to an enormous secret base in Oaxaca. A number of Cubans supposedly owned more than twenty thousand hectares there, most of which they employed for guerrilla training exercises using an "infinite number of

---

[52] Dariel Alarcón Ramírez, *Memorias de un soldado cubano: Vida y muerte de la revolución* (Barcelona: Tusquets Editores, 1997), 250–1.

[53] Condés Lara, *Represión y rebelión en México*, 263.

[54] "Dirección General de Inteligencia," May 1966, SPR – 540 – BIS5, SRE.

[55] "[PCM response to guerrilla training in Cuba]," December 6, 1966, DFS, Exp 11-4-66, Leg. 17, Hoja 436, AGN.

[56] "Actividades de la Central Campesina Independiente," July 3, 1966, IPS Caja 1022, AGN.

[57] Policía Judicial Federal, "[CCI planning agitation with help from Cuba]," October 6, 1966, GDO 206 (125), AGN.

[58] "[List of leftists receiving guerrilla training in the USSR]," August 25, 1966, DFS, Exp 11-4-66, Leg. 17, Hoja 104, AGN.

[59] "Informe general sobre Cuba," May 20, 1968, IPS Caja 2958 D, AGN.

high-power weapons" that they had amassed. According to the agent, the visit to the camp was to be a reward for the students' participation in different movements.[60] In 1967, the governor of the Federal District forwarded a report about guerrilla training to the Department of Political and Social Investigations. According to the document, a group of at least eight Mexican students had recently arrived in Mexico City from Havana, where they had taken a course in revolutionary warfare. "All of them are under orders to undertake a campaign of proselytism and training in the art of guerrilla warfare among their fellow students in various regions of our country," the report warned.[61]

Fear of communism went so deep among Mexico's security agents that even a lack of evidence could be interpreted as a plot. In April 1967, a member of the Federal Judicial Police reported that the "meager success of the most recent acts organized by the Mexican Communist Party and other leftists is intentional, as they want to distract the authorities of the Capital and give them [false] confidence." Once the security forces had let down their guard, believing that leftist groups were losing power, the communists would be free to agitate in other states of the republic, the agent contended.[62] This sort of logic negated the value of evidence and rested purely on speculation: the communists were planning to agitate the public, and any evidence to the contrary was a trick.

THE TRICONTINENTAL CONFERENCE

Though many of the intelligence reports may have sounded alarmist or paranoid, foreign communists were in fact actively encouraging revolutionary movements throughout the world in the 1960s. A major component of Cuba's foreign policy was hosting international conferences; one of the largest and most important was the January 1966 First Solidarity Conference of the Peoples of Africa, Asia, and Latin America, or the Tricontinental Conference. Unlike previous international gatherings like Lázaro Cárdenas's 1961 Latin American Peace Conference, the Tricontinental promoted an explicitly violent program of action. This shift in policy both responded to and provoked an increase in counterrevolutionary efforts on the part of government officials across the Americas.

---

[60] Policía Judicial Federal and Agente #399, "[Cuban guerrilla training camps in Oaxaca]," May 20, 1966, GDO 205 (124), AGN.
[61] "[Guerrilla training in Cuba]," June 9, 1967, IPS Caja 2966 B, AGN.
[62] Policía Judicial Federal, "[Communist plot]," April 26, 1967, GDO 207 (126), AGN.

The Tricontinental Conference was one of the largest international gatherings of revolutionaries and their supporters that the world had ever seen. According to the organizers, more than five hundred delegates from eighty-two countries attended, along with sixty-four observers and seventy-seven guests. One hundred and twenty-nine members of the foreign press from thirty-eight countries provided coverage.[63] Each of the three continents had about the same number of participants, which in theory provided equal representation. The Latin American countries with the biggest delegations were Cuba (41 members), Venezuela (15), and Chile (9).[64] Among the most famous Latin American leaders in attendance, besides Castro, were Salvador Allende of Chile and Luis Agusto Turcios Lima, a guerrilla leader from Guatemala. President Gamal Abdel Nasser of Egypt sent greetings and offered to host a subsequent tricontinental conference in Cairo. Messages of support arrived from Ho Chi Minh of Vietnam, Zhou Enlai of the People's Republic of China, Leonid Brezhnev of the Soviet Union, Kim Il Sung of North Korea, Walter Ulbricht of the German Democratic Republic, and Sukarno of Indonesia.[65]

At the time of the Tricontinental Conference, the Soviets, Chinese, and Cubans were engaged in a fierce competition for leadership of the so-called worldwide revolutionary movement. The Soviets were promoting peaceful coexistence with the United States and many Latin American governments, the Chinese were advocating armed struggle in the form of "people's wars," and the Cubans were pushing for the formation of guerrilla movements based on their *foco* theory.[66] Within Latin America, different groups either aligned themselves with one of the major communist powers or forged their own paths.

[63] General Secretariat of the OSPAAAL, *First Solidarity Conference of the Peoples of Africa, Asia, and Latin America*, 183. On the unique size and breadth of the conference, see also Maurice Halperin, *The Taming of Fidel Castro* (Berkeley: University of California Press, 1981), 186; Luis V. Manrara, *The Tricontinental Conference: A Declaration of War* (Miami: The Truth About Cuba Committee, 1966); OAS Special Consultative Committee on Security, *The "First Tricontinental Conference," Another Threat to the Security of the Inter-American System* (Organization of American States, 1966).

[64] OAS Special Consultative Committee on Security, *"The First Tricontinental Conference."*

[65] Ibid.

[66] On the conflict between Soviet, Chinese, and Cuban revolutionary efforts in Latin America, see Richard Gott, *Guerrilla Movements in Latin America* (Garden City, NJ: Doubleday, 1971), 34–5; Halperin, *The Taming of Fidel Castro*, 189; Domínguez, *To Make a World Safe for Revolution*, 67–72; Cole Blasier, "The Soviet Union in the Cuban-American Conflict," in *Cuba in the World*, ed. Cole Blasier and Carmelo Mesa-Lago (Pittsburgh: University of Pittsburgh Press, 1979), 37–52; Reeves, "Extracting the Eagle's Talons." On the Chinese concept of "people's war," see Cecil Johnson, *Communist China and Latin America, 1959–1967* (New York: Columbia University Press, 1970), 53–128.

The Mexican delegation included numerous leftist leaders who had gained political prominence in the 1950s and 1960s, as well as others were about make their mark on the national scene. Ramón Danzós Palomino, presidential candidate of the People's Electoral Front, attended, as did Othón Salazar of the Revolutionary Teachers' Movement; journalists Filomeno Mata, Victor Rico Galán, and Jorge Carrión; General Heriberto Jara; and Professor Alberto Bremauntz from the University of Michoacán.[67] Heading the delegation was a man whose role in Mexican politics would soon increase dramatically: Heberto Castillo Martínez. One of the founding members of the National Liberation Movement, Castillo had led the organization's committee for the defense of Cuba before gaining control of the entire movement in 1965. According to the director of intelligence in the Department of Federal Security, Castro paid Castillo to travel around Latin America promoting the Tricontinental Conference in the fall of 1965.[68] Security agents became even more concerned with Castillo's actions after the conference, especially when he started playing a lead role in the 1968 student movement.

Heberto Castillo's statements at the Tricontinental Conference gave the Mexican government significant cause for concern. Castillo declared that the National Liberation Movement operated under the principle that "only through the struggle for liberation can a contribution be made to that peace with dignity that ... requires in most cases a liberating war." He also asserted that imperialism could only be defeated "with weapons in hand." Castillo made it clear that this liberating war with weapons in hand needed to be fought across the Americas, including in Mexico. He denounced the Alliance for Progress and declared that the Mexican Revolution's program of agrarian reform had been betrayed and distorted since Cárdenas's departure from office. Castillo swore that the Mexicans were ready to undertake a fight to the death to free their country from American imperialism.[69]

Strident as it was, Castillo's speech was not the most heated of the Tricontinental Conference. Far from it. Fidel Castro delivered the closing address to the gathering, in which he declared that for the Cuban

[67] "Lista completa de los delegados mexicanos a la Conferencia Tricontinental de la Habana, Cuba, para los días del 3 al 10 de enero de 1966," AGN, from the personal collection of Sergio Aguayo.

[68] Fernando Gutiérrez Barrios, "[MLN support of Tricontinental Conference in Havana]," November 5, 1965, DFS, Exp 11-6-65, Leg. 15, Hoja 211, AGN.

[69] "Discursos de los jefes de las delegaciones a la Conferencia Tricontinental: México," *Política*, February 15, 1966.

revolutionaries, the battlefield against U.S. imperialism spanned the entire globe. He promised that revolutionary movements in any corner of the world could count on Cuban manpower. Castro also called for a common and simultaneous struggle throughout all of Latin America and specified that in "all or almost all" countries the struggle would take on violent forms.[70] His words broadcasted the increasingly internationalist thrust of Cuban foreign policy.[71]

Another Communist leader spontaneously pledged his government's support for revolutionary movements around the world. Sharaf R. Rashidov, the head of the Soviet delegation and first secretary of the Uzbek Communist Party, declared "the Soviet people always support popular wars of liberation and the armed struggle of oppressed peoples and provide them with every kind of aid."[72] He also reportedly expressed fraternal solidarity with revolutionaries in Venezuela, Peru, Colombia, and Guatemala.[73] U.S. journalists speculated that Rashidov's statement was an impulsive attempt to outflank the Chinese.[74] Attendees of the conference enthusiastically applauded his pledge, while U.S. intelligence agents gloated that it gave them the "perfect ammunition" for their propaganda operations against the gathering.[75]

Rashidov's speech reflected the Soviet Union's ambivalent approach to the Tricontinental Conference and to communist revolution in Latin America. On one hand, the Soviets favored the creation of a tricontinental revolutionary organization, hoping that it would dilute the heavy influence that the Chinese had enjoyed in the earlier Afro-Asian Solidarity Organization.[76] The Soviet delegate was the one who proposed that the conference attendees establish what became the Solidarity Organization of the

[70] General Secretariat of the OSPAAAL, *First Solidarity Conference of the Peoples of Africa, Asia, and Latin America.*

[71] On internationalism in Cuban foreign policy, see Gott, *Guerrilla Movements in Latin America*; Roberto F. Lamberg, "La formación de la línea castrista desde la Conferencia Tricontinental," *Foro Internacional* 8, no. 3 (31) (January 1, 1968): 278–301. Paul Dosal argues that Che Guevara had long been an internationalist, but that the Tricontinental Conference was the point when Castro pushed ahead with Che's plan to form an international fighting front. Paul J. Dosal, *Comandante Che: Guerrilla Soldier, Commander, and Strategist, 1956–1967* (University Park: Pennsylvania State University Press, 2003), 214.

[72] "Unión de Tres Continentes."

[73] John W. Finney, "O.A.S. Condemns Havana Meeting: Denounces Move for Wars of 'Liberation' in Americas," *New York Times*, February 3, 1966.

[74] Richard Eder, "Moscow Softens View on Revolts: Disclaimers of Stand Taken at Cuban Parley Reported," *New York Times*, February 17, 1966.

[75] Agee, *Inside the Company*, 464.

[76] Halperin, *The Taming of Fidel Castro*, 190.

Peoples of Africa, Asia, and Latin America (Organización de Solidaridad de los Pueblos de África, Asia, y América Latina, or OSPAAAL).[77] On the other hand, the conference's declaration of war against so-called neocolonial regimes contradicted the Soviet Union's attempts to establish friendly relations with many Latin American governments. Observers in Moscow considered the Tricontinental Conference "a brazen attempt by Cuba to exclude the Soviets from the leadership role in the Third World that they felt was rightfully theirs."[78] Furthermore, Castro and Rashidov's pledges to support wars of liberation around the world implicitly and explicitly required Soviet financial commitments.

The Tricontinental Conference's resolutions challenged the Soviet Union's official policy of peaceful coexistence and favored the opposing Chinese and Cuban programs of violent confrontation. The general declaration expounded upon the need for national liberation and social revolution as part of a "war to the death" against "the colonialist, neocolonialist, and imperialist system of oppression and exploitation." It proclaimed the right of all peoples to resort to "all forms of struggle that may be necessary, including armed struggle," in pursuit of independence. The conference attendees proclaimed solidarity with armed struggles in Venezuela, Guatemala, Peru, Portuguese Guinea, Mozambique, Angola, and the Congo. They claimed that the people of Africa, Asia, and Latin America had the right to answer imperialist violence with revolutionary violence.[79]

If this public promotion of revolutionary violence were not enough to worry Mexico's intelligence agents, they were also hearing rumors about secret plotting at the Tricontinental Conference. A week before the assembly began, agents from the Federal Judicial Police reported that Mexican communist leaders had formed a secret commission to send to Havana. Their mission supposedly was to receive orders in clandestine meetings outside of the spotlight of the conference. They would attend but not participate in the public events in order to avoid drawing attention to themselves.[80] None of the official publications about the conference mentioned the presence of Mexican Communist Party members,

---

[77] "Unión de Tres Continentes."
[78] James G. Blight and Philip Brenner, *Sad and Luminous Days: Cuba's Struggle with the Superpowers after the Missile Crisis* (Lanham, MD: Rowman and Littlefield, 2002), 109.
[79] "Primera Conferencia de Solidaridad de los Pueblos de África, Asia, y América," *Política*, February 1, 1966.
[80] Policía Judicial Federal, "[Secret communist meetings planned at Tricontinental Conference]," December 28, 1965, GDO 202 (121), AGN.

but an article in *El Sol de México* claimed that the communists and the socialists had paid to send their own delegates to Havana, separate from the National Liberation Movement's official delegation. Heberto Castillo reportedly expelled the second secretary of the PCM, Manuel Terrazas, from the liberation movement for leading the nonofficial delegation.[81] Lists of conference participants compiled by the State Department and Mexican intelligence agencies included both Castillo and Terrazas, but did not specify whether there were one or two Mexican delegations.[82]

Secret meetings most likely did take place at the Tricontinental Conference. Mario Monje, the secretary-general of the pro-Soviet Communist Party of Bolivia, later told journalist Jon Lee Anderson that "it was not the speeches that were being given [at the conference] that were important, but what was happening behind the scenes."[83] Monje claimed that the Cubans used the gathering to establish contacts with the more radical groups in attendance, encouraging them to create new guerrilla *focos* in Latin America.

While the Cubans may have conducted closed-door meetings with revolutionary groups at the Tricontinental Conference, they certainly made no secret of their desire to promote armed struggle throughout the Third World and especially in Latin America. The Havana-based organization that emerged from the conference, OSPAAAL, took a number of steps to enact the assembly's resolutions. In April 1966, it began publishing the *Tricontinental Bulletin*, a monthly magazine with Spanish, English, French, and Arabic editions.[84] The magazine provided news about anti-imperialist and anti-colonial events throughout the world, in addition to practical guides to guerrilla warfare and armed insurrection.[85] Later that year, the *New York Times* reported that OSPAAAL had announced plans to open schools in Cuba and North Korea where "political cadres and guerrilla experts" would train personnel involved in national liberation

---

[81] "'Liberación Nacional' quiere dirigir la agitación y riñe con el PPS y con el PCM: La pugna que se inició en la Tricontinental está debilitando la 'Semana del Vietcong.'" *El Sol de México*, March 17, 1966.

[82] George Ball, "Delegates to the Tricontinental Congress," February 7, 1966, RG 59 CFPF 1964–1966 Box 1553 CSM 6 AAPSO, NARA; "Lista completa de los delegados mexicanos a la Conferencia Tricontinental de la Habana, Cuba, para los días del 3 al 10 de enero de 1966."

[83] Anderson, *Che Guevara*, 684. Monje helped prepare Che's expedition in Bolivia before changing his mind and insisting that any armed insurgency in his country would have to be lead by his own countrymen – not the Cubans or Che. After a disastrous meeting with Guevara, Monje eventually revoked his party's support of Che's efforts.

[84] "World Solidarity with the Tricontinental," *Tricontinental Bulletin*, April 1966.

[85] Carlos Marighella, "Minimanual del guerrillero urbano," *Revista Tricontinental*, 1970.

movements.[86] The solidarity organization also published one of the most famous revolutionary documents of the decade: Che Guevara's "Message to the Tricontinental." The manifesto caused a sensation when it appeared in April 1967. In it, Guevara called for the initiation of a "worldwide conflagration ... a total war ... a constant and firm attack on all fronts." He claimed that liberation armies around the globe needed to create "two, three, or many Vietnams" in order to challenge the world system of imperialism. "Our soldiers must be ... violent, selective, and cold killing machine[s]," he argued.[87] Che had composed this missive on the eve of his secret departure from Cuba in early November 1966; by the time it was published in 1967, he was already in Bolivia, enacting his own call to arms.[88]

The promotion of violent revolution at the Tricontinental Conference prompted a swift backlash. According to ex-CIA agent Philip Agee, who was working in the Montevideo field office at the time, the U.S. government conducted an intense media campaign against the Tricontinental conference. The headquarters of the CIA spent months preparing the propaganda and encouraged local stations to try to place agents in the delegations.[89] The CIA's media campaign focused on two themes – portraying the Tricontinental Conference as an instrument of Soviet subversion and convincing the public that it was dangerous enough to require political, diplomatic, and military countermeasures. Headlines in the *New York Times* blared "Help for Vietcong is Urged at Havana," while the *Los Angeles Times* described the conference as a "hemispheric menace."[90] When the Soviet delegate Rashidov made his impulsive declaration of support for armed insurgencies, Washington pushed for prominent display of his speech in newspapers across the hemisphere. CIA agents and State Department officials in countries that maintained relations with the Soviet Union and Cuba, including Mexico, made sure to provide government officials with copies of Rashidov's statement.[91]

The reaction to Rashidov's speech was so vehement that his fellow Soviet leaders had to backpedal. In Uruguay, the foreign minister

[86] "Cuba Reports Plans to Train Guerrillas," *New York Times*, November 20, 1966.
[87] Ernesto Guevara, *Che Guevara Reader: Writings by Ernesto Che Guevara on Guerrilla Strategy, Politics and Revolution* (Melbourne: Ocean Press, 1997), 313.
[88] Anderson, *Che Guevara*, 718.
[89] Agee, *Inside the Company*, 463.
[90] "Help for Vietcong Is Urged at Havana," *New York Times*, January 14, 1966; "Hemispheric Menace," *Los Angeles Times*, February 20, 1966.
[91] Agee, *Inside the Company*, 464. Fulton Freeman, "Mexico City to Department of State," February 9, 1966, RG 59, CFPF 1964–66, Political and Defense, Communism, Folder CSM 6–AAPSO, NARA.

summoned the Soviet ambassador and demanded an explanation for the USSR's participation in the Tricontinental Conference. The Venezuelan government issued a statement that it was going to examine its diplomatic relations with countries represented at the assembly.[92] The Peruvian representative lodged a formal complaint with the Organization of American States, using Rashidov's declarations as evidence of Soviet intervention in Latin America.[93] All the Latin American members of the United Nations, except Mexico, filed a formal protest. In order to prevent further repercussions, representatives of the Soviet Union issued a public statement that Rashidov was speaking "privately" and not on behalf of the government.[94]

The Soviets' retraction was not enough to appease the Organization of American States. All the members of the OAS except Mexico and Chile approved a resolution condemning the Tricontinental Conference.[95] The Special Consultative Committee on Security prepared a study about the Havana gathering, which they presented in April 1966. Describing the conference as "the most dangerous and serious threat that international communism has yet made against the inter-American system," the OAS committee contended that it was a declaration of war against democracy.[96] The authors of the report observed that the conference was significant because it meant that the Cubans were no longer alone in their efforts to export revolution: now the Soviet Union had promised support to liberation movements around the world. "We are dealing with a war that is at the same time a revolution," the OAS security committee declared, "and with a prolonged struggle for universal domination." They recommended that member states respond with a coordinated propaganda campaign in favor of democracy, as well as increased cooperation in security and intelligence activities. Later, Operation Condor would enact similar plans for international military collaboration against subversives.[97]

Though Mexico refused to join the campaign against the Tricontinental Conference in the United Nations or the Organization of American States,

[92] Ibid., 468.
[93] "Peru Asks OAS Council to Meet on Intervention," *New York Times*, January 22, 1966; "Peru Protests Soviet Support of Subversives," *Los Angeles Times*, January 25, 1966.
[94] "Most Latin Members of U.N. Protest on Havana Parley," *New York Times*, February 8, 1966; Eder, "Moscow Softens View on Revolts: Disclaimers of Stand Taken at Cuban Parley Reported," *New York Times*, February 17, 1966.
[95] Finney, "O.A.S. Condemns Havana Meeting: Denounces Move for Wars of 'Liberation' in Americas," *New York Times*, February 3, 1966.
[96] OAS Special Consultative Committee on Security, "The First Tricontinental Conference."
[97] On Operation Condor, see John Dinges, *The Condor Years: How Pinochet and His Allies Brought Terrorism to Three Continents* (New York: New Press, 2004).

it had already taken independent measures to counteract the effects of the gathering. In an address for a select audience including ambassadors and former presidents at the Mexican Institute of International Law, Senator and ex-Foreign Minister Ezequiel Padilla called the Tricontinental Conference an "ominous example of subversion" and a "flagrant interventionist conspiracy of the totalitarian imperialisms against the security and integrity of our American countries."[98] *Excélsior* published a series of articles and editorials condemning the event and calling it a "meeting of hate."[99] A few months later, the newspaper *El Heraldo* and spokesmen of the National Action Party claimed that the Tricontinental Conference had provoked the 1966 student movement in UNAM.[100] The Minister of Agriculture, Juan Gil Preciado, blamed another student strike movement in 1967 on the gathering.[101] The conference's declarations about worldwide revolutions provided evidence for government officials' claims – and suspicions – that opposition and reform movements were part of an international communist conspiracy.[102]

SPYING ON CASTRO

In order to combat Cuba's revolutionary activities, Mexican officials used their embassy in Havana as a center not just of diplomacy, but also of espionage and intrigue. As the ties between Mexico and Cuba became increasingly exceptional throughout the 1960s, this source of information proved especially important for both the Mexican and U.S governments.

The Mexican ambassador to Cuba from 1965 to 1967, Fernando Pámanes Escobedo, proved to be particularly enthusiastic about

[98] Fulton Freeman, "U.S. Embassy in Mexico to State Department on Tri-Continental Conference," February 9, 1966, RG 59, CFPF 1964–66, Political and Defense, Communism, Folder CSM 6–AAPSO, NARA.

[99] Isaac M. Flores, "Quieren crear en Cuba un organismo para coordinar y apoyar actos subversivos," *Excélsior*, January 9, 1966; "Junta del odio," *Excélsior*, January 6, 1966; Isaac M. Flores, "Duros ataques a EU en la junta del odio," *Excélsior*, January 5, 1966.

[100] "Sepúlveda se tambalea," *Política*, March 15, 1966, 12.

[101] "Victoria estudiantil," *Política*, July 15, 1967.

[102] Fernando Gutiérrez Barrios, "[FEP and PCM agitation following Tricontinental Agreement]," February 2, 1967, DFS, Exp 11-141-67, Leg. 12, Hoja 222, AGN; Policía Judicial Federal and Agente #399, "[Communist agitation following Tricontinental Agreement]," July 6, 1966, GDO 206 (125), AGN. "Síntesis de antecedentes de 1966, 1967 del conflicto político y social conocido como movimiento estudiantil creado en el mes de julio de 1968," 1968, IPS Caja 2181 A, AGN; Comité 68 Pro Libertadores Democráticas, *Los procesos de México 68*, 50; Gutiérrez Oropeza, *Díaz Ordaz: el hombre, el gobernante*, (Mexico City: Gustavo de Anda, 1988) 42; Heberto Castillo, "Los represores del 68," *Proceso*, September 13, 1993.

undertaking intelligence work. During a luncheon at his residence in Mexico City with one of his close friends, U.S. Ambassador Fulton Freeman, Pámanes explained that he intended to expand the embassy's knowledge of what was going on in Cuba. Pámanes also mentioned that his family was remaining in Mexico, so he would be making frequent visits home. Freeman concluded that the Mexican ambassador had a "warm admiration" for the United States and would probably be amenable to sharing his observations on the Cuban situation during future informal meetings.[103]

Pámanes likely welcomed the excitement of espionage. A decorated army general and veteran of the Cristero Rebellion, he had served as a military attaché – and seen action – in Mexico's embassy in China during World War II.[104] He was thus disinclined to follow strict diplomatic protocol in his new posting in Cuba. As a summary of his activities in the files of the foreign ministry put it: "Ambassador Pámanes, during his mission in Cuba, undoubtedly guided by the best intentions, proposed to undertake intelligence work."[105] On multiple occasions, the foreign ministry warned the ambassador to refrain from activities outside those prescribed for his position, but he persisted.

Ambassador Pámanes sought out numerous sources for sensitive information about Cuba. He exchanged letters with anti-Castro groups and provided them with cameras to photograph Mexicans receiving guerrilla training on the island.[106] He interviewed a Cuban intelligence agent who sought asylum in Mexico about his employer and the schools for guerrilla warfare.[107] Pámanes cultivated another official seeking to leave the island, Dr. Yamil Kourí, who had been the director of the Cuban Center

---

[103] "[Freeman-Pámanes Lunch]," March 30, 1965, RG 59, Entry P2, ARC 602903, Box 2, NARA. On the friendship between Freeman and Pámanes, see Foreign Minister Raúl Roa to President Osvaldo Dorticós, Prime Minister Fidel Castro, and Comandante Manuel Piñeiro, "Memorandum," 23 March 1965, América Latina, México, 1963–1967 Ordinario 7, 1965, MINREX.

[104] Fernando Pámanes Escobedo, "Datos biográficos del C. General de División DEM Fernando Pámanes Escobedo," February 26, 1965, Leg. III–2940, SRE. On the Cristero Rebellion, see Jean A. Meyer, *La Cristiada*, 3rd ed. (Mexico: Siglo veintiuno editores, 1974); Matthew Butler, *Popular Piety and Political Identity in Mexico's Cristero Rebellion: Michoacán, 1927–29* (Oxford: Oxford University Press, 2004).

[105] "Expediente de Fernando Pámanes Escobedo," March 23, 1971, Leg. III – 2940, SRE.

[106] Ibid.

[107] "Dirección General de Inteligencia," May 1966, SPR – 540 – BIS5, SRE; Fernando Gutiérrez Barrios, "[Information from a man seeking asylum in the Mexican Embassy in Cuba]," April 2, 1966, DFS, Exp. 12-9-66, Leg. 17, Hoja 69, AGN.

of Scientific Investigations and Castro's personal physician. Dr. Kourí told the ambassador that he had information on numerous topics, including attempts to construct a nuclear reactor, plans to infiltrate Latin American universities, contraband weapons, foreign scientists who worked on the island, and Fidel's relationship with the communist old guard in Cuba. The doctor also knew intimate details about Castro's health, diet, and residence.[108] The Mexican foreign ministry ordered Ambassador Pámanes to cease questioning Dr. Kourí for fear of endangering his petition to the Cuban government for safe conduct.[109]

Fulton Freeman's hunch that Ambassador Pámanes would share his information with the United States proved correct. On at least one occasion, the Mexican official met with Francis Sherry, a CIA agent working undercover in the U.S. embassy. Pámanes told Sherry about political unrest in Cuba and the mobilization of thirty thousand troops along the southern coast in preparation for possible hostilities with Venezuela. He also described the unloading of what appeared to be Soviet ground-to-air missiles in the port of Mariel. A memorandum of the meeting circulated among officials in the CIA, the State Department, and the White House.[110]

Pámanes's questionable activities eventually caught up with him. According to an internal investigation conducted by Mexico's foreign ministry, the ambassador accepted bribes for asylum and helped refugees and exiles smuggle their possessions of value off the island. He also trafficked in Cuban cigars.[111] By 1967, Castro had become so frustrated that he refused to cooperate with Pámanes and suspended the repatriation of

[108] Fernando Pámanes Escobedo, "Kouri, Yamil H. (Dr.)," July 1, 1966, Leg. III – 5866 – 4, SRE.

[109] Dr. Kourí remained in the Mexican embassy in Havana for six years and seven months, waiting for the Cuban government to approve his request for safe conduct to Mexico. The Cubans denied the multiple petitions that the Mexicans made on his behalf, explaining that he was not the victim of political persecution but instead a common criminal guilty of felonious acts. In May 1972, Kourí voluntarily renounced the protection of the Mexican government and turned himself over to the Cuban authorities. After several years in Cuban prison, Kourí was freed in 1979 and found a position working in Harvard's Institute for International Development. In 1999, he was convicted of heading a group of conspirators that embezzled more than two million dollars of federal funds meant for AIDS research in Puerto Rico. See Mexican Embassy to Cuban Ministry of Foreign Relations, "Memorandum," November 17, 1969, América Latina, México, 1968–1969 Ordinario 8, 1969, MINREX; Ernesto Madero, "Caso del Dr. Yamil Kouri," December 7, 1978, Leg. III – 5866 – 4, SRE; *United States vs. Pagán Santini* (U.S. Court of Appeals, First Circuit 2006).

[110] Francis Sherry, "Conversation Between Embassy Officer and Mexican Ambassador to Cuba," June 12, 1967, RG 59, CFPF 67–69, POL Cuba-A, NARA.

[111] "Pámanes Escobedo Informe," July 24, 1967, File SPR-540-Bis 5, SRE.

U.S. citizens.[112] Pámanes lost his post, and a new ambassador, Miguel Covián Pérez, took his place.[113]

Pámanes's departure did not mark the end of attempts to use the Mexican embassy for intelligence purposes. In 1968, the Mexican foreign ministry created a new post of press counselor and attaché in its embassy in Havana. Humberto Carrillo Colón, the man who filled the post, was an undercover CIA agent on a mission to gather political, economic, and military information about Cuba. He also kept an eye on Mexico's embassy and its ambassador, Covián Pérez. The CIA provided special photographic and radio equipment to monitor military objectives, and Carrillo Colón used the official diplomatic mailbag to send his film and reports to the CIA station in Mexico City.[114]

Outraged, Cuban leaders risked endangering their relations with Mexico by denouncing Carrillo Colón. Fidel Castro personally intervened to try to convince the Mexican government to take action against the CIA spy in its midst. On September 3, 1969, the prime minister of Cuba and the president, Osvaldo Dorticós, summoned Mexican Ambassador Covián Pérez to a private meeting. The accusations against Carrillo Colón apparently caught the ambassador by surprise, and he asked for proof. Castro assured him that the Cuban government would not have risked "poisoning" their relations with Mexico without evidence, showed him some examples, and reminded Covián Pérez that the spy "has not only acted against the Cuban state, but against the Mexican state as well." Castro went on to insist: "We are not blaming the Mexican government, we are defending it against an attack by the CIA." He urged the ambassador to take action before Carrillo Colón had the chance to escape or destroy any additional evidence. Castro pointed out that the Cubans had shown a great deal of restraint and respect for the Mexican government by simply documenting Carrillo Colón's actions instead of arresting him in violation of his diplomatic immunity. At the end of the meeting, the ambassador promised to take whatever measures he could to limit the spy's actions while he awaited instructions from Mexico City.[115]

[112] "[Repatriation of American citizens now being held in Cuba]," September 15, 1967, NSF, Cuba, Bowdler File, Volume III (2 of 2), LBJ Library.

[113] "Covián en La Habana," *Política*, August 15, 1967.

[114] *El insólito caso del espía de la CIA bajo el manto de funcionario diplomático de la Embajada de México en Cuba* (Havana: Granma, 1969).

[115] "Entrevista efectuada por el Presidente Osvaldo Dorticós Torrado y el Primer Ministro Fidel Castro Ruz con el embajador de Méjico Sr. Miguel Cobián. Palacio de la Revolución, 3 de septiembre de 1969, Año del Esfuerzo Decisivo," América Latina, México, 1968–1969 Ordinario 8, 1969, MINREX.

At the same time that Castro and Dorticós were revealing the problem to Covián Pérez, Cuba's ambassador to Mexico presented Foreign Minister Antonio Carrillo Flores with a diplomatic note condemning the CIA's spy. Carrillo Flores rejected the note and recalled Carrillo Colón to Mexico. Cuban Foreign Minister Raúl Roa then flew to Mexico to deliver "indisputable proof" of Carrillo Colón's activities to President Díaz Ordaz.[116] In a private meeting at the president's residence, Roa demanded that the Mexican government punish Carrillo Colón or extradite him to Cuba for trial. Díaz Ordaz read over the evidence that Roa had brought with him, then returned it and remarked that the Cubans' accusations seemed legitimate. He went on to explain that what bothered him the most about the denunciation was the timing; Mexican-Cuban relations were already strained over the issue of recent hijackings of Mexican planes by people escaping to Cuba, and Díaz Ordaz did not want to see the negotiations over a new hijacking treaty derailed by the Carrillo Colón case.[117]

Though the meeting ended on friendly terms, Díaz Ordaz ultimately refused to extradite Carrillo Colón, and the spy remained free. The official mouthpiece of the Cuban government, *Granma*, retaliated by publishing a 164-page booklet titled *The Unusual Case of the CIA Spy under the Guise of Diplomatic Officer of the Mexican Embassy in Cuba*. Carrillo Colón gave an interview to the Mexican newspaper *El Universal* in which he publicly denied all the accusations.[118] Mexican journalists speculated that the CIA had masterminded the whole incident – including the disclosure – in order to cause friction between Mexico and Cuba.[119] Publicly, the mystery remained just that, but a classified internal history

[116] "Cuba Gives Spy 'Proof' to Mexico," *Washington Post*, September 13, 1969; "Roa of Cuba Flies to Talk with Díaz: Castro's Foreign Chief Sees Mexican President 2 Hours," *New York Times*, September 13, 1969.

[117] Luis Ojeda to Olexis, "Viaje a México el viernes 12 de septiembre, acompañando al co. Ministro, Dr. Raúl Roa, para entrevista con el Presidente de dicho país, Lic. Gustavo Díaz Ordaz, en relación con el caso del agente de la CIA, Humberto Carrillo Colón, Consejero, encargado de los asuntos de prensa de la Embajada de México en Cuba," September 19, 1969, América Latina, México, 1968–1969 Ordinario 8, 1969, MINREX. On the politics behind hijacking airplanes and forcing them to land in Cuba, see Teishan A. Latner, "Take Me to Havana! Airline Hijacking, U.S.-Cuba Relations, and Political Protest in Late Sixties America," *Diplomatic History* 39, no. 1 (2015): 16–44.

[118] Jorge Aviles R., "Raúl Roa vs. James Bond," *El Universal*, October 8, 1969.

[119] Horacio H. Quiñones, "[Article about Humberto Carrillo Colón]" *Buro de Investigación Política*, September 15, 1969, IPS Caja 2958 D, AGN; Manuel Buendía, *La CIA en México* (Mexico City: Ediciones Océano, 1984), 211–12.

of the CIA's Mexico City station confirmed a decade later that Humberto Carrillo Colón was indeed an undercover agent.[120]

CONCLUSION

It was extremely difficult, if not impossible, for Mexico's leaders to know exactly what role local and international communists played in the explosion of political activism that took place in Mexico in the 1960s. Security agents from multiple agencies reported that communist instigators were following orders and receiving support from the Soviet Union and Cuba. Prominent Mexican citizens attended international conferences where they exchanged ideas with foreign communist leaders and made declarations in favor of armed revolution. Diplomatic officials – and undercover CIA agents – working in the embassy in Havana claimed that Mexican citizens were matriculating through the guerrilla training schools in Cuba.

It was in this climate of uncertainty and insecurity that President Díaz Ordaz had to decide how to respond to various threats to his country's vaunted stability. Some of his intelligence agents were planting false evidence and spreading rumors of communist subversion, while other agents were finding that same evidence and reporting it as truth. The intelligence reports, when combined with prominent instances of genuine communist activity, were enough to convince Díaz Ordaz that his country was under attack. Increasingly, he resorted to violent repression, converting his critics into enemies.

[120] Goodpasture, "Mexico City Station History."

6

From Cold War to Dirty War

By the middle of the 1960s, the Mexican government's repeated acts of repression had begun producing the very phenomenon that it had been so desperate to avoid: a new revolutionary movement. Like the original revolution of 1910, this movement manifested itself in a variety of ways over the course of more than a decade. Though the various participants differed in their specific goals and strategies, they all sought fundamental political and social changes, and they all contributed to create a climate of instability.[1] Some expressions of this new revolutionary movement, like the student movement of 1968, were largely peaceful, but many others were not. The barriers that the Mexican government erected to democratic reform drove its most determined critics to resort to violence. Mexican officials' claims of conspiracies and subversion may have sounded paranoid, but guerrilla groups that sought to overthrow the government did, in fact, operate throughout Mexico from the mid-1960s until the early 1980s. According to recent estimates, nearly two thousand men and women joined some thirty or forty guerrilla groups in that period. The nation's leaders were so absorbed in their hunt for international communists that they ignored the many homegrown causes for discontent, and thus missed multiple opportunities to find negotiated

[1] I have chosen the term *movement* to capture the active and popular nature of these events and to connect them with earlier reformist movements, but the terms *process, situation,* or *attempt,* more common to sociological works on revolution, could also apply. On revolutionary processes, situations, and attempts, as opposed to successful revolutions, see Eric Selbin, *Modern Latin American Revolutions,* 2nd ed. (Boulder, CO: Westview Press, 1999); John Foran, *Taking Power: On the Origins of Third World Revolutions* (Cambridge: Cambridge University Press, 2005).

resolutions. Instead, the Mexican government unleashed a dirty war against its own citizens that took the lives of more than three thousand protesters, combatants, sympathizers, and family members.[2]

THE FIRST BATTLE

Shortly after Díaz Ordaz was elected president, the head of the Department of Federal Security submitted a report about suspicious activity in the mountains of Chihuahua. He claimed that communist guerrillas were planning an uprising for December and had already gone to the mountains to train. The intelligence agent's source, the secretary of the Independent Campesino Center, told him that the rebels had a copy of Che Guevara's guide to guerrilla warfare and were "studying it meticulously." The source also claimed that eighty soldiers had been sent to the mountains to suffocate the rebellion. Their failure to return or send word of their progress suggested that they might have joined the uprising.[3] The information in the intelligence report contained numerous overtones of the Cuban Revolution, in which many soldiers' reluctance to defend Fulgencio Batista and defection to Castro's guerrilla forces paved the way for the revolutionaries' triumph.

The intelligence report was partially correct: there was a guerrilla group forming in the state of Chihuahua. Arturo Gámiz and Salomón Gaytán had created the Popular Guerrilla Group (*Grupo Popular Guerrillero*) around the beginning of 1964 in order to demand land and political reforms and to defend the public against the violent repression that it suffered at the hands of state officials and caciques. Gámiz and Gaytán were local leaders of the Popular Socialist Party's General Union of Mexican Workers and Campesinos (*Unión General de Obreros y Campesinos Mexicanos*, or UGOCM) and members of the National Liberation Movement.[4] Gámiz, a rural schoolteacher who listened to Radio Habana

---

[2] Estimates of this death toll are constantly fluctuating, and do not include those who were tortured or harmed in other ways. See Jorge Luis Sierra Guzmán, *El enemigo interno: Contrainsurgencia y fuerzas armadas en México* (Mexico City: Centro de Estudios Estratégicos de América del Norte, 2003), 19–20; Calderón and Cedillo, "Introduction: The Unknown Mexican Dirty War," 8; Aguayo Quezada, "El impacto de la guerrilla en la vida mexicana," 91–8; FEMOSPP, *Informe Histórico Presentado a La Sociedad Mexicana*. I use the term *dirty war* to describe a long period of state-sponsored repression.

[3] Manuel Rangel Escamilla, "[Communist guerrillas in Chihuahua]," August 28, 1964, DFS, Exp 100-17-3-2-64, Leg. 1, Hoja 47, AGN.

[4] Castellanos, *México armado*, 73.

every morning, provided the ideological leadership while Gaytán, a *campesino*, acted as head of operations.[5] The Popular Guerrilla Group found another ideological guide in Pablo Gómez, a doctor, teacher, and leader of the Popular Socialist Party and the UGOCM. After becoming disillusioned with legal political channels after the 1964 elections, Gómez went to Mexico City and applied for permission to move to Cuba. When the authorities denied his request, he joined the guerrillas at the beginning of 1965.[6]

The Popular Guerrilla Group was the first in Mexico to base its strategy on the Cuban example. Its leaders had read Castro's "History Will Absolve Me" speech and studied Che Guevara's guide to guerrilla warfare.[7] They established a temporary headquarters in Mexico City in early 1965 in order to undertake military training, contact other revolutionary groups, and raise funds.[8] There, they received advice on strategy from a retired army captain, Lorenzo Cárdenas Barajas, who had helped instruct Fidel Castro's group of rebels during their time in Mexico almost a decade earlier and was likely serving as a spy for the Mexican government.[9] When the Department of Federal Security interrogated Cárdenas Barajas about his activities, he recalled that the Chihuahua group's members were already in excellent physical shape and merely needed an insider's expertise on engaging in battle with the Mexican military. He admitted that when he advised the guerrillas on how to prepare for an assault on an army barracks, he severely underestimated the number of soldiers that would be on guard.[10]

On September 23, 1965, the Chihuahua guerrillas made their mark on Mexican history. A few minutes before dawn, thirteen or so students, teachers, and *campesinos* of the Popular Guerrilla Group began their attack on the army barracks at Ciudad Madera. They planned to stage a lightning assault, seize weapons and money, and transmit a

[5] Padilla, "Rural Education, Political Radicalism, and Normalista Identity in Mexico after 1940," 353.
[6] Castellanos, *México armado*, 77. On the Popular Guerrilla Group, see also Elizabeth Henson, "Madera 1965: Primeros Vientos," in Herrera Calderón and Cedillo, eds. *Challenging Authoritarianism in Mexico*, 19–39.
[7] Víctor Orozco Orozco, "La guerrilla chihuahuense de los sesenta," in Oikión Solano and García Ugarte, eds., *Movimientos armados en México* ed., Vol. 2, 337–60, 342.
[8] Henson, "Madera 1965," 33.
[9] On Barajas's probable espionage and infiltration of the guerrilla group, see FEMOSPP, *Informe Histórico Presentado a La Sociedad Mexicana*, 261.
[10] Fernando Gutiérrez Barrios, "Extracto de la declaración rendida por Lorenzo Cárdenas Barajas," June 6, 1969, DFS, Versión Pública de Fidel Castro, Leg. 1, Hoja 288, AGN.

revolutionary message over the local radio before returning to the mountains, as Guevara's manual advised.[11] Just like Castro's ill-fated attack on the Moncada barracks, the Chihuahua group's plan failed. One hundred and twenty five soldiers guarded the barracks and repelled the assault for an hour and a half. At least five of the guerrillas managed to flee, but eight others died, including leaders Gómez, Gámiz, and Gaytán. Soldiers displayed the bodies of the fallen assailants in a row – the better for photographing and public viewing – then buried them in a common grave. "Since it was dirt that they were fighting for," the state governor quipped, "give them dirt until they are full of it."[12]

Just like the Cuban army's triumph at the Moncada barracks, the Mexican army's victory over the Chihuahua guerrillas was only the beginning of the war. CIA observers at the time of the attacks predicted accurately that the confrontation would "harden [Díaz Ordaz's] intolerance of activity designed to embarrass his administration."[13] By the same token, the events in Ciudad Madera also hardened the determination of opposition groups, and rural and urban guerrilla movements blossomed in Chihuahua and elsewhere across the country. Half a dozen armed groups emerged just within the state, and eight years later one of the most important urban guerrilla groups in Mexico, the 23rd of September Communist League, commemorated the date of the attack in their name.[14] Other revolutionary groups studied the failure of the Popular Guerrilla Group for lessons on what to avoid. Police arrested two survivors of the assault half a year later for suspected participation in further guerrilla activities as part of a communist plot.[15]

Accounts of the attack on the Chihuahua barracks helped generate support for the guerrillas' cause. Internationally renowned journalist Víctor Rico Galán, a close friend of Fidel Castro and Che Guevara, published a widely read report on the events at Ciudad Madera. He called the assault an act of desperation justified by years of abuse and concluded that peaceful change was impossible in Mexico.[16] A year later, police

---

[11] Castellanos, *México armado*, 63.

[12] "Sangre en Chihuahua," *Política*, October 1, 1965. The governor's comment played upon the double meaning of the Spanish word *tierra*, which can be translated as both "land" and "dirt." On the guerrillas in Chihuahua, see also José Santos Valdes, *Madera: Razón de un martirologio* (Mexico City: Imprenta Laura, 1968).

[13] CIA, "Insurgency in Northern Mexico," October 1, 1965. CREST Database, CIA-RD P79-00927A005000080001-0, NARA.

[14] Castellanos, *México armado*, 64.

[15] "Conjura roja en Chihuahua delatada por un cabecilla," *El Universal*, March 10, 1966.

[16] Castellanos, *México armado*, 81.

arrested Rico Galán and twenty-eight associates, including leaders of the People's Electoral Front and the doctors' strikes, in the preliminary stages of organizing an armed People's Revolutionary Movement (Movimiento Revolucionario del Pueblo). The Mexican ambassador in Havana, Fernando Pámanes Escobedo, sent a message to the Foreign Ministry upon learning of the arrests, in which he claimed that Rico Galán received "great quantities of money" from the Cuban government and recommended that officials submit the journalist to a "severe interrogation" about Cuban involvement with Mexican guerrillas.[17]

The events at Ciudad Madera continued to generate controversy three years later, when two books containing conflicting accounts appeared just as the student movement of 1968 erupted. A teacher and member of the Mexican Communist Party named José Santos Valdés published the first, a sympathetic account of the assault and a resounding condemnation of living conditions in the state of Chihuahua. Valdés, who had personally known Pablo Gómez and the other leaders of the Popular Guerrilla Group, explained that "the rebellion had been motivated by a local government that was inept, despotic, and dedicated to serving, protecting, and inform-ing the rich."[18] Shortly thereafter, someone writing under the pseudonym Prudencio Godines Jr. produced a direct challenge to Valdés's account. "Godines" claimed to be a former communist who had been trained in the Soviet Union and participated in the assault at Ciudad Madera following orders from Raúl Castro.[19] He accused José Santos Valdés, Víctor Rico Galán, Manuel Marcué Pardiñas, and other prominent leftists of leading the Popular Guerrilla Group into a trap in order to create martyrs for the communist cause. He contended that the people of Chihuahua didn't support the guerrillas because they were happy with their government. According to "Godines," the Soviet Union's efforts to conquer Mexico were failing because "the Mexican Revolution is humane and correct, while the Russian one is murderous and enslaving."[20] But, he warned, the communists were still at it; the Soviet Union, China, and Cuba were investing a great deal of money in "buying the consciousness of students," and they would "take advantage of any street brawl and force the police

[17] Condés Lara, *Represión y rebelión en México*, 175–91.
[18] Santos Valdes, *Madera: Razón de un martirologio*, 6.
[19] Prudencio Godines Jr., *¡Qué Poca Mad ... era La de José Santos Valdés!* (Mexico City, 1968), 59.
[20] Ibid., 156.

to intervene in order to accuse the government of being the enemy of the youth."[21]

Intelligence agents also consistently blamed the proliferation of guerrilla activity on a communist conspiracy. Agents of the Department of Federal Security, Department of Political and Social Investigations, and Federal Police independently claimed on numerous occasions that the Mexican Communist Party was training its members in the methods of guerrilla warfare.[22] The head of the DFS sent the federal prosecutor's office the text of a speech made by the leader of the PCM, Arnoldo Martínez Verdugo, at the party's fifteenth national congress in June 1967. The intelligence director transcribed the entire speech, underlining the most incriminating sections where Martínez Verdugo had proclaimed that Mexico required a new revolution consisting of armed struggle.[23]

To a certain extent, the intelligence agents had it right: the Mexican Communist Party had indeed resolved to pursue a new revolution using violent means. Martínez Verdugo told his fellow communists: "We need to prepare, so that the legal actions that today are the essential form of struggle of the masses to defend their rights can give way to the armed struggle as the principle form of revolutionary action."[24] Agents of the federal prosecutor's office acted upon the DFS's investigations by interrogating the communist leader about his promotion of revolution and violent warfare. Martínez Verdugo categorically denied that the communist party directed the actions of other groups. He also insisted that his statements about a new revolution were "a hypothesis derived from studying the political situation of the country."[25] Intelligence agents were, of course, conducting their own studies of Mexico's political situation, but they would form much different hypotheses about the causes of revolution.

---

[21] Ibid., 154.
[22] Policía Judicial Federal, "[Communist guerrilla training]," June 2, 1966, GDO 205 (124), AGN; "[PCM providing guerrilla training]," August 6, 1966, DFS, Exp 11-4-66, Leg. 18, Hoja 21, AGN; "Actividades del Partido Comunista Mexicano," 1966, IPS Caja 2181 A, AGN; Fernando Gutiérrez Barrios, "[PCM comité clandestino and guerrilla activity]," June 28, 1967, DFS, Exp 11-136-67, Leg. 17, Hoja 123, AGN; "[PCM guerrilla warfare preparations]," April 18, 1964, IPS Caja 1573 A, AGN; "[Communist activities]," July 9, 1967, IPS Caja 2966 C, AGN; "[PCM's guerrilla plans]," July 13, 1967, DFS, Exp 11-4-67, Leg. 20, Hoja 271, AGN.
[23] Fernando Gutiérrez Barrios, "[PCM leader's remarks]," July 3, 1967, DFS, Exp 11-4-67, Leg. 20, Hoja 285, AGN.
[24] Fabio Barbosa Cano, "Acción y búsqueda programática," in *Historia del comunismo en México*, ed. Arnoldo Martínez Verdugo (Mexico City: Grijalbo, 1985), 286.
[25] "[Interrogation of Arnoldo Martínez Verdugo]," July 11, 1967, IPS Caja 1456 A, AGN.

THE 1968 STUDENT MOVEMENT

July 26 proved to be a momentous day in both Cuban and Mexican history. On that date in 1953, Fidel Castro made an ill-fated attack on the Moncada Barracks that marked the beginning of the Cuban Revolution. Fifteen years later, a confrontation between students and police ignited a protest movement that spread across Mexico City and threatened to humiliate the government on the eve of the Olympic Games. Intelligence agents did not fail to note that the simmering student agitation came to a boil on Cuba's independence day. They concluded that students' admiration of the Cuban Revolution had finally been transformed into imitation. During and after the 1968 student movement, intelligence agents produced voluminous evidence that connected the uprising to Cuba and communism.

There were two main groups whose participation in the student movement served as "evidence" of an international conspiracy: the Mexican Communist Party and the communist-controlled National Center of Democratic Students. According to a report by the Federal Judicial Police used later in the prosecution of student movement leaders, the CNED held its first plenary meeting in early July 1968 in the city of Morelia. A few people who later played significant roles in the student movement attended and vowed to carry out disturbances across the country to create trouble for the government. They reportedly agreed that every month, beginning in July, they would execute "a distinct movement of agitation and incitement to rebellion against the government of the nation, with distinct pretexts such as support for Cuba and freedom for political prisoners."[26]

It appeared that the National Center of Democratic Students did not wait long to put its plan into action. Intelligence agents reported that the CNED, working in conjunction with the Mexican Communist Party, encouraged the confrontation between students and police on July 26 that helped spark the movement. The two communist groups had scheduled a demonstration that day in the center of Mexico City to celebrate the anniversary of the Cuban Revolution. It took place around the same time as a completely unrelated student march, also downtown, to protest police brutality in recent clashes among students. According to intelligence reports, the communists took advantage of the coinciding times and locations of the two demonstrations. First, two students who were

[26] FEMOSPP, *Los procesos de México*, 54.

members of both the Communist Party and the CNED tried to invite the student protestors from the second march to join their pro-Cuba rally. When that failed, leaders of the groups reportedly formed a plot to infiltrate the other protest and convince the students on the spot to join the rally. They would then threaten businesses, provoke the police, and blame the students. The members of the PCM and CNED agreed to arm themselves with sticks and stones to repel police.[27]

When they saw that a number of the participants from the student march had indeed joined up with the rally celebrating the Cuban Revolution, intelligence agents concluded that the communists' plan had worked. The pro-Castro speakers, they reported, had criticized the Mexican police and government, "inciting the crowd to violence," and the combined group began heading for the Zócalo. According to the official version of the events, the students broke windows and looted stores along the way until the riot police intervened.[28] Other witnesses contended that the police initiated the violence and destruction, attacking students uninvolved in the demonstrations. The students fled and took refuge in a few nearby schools, where they engaged in a prolonged battle with security forces.[29] Fighting lasted until the early morning hours of the next day, and then broke out again across the city when students learned that some of their comrades had been killed, injured, and arrested. As a result of the police's brutality, the uprising quickly spread over the following days to schools and universities across the city and country. Students seized hundreds of buses, barricaded streets, and started preparing Molotov cocktails.[30] The army stepped in and escalated the violence: one group of soldiers even used a bazooka to blast open the antique colonial doors of a high school, killing seven students who were hiding behind the doors.[31]

From the very beginning, government officials claimed to be victims of a conspiracy. On the night of July 26, police raided the offices of the Mexican Communist Party, the communist newspaper *La Voz*, and the National Center of Democratic Students. "We are facing an international communist conspiracy," the chief of police told the press. Other officials

[27] Fernando Gutiérrez Barrios, "[PCM recommends that pro-Cuba marchers arm themselves]," July 25, 1968, DFS, Exp 11-4-68, Leg. 23, Hoja 359, AGN.
[28] FEMOSPP, *Los procesos de México*. See also Mabry, *The Mexican University and the State*, 239.
[29] Jardón, *1968*, 30.
[30] "Síntesis de antecedentes de 1966, 1967 del conflicto político y social conocido como movimiento estudiantil creado en el mes de julio de 1968."
[31] Mabry, *The Mexican University and the State*, 244.

seconded this claim, including the general prosecutor, Julio Sánchez Vargas, and the minister of the interior, Luis Echeverría.[32] Judge Eduardo Ferrer Mac-Gregor issued an arrest warrant for fifteen leaders of the Communist Party and CNED for the crimes of damaging property, attacking public transportation, criminal association, and sedition. The warrant specified that they committed these offenses while trying to disturb public order and embarrass the national government in order to install a communist regime.[33]

Obliging members of the press picked up on the idea of an international conspiracy. Eduardo Arrieta of *El Universal Gráfico* published an article entitled "The 26 of July in Mexico," in which he claimed, "The young people of Mexico City were pushed by groups known to be interested in undermining order and national institutions." Drawing on popular press stereotypes of Mexican students as dangerous puppets and a subversive threat to peace and security, Arrieta sympathized with the thousands of residents of Mexico City who found their daily routines interrupted by the "unruly youngsters" and bemoaned the destruction of schools and office buildings. "There was a plan," he concluded. "It is no mere coincidence that during these days one of the many groups of instigators of the chaos took part in the anniversary celebration of the extinct 26 of July Movement."[34] *El Universal* also published a declaration by the extremist conservative student group MURO that blamed the events of July 26 on "Marxist agitators" and called for "all the weight of the law to fall on the intellectual authors of these barbarous acts."[35] Articles in *Excélsior, Novedades, Ovaciones, Revista de América,* and *Sucesos* all echoed the theme of communist subversion.[36]

---

[32] Jacinto Rodríguez Munguía, *1968: Todos los culpables* (Mexico City: Random House Mondadori, 2008), 30–1; "Mexican Students Fight Riot Police," *New York Times*, July 31, 1968.

[33] Judge Eduardo Ferrer Mac-Gregor, "[Arrest order for communists]," August 13, 1968, IPS Caja 1456 A, AGN.

[34] Eduardo Arrieta, "'26 de Julio' en México," *El Universal Gráfico*, August 2, 1968. On increasingly negative portrayals of students in the Mexican press in the 1950s and 1960s, see chapter 3 in Pensado, *Rebel Mexico*.

[35] González Ruiz, *MURO, Memorias y testimonios*, 375.

[36] Guillermo Estrada Unda, "76 agitadores rojos que instigaron los disturbios estudiantiles están detenidos; Algunos de ellos son extranjeros," *Novedades*, July 28, 1968; Adolfo Olmedo Luna, "Los rojos intentan azuzar más al estudiantado," *Ovaciones*, July 30, 1968; "El estado no puede permitir; ¿castrismo mexicano?," *Excélsior*, July 31, 1968; "Ingerencia de agentes extranjeros; Financió los motines el Partido Comunista," *Excélsior*, July 31, 1968; Raúl Torres Duque, "Los disturbios estudiantiles, pretexto para insidiosa campaña en el extranjero," *Ovaciones*, August 2, 1968; Francisco A. Gomez Jara, "Un 'mayo rojo' para el Politécnico," *Sucesos*, August 10, 1968; "Los mexicanos; Presente y pasado de las conjuras," *Revista de América*, August 24, 1968.

The Mexican Communist Party found itself in the difficult position of being blamed for a movement that had actually surpassed and overshadowed its own limited efforts to oppose the government. Led by muralist David Álfaro Siqueiros, the party issued a manifesto that claimed that subversive documents that the authorities had allegedly seized were actually CIA forgeries created to frame the communists. "The immediate causes of the events that have occurred since July 26 are found in the methods of governing that have been implanted in our country for some time," the manifesto argued, shifting the blame. "These methods are characterized by the use of public force and violence as a way of meeting popular anxieties and by the abuse of the so-called 'principle of authority,' which considers any popular protest as a threat to the regime." A reporter from the *New York Times* observed that the communists' critiques of the Mexican government "would appear to have the approval of a large number of students."[37] And yet, factionalism and conflicted loyalties prevented the PCM and other stalwarts of Mexico's Old Left from joining or even endorsing the New Leftist student movement.

U.S. Ambassador Fulton Freeman believed that the Mexican government possessed solid evidence of communist involvement in the July 26th confrontation between students and police. In a rather far-fetched report to Washington on the incidents, the ambassador posited that the Soviets had pressured the Mexican Communist Party to adopt more militant tactics in the lead-up to the Olympic Games. Freeman also suggested that the Cuban ambassador had known about the plans for agitation, and had absented himself from Mexico City on July 26th to avoid accusations of Cuban meddling.[38]

While the press and the U.S. ambassador were promoting the theory of a communist conspiracy, Mexican intelligence agents were busily trying to figure out if and how Cuba was involved. On August 19, 1968, as the movement built up steam, DFS agents composed a report based on the account of an anonymous informant. The source claimed that the president of the Mexican Communist Party, Hugo Ponce de León, as well as a woman named María Elena Díaz Alejo had each separately called the Cuban embassy to say that they were carrying out the student agitation. The Cuban official at the other end of the line cut them off, telling them not to discuss such

[37] Henry Giniger, "Reds Deny Role in Mexico Riots: Charge Leaflets Attributed to Party Are Forgeries," *New York Times*, August 6, 1969, 3.
[38] Fulton Freeman, "[Communist involvement in student demonstrations]," July 1968, Declassified Documents Reference System.

matters over the telephone.[39] The connections to Cuba mounted. The intelligence report also claimed that the director of the political science department at UNAM was a friend of Fidel Castro and a member of the Mexican Communist Party. This educator had supposedly signed one of the antigovernment fliers circulating in the university and sent instructions about street fighting to the students. The informant named another friend of Castro who received correspondence from the Cuban embassy and participated in the disturbances. A third "Castro-ite" (*castrista*) also reportedly took part in the student revolt.[40] On September 3, an official from the Department of Federal Security reported that two young Cuban women were working with a Mexican student to spread communist publications. The Mexican student also supposedly made frequent trips to Cuba.[41]

Participants in the student movement did make a number of public references to Cuba. While some students carried banners of Benito Juárez, Pancho Villa, Emiliano Zapata, and Demetrio Vallejo in their demonstrations, others marched under the iconic photograph of Che Guevara (see Figure 10).[42] Protesters bore signs that read "Cuba, 1956, Moncada: Mexico … When?" and "Che Has Not Died, He Lives Among Us."[43] When police arrested Heberto Castillo, they interrogated him about the origins of posters of Che and Fidel and signs that read "A Man – Castro; An Island – Cuba; An Ideal – Communism."[44] While they fell far short of proving Cuban involvement, the posters did demonstrate the students' admiration of Cuba and their desire to emulate their heroes.

Mexican officials received word that the Cuban embassy also showed a great deal of interest in student propaganda. The Mexican intelligence files contain a report, in English, describing a meeting between a Mexican university student involved in the protests – "Silvia" – and the Cuban embassy's cultural and press attaché and the commercial counselor. The meeting took place over breakfast in Sanborns, a popular local restaurant chain, on the morning of September 15. Silvia brought examples of propaganda leaflets distributed by the protesting students and the attaché

---

[39] "[People involved in student protests]," August 19, 1968, DFS, Exp 11-4-68, Leg. 32, Hoja 23, AGN.

[40] Ibid.

[41] "[Cuban propaganda distribution]," September 3, 1968, DFS, Exp 11-4-68, Leg 51, Hoja 164, AGN.

[42] Carr, *Marxism and Communism in Twentieth-Century Mexico*, 264.

[43] FEMOSPP, *Los procesos de México*, 71, 74.

[44] "Interrogatorio de Heberto Castillo Martínez," June 27, 1969, IPS Caja 2956, AGN.

FIGURE 10. Participants in the 1968 student movement marching behind a banner with the face of Che Guevara. "Student demonstrators march to the Presidential Palace to demand that the police chief be fired. One of a month-long series of student demonstrations."

Source: Bettmann/Corbis/AP Images, August 13, 1968. Courtesy of AP Images, ID Number 680813168.

"looked them over, read some of the printed matter, and laughed heart-ily."⁴⁵ Silvia's connections to the Cuban embassy probably predated the 1968 student movement. The intelligence report explained that she had been in contact with the previous cultural attaché, Abelardo Curbelo Padrón, a "known DGI [agent]."⁴⁶ Mexican intelligence agents suspected that Curbelo had given nine thousand pesos to the National Center of Democratic Students earlier that year.⁴⁷

Mexican leaders feared that the Cubans might provide weapons to the students. Beginning in August, the Mexican government put its navy and coastal military land units on alert for the possible infiltration of equipment from the island. This action came in response to claims that "the Cuban government would attempt to infiltrate arms into Mexico for use by students and student sympathizers during a planned demonstra-tion."⁴⁸ The fact that the Mexican government decided to put the navy and army on alert suggests that it took the threat of Cuban interference in the student movement extremely seriously.

Intelligence agents also suspected that the Cuban news agency Prensa Latina was involved in the student movement. A long report about the organization claimed that employees of the news agency were "intensely dedicated to student issues."⁴⁹ The report contained allegations that, under instructions from Havana, two representatives of Prensa Latina had traveled to Paris during the French student uprising of the spring of 1968. There, the Cubans had observed the methods used by the Parisian students and recruited some of them to go to Mexico to instruct stu-dents there. Intelligence agents and articles in U.S. newspapers referred to French "riot coaches" that had supposedly been involved in some of the earlier events of the Mexican student movement until police arrested them.⁵⁰

Prensa Latina hotly denied accusations that Cubans were involved in the Mexican student movement. In an article in the magazine *Bohemia*,

---

⁴⁵ "Cuban Embassy Contacts with Mexican Leftist Students," September 20, 1968, IPS Caja 2958 E, AGN.

⁴⁶ Ibid.

⁴⁷ "La embajada de Cuba y la marcha estudiantil por la Ruta de la Libertad"; "Central Nacional de Estudiantes Democráticos."

⁴⁸ "Mexican Military Alert for possible Cuban infiltration of arms destined for student use," August 24, 1968, NSF, Mexico, Box 60, Folder 6, Document 42c, LBJ Library.

⁴⁹ "Prensa Latina informe," November 25, 1968, DFS, Versión Pública de Fidel Castro, Leg. 1, Hoja 295 and Exp 65-92-69, Leg. 3, Hoja 132, AGN.

⁵⁰ "[Prensa Latina contacts with students]," May 4, 1970, DFS, Exp 65-92-70, Leg. 3, Hoja 241, AGN; "The Riots in Mexico City," *Chicago Tribune*, September 26, 1968.

a reporter from Prensa Latina accused the Mexican press of spreading "biased versions" of the movement. The reporter quoted from an article in *El Universal* that had claimed that "women of definite Cuban type, carrying flags of the Socialist Republic of Cuba, infiltrated the student movement that, when all is said and done, was directed by Castroism." Prensa Latina blamed "reactionary sectors" in Mexico for spreading misleading information in an effort to link Cuba with the movement.[51]

Mexico's Foreign Ministry tasked its ambassador to Cuba, Miguel Covián Pérez, with investigating Cuban media's connections with the student movement. President Díaz Ordaz received a message in September from a concerned citizen in Guerrero claiming that radio transmitters from Havana were "exhorting Mexican students to continue their battle against the Mexican government until they triumph."[52] Covián Pérez replied that the only Cuban radio coverage of the student movement was limited to the Prensa Latina reports that typically appeared in all the newspapers.[53] He sent copies back to Mexico City of all the stories in *Granma, Juventud Rebelde, El Mundo, El Socialista,* and *Girón* about the events in Mexico, and remarked that the Cuban press was covering the movement "without commentary, [which] this Mission interprets as an indication of the desires of the Cuban authorities to be objective in everything that has to do with our country."[54]

President Díaz Ordaz never publicly blamed the Cubans, but he did lend weight to the theory of an international conspiracy in his State of the Union address on September 1, 1968. "It is evident," he contended, "that non-student hands have intervened in the recent disturbances." Díaz Ordaz also explained to his audience how the recent violence throughout the country was part of a worldwide trend. "We situate these events within the frame of international information about similar bitter experiences in a great number of nations in which, from the beginning or after trying various solutions, they had to resort to force and only in that way were able to end the disturbances." The comparison to other countries conveyed a clear warning: the Mexican government was likewise ready

---

[51] "Dos meses de lucha estudiantil en México," *Bohemia,* September 20, 1968.
[52] Ricardo N. de la Peña, "[Telegram to President Gustavo Díaz Ordaz]," September 15, 1968, SRE, from the personal collection of Sergio Aguayo.
[53] Miguel Covián Pérez, "[Telegram to Mexico's Ministry of Foreign Affairs]," October 14, 1968, SRE, from the personal collection of Sergio Aguayo.
[54] Miguel Covián Pérez, "Recortes de prensa sobre disturbios estudiantiles en México," August 8, September 3, September 16, September 27, 1968 SRE, from the personal collection of Sergio Aguayo.

to use force if necessary. "We will do what we have to," Díaz Ordaz promised the nation.[55]

In blaming the student movement on an international conspiracy, Díaz Ordaz and his agents either willfully or unintentionally ignored the real causes of the protests. The students strove to make their goals clear, issuing a public list of demands that included a combination of immediate and larger political concerns. They called upon the government to release all its political prisoners, remove the head of the police and the army, disband the riot police, eliminate the crime of "social dissolution" from the constitution, and compensate the families of victims of government repression.[56] But Díaz Ordaz refused to meet with the student leaders or listen to their criticism of his government. In spite of very clear indications about what was actually causing the student movement, Díaz Ordaz chose to believe questionable evidence that supported what he wanted to think and continued to blame the protests on outside intervention.

THE TLATELOLCO MASSACRE

Two months passed, and the student movement swelled to include more than three hundred thousand people and showed little sign of abating. The students declared a strike, took over buildings on the campuses of UNAM and the National Polytechnic Institute, and organized massive marches in the streets of Mexico City. Bloody confrontations between protesters armed with Molotov cocktails and security forces bearing heavy artillery took place on an almost daily basis. The police arrested more than a thousand people, but most of the movement's leaders evaded capture. At the end of September, Díaz Ordaz sent the military to invade the UNAM and IPN campuses, in a clear violation of the principle of university autonomy. Even that failed to put an end to the movement.

Díaz Ordaz became desperate to regain control of his country before the eyes of the world would turn to Mexico for the Olympic Games. On the afternoon of October 2, ten days before the opening ceremonies, between five and fifteen thousand people gathered in Mexico City's Plaza de Tlatelolco. Most were students, but army personnel also ringed the area. Leaders of the National Strike Council (Consejo Nacional de Huelga) addressed the crowd from the fourth-floor balcony of one of

---

[55] "Gustavo Díaz Ordaz, al abrir el Congreso sus sesiones ordinarias, el 1 de septiembre de 1968," in *Mexico a través de los informes presidenciales*, Vol. 1: Los mensajes políticos (Mexico City: Secretaría de la Presidencia, 1976).

[56] Guevara Niebla, *La democracia en la calle*, 39.

the surrounding apartment buildings. Unbeknownst to the students and the soldiers, a top-secret group of ten officials armed with submachine guns were hiding in the buildings around the plaza. Other government agents with white gloves on one hand immersed themselves in the crowd. Shortly after six, a helicopter circled the plaza and dropped a couple of flares. The gunners in the buildings immediately opened fire on the students and army men below. The soldiers and the agents in the white gloves answered fire, shooting indiscriminately. The students found themselves trapped in a bloodbath that lasted hours, well into the night. By the time the shooting had stopped, scores of people lay dead and hundreds more were wounded. The events of October 2 subsequently became known as the Tlatelolco massacre.[57]

The government needed an excuse for the violence, and the cries of "international communist conspiracy" that had begun on July 26th became a chorus. Díaz Ordaz's press secretary told reporters that the "disturbances" were provoked by "international communist agitators ... under the influence of foreign interests that the whole world should know."[58] The minister of agriculture called the student movement "an international conspiracy to discredit Mexico," and the mayor of Mexico City, Alfonso Corona del Rosal, claimed that "forces outside the country" were paying students.[59] The Senate declared that "professional agitators" and "national and international elements who pursue extremely dangerous anti-Mexican goals" were to blame.[60] The main piece of evidence that the senators provided for their conclusion was the supposed presence of high-powered weapons among the students. *El Universal* also reported

[57] On the secret group of ten officials posted in the buildings, see Julio Scherer García and Carlos Monsiváis, *Parte de guerra: Tlatelolco 1968, Documentos del General Marcelino García Barragán* (Mexico City: Aguilar, 1999), 42; Morley, *Our Man in Mexico*, 269. On the agents in white gloves, see Mabry, *The Mexican University and the State*, 264. On the controversial issue of the number of deaths, see Kate Doyle, "The Dead of Tlatelolco: Using the Archives to Exhume the Past," *The National Security Archive Electronic Briefing Book* 201 (October 1, 2006), http://www.gwu.edu/~nsarchiv/NSAEBB/NSAEBB201/index.htm.

[58] "México: Abrieron fuego las tropas contra diez mil manifestantes," *Juventud Rebelde*, October 3, 1968.

[59] Ignacio Quiroz, "Los motines callejeros son una conspiración internacional para desprestigiar a la Nación," *El Sol de México*, October 5, 1968; "Se ataca a México desde el exterior; El titular de la SAG relaciona lo de aquí con el caso checo," *Excélsior*, October 5, 1968; Homero Bazan Viquez, "Fuerzas ajenas al país detrás del llamado conflicto estudiantil: Minoría pagada para quemar camiones, dice Corona del Rosal," *El Heraldo de México*, October 6, 1968.

[60] Luís Ernesto Cárdenas, "Declaración de la Gran Comisión del Senado sobre los recientes disturbios habidos en la capital," *El Nacional*, October 4, 1968.

that police found a great quantity of Russian weapons in the Plaza of Tlatelolco.[61] *La Prensa* claimed that police had arrested some foreigners with rifles and machine guns.[62] Journalists from *El Heraldo de México* blamed the violence on a "band of foreign agitators" and alluded to the presence of "Guevara in Tlatelolco."[63]

U.S. intelligence agents, meanwhile, had come to the opposite conclusion that international communists were not significantly involved. On October 5, 1968, President Lyndon Johnson received a cable from the CIA that began: "There is no hard evidence that either the Cuban or Soviet embassies in Mexico City masterminded the current disturbances." The message mentioned some unconfirmed reports that the Cubans had given "some moral or possibly financial assistance" but dismissed the likelihood of significant meddling. According to the CIA, the Cubans had avoided antagonizing the Mexican government and appeared reluctant to jeopardize their relationship with its leaders. The only evidence of international interference that the reports contained was, in the author's words, "circumstantial" – the appearance of several expensive student advertisements in the Mexico City press that would have cost thousands of dollars. The CIA reasoned that the money for the ads could have come from domestic sources.[64]

Mexican government officials' internal communications, however, reflected the same conspiracy theory that the press was broadcasting to the public, suggesting that Díaz Ordaz and others genuinely perceived themselves as victims of an international plot. A month after the end of the movement, police arrested Arturo Martínez Nateras, a known communist and secretary of foreign relations of the National Center of Democratic Students. Intelligence agents had been watching him for years and had noted his participation in various student uprisings, as well as his frequent trips to Cuba "for guerrilla training."[65] He had also reportedly received thousands of dollars from the Cuban embassy for CNED

---

[61] "Gran cantidad de armas de fabricación rusa, decomisadas," *El Universal*, October 3, 1968.

[62] "Extranjeros detenidos con rifles y ametralladoras," *La Prensa*, October 4, 1968.

[63] "Banda extranjera de agitadores, causa de los disturbios," *El Heraldo de México*, October 3, 1968; Agustín Barrios Gomez, "Guevara en Tlatelolco," *El Heraldo de México*, October 4, 1968.

[64] "Addendum to 'Mexican Student Crisis,'" October 5, 1968, NSF, Mexico, Box 60, Folder 6, Document 56a, LBJ Library.

[65] "Arturo Martínez Nateras," July 20, 1967, IPS Caja 2892 A, AGN. Nateras did, in fact, spend a year in the KOMSOMOL Communist Youth School in Moscow in 1964–5. Condés Lara, *Represión y rebelión en México*, 244n510.

activities in early 1968. The police claimed that when they arrested him in November 1968, Martínez Nateras possessed papers that he had authored that "revealed the direct influence that the Communist Party had played in the entire movement and in the activities of the National Strike Council."[66]

A general summary of the 1968 student movement that agents of the Department of Political and Social Investigations composed at the end of the year contained additional evidence of communist involvement. The author of the report accused the Mexican Communist Party and the National Center of Democratic Students of providing propaganda and orientation to the student movement. "There is an abundance of portraits of Che Guevara and [Demetrio] Vallejo, political propaganda in documents and phrases, signed by the CNED," the summary stated. Describing a protest march, the intelligence report claimed "the columns [of students] were protected with cordons and watched by militants of the Communist Party of Mexico and the Communist Spartacus League, who gave them orders to insult President Díaz Ordaz."[67] A separate report about the communist party claimed that it received money from members throughout the country, which it passed along to the leaders of the National Strike Council.[68]

Further claims of Cuban financial assistance to the student movement also emerged. In January 1969, agents from the Department of Political and Social Investigations reported that on September 10 of the previous year, an employee of the Cuban embassy had cashed a check from the National Bank of Cuba for more than $400,000 in the offshore Bank of the Atlantic. "This quantity was used in the financing of student disorders, especially to prepare actions that disturbed public order, most notably the meeting in Tlatelolco," the agents claimed. Photocopied below the intelligence information was a list of Cuban embassy officials with descriptions in English. The next page of the report specified that a British bank had given the Bank of the Atlantic permission to cash the check.[69]

The attorney general who prosecuted the leaders of the student movement promulgated the theory of an international conspiracy. Drawing primarily upon intelligence reports and semireliable confessions of

---

[66] "[PCM influence in student movement]," November 11, 1968, DFS, Exp 11-4-68, Leg. 57, Hoja 111, AGN.

[67] "Síntesis de antecedentes de 1966, 1967 del conflicto político y social conocido como movimiento estudiantil creado en el mes de julio de 1968."

[68] "Partido Comunista Mexicano," 1968, IPS Caja 2181 A, AGN.

[69] "[Cuban financing of student movement]," January 16, 1969, IPS Caja 2958 E, AGN.

students, the prosecution accused a whole group of defendants of participating in a "subversive plan of international scope." This plot was supposedly concocted outside of Mexico and implemented by the defendants "as leaders or members of the political organizations known as the Mexican Communist Party, the National Center of Democratic Students, the National Liberation Movement" and so on, down the line of left-wing organizations, ending with the National Strike Council. The prosecutor alleged that the conspiracy aimed to install a communist government.[70]

Some of the state's key evidence of an international plot involved Cuba. The first piece of evidence of a conspiracy that the prosecutor presented to the court was an edition of the Cuban newspaper *Granma* with the declarations of the First Conference of the Latin American Solidarity Organization, held in Havana in 1967. The prosecutor noted that the Mexican delegation had included Heberto Castillo Martínez, one of the defendants. He quoted some of the proclamations of the solidarity organization, including one declaring the "right and responsibility" of the people of Latin America to undertake revolution and another specifying the Marxist-Leninist orientation of the revolution.[71]

Despite the prosecutor's emphasis on the actions of groups and organizations, it was actually individual members of left-wing or communist organizations, rather than the groups as a whole, who played significant roles in the student movement. This became increasingly evident as the ideologically pluralistic National Strike Council emerged as the organizing force of the movement, rather than the Mexican Communist Party or the National Center of Democratic Students. The preexisting organizations had taken a back seat to the new strike council.

While the majority of the participants in the student movement were not associated with communist groups, some important and highly visible exceptions existed. CNED leader Arturo Martínez Nateras reportedly led meetings in which students suggested the need to take up arms "because the second phase of the Mexican Revolution had already begun."[72] Communist professors Heberto Castillo Martínez and Eli de Gortari led a group of educators who participated in the movement. Leftist journalist and *Política* editor Manuel Marcué Pardiñas was at the front of the marches and provided the students with propaganda.[73] Jesús

---

[70] FEMOSPP, *Los procesos de México*, 36.

[71] Ibid., 48.

[72] "Síntesis de antecedentes de 1966, 1967 del conflicto político y social conocido como movimiento estudiantil creado en el mes de julio de 1968."

[73] Perzabal, *De las memorias de Manuel Marcué Pardiñas*, 53.

Manuel Ovilla Maldujano, a member of the Mexican Communist Party and the National Center of Democratic Students, headed up brigades of UNAM and IPN students that visited high schools, private schools, and provincial schools to gain adherents for the movement. Dr. Fausto Trejo, a teacher and member of the Mexican Communist Party, spoke at numerous demonstrations.[74]

The theory of an international plot had staying power. One of the main instigators of the Tlatelolco massacre later claimed that he had defended the country against an international communist conspiracy. General Luis Gutiérrez Oropeza served as the chief of Díaz Ordaz's Presidential Guard and was most likely the person who ordered government officials with submachine guns to hide in the buildings around the plaza.[75] Twenty years after the fact, when he published his memoirs, he contended that Mexico had been suffering from "an acute communist infiltration" of numerous organizations, especially the educational system.[76] The communists' main goals supposedly included toppling the regime and sabotaging the Olympic Games. "Since the beginning of the government of Gustavo Díaz Ordaz," he explained, "the radical Left ... received precise orders from international communism to take advantage of the preparations for the Olympics in order to carry out in Mexico the part that the country had been assigned in the Worldwide Revolution."[77]

General Gutiérrez Oropeza placed most of the blame for student agitation throughout the 1960s on Lázaro Cárdenas and Heberto Castillo Martínez. He claimed that they began incorporating prominent educators and students into "Russian communism" when they founded the National Liberation Movement in 1961.[78] As further evidence of an international conspiracy, Gutiérrez Oropeza mentioned that Heberto Castillo had attended the Tricontinental Conference in Cuba, where he had praised the use of armed warfare to gain power. Following the congress in Havana, Castillo had supposedly joined Cuauhtémoc Cárdenas in a tour around Mexico, speaking with students and *campesinos* in order to gain adherents for an "aggression against the government." Gutiérrez Oropeza concluded that Castillo's tour of Mexico and visits to Cuba and

---

[74] "Síntesis de antecedentes de 1966, 1967 del conflicto político y social conocido como movimiento estudiantil creado en el mes de julio de 1968."

[75] Scherer García and Monsiváis, *Parte de guerra*, 42; Morley, *Our Man in Mexico*, 269.

[76] Luis Gutiérrez Oropeza, *Díaz Ordaz: el hombre, el gobernante*, 26.

[77] Ibid., 48.

[78] Ibid., 42.

the Soviet Union had helped the communists take over the universities of Veracruz, Oaxaca, Guerrero, Puebla, Sinaloa, UNAM, the IPN, and the National Teaching College.[79]

Gutiérrez Oropeza explicitly blamed Cárdenas, Castillo, and the communists for the student movement of 1968. He claimed that Castillo and the other teachers were confident that they could take advantage of the student conflict to stage a revolution in Mexico. Cárdenas, meanwhile, had supposedly provided aid and encouragement, in addition to convincing the UNAM rector to support the students. Gutiérrez Oropeza offered a bleak vision of what would have happened if Castillo and his followers had been allowed to triumph. "Beginning that fateful year, Mexico would have fallen into the communist orbit and we would now be another Cuba or Nicaragua."[80]

In his unpublished memoirs, Díaz Ordaz also insisted that his country was the target of an international conspiracy. These personal writings were not for public eyes and so probably contain the most unfiltered documentation available of the president's perception of the student movement. According to historian Enrique Krauze, who obtained the memoirs, Díaz Ordaz was convinced that the head of the Mexican Communist Party had received specific orders at an international Communist Party meeting in Sofia, Bulgaria, in 1967 to agitate among Mexican students for the purpose of disrupting the Olympic Games. The major responsibility for the student movement thus lay, in the president's eyes, with "international communist groups," especially "pro-Soviets and pro-Maoists." He also believed that the international communist movement funneled money to the students through the Cuban and Soviet embassies.[81] Díaz Ordaz thought that Heberto Castillo Martínez took charge of enacting the communist conspiracy and blamed the engineering professor for students' temporary seizure of the Zócalo on the night of August 27. He believed that on that occasion Castillo had established a claim to "maximum, indiscriminate, almost untouchable authority."[82] Díaz Ordaz interpreted a party on the UNAM's campus on September 15 to celebrate Mexican Independence as the professor's next step in creating a separate government and was convinced that students had called Castillo "the Little President." During the students' September 15 celebrations, they had invited Castillo to give the *grito*, or cry, of independence, a

[79] Ibid., 43.
[80] Ibid., 46.
[81] Krauze, *Biography of Power*, 704–6.
[82] Ibid., 707.

ceremonial action that Mexico's presidents perform every year.[83] "I realized," Díaz Ordaz reminisced, "that if we have 'little presidents' ... then they could form a 'little State' with a 'little President' within a State."[84]

Díaz Ordaz's personal version of the Tlatelolco massacre was in accord with his theory of an international conspiracy. He claimed that the students, armed with submachine guns, had attempted to seize the Ministry of Foreign Relations, whose headquarters overlooked the Plaza of Tlatelolco.[85] He denied the presence of police and soldiers in the buildings surrounding the plaza, insisting that there were only "young idealists" shooting down on their own people. In his conclusions about having fulfilled his duty, the president summarized what he saw as the crux of the conflict: "They want to change this Mexico of ours. They want to change it for another which [*sic*] we do not like. If we want to preserve it and we remain united, they will not change what is ours."[86] Who was the vague "they" that Díaz Ordaz blamed? Communists? Students? The rest of his memoir suggested that both groups tried to alter Mexico.

Díaz Ordaz made similar vague references to conspiracies when answering questions about the student movement in an interview he gave shortly before leaving office. When asked whether the government's response came too late, he answered "Look, this so-called student movement ... let's start from the beginning: those subversive attempts of 1958 and 1959, based in the workers' syndicates, failed. At that moment, the decision was made to concentrate all the attention on the students." The rest of the president's response continued in the same vein, always using the passive voice to avoid specifying the exact culprits. He saw the student uprising as part of a long-standing plot, contending, "An intense activity was undertaken since [1958 and 1959] to try to add the students to the attempts at subversion." In the president's eyes, those in charge of subverting Mexico's younger generation had achieved their purpose. "They succeeded in leading the students to violence," he told the interviewer.[87] Díaz Ordaz claimed that throughout his decade in power, first as minister of the interior and then as president, the government had used political methods to address the student problem. But by 1968 those methods were no longer enough. According to his account, someone had

[83] Heberto Castillo, *Si te agarran te van a matar* (Mexico City: Ediciones Océano, 1983), 71.
[84] Krauze, *Biography of Power*, 713.
[85] Ibid., 722–5.
[86] Ibid., 723–5.
[87] Carlos Aguilar Rodríguez, *Gustavo Díaz Ordaz: Su pensamiento, su palabra* (Mexico City, 1988), 100.

been determined to create problems for Mexico, using either workers or *campesinos* or students. "Their" efforts finally succeeded with the third group, and a reluctant government was forced to respond.

Other government officials, however, were less convinced of the existence of communist conspiracies. The man who was minister of defense in 1968, General Marcelino García Barragán, presented his version of the events in a letter to his son, which journalists Julio Scherer García and Carlos Monsiváis eventually obtained and published. According to the minister of defense, other government officials deserved the blame for most of the problems with the students. Minister of the Interior Luis Echeverría supposedly instructed the UNAM rector to lead a student demonstration in August in order to justify the army's earlier interventions at the end of July. "[Echeverría] did not imagine when he created this Civil Hero [the rector], that the consequences would be tragic for the country," García Barragán reflected.[88] The minister of defense also asserted that General Gutiérrez Oropeza had posted officials with submachine guns in the buildings surrounding the Plaza of Tlatelolco on orders from Díaz Ordaz.[89] The only time García Barragán mentioned communists was when he claimed that the UNAM rector had "heard the song of the communist sirens" and had begun to believe himself an actual hero of the people.[90] García Barragán accepted his own responsibility for the violent confrontation with the students, while also blaming Guitérrez Oropeza, Echeverría, and Díaz Ordaz.[91]

General García Barragán's belated confession of his own culpability was rare in government circles; both during and after the 1968 student movement, most Mexican officials stuck to the story of an international communist conspiracy. This theory allowed them to place the blame for Mexico's problems outside the country and it enabled them to avoid taking a hard look at some of the ways that they were failing to live up to the legacy of the Mexican Revolution.

RURAL INSURGENCIES IN GUERRERO

The student movement of 1968 was the most urgent and eye-catching manifestation of the new revolutionary movement, but it was far from the only threat that Mexico's leaders faced. In the state of Guerrero, two

---

[88] Scherer García and Monsiváis, *Parte de guerra*, 40.
[89] Ibid., 44.
[90] Ibid., 41.
[91] Ibid., 43.

insurgencies arose simultaneously that took advantage of the mountainous terrain and extensive community support to stage a protracted challenge to the Mexican government. Guerrero became one of the centers of Mexico's dirty war, as security forces waged a brutal campaign of terror against guerrillas and civilians alike.

The residents of Guerrero had long chafed under a combination of political repression, economic exploitation, and everyday violence at the hands of local authorities. In 1959, a loose coalition of students, workers, *campesinos*, and professionals formed the Guerrerense Civic Association (Asociación Cívica Guerrerense) to demand social justice and the rights promised them in the Constitution of 1917. A teacher named Genaro Vázquez Rojas became the president of the group and led the organization in its successful opposition to the abusive and corrupt governor, Raúl Caballero Aburto. Vázquez had a history of political activism; he had been fired from one of his early teaching posts for participating in Othón Salazar's Revolutionary Teachers' Movement, had attended Lázaro Cárdenas's Latin American Peace Conference, and had joined the National Liberation Movement.[92]

Local officials answered the civic association's reformist efforts with violence and repression. In December 1962, the civic association tried to build upon the foundations that it had laid in the anti-Aburtista campaign by participating in state and local elections. When the organization's members held a demonstration to protest the massive fraud that marred the election, police and soldiers tried to arrest Vázquez. He escaped, but the police instigated a gunfight in which seven protesters and one police officer died. Blamed for the death of the policeman, Vázquez had to go into hiding until Lázaro Cárdenas interceded with authorities on his behalf. State violence against the residents of Guerrero continued, however. In 1966, police arrested Vázquez outside the offices of the National Liberation Movement in Mexico City, and a court sentenced him to fourteen years of prison. He remained in prison for two years, until his followers arranged his escape in May 1968. Vázquez took to the hills, and his civic association became a guerrilla group called the National Revolutionary Civic Association (Associación Cívica Nacional Revolucionaria).

Another guerrilla group, the Party of the Poor (Partido de los Pobres), operated simultaneously in Guerrero. Members of this organization followed Lucio Cabañas, a teacher and a leader of the Federation of Socialist

---

[92] Castellanos, *México armado*, 112, 70.

Campesino Students of Mexico.[93] Cabañas, like Vázquez, had initially
resisted violent opposition to the government and tried for years to work
through reformist channels like the Guerrerense Civic Association, the
Revolutionary Teachers' Movement, the National Liberation Movement,
the Independent Campesino Center, and the People's Electoral Front.
When a group of followers of Arturo Gámiz arrived from Chihuahua in
1966 to ask him to help them spread their revolutionary Movement of
the 23rd of September to Guerrero, he declined.[94] In 1967, two more mas-
sacres, of five teachers and parents protesting outside a school in Atoyac
and at least twenty-three copra producers holding a peaceful demonstration in Acapulco, drove Cabañas to take up arms.[95]

Even though the rebellions in Guerrero grew out of specific local
conditions, their leaders drew inspiration from a wide range of times
and places. The movements combined a "constellation of radical traditions": histories of Mexican independence, memories of the 1910 revolution, military tactics from the Spanish Civil War and Southeast Asia,
ideological orientation from Marxist literature, and, most immediately,
inspiration from the Cuban Revolution.[96] The short-wave transmissions
of Cuba's Radio Rebelde reached Guerrero, spreading news of social justice, agrarian reforms, and nationalizations in Cuba and giving listeners
hope that change was possible in their own country as well.[97]

Both Vázquez and Cabañas sought to overthrow the PRI regime and
install a democratic, socialist government that would revive the Mexican
Revolution and the radicalism of the Cárdenas years. In order to achieve
these aims, the guerrillas proselytized among the public, developed
urban and rural networks of supporters, executed repressive caciques,
kidnapped important local and national figures, and assaulted military
targets. The Mexican Communist Party provided Cabañas's group with
weaponry, including M1 rifles, and in return the guerrillas occasionally
shared some of the money that they gained through their activities.[98]

Publicly, government officials denied the revolutionaries political
legitimacy by depicting them as simple criminals and social deviants.

---

[93] Jaime López, *10 años de guerrillas en México* (Mexico City: Editorial Posada, 1974).
[94] Baloy Mayo, *La guerrilla de Genaro y Lucio: Análisis y resultados*, 4th ed. (Mexico
City: Grupo Jaguar Impresiones, 2001), 45; Castellanos, *México armado*, 116–17.
[95] Castellanos, *México armado*, 116; Carr, *Marxism and Communism in Twentieth-Century
Mexico*, 233.
[96] Alexander Aviña, *Specters of Revolution: Peasant Guerrillas in the Cold War Mexican
Countryside* (New York: Oxford University Press, 2014), 4–5.
[97] Ibid., 68, 97.
[98] Condés Lara, *Represión y rebelión en México*, 257.

They claimed that the counterinsurgent military campaigns were targeting narcotics cultivators and bandits.[99] But in reality, the government fought a merciless war against the guerrillas and their communities that included mass detentions, torture, rape, destruction of property, executions, and disappearances. In 1968, IPS agents reported that there were thirty-six armed cells operating in Guerrero, each containing anywhere from eight to fifty members.[100] The military sent fourteen expeditions to Guerrero beginning in 1968 and devoted one-third of its men to pursuit of the guerrillas.[101] A former army official confessed that he and his fellow soldiers frequently killed their prisoners by burying them alive or throwing them out of helicopters into the ocean.[102] The DFS reported that members of the military lit *campesinos* on fire after forcing them to drink gasoline.[103] Vázquez died under questionable circumstances after an automobile accident in February 1972, while Cabañas held out until the end of 1974, when he was killed in combat. After years of fighting, the government's campaign of terror had "disappeared" nearly six hundred residents of the state, tortured countless others, and finally eliminated the two revolutionary groups.[104]

URBAN GUERRILLAS

At the same time that the Mexican government was battling Vázquez and Cabañas's groups in Guerrero, it faced urban insurgencies in other states and cities across the country. Like the groups in Guerrero, most of the other guerrilla organizations consisted of young people who had gained political experience in nonviolent contexts such as Christian student groups, strike committees, university federations, civic groups, popular mobilizations, and grassroots movements.[105] They opted for revolution as a last resort after becoming convinced that peaceful reform was impossible.

Though local conditions were the primary motivation for most of the members of the guerrilla groups, the Cuban Revolution continued

---

[99] Aviña, *Specters of Revolution*, 11.
[100] "Estado de Guerrero," 1968, IPS Caja 2181 A, AGN.
[101] Mayo, *La guerrilla de Genaro y Lucio*, 84.
[102] Sierra Guzmán, *El enemigo interno: Contrainsurgencia y fuerzas armadas en México*, 67–8.
[103] Aviña, *Specters of Revolution*, 147.
[104] Ibid., 153.
[105] On student participation and politicization in nonviolent organizations, see Calderón, "Contesting the State from the Ivory Tower," 52–65.

to play an inspirational role. Paquita Calvo Zapata, a communist student at UNAM and contributor to the magazine *Política*, founded one of the first urban guerrilla groups shortly after the Tlatelolco massacre, calling it the Zapatista Urban Front. Years later, she told journalist Elena Poniatowska that when she was arrested in September 1971, she reminded her five-year-old son of the famous Cuban leaders to help him understand what was happening. "Look, Tomás," she recalled saying, "I've spoken to you of Fidel, of Che, of Camilo, right? Well, you see, they are revolutionaries, I've told you that; and look, I have tried at least to be a revolutionary."[106] A few months after her arrest, Paquita and her husband sent Tomás to live in Cuba while she served out part of a thirty-year prison sentence.

Another massacre almost three years after the one in Tlatelolco further radicalized significant numbers of Mexican students. On June 10, 1971, seven thousand students in Mexico City organized a peaceful demonstration to show opposition to the government and solidarity with another movement in the northern state of Nuevo León. This was the first major protest that students in Mexico City had organized since Tlatelolco. As they began their march, riot police blocked their path, taunting and spraying tear gas. One thousand members of a government-trained clandestine paramilitary group known as the *Halcones* (falcons) appeared. They joined the riot police in attacking the students with clubs, bayonets, guns, and other weapons, while snipers took shots from surrounding buildings and the regular police stood by watching. Some of the marchers had brought their own guns to defend themselves, and a battle broke out. By the time peace had been restored four hours later, fifty of the protesters were dead, and two hundred more students and reporters were wounded. The events of June 10 became known as the Corpus Christi massacre.[107]

This was not the first time that extralegal paramilitary groups with close ties to the government had clashed with student activists. The agents in white gloves and the men with submachine guns who had instigated

---

[106] Elena Poniatowska, *Fuerte es el silencio* (Mexico City: Ediciones Era, 1980), 158.

[107] On the Corpus Christi massacre, see U.S. Embassy, "Telegram 3224 from the Embassy in Mexico to the Department of State, June 11, 1971," in *Foreign Relations of the United States, 1969–1976, American Republics*, Vol. E-10, doc. 462 (Washington, DC: U.S. Department of State, 2009); "Marcha estudiantil frenada por grupos de choque; 6 muertos," *Excélsior*, June 11, 1971, 1; "Muchos manifestantes iban armados, declara la Procuraduría," *Excélsior*, June 14, 1971, 1; Alan Riding, "A Few Corpses after the 'Dance' Was Over: Mexico," *New York Times*, June 20, 1971; Poniatowska, *Fuerte es el silencio*, 69–71, 144–5; Walker, *Waking from the Dream*, 27–9.

the Tlatelolco massacre had been members of a secret group called the Olympic Battalion that Díaz Ordaz had created shortly after the outbreak of the student movement of 1968 to maintain security for the Olympic Games.[108] Before that, Mexican officials with close connections to Díaz Ordaz had supported the anticommunist student group MURO and encouraged their violent activities. In 1968, members of MURO organized demonstrations to denounce the "Cuban infiltration" of the student movement, including one in front of the Basilica of Guadalupe during which fifteen thousand people chanted "We want one, two, three dead Che [Guevaras]! Long live Christ the King! Long live Díaz Ordaz!"[109] The Halcones were merely the latest version of the government's tactic of using clandestine groups to carry out its dirty work.

The Corpus Christi massacre also threatened to expose one of the many secret roles that the United States played in Mexico's dirty war. For years, the U.S. government had been training military officers, police, and other security officials from countries across Latin America, including Mexico.[110] Like U.S.-Mexican intelligence cooperation, these training programs were open secrets, something both governments preferred to keep quiet even in the face of widespread public suspicion. In January 1971, the U.S. ambassador had received an urgent request from the Mexican foreign minister to arrange for twenty Mexican security officials to receive special training in police work and crowd control in the United States. In messages back to Washington, the ambassador expressed concern that potential participants "might return to Mexico and play [a] leading role in the 'Halcones,' dealing harshly and perhaps even outside the law with student leaders and demonstrators." Nonetheless, the embassy and Department of State ultimately approved a modest training program. The man that the Mexican government chose to coordinate the program, Colonel Manuel Díaz Escobar, traveled to the United States in January 1971 to work out the details with USAID and FBI officials. When news of the Corpus Christi massacre broke and reporters identified Díaz Escobar as the leader of the Halcones, the U.S. embassy and State Department exchanged a series of worried telegrams to form a contingency plan in case the press learned of Díaz Escobar's connections to the

---

[108] Rodríguez Munguía, *1968: Todos los culpables.*

[109] Pensado, "To Assault with the Truth," 515–16.

[110] On U.S. training of Latin American security officials, see Lesley Gill, *The School of the Americas: Military Training and Political Violence in the Americas* (Durham, NC: Duke University Press, 2004). On Mexican involvement in the School of the Americas, see Jacinto Rodríguez Munguía, *Las nóminas secretas de Gobernación*, 8, 73.

United States.[111] Subsequent stories in the newspapers *Excélsior* and *La Prensa* correctly identified four leaders of the Halcones that were receiving police training in the United States, and the U.S. embassy became even more alarmed.[112]

Mexican officials stepped in to make sure that the U.S. training of Mexican paramilitaries remained hidden. In a press conference immediately following the massacre, Mexico City Mayor Alfonso Martínez Dominguez categorically denied that the Halcones existed, calling the group a "legend."[113] The under-secretary of the Foreign Ministry, José Gallástegui, reassured U.S. Deputy Chief of Mission John Kubisch in a meeting on June 18, "Not to worry – proper measures have been taken."[114] In a subsequent meeting with the U.S. Ambassador Robert McBride, Foreign Secretary Emilio Rabasa vowed that the Mexican government "assumed total responsibility for seeing that there was no harmful publicity insofar as [the] U.S. was concerned." Rabasa informed McBride that he had conferred with President Luis Echeverría, "who had known of this [training] program from its inception," and promised that "every possible measure had been taken to prevent publicity on [the] training program in [the] U.S."[115] These measures could have taken any form from bribery to destruction of materials to threats; the Mexican government, after all, had a wide variety of ways to influence the press.

With a masterstroke, President Echeverría not only managed to hide his own connections to the Halcones and those of the United States, but also to eliminate some of his political rivals within the government. Ever since entering office in 1970, he had been trying to present himself as a leftist, populist leader in order to distract from the role that he had played in the Tlatelolco massacre when he was minister of the interior. His policy of "democratic opening" (*apertura democrática*) that offered amnesty to the participants of the 1968 movement, educational reforms, and anticorruption campaign had created tensions with many members

---

[111] John B. Kubisch, "Telegram 3330 from the Embassy in Mexico to the Department of State, June 17, 1971," in *FRUS, 1969–1976, American Republics*, Vol. E-10, doc. 463; "Quiénes son los Halcones: Denuncia formal ante Sánchez Vargas de los fotógrafos y reporteros," *Excélsior*, June 13, 1971, 1.

[112] John B. Kubisch, "Telegram 3364 from the Embassy in Mexico to the Department of State, June 18, 1971," in *FRUS, 1969–1976, American Republics*, Vol. E-10, doc. 465.

[113] "Responsabiliza AMD a facciones divergentes," *Excélsior*, June 11, 1971, 1, 18.

[114] Ibid.

[115] Robert H. McBride, "Telegram 3558 from the Embassy in Mexico to the Department of State, June 25, 1971," in *FRUS, 1969–1976, American Republics*, Vol. E-10, doc. 466.

of the PRI's conservative factions.[116] Echeverría blamed the June 10 violence on right-wing elements within the government and declared to the public "If you are outraged, I am even more so.... The people responsible for this will be punished."[117] A few days after the massacre, he forced both the powerful mayor of Mexico City, Martínez Dominguez, and the police chief, Rogelio Flores Curiel, to resign.[118]

Instead of investigating Echeverría's involvement with the Halcones, the Mexican and U.S. media praised the president and focused on the paramilitary group's connections to his conservative opponents. "This is a first, unequivocal break with the past," an editorialist for *Excélsior* claimed, referring to Gustavo Díaz Ordaz and the events of 1968; Octavio Paz also praised the president's supposed efforts to pursue a new course and declared: "Echeverría deserves our trust."[119] "There have been widespread reports that the attack was sponsored by right-wing opponents of President Luis Echeverría Álvarez in the hope of provoking student rioting and forcing him to repress the left," the *New York Times* reported.[120] Carlos Fuentes told reporters that, in demanding the resignations of officials involved in the events of June 10, Echeverría had chosen democratization over repression.[121] Thousands of people participated in a march to the Zócalo to demonstrate their support for the president, and numerous individuals and organizations published fawning messages in the newspapers. One such announcement read: "Mr. President: You have such honor and such quality that you alone have saved the dignity of the Republic."[122] The media and most of the public celebrated the president's response to the massacre and remained ignorant of the role that he had played in instigating it.

While the Corpus Christi massacre gave Echeverría an opportunity to eliminate some of his political rivals, it also demonstrated the risks of peaceful protest and drove hundreds of young Mexicans to join

---

[116] Walker, *Waking from the Dream*, 25–9. On the question of Echeverría's populist credentials, see Amelia M. Kiddle and María L. O Muñoz, eds., *Populism in Twentieth Century Mexico: The Presidencies of Lázaro Cárdenas and Luis Echeverría* (Tucson: University of Arizona Press, 2010).

[117] "Se agredió quienes quieren expresarse con libertad: LE," *Excélsior*, June 12, 1971, 1.

[118] "Renunció Martínez Domínguez; O. Sentíez, nuevo regente," *Excélsior*, June 16, 1971, 1.

[119] "Ruptura con el pasado," *Excélsior*, June 16, 1971, 6; Octavio Paz, "El vocabulario político: Las palabras máscaras," *Excélsior*, June 16, 1971, 7.

[120] "Mexicans Begin a Secret-Army Inquiry," *New York Times*, June 17, 1971; "Mexico Says Inquiry Fails to Identify Students' Killers," *New York Times*, July 24, 1971.

[121] "Las renuncias, 'Obligadas,' " *Excélsior*, June 16, 1971, 1.

[122] Serafín Iglesias, "Serafín Iglesias dice," *Excélsior*, June 16, 1971.

revolutionary organizations in cities across the country. The Mexican government took the same public approach with the urban groups as it did with Vázquez and Cabañas's rural revolutions in Guerrero: it consistently denied the existence of guerrilla organizations and claimed that the frequent kidnappings, bank robberies, and sabotage were the actions of criminals, terrorists, bandits, thugs, and delinquents.[123]

Despite security agents' long-standing suspicions about Cuban support for Mexican guerrillas, the only time they found definitive proof of foreign connections it turned out to involve not Cuba, but North Korea. A group of Mexican students at the Patrice Lumumba University in Moscow founded the Revolutionary Action Movement (Movimiento de Acción Revolucionaria, or MAR) in 1966, seeking to spark a socialist revolution "under the guiding light of Guevarism and Vietnamese Marxism."[124] Having renounced "Soviet revisionism," the group knew that they would find no support in Moscow and began looking elsewhere. The founding members spent three months in Havana at the invitation of the Cuban government, but the Cubans refused to help because Mexico was the only country in Latin America that still maintained relations with Cuba. The Cubans did, however, put the young guerrillas in contact with the government of North Korea.[125] Fifty-three members of the group traveled to North Korea in 1969 and 1970, where they received military and doctrinal training.[126] They named the urban branch of their group after the date of the Tlatelolco massacre, *2 de Octubre*, and recruited students who had participated in the 1968 student movement. Mexican authorities first learned of the group when the owner of one of their safe houses, a former member of the Judicial Police of Veracruz, became suspicious and contacted the Federal Judicial Police.[127] In February 1971, police struck a significant blow to the organization when they arrested and imprisoned nineteen of its members.[128]

---

[123] E.g., see the article about the arrest of nineteen "bandits" in Mexico City who were holding up banks and other businesses to raise money to send to Genaro Vázquez and Lucio Cabañas in Guerrero. Carlos Borbolla and Luis Segura, "19 asaltos cometió la banda capturada por el Servicio Secreto: 3 de los bandidos eran viejos delincuentes," *Excélsior*, March 17, 1971.

[124] Verónica Oikión Solano, "In the Vanguard of the Revolution: The Revolutionary Action Movement and the Armed Struggle," in Calderón and Cedillo, eds., *Challenging Authoritarianism in Mexico*, 61–81, see p. 63.

[125] Condés Lara, *Represión y rebelión en México*, 33; Castellanos, *México armado*, 175.

[126] Oikión Solano, "In the Vanguard of the Revolution," 64, 75; Hodges and Gandy, *Mexico under Siege*, 147.

[127] Condés Lara, *Represión y rebelión en México*, 46–7.

[128] "Mexico Sees Plot by North Koreans," *New York Times*, March 16, 1971.

The news of the arrests filled Mexican papers for days, as the government used the incident to argue that their previous claims about international communist threats to national security had been correct. *Excélsior* ran a front-page story about the Revolutionary Action Movement that continued onto three additional pages, including photographs of all the arrested members and detailed background about the group's origins and training methods. "They declared that the purpose for which the North Korean military trained them was to impose a Marxist-Leninist regime in Mexico," officials from the Federal Public Ministry told journalists at a press conference. "To this end, they received theoretical drilling, in addition to studies in the use of all types of guns and heavy-duty explosives, urban and rural guerrilla warfare tactics, karate, and self-defense." By the time that the authorities had caught on to the organization's existence, its members had reportedly established schools and guerrilla training bases in Mexico City and across the central states of Veracruz, Guerrero, Hidalgo, San Luis Potosí, Querétaro, Michoacán, Guanajuato, Puebla, and Jalisco. The attorney general warned the shocked public that the initial arrests "had not completely resolved the matter," and that other members of the group remained at large.[129]

U.S. observers, meanwhile, tried to keep track of the confusing array of guerrilla groups and activities. Reporters for the *New York Times* contrasted Mexican leaders' claims that there were no guerrillas in the country with the frequent arrests, bank robberies, and bombings.[130] Journalist Alan Riding observed that it was especially difficult to determine what was going on in Mexico because the government referred to the revolutionaries as criminals at the same time that actual criminals and conservative terrorists posed as leftist revolutionaries to carry out crimes.[131] In 1974, FBI agents in Mexico City composed a list of the most important Mexican revolutionary, terrorist, and guerrilla groups, noting that:

No attempt has been made to characterize all revolutionary groups which have come to [our] attention as many such organizations have appeared on the scene

---

[129] Although the Mexican government arrested the members of the MAR in February, it waited until March to announce the arrests to the press. Victor Payan and M. Campos Diaz y Sanchez, "Consigna la Procuraduría a 20 'guerrilleros' entrenados en Corea," *Excélsior*, March 16, 1971, 1A, 13A, 14A, 15A. See also Manuel Campos Diaz y Sanchez and Federico Ortiz Jr., "Uno de los 19 presos amenazó con secuestros de personajes para liberarlos a ellos," *Excélsior*, March 17, 1971, 1A, 27A.

[130] "Mexico Says She Has No Guerrillas, Just Bandits," *New York Times*, August 7, 1971.

[131] Alan Riding, "Left and Right Tighten Vise: Mexico," *New York Times*, October 3, 1971.

and been identified in one or two isolated terrorist or revolutionary acts only to disappear and re-appear at a later time under a different name, comprised of subversives from several other groups.[132]

The FBI claimed that all of the most important guerrilla groups in Mexico were communist, and, indeed, many of them broadcast that ideological orientation in names such as the Armed Communist League, the Communist Spartacus League, and the 23rd of September Communist League.[133] The FBI considered the latter group the most dangerous in Mexico, along with Lucio Cabañas's Party of the Poor, the Korean-trained Revolutionary Action Movement, and the Student Revolutionary Front (Frente de Estudiantes Revoluccionarios, or FER).

The city of Guadalajara in the central state of Jalisco was host to two of these organizations; like Guerrero, it was a breeding ground for guerrilla groups. The Student Revolutionary Front originated there in 1970, and the 23rd of September Communist League formed in the same city three years later, uniting the FER with six other guerrilla groups. Both organizations were composed primarily of students, but they also reached out to workers, *campesinos*, and the urban poor. They saw themselves as the vanguard in an ideological and physical war against Mexico's elite and its government. The members of the earlier group had initially joined together to challenge the ultra-conservative leadership of the University of Guadalajara, and been radicalized and driven underground by a series of repressive measures. The leaders of the 23rd of September Communist League, or Liga, chose Guadalajara as the site for their initial organizational meeting in 1973 because the FER had already established a strong foundation there. The Liga united guerrilla groups in cities and rural areas all across Mexico, though it was strongest in Guadalajara, Mexico City, and Monterrey.[134]

Some of the guerrilla groups' more spectacular actions made it difficult for the Mexican government to deny that a revolutionary movement was

---

[132] LEGAT, Mexico City, "Characterization of Mexican Revolution, Terrorist, and Guerrilla Groups," March 11, 1974, Declassified Documents Reference System.

[133] Not all of the guerrilla groups adopted names that connoted communist ideology. Some, like the Zapatista Urban Front (*Frente Urbano Zapatista*), hearkened back to the Mexican Revolution, while others such as the Lacandones named themselves after local indigenous groups. Poniatowska, *Fuerte es el silencio*, 150–1.

[134] On the Student Revolutionary Front and the 23rd of September Communist League, see Calderón, "Contesting the State from the Ivory Tower"; Romain Robinet, "A Revolutionary Group Fighting against a Revolutionary State: The September 23rd Communist League against the PRI State (1973–1975)," in Calderón and Cedillo, eds., *Challenging Authoritarianism in Mexico*, 130–48.

taking place. In May 1973, members of the People's Armed Revolutionary Front (Fuerzas Revolucionarias Armadas del Pueblo, or FRAP), a group that had splintered off from the Student Revolutionary Front when it joined the 23rd of September Communist League, abducted the U.S. consul general in Guadalajara. They threatened to kill him unless the government agreed to release thirty political prisoners, many of them members of other guerrilla groups, and provide them with safe passage to Cuba.[135] President Echeverría acted quickly to meet the ransom requirements, as he had done two years earlier when Genaro Vázquez's group had abducted the rector of the Autonomous University of Guererro and demanded that the government fly nine prisoners to Cuba.[136] However, when the FRAP kidnapped Echeverría's father-in-law in 1974, the president was no longer willing to negotiate and sent in military police to arrest more than seven hundred people.[137] The 23rd of September Communist League coordinated a massive uprising in Culiacán, Sinaloa, in January 1974 that involved hundreds of militants and ten thousand farmworkers. The uprising only lasted a day, but five people lost their lives and the guerrillas were able to terrorize the city and seize vehicles, guns, and money.[138] Other revolutionary groups throughout the country flew hijacked airplanes to Cuba and dynamited U.S. consulates, conservative newspapers like *El Sol de México*, the national headquarters of the conservative PAN party, and the Ministry of the Interior.[139]

Eventually, however, the urban guerrilla groups crumbled under a combination of internal weakness and external repression. The new revolutionaries were unable to communicate a clear message to the public, they fought amongst themselves, and their propaganda brigades and attention-grabbing tactics failed to recruit enough new adherents to replace those killed or arrested by the government. Of the major urban organizations, the Student Revolutionary Front was the first to go when

---

[135] "U.S. Consul Seized by Mexican Group," *New York Times*, May 5, 1973.

[136] Richard Severos, "Mexico Flies 30 to Havana to Win Consul's Release," *New York Times*, May 7, 1973. On the kidnapping in Guerrero, see also Aviña, *Specters of Revolution*, 131; Orlando Ortiz, *Genaro Vázquez* (Mexico City: Editorial Diógenes, 1972), 127–42.

[137] Fernando Herrera Calderón, "From Books to Bullets: Youth Radicalism and Urban Guerrillas in Guadalajara," in Calderón and Cedillo, eds., *Challenging Authoritarianism in Mexico*, 106–29, see pp. 123–4.

[138] Robinet, "A Revolutionary Group Fighting Against a Revolutionary State," 139–40.

[139] LEGAT, Mexico City, "Characterization of Mexican Revolution, Terrorist, and Guerrilla Groups"; "Hijackers Gain Release of Six In Mexico and Fly On to Cuba," *New York Times*, November 9, 1972; Condés Lara, *Represión y rebelión en México*, 194–5.

debates over whether to join the 23rd of September Communist League in 1973 splintered the group.[140] The Liga began to disintegrate in 1974 after Mexican authorities captured and disappeared leader Ignacio Salas Obregón, though some of its members remained active until 1982 and 1983.[141] By 1975, most of the major guerrilla groups had ceased to operate, their members either jailed, in exile, or dead.[142] The Revolutionary Action Movement was one of the groups that held out the longest; after the mass arrests of 1971, the remaining members rebuilt and formed alliances with other groups. But factionalism, infiltration, arrests, and lack of popular support continued to plague the organization, and the MAR's influence waned until the last vestiges finally dissolved in 1979.[143]

CONCLUSION

In the mid-1960s, Mexican leaders' greatest fear became a reality: a new revolutionary movement exploded. Over the course of a decade, a combination of local, national, and international factors drove thousands of Mexican citizens to challenge their government and undermine its legitimacy. Violent repression, a lack of political and economic opportunity, and the inspiration of a successful revolution in Cuba all worked together to transform reform movements into revolutionary ones.

The Mexican government's inability to find a peaceful way to resolve conflicts like the student movement of 1968 heightened the Cold War into a dirty war. Thanks in part to unreliable information from their intelligence agents, Mexico's leaders misinterpreted the causes of the new revolutionary movement. Gustavo Díaz Ordaz believed that his country was the target of an international communist conspiracy, while Luis Echeverría considered the members of the guerrilla groups common criminals. Both leaders refused to acknowledge the depth of Mexico's social, economic, and political problems; both refused to acknowledge that their government had betrayed the legacy of the Mexican Revolution. Instead, they waged a merciless, largely hidden war against their own citizens.

---

[140] Calderón, "From Books to Bullets: Youth Radicalism and Urban Guerrillas in Guadalajara," 123.

[141] Robinet, "A Revolutionary Group Fighting Against a Revolutionary State," 141.

[142] Carr, *Marxism and Communism in Twentieth-Century Mexico*, 268.

[143] Condés Lara, *Represión y rebelión en México*, 71. Other historians argue that the MAR continued operating until the mid-1990s; see Oikión Solano, "In the Vanguard of the Revolution," 69–74.

Ultimately, the revolutionary movement failed. Conflicts over questions of ideology and strategy led to divisions within and among the revolutionary organizations. They faced an implacable enemy in the Mexican government, which was willing to use the dirty war tactics of torture, disappearances, and mass murder. And perhaps most critically, the guerrilla groups lacked the popular support that their revolution needed to succeed.

Conclusion

The Cuban Revolution changed the course of Mexican history. Before 1959, Mexico's leaders were secure in their control over the country. They had "institutionalized" the Mexican Revolution in a strong yet flexible web of organizations that claimed to protect the legacy of that revolution, including the National Campesino Confederation, the Confederation of Mexican Workers, the National Confederation of Popular Organizations, and, most importantly, the PRI. Mexico's leaders had also honed a number of practices to prevent opposition: they used the media to manipulate the public's access to information, their intelligence services to warn them of any potential threats, Article 145 of the Federal Penal Code to imprison critics, and their many security forces to keep order.

Yet all was not well in Mexico; the facades of the *pax PRIista* and the Mexican Miracle hid increasing levels of exploitation, discrimination, and inequality. Beginning in the 1940s, more and more Mexican citizens – politicians, *campesinos*, students, and workers – started organizing movements that criticized the government for failing to protect the rights enshrined in the Constitution of 1917. Mexico's leaders had to fend off a political challenge from the *henriquistas*, contend with the *jaramillistas* in Morelos, suppress student protests in Mexico City, and break strikes among multiple groups of workers. Though these movements all coincided with the early years of the global Cold War, they had little to do with international events or the geopolitical confrontation between communism and capitalism. Realizing this, Mexican leaders interpreted the movements as isolated incidents and remained confident in their control over the country.

A confluence of two events, one internal and one external, shattered that confidence and ushered in Mexico's Cold War. The first was the railroad movement of 1958–9, and the second, the Cuban Revolution. Communist involvement in the railroad movement added an international dimension to what was primarily a domestic conflict and stoked Mexican leaders' fears that foreign influences might threaten national security. At the same exact time that they were combating this insurgency among their own workers, President Adolfo López Mateos and Minister of the Interior Gustavo Díaz Ordaz watched as a guerrilla army that had started out as a tiny group of rebels managed to overthrow the Cuban government. The two simultaneous events sent a single message to Mexico's leaders: danger.

While the Mexican government was able to use a swift act of repression to crush the railroad movement, the Cuban Revolution proved to be a more durable threat that would repeatedly shape the domestic and international contours of Mexican politics for the next two decades. The Cuban example, the hope and fear that it inspired, intensified the tensions that already existed within Mexico into an undeclared state of war over questions of ideology, economics, culture, citizenship, and security. Thanks to the Cuban Revolution, the struggle over the legacy of the Mexican Revolution became Mexico's Cold War.

In the immediate aftermath of the Cuban Revolution, the Mexican public and government demonstrated enthusiastic support for Fidel Castro's new regime. Castro's defeat of a dictator, his economic reforms, and his defiant attitude toward the United States inspired obvious excitement among vast swaths of the Mexican population. López Mateos saw an opportunity to curry favor among sectors of the population that had begun to question the government's dedication to the Mexican Revolution. In speeches to domestic and international audiences, López Mateos expressed solidarity with Cuba's leaders and repeatedly stressed the similarities between the Cuban and Mexican Revolutions.

However, the friendship between the Mexican and Cuban governments had more symbolism than substance. In public, López Mateos used his country's solidarity with Cuba to shore up his revolutionary legitimacy and gain leftist support, but in private his intelligence agents were assisting U.S. operations against Castro. Mexican leaders and their security forces were eager to cooperate in surveillance and containment efforts because they believed that the Cubans were using Mexican territory to export revolution to the rest of Latin America. Castro, aware of Mexico's collaboration with the United States, conducted an equally superficial relationship with López Mateos. Castro and other Cuban officials praised the Mexican government's revolutionary legacy in public, while secretly condemning its hypocrisy and undertaking their own clandestine operations.

As the Cuban Revolution became more radical and the hostilities between the Cuban and U.S. governments escalated, Mexico's domestic politics reflected the increasing international tensions. Events in Cuba inspired admiration among some sectors of the Mexican population, and fear among others. Leftist groups and individuals, led by former president Lázaro Cárdenas, organized an international peace conference in March 1961 in an effort to capitalize upon the widespread enthusiasm for the Cuban Revolution and expand Cuba's reforms to other countries, including Mexico. When the Bay of Pigs invasion began a month later, close to a million people across the country took to the streets to protest. Inspired by Castro and emboldened by the outburst of public activism during the Bay of Pigs invasion, Mexican leftists began creating ambitious new groups that sought to restore the legacy of the Mexican Revolution, including the National Liberation Movement, the Independent Campesino Center, and the National Center of Democratic Students.

These national and international events redoubled the anxieties that were already mounting within Mexico's government and conservative sectors. The peace conference, the Bay of Pigs invasion, and the creation of the new leftist groups all fueled their fears that Cuba's communist revolution could spread to Mexico. Conservative politicians, students, religious leaders, and businessmen responded by creating their own new organizations, such as the Civic Front of Revolutionary Affirmation and MURO, that were more than willing to use violent tactics. The Mexican government also began resorting to more extreme measures to silence its critics, and ordered the military to assassinate agrarian leader Rubén Jaramillo and his family. By embracing the use of force, the Mexican government and the conservative sectors of society introduced a new, violent dimension to Mexico's Cold War.

At the same time that López Mateos was responding – and contributing – to the increasing domestic polarization, he also had to fend off renewed U.S. attempts to push him to take stronger measures against Cuba. The new U.S. president, John F. Kennedy, and his ambassador to Mexico, Thomas C. Mann, both tried to pressure Mexico into cutting relations with Cuba and became frustrated when López Mateos refused. The Cuban Missile Crisis proved to be a turning point in this relationship, as it forced Mexico's president to demonstrate that his country's loyalties were with the United States. The Kennedy assassination provided another test, after reports emerged of Lee Harvey Oswald's visit to the Cuban embassy in Mexico City. But the missile crisis had convinced U.S. leaders of the dangers of pursuing an open war against Castro and, instead of investigating the possible Cuban role in the assassination, the U.S. and Mexican governments worked together to hide it. By the time that the Organization of American States voted to isolate Cuba in 1964, U.S. officials had come around to the Mexican point of view and quietly supported Mexico's decision to maintain relations with Castro.

Thus by the middle of the 1960s, Mexico's leaders had managed to resolve most of the international problems that the Cuban Revolution had presented them; the internal Cold War, however, proved to be a greater challenge. For years, people like Lázaro Cárdenas, C. Wright Mills, and the editors of *Política* magazine had been warning that a new revolution could take place in Mexico. Over the course of his time serving as minister of the interior and then president, Gustavo Díaz Ordaz became increasingly convinced that communists were working to create just such a revolution. Security officials from multiple agencies warned him that communist instigators were following orders and receiving support from the Soviet Union and Cuba. Mexican activists attended international gatherings like the Tricontinental Conference in Havana, where they exchanged ideas with foreign communist leaders and made declarations in favor of armed revolution. Diplomatic officials in the Mexican embassy in Havana claimed that Mexican citizens were matriculating through the Cuban guerrilla training schools. These intelligence and diplomatic reports, when combined with prominent instances of genuine communist activity, were enough to convince Díaz Ordaz that Mexico and its government were under attack. Instead of defusing the situation by pursuing reforms or engaging in dialogue, he unleashed a dirty war against his own citizens, converting the government's critics into its enemies.

Ironically, the Mexican government's repeated acts of repression produced the very thing that it had been so desperate to avoid: a new revolutionary movement. Like the original revolution of 1910, this new uprising had a variety of causes and manifested itself in a number of ways over the course of more than a decade. And as in 1910, foreign countries and their citizens for the most part played only supporting roles in Mexico's new revolution; Cuba provided inspiration, while the United States contributed weapons and training for security forces. Some participants in the new revolution, including the students in 1968, used predominantly peaceful tactics, but many others, such as the members of rural and urban guerrilla groups, did not. In towns and cities across the country, brutality on the part of Mexican officials, economic exploitation, and a lack of political opportunities all combined to transform reformers into revolutionaries.

It was government violence that, more than anything else, escalated Mexico's Cold War into a new revolutionary movement, and it was government violence that ultimately ended the war. In the name of national security, Mexico's army, police, and paramilitaries waged a merciless campaign of terror not only against the guerrilla groups, but also against anyone who supported or sympathized with the new revolution. Already crippled by their inability to form lasting alliances or gain significant public support, the guerrillas crumbled under the onslaught of arrests, torture, disappearances, and mass murder. At the same time, the Mexican government slowly, haltingly, undertook a series of democratic openings that further deterred its citizens from joining the new revolution by opening a peaceful path to reform. Mexico's Cold War came to a close in the early 1980s, when the last Mexican guerrilla army inspired by the Cuban Revolution finally disappeared.

What were the effects of Mexico's Cold War? Why did it matter? On the international level, Mexican leaders' decision to use their relations with Castro to shore up their revolutionary legitimacy at home presented the United States with a challenge and Cuba with an opportunity. Mexico's refusal to join the hemispheric efforts to isolate Castro forced U.S. leaders to reevaluate their priorities and tactics. After witnessing the destabilizing effect that the Bay of Pigs invasion had on Mexico, and listening to López Mateos's arguments about the need to maintain his government's revolutionary legitimacy, Kennedy conceded that supporting Mexico's stability was more important than cutting off all of Cuba's points of access to the Latin American mainland. Castro took advantage of this open door, though it remains impossible to know to what extent. It appears that the connection with Mexico helped the Cubans build their own news service and allowed them to provide limited support to revolutionary activities in neighboring countries; the Mexican connection may even have given the Cubans the opportunity to encourage Oswald to assassinate Kennedy. What is clear, however, is that López Mateos's decision to maintain relations with Cuba heightened Mexico's international status as a center of diplomacy, espionage, and intrigue.

On the national level, Mexico's Cold War ended the government's ability to use the legacy of the Mexican Revolution as an effective source of legitimacy. Mexico's leaders knew that comparisons between the Cuban and Mexican revolutions were inevitable. In the first years after the Cuban Revolution, López Mateos tried to capitalize on the widespread enthusiasm for Castro by connecting the two events in the minds of the Mexican public. As the Cuban Revolution became increasingly radical and Castro joined the communist camp, however, López Mateos stopped drawing similarities between the two revolutions and shifted to a policy of defending Cuba on principle. While Mexico's defense of Cuba did inspire gratitude and even occasional pride from the domestic Left, it was not enough to rescue Mexico's revolutionary legacy. Within a few years, it became obvious that Cuba's revolution had eclipsed Mexico's in terms of redistribution of wealth and power. Furthermore, Mexican leaders' fears of communist subversion led them to adopt increasingly counterrevolutionary measures that did even greater damage to their reputation. The combination of a real revolution next door and a dirty war at home exposed beyond a doubt the fact that Mexico's government no longer embodied the legacy of the Mexican Revolution.

And yet, the PRI managed to stay in power for forty years after the Cuban Revolution, because the revolutionary legitimacy that Mexico's leaders were so desperate to maintain turned out not to be that crucial after all. Looking back now, it is apparent that even though much, if not most, of the Mexican population wanted reform, relatively few wanted revolution. But Mexican and U.S. leaders during the Cold War did not have the benefit of this hindsight; the information available to them at the time told them that a small band of dedicated fighters had been able to overthrow the Cuban government, and that a similar insurgency was growing in Mexico. The mass demonstrations, the riots, the explosion of political activism, and the proliferation of guerrilla groups all led them to believe that Mexico's stability was in danger. It was only after Mexican leaders faced and defeated a new revolutionary movement that it became clear that Mexico's government was strong enough to withstand the loss of its revolutionary legacy.

Bibliography

Archival Sources

Archives Direct UK
Archivo General de la Nación, Mexico City
    Fondo Dirección Federal de Seguridad
    Fondo Dirección General de Investigaciones Políticas y Sociales
    Fondo Policía Judicial Federal
    Fondo Presidencial de Adolfo López Mateos
    Fondo Presidencial de Gustavo Díaz Ordaz
Central Intelligence Agency FOIA Electronic Reading Room
Columbia University Rare Book and Manuscript Library
    Mexican Communist Party Records
Declassified Documents Reference System
Dirección de Servicios de Investigación y Análisis de México
John F. Kennedy Presidential Library, Boston, Massachusetts
    National Security Files
    White House Files
    Oral History Interviews
LANIC Castro Speech Database
Lyndon B. Johnson Presidential Library, Austin, Texas
    National Security Files
    Recordings of Telephone Conversations – White House Series
    Country Files
Mary Ferrell Foundation Digital Archive
Ministerio de Relaciones Exteriores, Havana
Ministerio de Relaciones Exteriores, Panama City
National Security Archive, George Washington University, Washington, DC
Nettie Lee Benson Latin American Collection, University of Texas, Austin, Texas
    U.S. State Department Files Microfilm Collection
Secretaría de Relaciones Exteriores, Mexico City
U.S. Library of Congress, Washington, DC

Foreign Affairs Oral History Collection of the Association for Diplomatic Studies and Training
Manuscript Division
Newspaper, Periodical, and Government Publications Division
Prints and Photographs Division
U.S. National Archives, College Park, Maryland
CIA CREST Database
Record Group 59: State Department
Record Group 233: U.S. House of Representatives (John F. Kennedy Assassination Records Collection)
Record Group 263: Central Intelligence Agency (John F. Kennedy Assassination Records Collection)

Periodicals

Brazil
Última Hora
Cuba
Bohemia
Girón
Granma
Juventud Rebelde
Prensa Latina
Revista Tricontinental
Revolución
El Socialista
Tricontinental Bulletin
England
The London Times
Mexico
Boletín de Información de la Embajada de Cuba
Boletín Informativo del Consulado de Cuba en Mérida
Buro de Investigación Política
El Día
Diario de Morelos
Excélsior
El Heraldo de México
Jueves de Excélsior
El Nacional
Novedades
Ovaciones
Política
¿Por Qué?
La Prensa
Proceso
Revista de América
Revista de Revistas

¡*Siempre!*
El Sol de México
Sucesos
El Universal
El Universal Gráfico
La Voz de México
La Voz de Michoacán
Nicaragua
Novedades
United States
Chicago Defender
Chicago Tribune
Look Magazine
Los Angeles Times
New York Herald Tribune
New York Times
Readers' Digest
Time Latin America
Tri-State Defender
Washington Daily News
Washington Post
U.S. News and World Report

Printed Primary Sources

Anonymous. *El insólito caso del espía de la CIA bajo el manto de funcionario diplomático de la Embajada de México en Cuba.* Havana: 1969.

Agee, Philip. *Inside the Company: CIA Diary.* New York: Stonehill Publishing Company, 1975.

Aguilar Rodríguez, Carlos. *Gustavo Díaz Ordaz: Su pensamiento, su palabra.* Mexico City, 1988.

Alarcón Ramírez, Dariel. *Memorias de un soldado cubano: Vida y muerte de la revolución.* Barcelona: Tusquets Editores, 1997.

Álvarez Garín, Raúl, and Gilberto Guevara Niebla. *Pensar el 68.* Mexico City: Cal y arena, 1988.

Álvarez Quiñones, Roberto. "Entrevista con el internacionalista mexicano Guillén Zelaya Alger, expedicionario del 'Granma.'" In *México y Cuba: Dos pueblos unidos en la historia*, edited by Martha López Portillo de Tamayo, Vol. 2: 420–5. Mexico City: Centro de Investigación Científica Jorge L. Tamayo, 1982.

Borge, Tomás. *The Patient Impatience: From Boyhood to Guerrilla: A Personal Narrative of Nicaragua's Struggle for Liberation.* Willimantic, CT: Curbstone Press, 1989.

Bremauntz, Alberto. *México y la revolución socialista cubana.* Morelia: Universidad Michoacana de San Nicolas de Hidalgo, 1966.

Setenta años de mi vida: Memorias y anécdotas. Mexico City: Ediciones Jurídico Sociales, 1968.

Cárdenas, Lázaro. *Palabras y documentos públicos de Lázaro Cárdenas, 1928–1970*, n.d.
  Epistolario de Lázaro Cárdenas. Mexico City: Siglo XXI, 1975.
  Obras: Apuntes 1957/1966. Vol. 3. Mexico City: Universidad Nacional Autónoma de México, 1986.
  Apuntes: Una selección. Mexico City: Universidad Nacional Autónoma de México, 2003.
Castillo, Heberto. *Si te agarran te van a matar.* Mexico City: Ediciones Océano, 1983.
Castro Hidalgo, Orlando. *Spy for Fidel.* Miami: E. A. Seemann Pub, 1971.
Castro Ruz, Fidel. *La cancelación de la deuda externa y el nuevo órden económico internacional como única alternativa verdadera. Otros asuntos de interés político e histórico.* Havana: Editora Política, 1985.
Casuso, Teresa. *Cuba and Castro.* New York: Random House, 1961.
Comisión Nacional de Cultura y Propaganda de la Federación Nacional Ferroviaria de Cuba. *Los trabajadores, los sindicatos, y la producción.* Havana: 1960.
Comité 68 Pro Libertadores Democráticas and Fiscalía Especial FEMOSPP. *Los procesos de México 68: La criminalización de las víctimas.* México: Genocidio y delitos de lesa humanidad, documentos básicos 1968–2008. Mexico City: Comité 68 Pro Libertades Democráticas, 2008a.
  Informe histórico presentado a la sociedad mexicana. México: Genocidio y delitos de la humanidad, documentos fundamentales, 1968–2008. México, D.F.: Comité 68 Pro Libertades Democráticas, 2008b.
Corona del Rosal, Alfonso. *Mis memorias políticas.* Mexico City: Grijalbo, 1995.
Cosío Villegas, Daniel. *Ensayos y notas.* Vol. 1. Mexico City: Editorial Hermes, 1966.
Díaz Ordaz, Gustavo. *Primer informe de Díaz Ordaz.* Mexico City: Secretaría de Gobernación, 1965.
  "El Lic. Gustavo Díaz Ordaz, al abrir el Congreso sus sesiones ordinarias, el 1 de septiembre de 1966." In *Los presidentes de México ante la nación.* Vol. 4. Mexico City: Imprenta de la Cámara de Diputados, 1966.
  "Gustavo Díaz Ordaz, al abrir el Congreso sus sesiones ordinarias, el 1 de septiembre de 1968." In *Mexico a través de los informes presidenciales.* Vol. 1: Los mensajes políticos. Mexico City: Secretaría de la Presidencia, 1976.
Farías, Luis M. *Así lo recuerdo: Testimonio político.* Mexico City: Fondo de Cultura Económica, 1992.
Fonseca, Carlos. *Obras.* Vol. 1. Managua: Editorial Nueva Nicaragua, 1982.
Foreign Relations of the United States, 1952–1954, American Republics. Vol. 4. Washington, DC: U.S. Government Printing Office, 1983.
Foreign Relations of the United States, 1955–1957, American Republics. Vol. 6. Washington, DC: U.S. Government Printing Office, 1987.
Foreign Relations of the United States, 1958–1960, American Republics. Vol. 5. Washington, DC: U.S. Government Printing Office, 1991.
Foreign Relations of the United States, 1958–1960, Cuba. Vol. 6. Washington, DC: U.S. Government Printing Office, 1991.

Foreign Relations of the United States, 1961–1963, American Republics. Vol. 12. Washington, DC: U.S. Government Printing Office, 1996.

Foreign Relations of the United States, 1969–1976, American Republics. Vol. E-10. Washington, DC: U.S. Government Printing Office, 2009.

Gadea, Hilda. *Ernesto: A Memoir of Che Guevara.* Translated by Carmen Molina and Walter I. Bradbury. New York: Doubleday and Company, 1972.

General Secretariat of the OSPAAAL. *First Solidarity Conference of the Peoples of Africa, Asia, and Latin America.* Havana, 1966.

Godines, Prudencio, Jr. *¡Qué Poca Mad … era La de José Santos Valdés!* Mexico City, 1968.

Guerra Leal, Mario. *La grilla.* Mexico City: Editorial Diana, 1978.

Guevara Niebla, Gilberto. *La democracia en la calle: Crónica del movimiento estudiantil mexicano.* Mexico City: Siglo Veintiuno Editores, 1988.

1968: Largo camino a la democracia. Mexico City: Cal y Arena, 2008.

Gutiérrez Oropeza, Luis. *Díaz Ordaz: el hombre, el gobernante.* Mexico City: Gustavo de Anda, 1988.

Hoover, J. Edgar. *Exposé of Soviet Espionage, May 1960: For the Use of the Subcommittee to Investigate the Administration of the Internal Security Act and Other Internal Security Laws.* Washington, DC: U.S. Government Printing Office, 1960.

House of Representatives Subcommittee on Inter-American Affairs. *Communist Activities in Latin America, 1967.* Washington, DC: U.S. Government Printing Office, 1967.

Jardón, Raúl. *1968: El fuego de la esperanza.* Mexico City: Siglo Veintiuno Editores, 1998.

Leu, Hans-Joachim, and Freddy Vivas, eds. *Las relaciones interamericanas: Una antología de documentos.* Caracas: Universidad Central de Venezuela, 1975.

Llovio-Menéndez, José Luis. *Insider: My Hidden Life as a Revolutionary in Cuba.* Toronto: Bantam Books, 1988.

Lombardo Toledano, Vicente. "La Conferencia Tricontinental y la Revolución Mexicana." In *Escritos sobre Cuba: Análisis de su proceso político, 1928–1967*, 433–7. Mexico City: Centro de Estudios Filosóficos, Políticos y Sociales Vicente Lombardo Toledano, 2003.

López Mateos, Adolfo. "El Lic. Adolfo López Mateos, al abrir el Congreso sus sesiones ordinarias, el 1 de septiembre de 1960." In *Los presidentes de México ante la nación.* Vol. 4. Mexico City: Cámara de Diputados, 1966.

López Portillo de Tamayo, Martha, ed. *México y Cuba: Dos pueblos unidos en la historia.* Vol. 2. Mexico City: Centro de Investigación Científica Jorge L. Tamayo, 1982.

Los presidentes de México: Discursos políticos 1910–1988. Vol. 4. Mexico City: El Colegio de México, 1988.

Manrara, Luis V. *The Tricontinental Conference: A Declaration of War.* Miami: The Truth About Cuba Committee, 1966.

Masetti, Jorge. *In the Pirate's Den: My Life as a Secret Agent for Castro.* San Francisco: Encounter Books, 2002.

Mills, C. Wright. *Listen, Yankee: The Revolution in Cuba.* New York: McGraw-Hill Book Company, 1960.

Morrison, Delesseps S. *Latin American Mission: An Adventure in Hemisphere Diplomacy.* New York: Simon and Schuster, 1965.

Nixon, Richard. "Cuba, Castro, and John F. Kennedy." *Readers' Digest*, Vol. 85. November 1964.

OAS Special Consultative Committee on Security. *The "First Tricontinental Conference," Another Threat to the Security of the Inter-American System.* Washington, DC: Organization of American States, 1966.

Perzabal, Carlos. *De las memorias de Manuel Marcué Pardiñas.* Mexico City: Editorial Rino, 1997.

Poniatowska, Elena. *Palabras cruzadas.* Mexico City: Editorial Era, 1961.

Fuerte es el silencio. Mexico City: Ediciones Era, 1980.

Presencia internacional de Adolfo López Mateos. Vol. 1. Mexico City: Talleres Gráficos de la Nación, 1963.

Roig, Pedro L. *Como trabajan los espías de Castro: Como se infiltra el G2.* Miami: Duplex Paper Products of Miami, 1964.

Salinas Price, Hugo. *Mis años con Elektra: Memorias.* Mexico City: Editorial Diana, 2000.

Santos Valdes, José. *Madera: Razón de un martirologio.* Mexico City: Imprenta Laura, 1968.

Secretaría de Industria y Comercio. *Anuario estadístico de los Estados Unidos Mexicanos, 1962–1963.* Mexico City: Talleres Gráficos de la Nación, 1965.

Senate Committee on the Judiciary. *Cuban Aftermath–Red Seeds Blow South: Implications for the United States of the Latin American Conference for National Sovereignty and Economic Emancipation and Peace.* Washington, DC: U.S. Government Printing Office, 1961.

Senate Select Committee to Study Governmental Operations with Respect to Intelligence Activities. *The Investigation of the Assassination of President John F. Kennedy: Performance of the Intelligence Agencies.* Vol. 5. Washington, DC: U.S. Government Printing Office, 1976.

Senate Subcommittee to Investigate the Administration of the Internal Security Act and Other Internal Security Laws. *Communist Threat to the United States through the Caribbean.* Washington, DC: U.S. Government Printing Office, 1959.

Suárez, Luís. *Cárdenas: Retrato inédito, testimonios de Amalia Solorzano de Cárdenas y nuevos documentos.* Mexico City: Editorial Grijalbo, 1987.

Tamayo, Jorge L. *Obras de Jorge L. Tamayo.* Vol. 9: Cartas. Mexico City: Centro de Investigación Científica Jorge L. Tamayo, 1986.

United States v. Pagán Santini (U.S. Court of Appeals, First Circuit 2006).

Secondary Sources

Anonymous. "Book review of 'Inside the Company: CIA Diary' by Philip Agee." *Studies in Intelligence* 19, no. 2 (Summer 1975): 35–8.

De Tuxpan a La Plata. Havana: Editora Política, 1985.

Aguayo, Sergio. *1968: Los archivos de la violencia.* Mexico City: Editorial Grijalbo, 1998.

La Charola: Una historia de los servicios de intelligencia en México. Mexico City: Grijalbo, 2001.

"El impacto de la guerrilla en la vida mexicana: Algunas hipótesis." In *Movimientos armados en México, siglo XX*, edited by Verónica Oikión Solano and Marta Eugenia García Ugarte, Vol. 1: 91–8. Zamora: El Colegio de Michoacán, 2006.

Aguilar Ayerra, Carolina. *Por siempre Vilma*. Havana: Editorial de la Mujer, 2008.

Aguilar Camín, Héctor, and Lorenzo Meyer. *A la sombra de la revolución mexicana*. Mexico City: Cal y arena, 1989.

Alegre, Robert F. *Railroad Radicals in Cold War Mexico: Gender, Class, and Memory*. Lincoln: University of Nebraska Press, 2013.

Alexander, Robert J. *Trotskyism in Latin America*. Stanford, CA: Hoover Institution Press, 1973.

Anderson, Jon Lee. *Che Guevara: A Revolutionary Life*. New York: Grove Press, 1997.

Andrew, Christopher. "Intelligence in the Cold War." In *The Cambridge History of the Cold War*, edited by Melvyn P. Leffler and Odd Arne Westad, Vol. 2: Crises and Détente: 417–37. Cambridge: Cambridge University Press, 2010.

Avalos, Daniel Jacinto. *La guerrilla del Che y Masetti en Salta – 1964: Ideología y mito en el Ejército Guerrillero del Pueblo*. 2nd ed. Salta: Ediciones Política y Cultura, 2005.

Aviña, Alexander. "The New Left in Latin America," *Oxford Bibliographies Online*. DOI: 10.1093/OBO/9780199766581-0040. Accessed March 13, 2015.

Specters of Revolution: Peasant Guerrillas in the Cold War Mexican Countryside. New York: Oxford University Press, 2014.

Barbosa Cano, Fabio. "Acción y búsqueda programática." In *Historia del comunismo en México*, edited by Arnoldo Martínez Verdugo, 273–320. Mexico City: Grijalbo, 1985.

Becker Lorca, Arnulf. *Mestizo International Law: A Global Intellectual History, 1842–1933*. Cambridge: Cambridge University Press, 2014.

Bell, Wendell. "Independent Jamaica Enters World Politics: Foreign Policy in a New State." *Political Science Quarterly* 92 (1977–8): 683–703.

Benjamin, Thomas. *La Revolución: Mexico's Great Revolution as Memory, Myth, and History*. Austin: University of Texas Press, 2000.

Bethell, Leslie, and Ian Roxborough. "The Impact of the Cold War on Latin America." In *Origins of the Cold War: An International History*, edited by Melvyn P. Leffler and D. S. Painter, 299–316. 2nd ed. New York: Routledge, 2005.

Blancarte, Roberto. *Historia de la Iglesia Católica en México*. Mexico City: Fondo de Cultura Económica, 1992.

Blasier, Cole, and Carmelo Mesa-Lago, eds. *Cuba in the World*. Pittsburgh, PA: University of Pittsburgh Press, 1979.

Blight, James G., and Philip Brenner. *Sad and Luminous Days: Cuba's Struggle with the Superpowers after the Missile Crisis*. Lanham, MD: Rowman and Littlefield, 2002.

Bobadilla González, Leticia. *México y la OEA: Los debates diplomáticos, 1959–1964*. Mexico City: Secretaría de Relaciones Exteriores, 2006.

Bolívar Meza, Rosendo. *Lombardo: Su pensamiento político.* Mexico City: Universidad Obrera de México, 2006.

Boyer, Christopher R. *Becoming Campesinos: Politics, Identity, and Agrarian Struggle in Postrevolutionary Michoacán, 1920–1935.* Stanford, CA: Stanford University Press, 2003.

Brandenburg, Frank. *The Making of Modern Mexico.* Englewood Cliffs, NJ: Prentice Hall, 1964.

Brands, H. W. *The Specter of Neutralism: The United States and the Emergence of the Third World, 1947–1960.* New York: Columbia University Press, 1989.

Brands, Hal. *Latin America's Cold War.* Cambridge, MA: Harvard University Press, 2010.

Buchenau, Jürgen. *In the Shadow of the Giant: The Making of Mexico's Central America Policy, 1876–1930.* Tuscaloosa: University of Alabama Press, 1996.

"¿En defesa de una 'Cuba Libre'? México entre el nacionalismo cubano y la expansión de Estados Unidos." In *México y el Caribe: vínculos, intereses, región,* edited by Laura Muñoz Mata, Vol. 2: 221–50. San Juan Mixcoac: Instituto de Investigaciones Dr. José María Luis Mora, 2002.

"Por una guerra fría más templada: México entre el cambio revolucionario y la reación estadounidense en Guatemala y Cuba." In *Espejos de la guerra fría: México, América Central y el Caribe,* edited by Daniela Spenser, 119–50. Mexico City: Centro de Investigaciones y Estudios Superiores en Antropología Social, 2004.

Buendía, Manuel. *La CIA en México.* Mexico City: Ediciones Océano, 1984.

Butler, Matthew. *Popular Piety and Political Identity in Mexico's Cristero Rebellion: Michoacán, 1927–29.* Oxford: Oxford University Press, 2004.

Calderón, Fernando Herrera. "Contesting the State from the Ivory Tower: Student Power, Dirty War and the Urban Guerrilla Experience in Mexico, 1965–1982." PhD diss., University of Minnesota, 2012a.

"From Books to Bullets: Youth Radicalism and Urban Guerrillas in Guadalajara." In *Challenging Authoritarianism in Mexico: Revolutionary Struggles and the Dirty War, 1964–1982,* edited by Fernando Herrera Calderón and Adela Cedillo, 106–29. New York: Routledge, 2012b.

Calderón, Fernando Herrera, and Adela Cedillo. "Introduction: The Unknown Mexican Dirty War." In *Challenging Authoritarianism in Mexico: Revolutionary Struggles and the Dirty War, 1964–1982,* edited by Fernando Herrera Calderón and Adela Cedillo, 1–18. New York: Routledge, 2012.

Camp, Roderic A. *Intellectuals and the State in Twentieth Century Mexico.* Austin: University of Texas Press, 1985.

Politics in Mexico: The Democratic Consolidation. 5th ed. Oxford: Oxford University Press, 2006.

Carey, Elaine. *Plaza of Sacrifices: Gender, Power, and Terror in 1968 Mexico.* Albuquerque: University of New Mexico Press, 2005.

Carr, Barry. *Marxism and Communism in Twentieth-Century Mexico.* Lincoln: University of Nebraska Press, 1992.

Castañeda, Jorge G. *Utopia Unarmed: The Latin American Left after the Cold War.* New York: Vintage Books, 1994.

Perpetuating Power: How Mexican Presidents Were Chosen. New York: The New Press, 2000.

Castellanos, Laura. *México armado 1943–1981*. Mexico City: Ediciones Era, 2007.

Chabat, Jorge. "Condicionantes del activismo de la política exterior mexicana (1960–1985)." In *Fundamentos y prioridades de la política exterior de México*, edited by Humberto Garza Elizondo, 89–114. Mexico City: El Colegio de México, 1986.

Chase, Michelle. "The Trials: Violence and Justice in the Aftermath of the Cuban Revolution." In *A Century of Revolution: Insurgent and Counterinsurgent Violence during Latin America's Long Cold War*, edited by Greg Grandin and Gilbert M. Joseph, 163–98. Durham, NC: Duke University Press, 2010.

Chávez de la Lama, Ignacio. *La madre de todas las "huelgas": La UNAM en 1966*. Monterrey: Universidad Autónoma de Nuevo León, 2011.

Childs, Matt D. "An Historical Critique of the Emergence and Evolution of Ernesto Che Guevara's Foco Theory." *Journal of Latin American Studies* 27, no. 3 (October 1995): 593–624.

Colman, Jonathan. *The Foreign Policy of Lyndon B. Johnson: The United States and the World, 1963–69*. Edinburgh: Edinburgh University Press, 2010.

Condés Lara, Enrique. *Represión y rebelión en México (1959–1985)*. Vol. 1 and 2. Mexico City: Miguel Ángel Porrúa, 2007.

Represión y rebelión en México (1959–1985). Vol. 3. Mexico City: Miguel Ángel Porrúa, 2009.

Cosío Villegas, Daniel. *El sistema político mexicano: las posibilidades de cambio*. Mexico City: Editorial Joaquin Mortiz, 1972.

Costigliola, Frank. "U.S. Foreign Policy from Kennedy to Johnson." In *The Cambridge History of the Cold War*, edited by Melvyn P. Leffler and Odd Arne Westad, Vol. 2: Crises and Détente: 112–33. Cambridge: Cambridge University Press, 2010.

Couturier, Edith B. "Mexico." In *Latin American Foreign Policies*, edited by Harold Davis and Larman Wilson, 117–35. Baltimore: Johns Hopkins University Press, 1975.

Covarrubias-Velasco, Ana. "Mexican-Cuban Relations, 1959–1988." PhD diss., Oxford University, 1994.

"Cuba and Mexico: A Case for Mutual Non-Intervention." *Cuban Studies* 26 (1996): 121–41.

Craig, Campbell, and Fredrik Logevall. *America's Cold War: The Politics of Insecurity*. Cambridge, MA: Belknap Press of Harvard University Press, 2009.

Crespi, Roberto Simón. "José Revueltas (1914–1976): A Political Biography." *Latin American Perspectives* 6, no. 3 (July 1, 1979): 93–113.

Darnton, Christopher. *Rivalry and Alliance Politics in Cold War Latin America*. Baltimore: Johns Hopkins University Press, 2014.

Dávila Peralta, Nicolás. *Las santas batallas: El anticomunismo en Puebla*. Puebla: Litografía Magno Graf, 2001.

Davis, Diane E. *Urban Leviathan: Mexico City in the Twentieth Century*. Philadelphia: Temple University Press, 1994.

De Garay, Graciela, ed. *Gilberto Bosques: Cuba 1953–1964*. Jalisco: El Colegio de Jalisco, 2007.

Delgado, Álvaro. *El Yunque: La ultraderecha en el poder*. Mexico City: Editorial Grijalbo, 2003.

Domínguez, Jorge I. *To Make a World Safe for Revolution: Cuba's Foreign Policy.* Cambridge, MA: Harvard University Press, 1989.

Domínguez, Jorge I., and Juan Lindau. "The Primacy of Politics: Comparing the Foreign Policies of Cuba and Mexico." *International Political Science Review/Revue internationale de science politique* 5, no. 1 (1984): 75–101.

Dosal, Paul J. *Comandante Che: Guerrilla Soldier, Commander, and Strategist, 1956–1967.* University Park: Pennsylvania State University Press, 2003.

Doyle, Kate. "Double Dealing: Mexico's Foreign Policy Toward Cuba." *The National Security Archive Electronic Briefing Book* (March 2, 2003). http://www.gwu.edu/~nsarchiv/NSAEBB/NSAEBB83/index.htm#sidebar.

"The Dead of Tlatelolco: Using the Archives to Exhume the Past." *The National Security Archive Electronic Briefing Book* 201 (October 1, 2006). http://www.gwu.edu/~nsarchiv/NSAEBB/NSAEBB201/index.htm.

Dudziak, Mary. *Cold War Civil Rights: Race and the Image of American Democracy.* Princeton, NJ: Princeton University Press, 2000.

Dumois, Conchita, and Gabriel Molina. *Jorge Ricardo Masetti: El Comandante Segundo.* Havana: Editorial Capitán San Luis, 2012.

Duncan, W. Raymond. *The Soviet Union and Cuba: Interests and Influence.* New York: Praeger, 1985.

Dwyer, John J. *The Agrarian Dispute: The Expropriation of American-Owned Rural Land in Postrevolutionary Mexico.* Durham, NC: Duke University Press, 2008.

Eckstein, Susan. *The Poverty of Revolution: The State and the Urban Poor in Mexico.* Princeton, NJ: Princeton University Press, 1977.

Estrada, Ulises. *Tania: Undercover with Che Guevara in Bolivia.* Melbourne: Ocean Press, 2005.

Estrada Rodríguez, Gerardo. *1968, estado y universidad: Orígenes de la transición política en México.* Mexico City: Plaza Janés, 2004.

Evans, Peter B., Harold Karan Jacobson, and Robert D. Putnam, eds. *Double-Edged Diplomacy: International Bargaining and Domestic Politics.* Berkeley: University of California Press, 1993.

Faber, Sebastian. *Exile and Cultural Hegemony: Spanish Intellectuals in Mexico, 1939–1975.* Nashville: Vanderbilt University Press, 2002.

Fallaw, Ben. *Religion and State Formation in Postrevolutionary Mexico.* Durham, NC: Duke University Press, 2013.

Fein, Seth. "Myths of Cultural Imperialism and Nationalism in Golden Age Mexican Cinema." In *Fragments of a Golden Age: The Politics of Culture in Mexico Since 1940,* edited by Gilbert Joseph, Anne Rubenstein, and Eric Zolov, 159–98. Durham, NC: Duke University Press, 2001.

"New Empire into Old: Making Mexican Newsreels the Cold War Way." *Diplomatic History* 28, no. 5 (November 2004): 703–48.

Fernández, Claudia, and Andrew Paxman. *El Tigre: Emilio Azcárraga y su imperio Televisa.* Mexico City: Grijalbo, 2000.

Fernández Christlieb, Fátima. *Los medios de difusión másiva en México.* Mexico City: Juan Pablos Editor, 1982.

Foos, Paul W. *A Short, Offhand, Killing Affair: Soldiers and Social Conflict during the Mexican-American War.* Chapel Hill: University of North Carolina Press, 2002.

Foran, John. *Taking Power: On the Origins of Third World Revolutions.* Cambridge: Cambridge University Press, 2005.

Freedman, Lawrence. *Kennedy's Wars: Berlin, Cuba, Laos, and Vietnam.* New York: Oxford University Press, 2000.

Friedman, Max Paul. "Retiring the Puppets, Bringing Latin America Back In: Recent Scholarship on United States-Latin American Relations." *Diplomatic History* 27, no. 5 (November 2003): 621–36.

Gaddis, John Lewis. *Strategies of Containment: A Critical Appraisal of Postwar American National Security Policy.* New York: Oxford University Press, 1982.

We Now Know: Rethinking Cold War History. Oxford: Clarendon Press, 1998.

Gallegos Nájera, José Arturo. *La guerrilla en Guerrero: testimonios sobre el Partido de los Pobres y las Fuerzas Armadas Revolucionarias.* Chilpancingo: Grupo Editorial Lama, 2004.

Garcés Contreras, Guillermo. *México: Cincuenta años de política internacional.* Mexico City: Partido Revolucionario Institucional and Instituto de Capacitación Política, 1982.

Geary, Daniel. *Radical Ambition: C. Wright Mills, the Left, and American Social Thought.* Berkeley: University of California Press, 2009.

Gill, Lesley. *The School of the Americas: Military Training and Political Violence in the Americas.* Durham, NC: Duke University Press, 2004.

Gillingham, Paul. "Preface." In *Dictablanda: Politics, Work, and Culture in Mexico, 1938–1968*, edited by Paul Gillingham and Benjamin T. Smith, vii–xiv. Durham, NC: Duke University Press, 2014a.

"'We Don't Have Arms, But We Do Have Balls': Fraud, Violence, and Popular Agency in Elections." In *Dictablanda: Politics, Work, and Culture in Mexico, 1938–1968*, edited by Paul Gillingham and Benjamin T. Smith, 149–72. Durham, NC: Duke University Press, 2014b.

Gilly, Adolfo. *Tres imágenes del General.* Mexico City: Taurus, 1997.

Gleijeses, Piero. *Conflicting Missions: Havana, Washington, and Africa, 1959–1976.* Chapel Hill: University of North Carolina Press, 2002.

The Cuban Drumbeat: Castro's Worldview: Cuban Foreign Policy in a Hostile World. London: Seagull Books, 2009.

Gleizer, Daniela. *Unwelcome Exiles: Mexico and the Jewish Refugees from Nazism, 1933–1945.* Translated by Susan Thomae. Leiden, The Netherlands: Brill, 2014.

González de Bustamante, Celeste. *"Muy Buenas Noches": Mexico, Television, and the Cold War.* Lincoln: University of Nebraska Press, 2012.

González Casanova, Pablo. *Democracy in Mexico.* Translated by Danielle Salti, 2nd ed. New York: Oxford University Press, 1970.

El estado y los partidos políticos en México: Ensayos. Mexico City: Ediciones Era, 1981.

La democracia en México. 2nd ed. Mexico City: Ediciones Era, 1991.

González Compeán, Miguel, Leonardo Lomelí, and Pedro Salmerón Sanginés, eds. *El partido de la revolución: Institución y conflicto, 1928–1999.* Mexico City: Fondo de Cultura Económica, 2000.

González Ruiz, Edgar. *MURO: Memorias y testimonios: 1961–2002.* 2nd ed. Puebla: Gobierno del Estado de Puebla: Benemérita Universidad Autónoma de Puebla, 2004.

Gosse, Van. *Where the Boys Are: Cuba, Cold War America and the Making of a New Left*. London: Verso, 1993.

Gott, Richard. *Guerrilla Movements in Latin America*. Garden City, NJ: Doubleday, 1971.

Grabendorff, Wolf. "La función interna de la política exterior mexicana." *Nueva Sociedad*, no. 31–2 (October 1977): 94–6.

Grandin, Greg. *The Last Colonial Massacre: Latin America in the Cold War*. Chicago: University of Chicago Press, 2004.

Grandin, Greg, and Gilbert Joseph, eds. *A Century of Revolution: Insurgent and Counterinsurgent Violence during Latin America's Long Cold War*. Durham, NC: Duke University Press, 2010.

Guillo Deza, Concepción. "Cómo financió Castro la Revolución Cubana." In *México y Cuba: Dos pueblos unidos en la historia*, edited by Martha López Portillo de Tamayo, Vol. 2: 416–19. Mexico City: Centro de Investigación Científica Jorge L. Tamayo, 1982.

Halperin, Maurice. *The Taming of Fidel Castro*. Berkeley: University of California Press, 1981.

Hamilton, Nora. *The Limits of State Autonomy: Post-Revolutionary Mexico*. Princeton, NJ: Princeton University Press, 1982.

Harmer, Tanya. *Allende's Chile and the Inter-American Cold War*. Chapel Hill: University of North Carolina Press, 2011.

Heale, M. J. *American Anticommunism: Combating the Enemy within, 1830–1970*. Baltimore: Johns Hopkins University Press, 1990.

Heinrichs, Waldo. "Lyndon B. Johnson: Change and Continuity." In *Lyndon Johnson Confronts the World: American Foreign Policy, 1963–1968*, edited by Warren I. Cohen and Nancy Bernkopf Tucker, 9–30. New York: Cambridge University Press, 1994.

Henson, Elizabeth. "Madera 1965: Primeros vientos." In *Challenging Authoritarianism in Mexico: Revolutionary Struggles and the Dirty War, 1964–1982*, edited by Fernando Herrera Calderón and Adela Cedillo, 19–39. New York: Routledge, 2012.

Heredia, Blanca. "La relación entre política interna y política exterior: Una definición conceptual: El caso de México." In *Fundamentos y prioridades de la política exterior de México*, edited by Humberto Garza Elizondo, 135–66. Mexico City: El Colegio de México, 1986.

Hernández Rodríguez, Rogelio. "Strongmen and State Weakness." In *Dictablanda: Politics, Work, and Culture in Mexico, 1938–1968*, edited by Paul Gillingham and Benjamin T. Smith, 108–25. Durham, NC: Duke University Press, 2014.

Herrera, Hayden. *Frida, a Biography of Frida Kahlo*. New York: Perennial Library, 1983.

Herrera Franyutti, Alfonso. *Martí en México: Recuerdos de una época*. Mexico City: Consejo Nacional para la Cultura y las Artes, 1996.

Herring, George C. "The Cold War and Vietnam." *OAH Magazine of History* 18, no. 5 (October 1, 2004): 18–21.

Hershberg, James G., and Christian F. Ostermann, eds. "The Global Cuban Missile Crisis at 50." *Cold War International History Project Bulletin*, no. 17–18 (Fall 2012).

Hodges, Donald, and Ross Gandy. *Mexico under Siege: Popular Resistance to Presidential Despotism*. London: Zed Books, 2002.

Holland, Max. *The Kennedy Assassination Tapes*. New York: Knopf, 2004.

Huggins, Martha Knisely. *Political Policing: The United States and Latin America*. Durham, NC: Duke University Press, 1998.

Iber, Patrick. "The Imperialism of Liberty: Intellectuals and the Politics of Culture in Cold War Latin America." PhD diss., University of Chicago, 2011.

   "Paraíso de espías. La ciudad de México y la Guerra Fría." *Nexos*. April 1, 2014. http://www.nexos.com.mx/?p=20004.

Jackson, D. Bruce. *Castro, the Kremlin, and Communism in Latin America*. Baltimore: Johns Hopkins Press, 1969.

Jervis, Robert. *Perception and Misperception in International Politics*. Princeton, NJ: Princeton University Press, 1976.

Johnson, Cecil. *Communist China and Latin America, 1959–1967*. New York: Columbia University Press, 1970.

Joseph, Gilbert M. "What We Now Know and Should Know: Bringing Latin America More Meaningfully into Cold War Studies." In *In from the Cold: Latin America's New Encounter with the Cold War*, edited by Gilbert M. Joseph and Daniela Spenser, 3–46. Durham, NC: Duke University Press, 2008.

Joseph, Gilbert M., and Jürgen Buchenau. *Mexico's Once and Future Revolution: Social Upheaval and the Challenge of Rule since the Late Nineteenth Century*. Durham, NC: Duke University Press, 2013.

Kaiser, David E. *The Road to Dallas: The Assassination of John F. Kennedy*. Cambridge, MA: Belknap Press of Harvard University Press, 2008.

Karabell, Zachary. *Architects of Intervention: The United States, the Third World, and the Cold War, 1946–1962*. Baton Rouge: Louisiana State University Press, 1999.

Katz, Friedrich. "International Wars, Mexico, and U.S. Hegemony." In *Cycles of Conflict, Centuries of Change: Crisis, Reform, and Revolution in Mexico*, edited by Elisa Servín, Leticia Reina, and John Tutino, 184–210. Durham, NC: Duke University Press, 2007.

   "Violence and Terror in the Mexican and Russian Revolutions." In *A Century of Revolution: Insurgent and Counterinsurgent Violence during Latin America's Long Cold War*, edited by Greg Grandin and Gilbert Joseph, 45–61. Durham, NC: Duke University Press, 2010.

Kaufman Purcell, Susan. *The Mexican Profit-Sharing Decision: Politics in an Authoritarian Regime*. Berkeley: University of California Press, 1975.

Keohane, Robert O. "The Big Influence of Small Allies." *Foreign Policy*, no. 2 (April 1971): 161–82.

Kiddle, Amelia M., and María L. O. Muñoz, eds. *Populism in Twentieth Century Mexico: The Presidencies of Lázaro Cárdenas and Luis Echeverría*. Tucson: University of Arizona Press, 2010.

Kirk, John M., and Peter McKenna. *Canada-Cuban Relations: The Other Good Neighbor Policy*. Gainesville: Gainesville University Press of Florida, 1997.

Kissinger, Henry A. "Domestic Structure and Foreign Policy." *Daedalus* 95, no. 2 (Spring 1966): 503–29.

Knight, Alan. *The Mexican Revolution*, 2 vols. Cambridge: Cambridge University Press, 1986.

"Cardenismo: Juggernaut or Jalopy?" *Journal of Latin American Studies* 26, no. 1 (February 1, 1994): 73–107.

"Mexico's Three Fin de Siècle Crises." In *Cycles of Conflict, Centuries of Change: Crisis, Reform, and Revolution in Mexico*, edited by Elisa Servín, Leticia Reina, and John Tutino, 153–83. Durham, NC: Duke University Press, 2007.

"Lázaro Cárdenas." In *Gobernantes mexicanos*, edited by Will Fowler, Vol. 2: 179–208. Mexico City: Fondo de Cultura Económica, 2008.

"The Myth of the Mexican Revolution." *Past and Present*, no. 209 (November 2010): 223–73.

Knight, Alan, and W. G. Pansters, eds. *Caciquismo in Twentieth-Century Mexico*. London: Institute for the Study of the Americas, 2005.

Knorr, Klaus. "Threat Perception." In *Historical Dimensions of National Security Problems*, edited by Klaus Knorr, 78–119. Lawrence: University Press of Kansas, 1976.

Krauze, Enrique. *Mexico: Biography of Power*. New York: HarperCollins, 1997.

LaFeber, Walter. "Thomas C. Mann and the Devolution of Latin American Policy: From the Good Neighbor to Military Intervention." In *Behind the Throne: Servants of Power to Imperial Presidents, 1898–1968*, edited by Thomas J. McCormick and Walter LaFeber, 166–203. Madison: University of Wisconsin Press, 1993.

Lamberg, Roberto F. "La formación de la línea castrista desde la Conferencia Tricontinental." *Foro Internacional* 8, no. 3 (31) (January 1, 1968): 278–301.

Latner, Teishan A. "Take Me to Havana! Airline Hijacking, U.S.-Cuba Relations, and Political Protest in Late Sixties America," *Diplomatic History* 39, no. 1 (2015): 16–44.

Lawson, Chappell H. *Building the Fourth Estate: Democratization and the Rise of a Free Press in Mexico*. Berkeley: University of California Press, 2002.

Leffler, Melvyn P. *The Specter of Communism: The United States and the Origins of the Cold War, 1917–1953*. New York: Hill and Wang, 1994.

Leffler, Melvyn P., and Odd Arne Westad, eds. *The Cambridge History of the Cold War*. 3 vols. Cambridge: Cambridge University Press, 2010.

LeoGrande, William M., and Peter Kornbluh. *Back Channel to Cuba: The Hidden History of Negotiations between Washington and Havana*. Chapel Hill: University of North Carolina Press, 2014.

Lettieri, Michael Joseph. "Wheels of Government: The Alianza de Camioneros and the Political Culture of PRI Rule, 1929–1981," PhD diss., University of California San Diego, 2014.

Leyva de Varona, Adolfo. "Cuban-Mexican Relations during the Castro Era: A Historical Analysis." PhD diss., University of Miami, 1994.

Loaeza, Soledad. "El Partido Acción Nacional: La oposición leal en México." *Foro Internacional* 14, no. 3 (55) (January 1, 1974): 352–74.

"Notas para el estudio de la Iglesia en el México contemporáneo." In *Religión y política en México*, edited by Martín De la Rosa and Charles A. Reilly, 42–58. Mexico City: Siglo Veintiuno Editores, 1985.

Clases medias y política en México. La querella escolar, 1959–1963. Mexico City: El Colegio de México, 1988.

"Gustavo Díaz Ordaz: Las insuficiencias de la presencia autoritaria." In *Gobernantes mexicanos*, edited by Will Fowler, Vol. 2: 287–335. Mexico City: Fondo de Cultura Económica, 2008.

Logevall, Fredrik. "Politics and Foreign Relations." *The Journal of American History* 95, no. 4 (March 2009): 1074–8.

Lomnitz, Larissa Adler de, Rodrigo Salazar Elena, and Ilya Adler. *Symbolism and Ritual in a One-Party Regime: Unveiling Mexico's Political Culture.* Tucson: University of Arizona Press, 2010.

López, Jaime. *10 años de guerrillas en México.* Mexico City: Editorial Posada, 1974.

Lynd, Staughton. "The New Left." *Annals of the American Academy of Political and Social Science* 382 (March 1969): 64–72.

Mabry, Donald J. *The Mexican University and the State: Student Conflicts, 1910–1971.* College Station: Texas A&M University Press, 1982.

Marnham, Patrick. *Dreaming with His Eyes Open: A Life of Diego Rivera.* New York: Knopf, 1998.

Martínez della Rocca, Salvador. *Estado y universidad en México, 1920–1968: Historia de los movimientos estudiantiles en la UNAM.* Mexico City: J. Boldó i Climent, 1986.

Martínez Rivera, Gastón. *La lucha por la democracia en México.* Mexico City: Grupo Editorial Cenzontle, 2009.

Mayo, Baloy. *La guerrilla de Genaro y Lucio: Análisis y resultados.* 4th ed. Mexico City: Grupo Jaguar Impresiones, 2001.

McClintock, Michael. *Instruments of Statecraft: U.S. Guerrilla Warfare, Counterinsurgency, and Counter-Terrorism, 1940–1990.* New York: Pantheon Books, 1992.

McCaughan, Edward J. *Reinventing Revolution: The Renovation of Left Discourse in Cuba and Mexico.* Boulder, CO: Westview Press, 1997.

McKercher, Asa. "'The Most Serious Problem'? Canada-U.S. Relations and Cuba, 1962." *Cold War History* 12, no. 1 (February 2012): 69–88.

McMahon, Robert J. "U.S. National Security Policy from Eisenhower to Kennedy." In *The Cambridge History of the Cold War*, edited by Melvyn P. Leffler and Odd Arne Westad, Vol. 1: Origins: 288–311. Cambridge: Cambridge University Press, 2010.

Mencía, Mario. "La insurrección cubana y su tránsito por México." In *México y Cuba: Dos pueblos unidos en la historia*, edited by Martha López Portillo de Tamayo, Vol. 2: 279–301. Mexico City: Centro de Investigación Científica Jorge L. Tamayo, 1982.

Meyer, Lorenzo. *La segunda muerte de la revolución mexicana.* Mexico City: Cal y arena, 1992.

"México y la soberanía relativa. El vaivén de los alcances y los límites." *Foro Internacional* 48, no. 4 (194) (October 1, 2008): 765–84.

Middlebrook, Kevin J. *The Paradox of Revolution: Labor, the State, and Authoritarianism in Mexico.* Baltimore: Johns Hopkins University Press, 1995.

254 *Bibliography*

Monsiváis, Carlos, and Julio Scherer. *Tiempo de saber: Prensa y poder en México.* Mexico City: Nuevo Siglo Aguilar, 2003.

Moreno, Julio. *Yankee Don't Go Home!: Mexican Nationalism, American Business Culture, and the Shaping of Modern Mexico, 1920–1950.* Chapel Hill: University of North Carolina Press, 2003.

Morley, Jefferson. *Our Man in Mexico: Winston Scott and the Hidden History of the CIA.* Lawrence: University Press of Kansas, 2008.

Moulton, Aaron Coy. "Building Their Own Cold War in Their Own Backyard: The Transnational, International Conflicts in the Greater Caribbean Basin, 1944–1954," *Cold War History,* Advanced Access, published February 3, 2015, DOI: 10.1080/14682745.2014.995172.

Nagengast, Carole. "Violence, Terror, and the Crisis of the State." *Annual Review of Anthropology* 23 (January 1, 1994): 109–36.

Narváez, Rubén. *La sucesión presidencial: Teoría y práctica del tapadismo.* 2nd ed. Mexico City: Instituto Mexicano de Sociología Política, 1981.

Navarro, Aaron. *Political Intelligence and the Creation of Modern Mexico, 1938–1954.* University Park: Pennsylvania State University Press, 2010.

Newman, John. *Oswald and the CIA: The Documented Truth about the Unknown Relationship between the U.S. Government and the Alleged Killer of JFK.* New York: Skyhorse Publishing, 2008.

Niblo, Stephen R. *War, Diplomacy, and Development : The United States and Mexico, 1938–1954.* Wilmington, DE: Scholarly Resources, 1995.

Mexico in the 1940s: Modernity, Politics, and Corruption. Wilmington, DE: Scholarly Resources, 1999.

Oikión Solano, Verónica. "In the Vanguard of the Revolution: The Revolutionary Action Movement and the Armed Struggle." In *Challenging Authoritarianism in Mexico: Revolutionary Struggles and the Dirty War, 1964–1982,* edited by Fernando Herrera Calderón and Adela Cedillo, 61–81. New York: Routledge, 2012.

Ojeda, Mario. *Alcances y límites de la política exterior de México.* Mexico City: El Colegio de México, 1976.

México y Cuba revolucionaria: Cincuenta años de relación. Mexico City: El Colegio de México, 2008.

O'Malley, Ilene V. *The Myth of the Revolution: Hero Cults and the Institutionalization of the Mexican State, 1920–1940.* New York: Greenwood Press, 1986.

Orozco Orozco, Víctor. "La guerrilla chihuahuense de los sesenta." In *Movimientos armados en México, siglo XX,* edited by Verónica Oikión Solano and Marta Eugenia García Ugarte, Vol. 2: 337–60. Zamora: El Colegio de Michoacán, 2006.

Ortiz, Orlando. *Genaro Vázquez.* Mexico City: Editorial Diógenes, 1972.

Padgett, Leon Vincent. *The Mexican Political System,* 2nd ed. Boston: Houghton Mifflin, 1976.

Padilla, Tanalís. *Rural Resistance in the Land of Zapata: The Jaramillista Movement and the Myth of the Pax Priísta, 1940–1962.* Durham, NC: Duke University Press, 2008.

"Rural Education, Political Radicalism, and Normalista Identity in Mexico after 1940." In *Dictablanda: Politics, Work, and Culture in Mexico,*

1938–1968, edited by Paul Gillingham and Benjamin T. Smith, 341–59. Durham, NC: Duke University Press, 2014.

Padilla, Tanalís, and Louise E. Walker. "Spy Reports: Content, Methodology, and Historiography in Mexico's Secret Police Archive." *Journal of Iberian and Latin American Research* 19, no. 1 (July 2013): 1–111.

Pansters, Will. *Politics and Power in Puebla: The Political History of a Mexican State, 1937–1987*. Amsterdam: Centre for Latin American Research and Documentation, 1990.

——— "Tropical Passion in the Desert: Gonzalo N. Santos and Local Elections in Northern San Luis Potosí, 1943–1958." In *Dictablanda: Politics, Work, and Culture in Mexico, 1938–1968*, edited by Paul Gillingham and Benjamin T. Smith, 126–48. Durham, NC: Duke University Press, 2014.

Paolucci, Gabriella. "Sartre's Humanism and the Cuban Revolution." *Theory and Society* 36, no. 3 (May 2007): 245–63.

Paterson, Thomas G. "Introduction: John F. Kennedy's Quest for Victory and Global Crisis." In *Kennedy's Quest for Victory: American Foreign Policy, 1961–1963*, edited by Thomas G. Paterson, 3–23. New York: Oxford University Press, 1989.

——— *Contesting Castro: The United States and the Triumph of the Cuban Revolution*. New York: Oxford University Press, 1994.

Paxman, Andrew. "William Jenkins, Business Elites, and the Evolution of the Mexican State: 1910–1960." PhD diss., University of Texas, 2008.

Pellicer de Brody, Olga. *México y la revolución cubana*. Mexico City: El Colegio de México, 1972.

Pellicer de Brody, Olga, and Esteban L. Mancilla. *Historia de la Revolución Mexicana 1952–1960: El entendimiento con los Estados Unidos y la gestación del desarrollo estabilizador*. Vol. 23. Mexico City: El Colegio de México, 1978.

Pellicer de Brody, Olga, and José Luis Reyna. *Historia de la Revolución Mexicana, periodo 1952–1960: El afianzamiento de la estabilidad política*. Vol. 22. Mexico City: El Colegio de México, 1978.

Pensado, Jaime. "Political Violence and Student Culture in Mexico: The Consolidation of Porrismo during the 1950s and 1960s." PhD diss., University of Chicago, 2008.

——— *Rebel Mexico: Student Unrest and Authoritarian Political Culture during the Long Sixties*. Stanford, CA: Stanford University Press, 2013.

——— "'To Assault with the Truth': The Revitalization of Conservative Militancy in Mexico during the Global Sixties." *The Americas* 70, no. 3 (January 2014): 489–521.

Pérez, Louis A. *Cuba and the United States: Ties of Singular Intimacy*. Athens: University of Georgia Press, 1990.

Pérez Arce, Francisco. *El principio: 1968–1998, años de rebeldía*. Mexico City: Ítaca, 2007.

Pérez-Stable, Marifeli. *The Cuban Revolution: Origins, Course, and Legacy*. 2nd ed. New York: Oxford University Press, 1999.

——— *The United States and Cuba: Intimate Enemies*. New York: Routledge, 2011.

Poitras, Guy. "Mexico's 'New' Foreign Policy." *InterAmerican Economic Affairs* 28 (1974): 59–77.

Poo Hurtado, Jorge. "Los protagonistas olvidados." In *Asalto al cielo: Lo que no se ha dicho del 68*, edited by Rogelio Carvajal Dávila, 121–30. Mexico City: Editorial Océano, 1998.

Preston, Julia. *Opening Mexico: The Making of a Democracy*. New York: Farrar, Straus and Giroux, 2004.

Putnam, Robert D. "Diplomacy and Domestic Politics: The Logic of Two-Level Games." *International Organization* 42, no. 3 (July 1988): 427–60.

Rabe, Stephen G. *The Most Dangerous Area in the World: John F. Kennedy Confronts Communist Revolution in Latin America*. Chapel Hill: University of North Carolina Press, 1999.

   The Killing Zone: The United States Wages Cold War in Latin America. New York: Oxford University Press, 2012.

Rangel Hernández, Lucio. *La Universidad Michoacana y el movimiento estudiantil, 1966–1986*. Morelia: Universidad Michoacana de San Nicolás de Hidalgo, Instituto de Investigaciones Históricas, 2009.

Rankin, Monica A. *¡México, La Patria! Propaganda and Production during World War II*. Lincoln: University of Nebraska Press, 2009.

Rath, Thomas. *Myths of Demilitarization in Postrevolutionary Mexico, 1920–1960*. Chapel Hill: University of North Carolina Press, 2013.

Reeves, Michelle. "Extracting the Eagle's Talons: The Soviet Union in Cold War Latin America." PhD diss., University of Texas, Austin, 2014.

Reyes, Mauricio. "Política interna y política exterior en México desde 1950 hasta 1964." In *Fundamentos y prioridades de la política exterior de México*, edited by Humberto Garza Elizondo, 135–66. Mexico City: El Colegio de México, 1986.

Rivas O., René. *La izquierda estudiantil en la UNAM: Organizaciones, movilizaciones y liderazgos (1958–1972)*. Mexico City: Universidad Nacional Autónoma de México, Facultad de Estudios Superiores Aragón, 2007.

Robbins, Carla Anne. *The Cuban Threat*. New York: McGraw-Hill, 1983.

Robinet, Romain. "A Revolutionary Group Fighting Against a Revolutionary State: The September 23rd Communist League Against the PRI State (1973–1975)." In *Challenging Authoritarianism in Mexico: Revolutionary Struggles and the Dirty War, 1964–1982*, edited by Fernando Herrera Calderón and Adela Cedillo, 130–48. New York: Routledge, 2012.

Robinson, Cecil, ed. *The View from Chapultepec: Mexican Writers on the Mexican-American War*. Tucson: University of Arizona Press, 1989.

Rodríguez, Victoria E., and Peter M. Ward. "Disentangling the PRI from the Government in Mexico." *Mexican Studies/Estudios Mexicanos* 10, no. 1 (January 1, 1994): 163–86.

Rodríguez Castañeda, Rafael. *Prensa vendida. Los presidentes y los periodistas: 40 años de relaciones*. Mexico City: Grijalbo, 1993.

Rodríguez Menier, Juan Antonio. *Cuba por dentro: El MININT*. Miami: Ediciones Universal, 1994.

Rodríguez Munguía, Jacinto. *Las nóminas secretas de Gobernación*. Mexico City: LIMAC (Libertad de Información-México A.C.), 2004.

   La otra guerra secreta: Los archivos prohibidos de la prensa y el poder. Mexico City: Random House Mondadori, 2007.

1968: Todos los culpables. Mexico City: Random House Mondadori, 2008.

Roel García, Santiago, ed. *Genaro Estrada: Diplomático y escritor.* Mexico City: Secretaría de Relaciones Exteriores, 1978.

Ros, Enrique. *Castro y las guerrillas en Latinoamérica.* Miami: Ediciones Universal, 2001.

Rosenau, James. "Introduction." In *Domestic Sources of Foreign Policy,* edited by James Rosenau, 1–10. New York: The Free Press, 1967.

Rosenau, James N., ed. *Linkage Politics: Essays on the Convergence of National and International Systems.* New York: Free Press, 1969.

Ross, Stanley R. *Is the Mexican Revolution Dead?* New York: Knopf, 1966.

Rot, Gabriel. *Los orígenes perdidos de la guerrilla en la Argentina: La historia de Jorge Ricardo Masetti y el Ejército Guerrillero del Pueblo.* Buenos Aires: Ediciones El Cielo por Asalto, 2000.

Roxborough, Ian. "Mexico." In *Latin America between the Second World War and the Cold War, 1944–1948,* edited by Leslie Bethell and Ian Roxborough, 190–216. Cambridge: Cambridge University Press, 1992.

Rubin, Jeffrey W. *Decentering the Regime: Ethnicity, Radicalism, and Democracy in Juchitán, Mexico.* Durham, NC: Duke University Press, 1997.

"Contextualizing the Regime: What 1938–1968 Tells Us about Mexico, Power, and Latin America's Twentieth Century." In *Dictablanda: Politics, Work, and Culture in Mexico, 1938–1968,* edited by Paul Gillingham and Benjamin T. Smith, 379–95. Durham, NC: Duke University Press, 2014.

Scherer García, Julio, and Carlos Monsiváis. *Parte de guerra: Tlatelolco 1968, Documentos del General Marcelino García Barragán. Los hechos y la historia.* Mexico City: Aguilar, 1999.

Schers, David. "The Popular Sector of the Partido Revolucionario Institucional in Mexico." PhD diss., Tel Aviv University, 1972.

Schmidt, Arthur. "Making It Real Compared to What? Reconceptualizing Mexican History since 1940." In *Fragments of a Golden Age: The Politics of Culture in Mexico since 1940,* edited by Gilbert Joseph, Anne Rubenstein, and Eric Zolov, 23–68. Durham, NC: Duke University Press, 2001.

Schreiber, Rebecca Mina. *Cold War Exiles in Mexico: U.S. Dissidents and the Culture of Critical Resistance.* Minneapolis: University of Minnesota Press, 2008.

Selbin, Eric. *Modern Latin American Revolutions.* 2nd ed. Boulder, CO: Westview Press, 1999.

Service, Robert. *Trotsky: A Biography.* Cambridge, MA: Belknap Press of Harvard University Press, 2009.

Servín, Elisa. *Ruptura y oposición: El movimiento henriquista, 1945–1954.* Mexico City: Cal y arena, 2001.

"Propaganda y Guerra Fria: la campaña anticomunista en la prensa mexicana del medio siglo." *Signos Históricos,* no. 11 (2004): 9–39.

La oposición política: Otra cara del siglo XX mexicano. Herramientas para la historia. Mexico City: Centro de Investigación y Docencia Económicas: Fondo de Cultura Económica, 2006.

Shenon, Philip. *A Cruel and Shocking Act: The Secret History of the Kennedy Assassination*. New York: Henry Holt and Company, 2013.

Sherman, John W. *The Mexican Right: The End of Revolutionary Reform, 1929–1940*. Westport, CT: Praeger, 1997.

Sierra Guzmán, Jorge Luis. *El enemigo interno: Contrainsurgencia y fuerzas armadas en México*. Mexico City: Centro de Estudios Estratégicos de América del Norte, 2003.

"Armed Forces and Counterinsurgency: Origins of the Dirty War (1965–1982)." In *Challenging Authoritarianism in Mexico: Revolutionary Struggles and the Dirty War, 1964–1982*, edited by Fernando Herrera Calderón and Adela Cedillo, 182–97. New York: Routledge, 2012.

Smith, Arthur K. "Mexico and the Cuban Revolution: Foreign Policy-Making in Mexico Under President Adolfo López Mateos (1958–1964)." PhD diss., Cornell University, 1970.

Snodgrass, Michael. "The Golden Age of Charrismo: Workers, Braceros, and the Political Machinery of Postrevolutionary Mexico." In *Dictablanda: Politics, Work, and Culture in Mexico, 1938–1968*, edited by Paul Gillingham and Benjamin T. Smith, 175–95. Durham, NC: Duke University Press, 2014.

Spenser, Daniela. *The Impossible Triangle: Mexico, Soviet Russia, and the United States in the 1920s*. Durham, NC: Duke University Press, 1999.

Stevens, Evelyn P. "Legality and Extra-Legality in Mexico." *Journal of Interamerican Studies and World Affairs* 12, no. 1 (January 1, 1970): 62–75.

Protest and Response in Mexico. Cambridge, MA: Massachusetts Institute of Technology, 1974.

Story, Dale. *The Mexican Ruling Party: Stability and Authority*. New York: Praeger, 1986.

Super, John C. "'Rerum Novarum' in Mexico and Quebec." *Revista de Historia de América*, no. 126 (January 1, 2000): 63–84.

Suri, Jeremi. *Power and Protest: Global Revolution and the Rise of Detente*. Cambridge, MA: Harvard University Press, 2003.

ed. *The Global Revolutions of 1968: A Norton Casebook in History*. New York: W. W. Norton, 2007.

Szulc, Tad. *Fidel: A Critical Portrait*. New York: Morrow, 1986.

Taffet, Jeffrey F. *Foreign Aid as Foreign Policy: The Alliance for Progress in Latin America*. New York: Routledge, 2007.

Tatum, Chuck, and Harold Hinds. "Eduardo Del Río (Rius): An Interview and Introductory Essay." *Chasqui* 9, no. 1 (November 1, 1979): 3–23.

Thomas, Ann Van Wynen, and A. J. Thomas. *Non-Intervention: The Law and Its Import in the Americas*. Dallas: Southern Methodist University Press, 1956.

Trevizo, Dolores. *Rural Protest and the Making of Democracy in Mexico, 1968–2000*. University Park: Pennsylvania State University Press, 2011.

Trubowitz, Peter. *Politics and Strategy: Partisan Ambition and American Statecraft*. Princeton, NJ: Princeton University Press, 2011.

Tunstall Allcock, Thomas. "Becoming 'Mr. Latin America': Thomas C. Mann Reconsidered." *Diplomatic History* 38, no. 5 (2014): 1017–45.

Vargas Llosa, Mario. "Mexico: The Perfect Dictatorship." *New Perspectives Quarterly* 8, no. 1 (1991): 23–5.

Vaughan, Mary K. *Cultural Politics in Revolution: Teachers, Peasants, and Schools in Mexico, 1930–1940.* Tucson: University of Arizona Press, 1997.

Villalpando César, José Manuel. *Las balas del invasor: La expansión territorial de los Estados Unidos a costa de México.* Mexico City: Miguel Angel Porrúa, 1998.

Walker, Louise E. *Waking from the Dream: Mexico's Middle Classes after 1968.* Stanford, CA: Stanford University Press, 2013.

Westad, Odd Arne. *The Global Cold War.* Cambridge: Cambridge University Press, 2007.

White, Anthony. *Siqueiros: A Biography.* Encino, CA: Floricanto Press, 1994.

White, Christopher M. *Creating a Third World: Mexico, Cuba, and the United States during the Castro Era.* Albuquerque: University of New Mexico Press, 2007.

Wilson, Larman C. "International Law and the United States Cuban Quarantine of 1962." *Journal of Inter-American Studies* 7, no. 4 (October 1, 1965): 485–92.

Winn, Peter. *Weavers of Revolution: The Yarur Workers and Chile's Road to Socialism.* New York: Oxford University Press, 1986.

Womack, John. *Zapata and the Mexican Revolution.* New York: Vintage Books, 1970.

Wright, Thomas C. *Latin America in the Era of the Cuban Revolution.* Westport, CT: Praeger, 2001.

Yankelevich, Pablo, ed. *México, país refugio: La experiencia de los exilios en el siglo XX.* Mexico City: Plaza y Valdés, 2002.

Zolov, Eric. *Refried Elvis: The Rise of the Mexican Counterculture.* Berkeley: University of California Press, 1999.

"Expanding Our Cultural Horizons: The Shift From an Old to a New Left in Latin America." *A contra corriente* 5, no. 2 (Winter 2008): 47–73.

"'Cuba sí, yanquis no!': el saqueo del Instituto Cultural México-Norteamericano en Morelia, Michoacán, 1961." In *Espejos de la guerra fría: México, América Central y el Caribe*, edited by Daniela Spenser, 175–214. Mexico City: Centro de Investigaciones y Estudios Superiores en Antropología Social, 2004.

Index

and Latin American Peace
Conference, 93, 94
records, 7
Department of State (U.S.), 26, 38, 66, 69,
71, 89, 130, 133, 165, 188
DFS. *See* Department of Federal Security
(Mexico)
DGI. *See* General Intelligence Department
Díaz, Porfirio, 14
Díaz Alejo, María Elena, 205
Díaz Escobar, Manuel, 223
Díaz Ordaz, Gustavo
anti-communism, 168, 174, 178,
230, 235
assassination rumors, 154, 155
and CCI, 115, 117
and the CIA, 25, 26, 27, 64
and Cuba, 165, 175, 233
and Cuban Missile Crisis, 138, 139, 140
and doctors' movement, 168
and Dorticós visit, 61
election, 148, 155, 156, 168
and FEP, 153
and guerrillas, 197
and Humberto Carrillo Colón, 194
insults, 175, 213
and intelligence services, 7
and Kennedy assassination, 142
and Latin American Peace
Conference, 93
and MLN, 108, 111
and 1968 student movement, 209, 210,
216, 217
and Olympic Battalion, 223
and Olympic Games, 210
and *Política*, 176
and railroad movement, 40
reaction to Ciudad Madera attack, 199
and student protests, 168, 170, 173
and Tlatelolco massacre, 212, 215, 217,
218, 225
warning to students, 170, 209
dictablanda, 16
Dillon, C. Douglas, 70
Dirección de Asuntos Latinoamericanos.
See Department of Latin American
Affairs (Cuba)
Dirección Federal de Seguridad. See
Department of Federal Security
(Mexico)
Dirección General de Inteligencia. *See*
General Intelligence Department

*Dirección General de Investigaciones
Políticas y Sociales. See* Department
of Political and Social Investigations
(Mexico)
dirty war, 197, 197n2, 211, 221, 222, 223,
230, 231, 235, 236, 237
doctors' movement, 168
Dominican Republic, 52, 74, 80, 176
domino theory, 174
Dorticós Torrado, Osvaldo, 3, 61–4, 65,
85, 98, 143, 176, 193
Dulles, Allen, 91
Durán, Silvia, 141–7

Eastland, James O., 84
Echeverría, Luis, 22n33
and the CIA, 26
and Corpus Christi massacre,
224, 225
and elections of 1964, 155
and guerrilla groups, 229, 230
and Halcones, 224, 225
and intelligence services, 7
and Kennedy assassination, 142, 143
and 1968 student movement, 204, 218
Ecuador, 3n10, 80
Egypt, 183
Eisenhower, Dwight, 38, 66, 69, 98, 128
El Diario de la Tarde, 93
El Diario de México, 93
El Dictámen, 80
elections
and corruption, 16, 18, 29, 156, 219
on local level, 18n21
of 1946, 29, 30
of 1952, 29, 30
of 1958, 39, 147
of 1964, 147, 150, 151, 155, 156, 198
reform efforts, 106, 150, 236
El Fígaro, 93
El Heraldo, 190
El Heraldo de México, 212
Elías Calles, Plutarco, 17
El Liberal, 111
El Nacional, 22, 114, 115, 130,
157, 158
El Popular, 93
El Sol de México, 187, 229
El Sol de Monterrey, 114
El Universal, 22, 35, 93, 194, 209, 211
El Universal Gráfico, 204
embutes, 22